Landmarks in Rhetoric and Public Address

THE SELECTED
WRITINGS OF
JOHN WITHERSPOON

Edited by
Thomas P. Miller

Southern Illinois University Press
Carbondale

Cover illustration: John Witherspoon, lithograph based on a painting by
C. W. Peale; Library of Congress

Cataloging data may be obtained from the U.S. Library of Congress.
Library of Congress Control Number: 2015944974

Printed on recycled paper. ♻

The paper used in this publication meets the minimum requirements of
American National Standard for Information Sciences—Permanence of
Paper for Printed Library Materials, ANSI Z39.48-1992. ∞

CONTENTS

Preface to the Paperback Edition

In the twenty-five years since the publication of the hardcover edition of this collection, studies of rhetoric and the eighteenth century have changed in ways that brought new perspectives on John Witherspoon. The first professor in the United States to publish his lectures on rhetoric, Witherspoon was also a widely influential practitioner of the art. From his arrival in New Jersey in 1768 until shortly before his death in 1794, he taught courses in rhetoric and moral philosophy at Princeton, where he served as president. As a member of the Second Continental Congress and a signatory of the Declaration of Independence, Witherspoon was one of the most influential religious leaders of the Revolutionary period. His lectures, writings, and sermons document the theories of rhetoric and moral philosophy that shaped the Declaration and the Constitution. James Madison studied with Witherspoon at Princeton, and Thomas Jefferson also studied rhetoric and moral philosophy with a Scottish college graduate, William Small. Witherspoon was one of the most noted members of the generation of Scottish immigrants who founded the expanding numbers of colleges and academies that shaped US education into the nineteenth century.

Recently scholars have reassessed the impact of Scottish rhetoric and moral philosophy in Revolutionary America. Two notable studies of Witherspoon are J. Blake Scott's "John Witherspoon's Normalizing Pedagogy of Ethos" and Mark Garrett Longaker's *Rhetoric and the Republic: Politics, Civic Discourse, and Education in Early America*. Both Scott and Longaker analyze how Witherspoon's writings and courses met the needs of enterprising colonials who resented genteel refinements but also sought to raise their own social standing through higher education. Longaker examines Witherspoon's writings from the standpoint of "New Jersey's freeholding bourgeoisie" who sought "equal participation in the capitalist British Atlantic economy," while Scott focuses on how Witherspoon appealed to the "elite class" by combining "elements of civic and belletristic rhetoric in his notion of ethos." Scott maintains that Witherspoon's "normalizing pedagogy" combined belletristic and civic dimensions in ways that I had failed to consider in my earlier examinations of Witherspoon's and Blair's perspectives. In retrospect, this criticism seems well founded, and I recommend that readers consider Longaker's and Scott's analyses as useful complements to the introduction that follows.

My perspective on Witherspoon has also expanded in the decades since I published the first edition. I have published a two-volume history of college English studies: *The Formation of College English: Rhetoric and Belles Lettres in the British Cultural Provinces* focuses on the transition from classical to modern cultural studies in the English dissenting academies and Scottish and Irish colleges, while *The Evolution of College English: Literacy Studies from the Puritans to the Postmoderns* expanded the field of study to consider the transition from classical to modern literatures as one example of a historical formation in which literature and the literate evolved in tandem with broader changes in literate technologies, economies, and epistemologies. While we do not generally include oratorical and belletristic conceptions of literature within the sphere of literary studies, we may have reached the historical standpoint where we can see that a modern conception of literature held an institutional position vis-à-vis the literate culture that was in some ways comparable to that which the classics occupied in a previous era. From such a vantage point, we can perhaps reassess how our own pedagogies serve "normalizing" purposes within professional hierarchies that reproduce broader class structures, in part by positioning literature on an aesthetic plane divorced from the domains of business writing, public journalism, and other nonliterary genres.

While Witherspoon does not have a place in the history of literature as traditionally understood, he occupied a pivotal position in the broader transition from classical to modern cultural studies. He taught one of the first college courses in composition in America, though he is more often recognized for teaching one of the capstone courses in moral philosophy that shaped the Revolutionary generation's assumptions about natural laws, personal duties, political structures, and cultural hierarchies. Witherspoon's impact has been recognized in works such as Daniel Robinson's "Scottish Enlightenment and the American Founding," which begins with Witherspoon to explain how Scottish models of human psychology, moral epistemology, and political economy shaped the formation of the American national identity. Witherspoon is recognized as the principal conduit for the transmission of commonsense moral philosophy into the pragmatic tradition, as discussed in Segrest's *America and the Political Philosophy of Common Sense*. Witherspoon's philosophy of common sense is examined in the introduction. New dimensions of that philosophy emerge if we examine the critiques of Longaker and Scott together with broader research on the culture of the book in the eighteenth century. Witherspoon's composition course takes on new significance when we recognize that its concern for standard usage and the formal conventions of spelling, punctuation, and paragraphing are harbingers of the characteristic concerns of a print economy and begin to consider those concerns as integral to formation of the modern student subject and the modern "birth of the author."

As we have come to terms with such developments, we have become more attuned to the circulation of ideas and practices through transatlantic cultural and political networks in the late eighteenth century. For example, Manning and Cogliano's edited collection *The Atlantic Enlightenment* examines the "exchanges and circulations—commercial, material, spiritual, intellectual and imaginative" (1). As Manning, Cogliano, and their contributors explain, the Enlightenment has come to be understood as "a culturally dense symbolic experience in which ideas, beliefs, and consciousness itself were transformed" (4). This interpretive framework is highly rhetorical and deeply rooted in the sort of pedagogical and institutional practices that Witherspoon helped to transform, not with the originality of his ideas but with the breadth of his engagements in religion, education, and politics on both sides of the Atlantic, as Daniel W. Howe discusses in "John Witherspoon and the Transatlantic Enlightenment" in Manning and Cogliano's collection.

These recent works can help us better assess the continuities among the writings included in this collection, as I discuss in the following preface and introduction. My work on this collection, and on the publications that have followed it, has been supported by two fellowships from the National Endowment for the Humanities, which provides absolutely vital support to research in the humanities. My own research has depended far more on the support of my wife and family. In my original preface, I dedicated the hardcover edition to my wife, Kerstin Miller, and our unborn child. Marcus and his sister Melina have now grown into young adults, and I rededicate this volume to them with appreciation for all that they have done, and faith in what they will do.

Bibliography

Howe, Daniel W. "John Witherspoon and the Transatlantic Enlightenment." Manning and Cogliano 61–80.

Longaker, Mark Garrett. *Rhetoric and the Republic: Politics, Civic Discourse, and Education in Early America.* Tuscaloosa: U of Alabama P, 2007.

Manning, Susan, and Francis D. Cogliano, eds. *The Atlantic Enlightenment.* Burlington, VT: Ashgate Publishing, 2008.

Miller, Thomas P. *The Evolution of College English: Literacy Studies from the Puritans to the Postmoderns.* Pittsburgh: Pittsburgh UP, 2011.

——. *The Formation of College English: Rhetoric and Belles Lettres in the British Cultural Provinces.* Pittsburgh: Pittsburgh UP, 1997.

Robinson, Daniel. "Scottish Enlightenment and the American Founding," *The Monist* 90.2 (2007): 170–81.

Scott, J. Blake. "John Witherspoon's Normalizing Pedagogy of Ethos." *Rhetoric Review* 16.1 (Autumn 1997): 58–75.

Segrest, Scott Philip. *America and the Political Philosophy of Common Sense.* Columbia: U of Missouri P, 2009.

Preface to the Cloth Edition

By most accounts, John Witherspoon's *Lectures on Eloquence* is the first American rhetorical treatise. From his arrival in America in 1768 until shortly before his death in 1794, Witherspoon taught rhetoric and moral philosophy at Princeton, where he served as president. As a member of the Continental Congress, signatory of the Declaration of Independence, and founder of the American Presbyterian Church, he was in fact too busy practicing rhetoric to publish on it, and his *Lectures* were published posthumously, first appearing in 1801 in his *Works* and then in a separate edition with his *Lectures on Moral Philosophy* in 1810. One can only speculate what sort of an effect his rhetorical theory might have had if he had published it twenty years earlier. Witherspoon defined rhetoric quite differently from his former college classmate Hugh Blair, whose *Lectures on Rhetoric and Belles Lettres* (1789) came to dominate the origin of college English studies at the turn of the century. Where Blair helped institutionalize a rhetoric defined by its ties to polite literature, Witherspoon reiterated the classical relationship between rhetoric and the twin studies of moral philosophy—ethics and politics. Blair and Witherspoon differed on practical as well as theoretical matters. Despite the fact that Witherspoon shared a common educational background with Blair and other leaders of the Moderate party in the Scottish church, he opposed their cultural liberalism and political conservatism. While the Moderates sought to liberalize Scottish cultural and religious attitudes and Witherspoon remained a staunch Calvinist, it was he who became an advocate of revolution and they who spoke for the ruling British political interests.

Most readers of this Landmarks in Rhetoric and Public Address series are probably more interested in the history of rhetoric than in Scottish church politics or American colonial education, yet one cannot understand Witherspoon's contributions to the rhetorical tradition unless one knows something about the rhetorical contexts he was addressing. I have thus chosen to publish Witherspoon's lectures on rhetoric and moral philosophy along with his most important responses to the public affairs of the time, and in the introduction that follows I have attempted to locate Witherspoon's theories of rhetoric and moral philosophy in the context of his public career in Scotland and America.

Whatever success I have had has been due to the support of those who have contributed to this project. Most important has been Richard Sher, who has served as a principal reviewer for this book. Professor Sher's *Church and University in the Scottish Enlightenment: The Moderate Literati of Edinburgh* (1984) sets a standard for scholarly inquiry that I do not pretend to have equaled, but I have benefited greatly from his criticisms of my insensitivity to the Moderates and of other issues. Of course any misjudgments I have made on these or other matters are completely attributable to my own shortcomings. I have also benefited from the responses of Ronald F. Reid, Wilbur Samuel Howell, and Michael S. Halloran, who wanted to see the *Lectures on Eloquence* in print so badly that he allowed me to edit them when he saw that his schedule would not soon allow him to do so.

The needed archival research in Britain and America has been generously supported by several organizations. Research in Scotland in the summer of 1986 and at Princeton in December 1986 was supported by various offices of Southern Illinois University: the Department of English, the College of Liberal Arts, the Office of International Programs, and the Mini-Sabbatical Program. The National Endowment for the Humanities supported further research in Scotland in 1987 that enabled me to complete the introduction and also continue my work on a book on eighteenth-century college English studies. But most of all I am indebted to my wife, Kerstin Miller, who helped with specific tasks like collating editions and with the more general challenge of understanding what it is that I do. I would like to dedicate my work on this project to her and to the baby who, hopefully, will be delivered into the world just before this book is.

The Selected Writings
of John Witherspoon

INTRODUCTION

Those who have given the history of oratory have . . . given us the history of the teachers of that art rather than its progress and effects.

—John Witherspoon

JOHN WITHERSPOON has been widely recognized as one of the first important teachers of rhetoric and moral philosophy in America. However, Witherspoon's criticism of "those who have given us the history of oratory" is an appropriate comment on much that has been written about him. Too little attention has been paid to the relationship between his teaching and the "progress and effects" of political debate in the eighteenth century. Witherspoon was much more than a teacher of rhetoric, he was an influential practitioner of that art. He was a leader of the Presbyterian Church in Scotland and America, a president of Princeton University, and a well-known spokesman for independence. Witherspoon was quite possibly the most influential religious and educational leader in Revolutionary America and the only clergyman to sign the Declaration of Independence. Witherspoon's public career had strong continuities with his theories of moral philosophy and rhetoric, for in the classroom he stressed civic ethics, political rights, and the public responsibilities of the citizen orator. When one considers that Witherspoon taught the generation who created the American republic, most notably James Madison, then one can see just how important Witherspoon is to understanding the relationship between public political practice and theories of rhetoric and moral philosophy in the eighteenth century.

Witherspoon is also interesting because his life and writings provide direct links between the Scottish Enlightenment and the American Revolution. Scottish professors were at the time redefining classical rhetoric and moral philosophy to suit the social needs of their time, and Americans proved to be their most responsive students. Scottish rhetoricians like Hugh Blair and George Campbell defined the study of English composition, literature, and rhetoric in American colleges into the latter half of the nineteenth century, and Thomas Reid's common-sense moral

1

philosophy was equally predominant. Other Scotsmen like Francis Hutcheson, Adam Smith, David Hume, and Adam Ferguson were also
widely influential in moral philosophy and in the fields that developed
out of it—economics, political science, psychology, and sociology. The
Scots' contributions to the origins of the social sciences were rooted in a
well-defined civic tradition. Hutcheson, the earliest of the major Scottish
moral philosophers, was heavily influenced by Cicero, and Hutcheson's
Whig political philosophy followed in the tradition of Commonwealth
writers like James Harrington, who sought to justify a mixed form of
government after the Restoration. According to the work of Caroline
Robbins and J. G. A. Pocock, these writers were themselves drawing on
classical civic humanists like Aristotle and Cicero in order to revive the
ideal of the politically active citizen who speaks for public virtue against
self-interested factions and kings. Aristotle and Cicero were the sources
for this tradition in rhetoric and moral philosophy, and it was the Scots
more than any other group who translated classical rhetoric and moral
philosophy into English. Like the Commonwealth writers and classical
civic humanists, Scots after the Union with England in 1707 faced a
radically different political world, for the Union called accepted social
traditions into question and made English the only way of talking about
them. Colonial Americans were also trying to understand what it meant
to be political and cultural provincials in an expanding empire, and
many looked to Scottish sources for answers.

Witherspoon was instrumental in introducing Scottish moral philosophy and rhetoric to America, and his public career amply documents
the complex social background that shaped rhetoric and moral philosophy in eighteenth-century Scotland and America. When Witherspoon
was born in 1723, Scotland was struggling to define a place for itself in
the British Empire after a century of incessant political and religious
conflict, a state of affairs that helped to strengthen the Scots' concern
for the study of contemporary social affairs and English culture. At
Edinburgh University, Witherspoon studied alongside Hugh Blair under John Stevenson, who was one of the first to teach English in a
systematic way. After graduation Witherspoon became a leader of the
traditional Calvinist opponents of the Moderate Presbyterians, who
aligned themselves with the high culture and political interests of Britain. In 1768 he came to America to become president of Princeton,
then called the College of New Jersey. There he introduced the study
of Scottish moral philosophy and rhetoric in an effort to broaden the
curriculum and make it more responsive to the social and intellectual
needs of the generation who created the American republic. Soon after
his arrival in America, Witherspoon became a leader of the American
Presbyterian Church, and he was instrumental in making it a public

advocate of independence. In 1776, he joined the Continental Congress, where he spoke decisively for the Declaration of Independence, and until his death in 1794, Witherspoon remained a leading figure in American politics, education, and religion.

The works included in this volume span the wide-ranging concerns of Witherspoon's public career in Scotland and America, but a number of hard choices had to be made in selecting from Witherspoon's four volumes of published writings. I have sought to present a unified view of Witherspoon as a social leader and educational reformer in order to let readers examine his works on rhetoric and moral philosophy in the social context of his public career. Of the numerous sermons and theological tracts that Witherspoon wrote in Scotland, *Ecclesiastical Characteristics* (1753) is by far the most influential and the most interesting because it offers insights into the tension between the Scots' social philosophy and the political conflicts that followed the Union. As president of Princeton, Witherspoon published *Address . . . in Behalf of the College of New Jersey* (1772), which provides a useful picture of educational reform in the period. The sermon that Witherspoon first preached to graduating students in 1775, *Christian Magnanimity,* puts forward the ideal of public service that informed his educational reforms and his general social philosophy. The continuity between his public roles as minister and politician is clearly documented by his sermon *The Dominion of Providence over the Passions of Men* (1776), one of the most significant statements of support for the Revolution to be delivered from an American pulpit. Few of Witherspoon's orations in Congress are extant, but the surviving portion of his speech "Upon the Confederation" offers a sample of his rhetorical practice in that forum. These sermons, pamphlets, and speeches provide a historical context for the *Lectures on Moral Philosophy* and *Lectures on Eloquence.*

Witherspoon's Early Intellectual Development

Witherspoon was born in 1723 into a Scotland quite different from the one he left in 1768, for in a very real way he came of age with the Scottish Enlightenment. Many Scots had hoped that the Union of Parliaments with England in 1707 would bring an end to a century of debilitating religious and political turmoil; however, the unrest continued through the Jacobite rebellions of 1715 and 1745 and through several major schisms in the Presbyterian Church. The conflicts in the Church receded when the Moderates assumed control with the support of British party politics in the 1750s, and the general political unrest ended with the Highland clearances and increased emigration to America.

Witherspoon first became acquainted with his future opponents in the Scottish Church when he studied at Edinburgh University from 1736 to 1745 along with Hugh Blair, Alexander Carlyle, and William Robertson, who became leaders of the Moderate party in the church. The reformation of Edinburgh University that established it as one of the most progressive educational institutions in Europe had begun in 1708 under Principal Carstares, who broadened the curriculum beyond the traditional classical subjects and abolished the archaic regenting system of having students spend their whole career under a single teacher (Grant 1: 363). However, students still matriculated under a principal instructor, and both Witherspoon and Blair registered under John Stevenson, Professor of Logic and Metaphysics from 1730 to 1777. Stevenson had a formative impact on Witherspoon's and Blair's development according to their biographers (Collins 1: 14; Schmitz 11). Stevenson made two crucial educational reforms. He started the custom of lecturing largely in English, which was essential to the continuing movement away from classicism, and he was also one of the first to integrate Lockean philosophy into the college curriculum ("Account of Gordon" 22; "Account of Erskine"; Bower 2: 279).

While few records of Stevenson's classes remain, he apparently gave considerable emphasis to English rhetoric and belles lettres. Bower states that Stevenson started the practice of having students compose, deliver, and defend essays on philosophical topics in English as well as Latin (2: 280). About half of the student essays that remain are in English, and they suggest that Stevenson emphasized belletristic topics like taste. Thomas Sommerville, a Moderate clergyman who studied under Stevenson, praised his lectures on "the cardinal points of criticism," which included "many excellent examples and useful practical rules of composition" (13). Stevenson's students were interested in the study of English because they were well aware of the boundaries that their provincial dialect placed upon them. As a student wrote in the class, "the History of our own Country" shows that one must master the "art of making himself agreeable by the charms of a well regulated conversation," which is "the most natural and certain method of rising in the world and making one's fortune" (Drummond 101). The *Autobiography* of Witherspoon's classmate Alexander Carlyle gives the fullest account of Stevenson's course. According to Carlyle, Stevenson made "a judicious selection from the French and English critics"; discussed works by Aristotle, Longinus, Heineccius, and Locke; and presented "a compendious history of the ancient philosophers" (48). Stevenson also lectured on the rhetorical theory of Cicero and Quintilian, and students read three of the authors who would become the standards of early college English studies: Dryden, Pope, and Addison, who are regularly cited in Stevenson's students' essays (Henderson 373; "Account of Gordon").

Witherspoon said that any similiarity between his and Blair's perspectives was due to Stevenson's course (Collins 1: 14). However, one could argue that the basic difference between their perspectives is also evident in their work for that course. Blair wrote an essay on the nature of beauty, just the sort of belletristic topic that predominates in his *Lectures on Rhetoric and Belles Lettres* (Schmitz 12–13). Just as Blair's studies foreshadowed some of his later concerns, Witherspoon's interest in moral philosophy is apparent in his Latin thesis on the immutability of the soul (which is translated and reproduced in Rich). He draws heavily on Ciceronian moral philosophy, while also citing Berkeley and Locke. From these sources, Witherspoon creates a rudimentary form of common-sense philosophy to demonstrate the continuity of reason and revelation. He synthesizes Christian and Ciceronian arguments for the immortality of the soul with a loosely adopted Lockean method to support his conclusion, which he holds to be "so common to all races and to almost all men . . . it seems justifiable to count it among those natural conceptions of ours, which divine truth does not permit to be false" (Rich 164; see also 166). He asserts six final conclusions that he obviously holds to be self- evident because he offers no specific proof for them, including the ideas that space and matter are givens, the world did not always exist, and "Men are by nature free" (Rich 168). By founding these ideas on common sense, Witherspoon foreshadows the response that he and the major Scottish moral philosophers would take to the skepticism of Hume. Witherspoon's inclusion of natural rights as similarly self-evident is important because it shows his early familiarity with the political theories that he would draw on in his own teaching.

Witherspoon's interest in Cicero is not surprising because he remained one of the best-known authorities in moral philosophy until the Scots became predominant later in the century (Phillipson). Records of other Edinburgh professors offer further evidence of Cicero's influence. John Pringle, who would later become president of the Royal Society of London and a friend of Franklin, began lecturing on ethics and political philosophy as assistant professor of moral philosophy at Edinburgh in 1734, and Witherspoon would probably have heard his lectures. The lecture notes that remain from Pringle's courses are in English, and he regularly had his students write essays in English and Latin ("Account of Erskine" 75). Carlyle discusses the importance of Bacon and especially Pufendorf in his studies under Pringle (Carlyle 41), but Pringle apparently covered a wide range of classical and modern authorities, including Cicero, the Commonwealth writers, Shaftesbury, and Hutcheson (Fechner 75). A set of lectures by Pringle entitled "Lectures from Cicero" documents the strong continuities between Cicero and the developing emphases of Scottish moral sense philosophy. Pringle moves easily back and forth from explicating Ciceronian moral philosophy to developing one of the basic themes of Scottish moral philosophy, the theme that social virtue is based in a moral sense that gives us pleasure when we respond with approbation to disinterested "benevolence" in others (Pringle 77–80). James Beattie, the important Aberdeen moral philosopher, delivered a similar set of lectures on Cicero as late as 1778.

Such continuities are important because moral philosophy was central to the Scots' ongoing educational reforms, as can be seen by merely noting who was teaching it. The Glasgow chair in moral philosophy was held by Francis Hutcheson (1730–1746), founder of Scottish moral sense philosophy; Adam Smith (1752–1764), who wrote on moral sentiments as well as economics; and Thomas Reid (1764–1780), whose common-sense moral philosophy dominated the field into the next century. A related line of development can be traced through Edinburgh's moral philosophy chair from Pringle to Adam Feguson (1764–1785) to Dugald Stewart (1785–1810), an influential Scottish common sense philosopher, who ties the Edinburgh line to the Glasgow line through his studies under Reid. Such academic genealogies emphasize an important dimension of the sociointellectual context of Witherspoon's early development: the professors of the Scottish Enlightenment were part of a closely knit group of intellectuals who heavily influenced each other's ideas, and these ideas evolved as a unified philosophical movement in the universities, with the study of moral philosophy playing a particularly central role. For these teachers, moral philosophy's importance was not merely academic. Scottish professors saw themselves as spokesmen for polite refinement and social progress, and they were interested in moral philosophy and rhetoric and belles lettres because they wanted to understand and speak to the social world created by the Union. To further this effort, Scottish educators established a curriculum that gave considerable emphasis to contemporary British culture and social affairs, and outside the classroom they joined with other educated Scots in literary societies intended to "improve" Scottish life and letters.

As a traditional Presbyterian, Witherspoon steadfastly opposed the literati's efforts to spread polite secular culture in Scotland, but he was of two minds about the literati's major intellectual source, Francis Hutcheson. Hutcheson and his principal philosophical predecessor, Shaftesbury, are the primary ideological opponents of Witherspoon's first significant work, *Ecclesiastical Characteristics*, which takes its name from Shaftesbury's *Characteristics of Men, Manners, Opinions, Times* (1711). Hutcheson was a basic source for the social and intellectual outlook of the Moderate clergymen, who deemphasized the traditional Calvinist theme of the spiritual regeneration of the elect and preached instead on less divisive and more refined topics, topics like the social duties of Christianity and the moral value of polite studies. Hutcheson himself had taught these themes to those who studied at Glasgow. However, while Hutcheson was an early spokesman for the Moderate outlook that Witherspoon opposed, Hutcheson is also the main source for Witherspoon's *Lectures on Moral Philosophy*. Hutcheson was also an important source for the educational and political reforms that Witherspoon would help to promote in America (see Norton). Hutcheson is thus central to the most curious aspect of Witherspoon's career: Why was Witherspoon an opponent of the "liberalization" of Scottish society, which Hutcheson helped to inspire, and a proponent of the "liberal" American politics that Hutcheson also influenced? Answering this question will also help answer the broader question of how the development of moral philosophy and rhetoric was shaped by the social contexts of post-Union Scotland and pre-Independence America.

Hutcheson and Witherspoon's Ecclesiastical Characteristics

While Hutcheson's studies and early teaching were heavily influenced by Cicero (see William Scott 182–97), Shaftesbury is clearly his source for the moral sense. Against Hobbes's view that self interest is the dominant force in human nature and society, Shaftesbury takes the perspective that people have a "proportionableness, constancy and regularity in all their passions and affections" that create "the economy of a particular creature, both with respect to himself, and to the rest of his species" (1: 291, 289). The "economy of the passions" that harmonizes selfish and social affections in the individual is the microcosm of the "economy of the species or kind" that makes "the *private interest* and *good* of every-one . . . work towards the *general good*" (1: 336, 338). Thus, ethics and politics are conceived in aesthetic terms like balance and harmony, and the private interest and selfish affections are shown to be in harmony with the common good and public-spirited benevolence. For Shaftesbury, "the public interest and one's own" are not only "consistent but inseparable" (1: 282). Shaftesbury opposes this reasoned understanding of the common good to the unenlightened fanaticism that leads to factionalism, for this whole line of thought was meant to justify the reasoned involvement of the educated, not the voice of the mob. Hutcheson agrees with Shaftesbury that "sympathy or fellow-feeling" is the basis for both moral sentiment and social economy (*Introduction to Moral Philosophy* 21). Like Shaftesbury, Hutcheson views the natural state as a state of "peace and good-will, of innocence and beneficence, and not of violence, war, and rapine" as Hobbes had argued (*Introduction* 139). Unlike Hobbes, Hutcheson emphasizes the natural rights that persist from the state of nature to the state of civilized society, which he defines in utilitarian terms as "a society of free men united under one government for their common interest" (*Introduction* 283). According to Hutcheson, rulers have no "divinely nominated" right to power, only that authority given them by the social contract; and "there can be no right to power except what is either founded upon, or speedily obtains, the hearty consent of the body of the people" (286–87). Hutcheson's philosophy of natural rights—which includes rights to religious freedom, happiness, representation, and economic opportunity—gave intellectual support to the American Revolution, which was justified by the argument that the governed had the right and the obligation to change the system of government when it ceased to serve their needs (303).

Like Cicero, Hutcheson treats human beings as social creatures whose interests and general well-being are closely tied to the common good of society. As a result, questions about morality lead directly to discussions of civic ethics. However, Hutcheson conceives of ethics in terms of the moral sense and treats political "economy" in terms of moral-aesthetic harmony, and these conceptualizations create basic tensions in his social philosophy. Hutcheson's efforts to harmonize the needs of the individual and the public good lead him to dismiss conflicts between competing groups within society as merely the expression of unenlightened self-interest. At such points, his speculations about moral sentiments lead to a sentimental moralism that repeatedly insists that conflicts of interest can be easily avoided because "such as sincerely aim at acting the virtuous part, will always easily discern what equity and humanity require, unless, they are too much influenced by selfishness" (*Introduction* 155). This sentimentality is also evident in Hutcheson's belief that "sympathy or fellow-feeling" naturally evolves from relationships to the family, to neighbors, to fellow citizens, to all mankind. Such continuity of collective experience is highly problematic, particularly in a heterogeneous society like eighteenth-century Scotland, where political and religious differences left many of the Lowlanders with little sympathy for their fellow Scots in the Highlands. Educated Scots were sympathetic to Hutcheson's view that aesthetic studies improve individual morality and advance social harmony by refining one's sensibility. This view justified the moral value of polite literature against traditional Calvinists, who saw it as a worldly distraction that was unfit for clergymen and unhealthy for the public. The moral-aesthetic assumptions of Hutcheson's social philosophy also justified both the social authority of the literati, who claimed to speak for refined taste and enlightened social harmony, and the assimilation of Scotland into Britain, which offered a more enlightened culture than had been provided by Scotland's traditional religious and political factionalism.

In addition to supplying the public justification for secular studies, such attitudes fostered an educational philosophy that redefined the traditional relationship between moral philosophy and rhetoric by subordinating rhetoric to belles lettres. Rhetoric and the twin studies of moral philosophy—ethics and politics—were integrally related for Aristotle and Cicero, the primary classical sources in both moral philosophy and rhetoric. In the eighteenth century the relationship between moral philosophy and rhetoric and belles lettres is close and vital, as is evident in the careers of major figures like Adam Smith, who lectured on rhetoric and belles lettres from 1748–1751 at the same time that he was delivering his influential public lectures on political economy and jurisprudence; James Beattie, who developed his belletristic literary theories while holding a chair of moral philosophy at Aberdeen; and Hutcheson, who published on both literary topics and moral philosophy. Works on moral philosophy often included topics related to the individual (ethics and psychology), to society (political history and philosophy, economics, and jurisprudence), as well as to language and literature. Hutcheson himself had explicitly included rhetoric along with poetry and art as a study that strengthened sympathetic moral feelings through aesthetic refinement (*Introduction* 20), but this is a quite different justification of rhetoric than that advanced by classical civic humanists like Aristotle and Cicero, who saw rhetoric and moral philosophy as related disciplines because they shared a concern for political action and civic ethics. While traces of the classical interest in political rhetoric can be seen in works like Hugh Blair's *Lectures on Rhetoric and Belles Lettres,* political discourse is given far less attention than literary issues like sublimity and genius because they better exemplify the continuity between morality and aesthetics that was as important to Blair as it was to Hutcheson (see Miller).

Hutcheson has traditionally been seen as the founder of the Scottish Enlightenment, not just because he introduced some of its characteristic concerns but also because he helped to create an intellectual environment where secular inquiry could be defended against orthodox Calvinists, who were appalled that ministers would attend the theater, let alone begin to write plays, as John Home would do, or defend skeptics like Kames and Hume, as leading Moderates would do. However, the aestheticism of Hutcheson's civic ethics and the easy optimism of his social philosophy provided a rather thin foundation for the study of political rhetoric, for civic ethics, and for civic humanism in general. His emphasis on the natural rights of the governed did justify revolutions against governments that failed to serve the common good; however, his moral-aesthetic model of the common good tended to treat the conflicting interests within society as the expressions of narrow self-interests that disrupted the harmony of the general economy, an economy that was best understood by those with the polite refinement necessary to appreciate its balance, proportion, and harmony—in short men of letters like Hutcheson and the Moderate literati. In the practice of the literati, one can see that Hutcheson's moral philosophy did serve to empower the politely educated as the voice of enlightened harmony while his moral-aesthetic assumptions tended to depict opposing political groups as self-serving and unreasonable factions.

How did Witherspoon respond to all of this? From his first publication, an article criticizing Kames's *Essays on Principles of Morality and Natural Religion* (1753), Witherspoon opposed the skepticism and the easy moralism that he saw developing in Scottish moral philosophy in the wake of Hutcheson. In the same year Witherspoon also wrote *Ecclesiastical Characteristics,* and according to his *Serious Apology for the Ecclesiastical Characteristics* (1763), the work was intended as a direct response to Hutcheson (*Works* 3: 277). *Ecclesiastical Characteristics* went through more than ten editions to become his best known work. In it, he satirizes those who use terms like "beauty, order, proportion, harmony" to describe human nature as "a little glorious piece of clock-work, a wheel within a wheel, or rather a pendulum in this grand machine" (68, 81). He ridicules the whole idea that aesthetics can provide a model for morality: "According to modern discoveries, there is a great analogy between the 'moral virtues,' or if you will, the 'science of morals,' and the 'fine arts'; and it is on account of this analogy that most of the present reigning expressions upon the subject of morals are borrowed from the arts, as 'beauty, order, proportion, harmony, decency'" (68). Witherspoon rejects the closely related assumption that an enlightened individual can understand what is best for society because his Calvinism led him to view human understanding as itself highly fallible (167–68). Witherspoon also criticizes the "good of-the-whole scheme" of moral philosophy because it contributes to the Moderates' elitist and intolerant political practice, "a transcript in miniature" of the "order, proportion, and unity of design in the universal system" (80, 100). Because the Moderates assume that they know the "good of the whole," according to Witherspoon, they conclude that "an illustrious and noble end sanctifies the means of attaining it," and since these philosophical principles are evident to all reasonable men, only those driven by faction and self-interest would oppose the larger good the Moderates offered (87, 95).

Obviously, Witherspoon is being less than fair to the targets of his irony, but there is merit to his argument that a moral philosophy that idealizes harmony and proportion strengthens the opinion among the educated that they are the voice of enlightened social harmony because only they have the rational detachment and critical acumen to understand the delicate balance of the social economy. As we will see in the next section, the Moderates did act as if their polite refinement gave them an awareness of the common good unavailable to those who were driven by "enthusiasm," "faction," and "fanaticism." In response to these elitist tendencies, Witherspoon consistently argues for a stronger concern for the voice of the public—an educated public to be sure, but not necessarily a politely educated one—and a greater sensitivity to the fallibility of human understanding, particularly in matters of conscience. As a traditional Calvinist, he was far more pessimistic about the ability of any philosophy to achieve a reliable conception of the common good. He repeatedly argues that the fallibility of human understanding makes human authority equally fallible. Thus, individuals have only their consciences to rely on, and when their consciences tell them to resist civil authority, then they have a natural right and a civic duty to do so. The Moderates denied this right because they saw it as threatening to the harmony of the group. In Witherspoon's conflict with the Moderates, one can see his ambivalent attitudes to Scottish moral philosophy develop into a political philosophy that would lead him to support the cause of revolution in America, while the Moderates remained loyal to the common good of the Empire.

The Conflict with the Moderates and Ecclesiastical Characteristics

Witherspoon opposed the Moderates on a variety of social and religious issues, but the most important political conflict centered on the question of who would select local ministers, an important question because they were the major social authorities in many communities. The issue had not been clearly resolved since the Revolution Settlement of 1690, which had established a compromise between the rights of congregations and upper-class patrons. In the 1750s, church patronage became involved with the exercise of political party patronage when the managers of British interests in Scotland began to work in concert with the Moderates to insist uncompromisingly upon church patronage as a means of local political control. The Moderates have recently attracted considerable scholarly attention, some of it quite sensitive to their goals and assumptions (see Sher), but the traditional view has been that they were a conservative social elite who identified themselves with the ruling political interest. For example, Smout views them as "the mouthpiece of the lairds" who were insensitive to the culture and social problems of the common people (Smout 330, 238; see also Craig; Shaw). Against the Moderates' efforts to establish strong centralized control over local churches, Witherspoon and his allies in the "Orthodox" or "Popular" party supported the right of congregations to be involved in the choice of their clergy on the grounds that forcing unpopular ministers on congregations weakened the Church's social authority and subverted its traditional democratic structure.

In 1751 William Robertson, Hugh Blair, and the other founders of the Moderate party failed to persuade the General Assembly of the church to assert its authority over regional presbyteries who refused to settle unpopular ministers. To justify their dissent from the Assembly's decision, Robertson and several other Moderates wrote "Reasons of Dissent," which Morren calls *"the Manifesto of the Moderate Party"* (see Morren 1: 197–99) The pamphlet opens by straightforwardly rejecting the common argument that the right to follow one's conscience gave local congregations and presbyteries the right to dissent from the decisions of the General Assembly: "When men are considered as individuals, we acknowledge that they have no guide but their own understanding, and no judge but their own conscience. But we hold it for an undeniable principle, that as members of society, they are bound in many cases to follow the judgment of society" (Robertson et al. 1: 231). The pamphlet goes on to equate "liberty of conscience" with "anarchy and confusion" (1: 233) and to identify the judgment of the General Assembly as "absolute and final" (1: 231). By thus defining the Moderates as the party of social order, the authors succeeded in gaining the support of the gentry and the ruling political faction. With this support, the Moderates convinced the General Assembly in 1752 to begin enforcing centralized control and settle ministers supported by local patrons, even when the minister was rejected by his local congregation.

In "Answers to the Reasons of Dissent," Witherspoon and his allies argued against the Moderates on the grounds that individuals have both "a right" and "an indispensable duty" to follow their conscience because it speaks from God, a higher power than any civil authority (Witherspoon et al. 1: 244). Therefore, it is a *"self-evident* maxim" that "no man is to be constructed an open transgressor of the laws of Christ, *merely* for not obeying the commands of any Assembly of fallible men" (1: 251). According to this view, the Moderates' efforts to assume absolute authority and thus "destroy *liberty of conscience*" are both inappropriate to a religious society and politically unacceptable because even the highest civil authorities had been limited by the Constitution since the days of the Commonwealth (1: 256). This line of reasoning is important because it shows that Witherspoon had a practical understanding of the continuity between the Commonwealth tradition and his own faith in the primacy of the individual's relationship to God. The Commonwealth writers had rejected the divine right of kings because kings were as humanly fallible as their subjects, who had their own natural and inalienable rights as children of God. In his defense of the "self-evident" right of active dissent, Witherspoon argues that the Moderates' philosophical systems and polite refinement do not make them any less humanly fallible, and thus all societies must recognize the inalienable right to act on conscience.

In *Ecclesiastical Characteristics* (1753), Witherspoon returns again and again to the irony that the Moderates were attacking orthodoxy as a source of factionalism while at the same time they were establishing themselves as the ruling faction. According to his ironical critique, the Moderates' governed by "authority" rather than reasoned argument because they assumed that "the principles of moderation being so very evident to reason, it is a demonstration that none but unreasonable men can resist their influence" (94). In practice, the Moderates did tend to resist public opinion and rely on the political support of the upper classes in a way that created considerable alienation within the Church. This alienation can be seen in the rising numbers of seceders, which reached 100,000 by 1765 (Sloan, *Scottish Enlightenment* 110). The Moderates' alliance with the upper classes is the target of four of the twelve maxims of *Ecclesiastical Characteristics*. According to Witherspoon, Moderate Christianity would be perfected when it became an entirely patrician religion, "when we shall have driven away the whole common people to the Seceders, who alone are fit for them, and captivated the hearts of the gentry to a love of our solitary temples" (101). This gentrification of the Church would be accomplished by preaching the polite refinement that the upper classes find more comforting than the dark orthodoxies of Calvinism. Witherspoon's criticisms in maxim four of the Moderates' polite sermonizing on social duties show that his sense of the practical applications of rhetoric and moral philosophy was quite different from that found in Blair's *Sermons* (1777–1801).

If one reads the *Ecclesiastical Characteristics* in the context of Witherspoon's conflict with the Moderates, one can see the practical political origins of his developing social philosophy. He criticized the aestheticism and moralism of Hutcheson and Shaftesbury because he saw how it could lead educated leaders in practice to assume that they knew better than the public, and he spoke for the rights of the public not because he was a radical democrat but because he was a religious conservative concerned with practical public piety, which he saw as essential to spiritual and economic prosperity. In America this conservative orientation would lead him to support the American Revolution, while Moderates like Hugh Blair and George Campbell were strong public opponents of both the American and French revolutions. However, it is important to note that while the traditionalists in the Scottish Church generally tended to be more supportive of democracy at home and abroad, it was the Moderates who spoke out for freedom of inquiry and religious tolerance when traditional Scots called for the suppression of skeptics like Hume or rioted against offering Catholics basic civil rights. What such facts emphasize is that terms like "liberal" and "conservative" are virtually meaningless unless one closely attends to what they actually meant in social practice. In the social practices of the Moderates, one can see that the liberal political ideals of Hutcheson could lead to conservative political practices, but in America these same ideals could be revolutionary because the social situation of pre-Independence America was quite different from post-Union Scotland (see Hook).

Witherspoon and the Scottish Emigration to America

When Witherspoon was persuaded to come to Princeton in 1768, he found much that was familiar to him, particularly in the Presbyterian Church. Total immigration of Scots and Scots-Irish in the eighteenth century would reach between 200,000 and 300,000, making those of Scottish descent around 10 percent of the American population by 1790 (see Sloan, *Scottish Enlightenment* 36; Brock 13; and Henretta 124–28). As in Scotland, the Presbyterian Church was divided between more established clergy and "New Light" evangelical populists. New Light clergy like Gilbert Tennent, Samuel Finley, and Samuel Davies had established Princeton in 1742 as an alternative to the established universities, and in 1768 they convinced Witherspoon to become president because they wanted to circumvent the established clergy's efforts to gain control of Princeton (see Butterfield). In America, as in Scotland, New Light revivalists toured the countryside preaching that damnation awaited anyone who had not experienced spiritual "regeneration," "the great foundation of true religion and social virtue" (Davies 191). Like their Scottish counterparts, the American evangelicals criticized the established clergy for being too coolly rational and too concerned with worldly advancement and social refinement. In America, however, the established clergy failed to inspire the younger generation, as professors like Hutcheson, Robertson, Blair, and others had been able to do; and the conflict was not resolved through patronage because America was farther removed from the machinations of British party politics.

Both Scotland and America witnessed popular evangelical movements between the 1730s and 1760s (Landsman 227–55). On both sides of the Atlantic, evangelicals like George Whitefield, whom Witherspoon holds forth as a model in his "Lectures on Eloquence," preached on the populist theme that God's law overruled earthly authorities and bestowed natural rights on all. However, in America the "Great Awakening" of anti-establishmentarian evangelism contributed in a decisive way to the political awakening of the public. In fiery tent revival sermons and pamphlets such as Gilbert Tennent's *Danger of an Unconverted Ministry* (1740), New Light clergymen reasoned from the equality of all before God to attack the established clergy and argue that the only legitimate source of religious authority was a personal emotional regeneration of the spirit, an experience particularly essential to clergymen but accessible to the uneducated and educated alike. These criticisms of institutionalized authorities often created considerable social unrest. The New Lights often condemned the local minister by name, and their tent revivals sometimes led to the founding of new churches and reading societies, where people read and wrote with others who had also placed themselves outside the reach of the community's religious authorities. Throughout the colonies, the Great Awakening created a heated debate that put terms like "natural rights" and "personal freedom" at the center of a public dialogue that was unprecedented in scope and intensity (see Baldwin).

American evangelicals had a more significant political impact because they spoke to a public quite different from post-Union Scotland. In Scotland advocates of Enlightenment like the Moderates worked to transform a traditional sectarian society into an integral part of Britain. As a result, the Presbyterian Church, which had been a traditional bastion of the Scottish national identity, was divided between defenders of traditional religious values and those who sought to use the Church to spread polite British culture in Scotland. As a result, the opposition of religion and Enlightenment became intensely political and intensely divisive. On the other side of the Atlantic the rising debate over America's place in the British Empire was beginning to establish a consensus that Americans were economically, politically, and morally justified to resist Britain. The colonies were becoming increasingly unified against the Stamp Act of 1765 and other such policies when Witherspoon arrived from Scotland. Thus, by emigrating to America, Witherspoon stepped from a province that was deeply divided over how to respond to British political and cultural influences to another British province that was increasingly unified in its opposition to outside control. In America the tension between the advocates of reason and revelation was not exacerbated by political divisions because religious and secular leaders largely worked together to oppose Britain and establish a national government and a governing elite. Thus, while religious revivalism and political reform had clear continuities on both sides of the Atlantic, in America this continuity contributed to the development of a national leadership that was ready to apply the public debates over religious rights and authorities to secular politics.

American revivalists had a particularly important impact on higher education. Evangelicals founded four out of the six colleges that were established in the period. While the Scottish literati supported educational reform as a means to spread polite culture in Scotland, in America it was often evangelicals who turned to educational reform in order to prepare clergy to speak to the public in less refined and more moving language. However, these educators did not intend to make colleges into seminaries, and in fact their reforms contributed to the production of a generation of leaders who spoke not from the pulpit but the political forum. Garry Wills has emphasized the important role that Scottish educators played in this development: "The education of our revolutionary generation can be symbolized by this fact: At age sixteen Jefferson *and* Madison *and* Hamilton were all being schooled by Scots who had come to America as adults" (*Explaining* 63). According to Jefferson's *Autobiography,* his studies in rhetoric, belles lettres, and moral philosophy at William and Mary under William Small "probably fixed the destinies of my life" (20). Madison considered his studies in these same pivotal subjects under Witherspoon so important that he stayed on after graduation to pursue them. However, the impact of Scottish moral philosophy and rhetoric cannot be identified with a few isolated figures, no matter how important they were, because the rising status of the study of moral philosophy and rhetoric in English was part of a broad educational and social development, and it is this broader development that forms the context for Witherspoon's own writings on rhetoric and moral philosophy.

The Origins of English Rhetoric and Scottish Moral Philosophy in America

The revivalists who founded and led Princeton had strong ties with the Scottish universities and the English dissenting academies, which were far more innovative than the English universities. The influence of the Scottish universities in America had important implications for both moral philosophy and English studies because the traditional arts curriculum that the older American universities had adopted from the English universities severely limited the study of contemporary life and letters. Rhetoric was traditionally studied in Latin, the language of the academy, not the public forum; and the predominance of Peter Ramus's rhetorical theory split language studies in half by limiting rhetoric to style and allotting invention to the province of logic, specifically the syllogistic logic of Aristotle. Ramus's stylistic rhetoric and the formulaic logic of Aristotelianism suited the Puritans' ambivalent attitudes to the worldliness of classical learning, for they studied the classics intensively, not extensively, in order to master the stylistic forms of the educated language. The limited concerns of the traditional curriculum cut rhetoric off from the civic vision of classical rhetoric. Despite the reigning classicism, classical civic humanists like Isocrates, Cicero, and Quintilian were rarely studied in the seventeenth and early eighteenth centuries (see Guder 38–41; Guthrie, "Rhetorical Theory in Colonial America" 48–49; and Morrison, *Harvard* 172–73, 175n).

The limitations that this scholasticism placed on rhetoric are most evident in the extensive reliance on syllogistic disputations. To demonstrate what they had learned, students delivered ritualized syllogistic disputations that laid down time-worn theses and defended them against opponents' refutations, which were often as well known as the original theses. These formulaic disputations were both the principal vehicle and the end of instruction until the middle of the eighteenth century. Students recited them in class and delivered them upon important occasions like commencement to demonstrate that they had mastered the logical and rhetorical forms of the educated community. This ritualized display of accepted wisdoms had come down to colonial America virtually unchanged from the time of Abelard according to Morrison (*Harvard* 143). However, in the 1770s Latin syllogistic disputations began to be replaced by forensic debates in English (see Bohman 65). This adoption of the informal style of debate common in public life is one of the most significant indications of the developing reorientation of American higher education in the period. With the institution of a more socially applicable form of debate in the commencement speeches of the 1770s, students were called on to demonstrate their ability to use the contemporary idiom to address public issues, not the abstractions of scholastic epistemology and ontology.

The introduction of debates in English was not the only example of the emerging interest in English studies. As early as 1722 Harvard students were studying English literature and composition in philosophical societies, and at about the same time the predominant stylistic rhetoric began to be questioned in the classroom as well (see Potter 66–

70). In 1754 a committee was established at Harvard to promote oratory in English as well as Latin, and in 1766 a tutor was appointed to teach "Elocution, composition in English, Rhetoric, and other parts of the Belles Lettres" (qtd. in Quincy 2: 124, 133). The first professorship of English in America was established at the College of Philadelphia in 1755. In 1763 at King's College (Columbia) the curriculum was reorganized to give more emphasis to public speaking (Aly 36). And at Yale, English debates were begun around 1751; English was apparently first taught in 1767; and rhetoric and belles lettres were being taught by the president in 1776 (Kelly 80). While classical studies remained dominant, they were also affected by the increasing interest in the contemporary idiom. Cicero and Aristotle were studied more widely, and in ways better suited to public life. For example, at King's College the same reorganization that gave new emphasis to oratory introduced the study of Aristotle's works on ethics and politics, and Cicero's rhetorical theory was more broadly examined (Aly 36). According to Guthrie, by 1750 Quintilian and Cicero achieved a widespread influence in rhetorical studies that the truncated rhetoric of Ramus had denied them in the previous century, and at the same time neo-Ciceronian works like John Ward's *A System of Oratory* also became popular ("Development of Rhetorical Theory in America: II" 15; "Rhetorical Theory in Colonial America" 54).

At the same time that English studies were gaining importance, Scottish moral philosophy was also becoming influential. The best known Scottish moral philosopher in America in the first half of the eighteenth century was Francis Hutcheson, who was studied at Harvard almost from the time of his first publication in 1725 (Fiering 106). Other Scots were also well known. David Fordyce's "Elements of Moral Philosophy," which was included in Dodsley's extremely popular *Preceptor,* was used as the standard ethics text at Harvard after its publication in 1748 (Morrison, *Three Centuries* 89). Fordyce himself cites Hutcheson as a source for his view that the "counterpoise" between "*Private*" and "*Public*" affections balances the self-interest against the public interest in a state of "calm dispassionate BENEVOLENCE" ("Elements" 2: 278, 279). These social philosophies had explicit educational implications. Fordyce recommends broadening the curriculum beyond the classics to include a stronger concern for contemporary life ("Elements" 2: 276). Fordyce's ambivalence to the dominance of classical studies is evident in his satiric portrait of a classical "book-worn" scholar who is so alienated from contemporary society that he cannot even name a prime minister. This classicist knows everything about ancient writers, everything except for the basic fact that they were themselves committed to an active public life (*Dialogues* 95). Like other Scots, Fordyce placed moral philosophy at the center of his educational philosophy: "This *Moral Art or Science,* which unfolds our Duty and Happiness, must be a proper Canon or Standard, by which the Dignity and Importance of every other Art and Science are to be ascertained" ("Elements" 2: 243).

Fordyce, Hutcheson, and Thomas Reid's teacher George Turnbull are the major sources of Franklin's *Proposals for the Education of Youth* (1749), which put forth an alternative to the traditional classical education. Franklin helped institute this alternative by founding the Academy and Charitable School of Philadelphia in 1751, which became the College of Philadelphia in 1755. With the new charter of 1755, two Scottish college graduates assumed control of the reorganized college: Provost William Smith, who had been hired to teach juniors and seniors logic, rhetoric, and moral philosophy in 1754, and Vice-provost Francis Alison, who took over the teaching of moral philosophy from Smith soon afterwards (Cheyney 43). Drawing on his own Scottish education, Smith instituted a curriculum that contained more than the accepted classical and religious subjects. One-third of the students' studies was devoted to contemporary science, language, and culture (Rudolph 32). Smith's educational philosophy is clearly expressed in pamphlets like *Some Thoughts on Education* (1752), where he cites Shaftesbury and Hutcheson's arguments that a liberal education oriented to public life is far better than either that "Pedantry and School Learning, which lies amidst the Dregs of Ancient Literature; or that of the fashionable illiterate World, which aims merely at the Character of the fine Gentleman" (10). Alison's moral philosophy course closely followed Hutcheson, which is not surprising since Alison had studied under him at Glasgow. Like Hutcheson, Alison emphasized such political issues as the social contract and natural rights (see McAllister). Before coming to Philadelphia, Alison had run his own Presbyterian academy, where he had instituted a curriculum that gave considerable attention to English composition and Scottish moral philosophy (Sloan, *The Great Awakening* 176).

Educational Reform at Princeton

The best source on the curriculum, entrance requirements, and daily routine that Witherspoon found when he arrived at Princeton is Samuel Blair's *Account of the College of New Jersey* (1764). The school gave less emphasis to classical and religious studies than colleges like Harvard, and new attention was being given to natural philosophy, moral philosophy, and English. Students studied Shakespeare, Milton, and Addison and delivered syllogistic and forensic orations in the evenings in English as well as Latin. These orations were intended not merely as rote repeti-

tions of classroom material but as opportunities to explore issues that
the students had independently researched in the college library (26).
Blair states that Princeton's purpose was to spread "Science and
Religion," but he is as careful as his predecessors to emphasize that
Princeton was organized "to cherish a spirit of liberty and free
enquiry," rather than to instill a specific religious viewpoint. From
the start, Tennent and Davies and the other leaders of Princeton had
emphasized that it was not a private religious seminary but "a public
seminary of learning" (Tennent and Davies 182). Like Blair, Tennent
and Davies did emphasize the congruence of religion and "her
constant attendant," science (178). According to Davies, science and
religion are bound irrevocably to the public interest, without which
"all the valuable ends of a liberal education will be lost" (189). The
curriculum under Blair reflects this concern for educating public
leaders, not classical scholars or theologians. Classical studies dominated only the first year and a half, after which students moved
on to science, math, logic, rhetoric, history, geography, and moral
philosophy. The only religious study mentioned is the option of
Hebrew in the junior year for aspiring clergymen. Far more significant
than such studies is the fact that the final year was devoted to review
and to "composition," including weekly public speaking exercises
continued from the previous year (Samuel Blair 24–25).

   When Witherspoon arrived at Princeton, he thus found a curriculum
that represented some of the most significant innovations of the period.
Under Witherspoon these reforms would have a major impact on the
American Revolution. While Princeton was smaller than Harvard and
Yale, its student population was less regionalized than either. According
to McLachlan, 90 percent of Harvard's students came from Massachu-
setts; 75 percent of Yale's students came from Connecticut; and other
schools like William and Mary drew almost entirely on their own specific
areas. However, Princeton's students came from all the colonies and
from a wider cross section of colonial society because Princeton was the
cheapest college and had strong support from the popular evangelical
movement (xix–xx). Under Witherspoon, several Indians and blacks
attended Princeton, including the important teacher and minister John
Chavis (Collins 2: 217). For its comparatively small size, Princeton made
a large contribution to the emerging national leadership. For example,
nine of the twenty-five college graduates at the Constitutional Conven-
tion in 1787 were from Princeton (including five who had graduated
under Witherspoon), while only four came from Yale and three from
Harvard (Norris 73). The Constitution itself was shaped by Princeton
graduates: Madison inspired the Virginia Plan to establish representation by population, and other Princeton graduates sponsored the New

Jersey Plan of state representation and the compromise solution to combine the two plans (Norris 74–75).

After arriving at Princeton, Witherspoon made a number of changes in everything from the college-sponsored grammar school to the institution of graduate studies. He increased the attention given to English in the grammar school, which he personally administered (Collins 1: 110). In a letter advising teachers on how to prepare their students for Princeton, he also encouraged them to teach more English (rptd. *New Jersey Archives* 2nd Series 4: 225). Beginning in 1769, he wrote several newspaper articles stressing the emphasis given to English in the grammar school and announcing the regular program of public Latin and English exercises (rptd. *New Jersey Archives* 1st series 26: 269, 383–84, 525–26, 568–69). In 1769 he also added reading and writing English to the college's entrance requirements (Wertenbaker 91–92). According to Guder's detailed analysis of the curriculum, under Witherspoon English was studied in all four years, including Lowth's *English Grammar,* Holme's *Rhetoric,* Sheridan's *Rhetorical Grammar,* and Witherspoon's own course in rhetoric and criticism in the last two years (169–70). Witherspoon believed that a college would be "very imperfect" if it did not teach students "taste, propriety and accuracy in that language which they must speak and write all their life" (*Druid,* in *Works* 4: 458). This orientation to life beyond the classroom is also evident in the graduate program that Witherspoon established, a program of studies intended not just to prepare students for the traditional scholarly professions, but to "fit young Gentlemen for serving their Country in public Stations" (rptd. *New Jersey Archives* 1st series 26: 306). When Madison stayed on after graduation to pursue this course of studies, he became Princeton's first graduate student outside of divinity (Thorp et al. 6–9).

According to Bohman, Witherspoon developed the most extensive program of oratorical study in revolutionary America (68). The students' diaries and letters are full of references to their compositions. Virtually every evening students gathered for speeches and debates in the main hall. These exercises, which sometimes included dramatic performances, were attended by the whole school as well as by townspeople and visiting dignitaries, who would occasionally offer comments and suggestions. One of the student orations aptly expressed the underlying assumption of this program: "Any Person of Tolerable Genius, may by Application acquaint himself with all the Rules of Oratory, but if he has never practised Speaking in Public, if he should be brought before an august Assembly to deliver some important Harangue, he would appear ridiculous to all" (Fithian, "Exercises"). As this student suggests, the purpose of combining classroom instruction with extensive public practice was to prepare students to speak to the practical problems of public

life. These orations had become so important by the end of Witherspoon's tenure that they were covered by a whole section of the college
Laws of 1794 (Guder 202; see also Broderick).

To support the students' work in English composition and criticism,
in 1769 Witherspoon reactivated the student philosophical societies that
had been suppressed shortly before. These societies were renamed the
Whig and the Cliosophic to avoid reawakening the divisiveness that had
marred their predecessors. Among the founders of the Whig and the
Clio were James Madison, Henry Lee, and Aaron Burr. Virtually all the
early records of these societies were destroyed during the Revolution
or by the fire of 1802. However, the "Cliosophic Society Minutes" of
the last decade of the eigtheenth century note that "the objects of the
institution are the same that it embraced before the revolution and are
pursued on the same plan." These minutes give intriguing glimpses of
how important these societies were to the students' education, particularly to their study of rhetoric and politics. Members took pseudonmyms
like "Addison," "Steele," "Hume," "Fenelon," and "Longinus" and debated issues like the rights of women, religious tolerance, equal opportunity for the poor, foreign affairs, and government immigration policies.
Members also criticized and edited the orations that their peers planned
to deliver before the assembled college, and students were fined for
reading essays in public or in class if they had not first undergone this
process of peer editing ("Clio. Minutes" May 15, 1793; January 22,
1794; and February 12, 1794).

To promote Princeton's reputation and attract students, Witherspoon wrote *An Address to the Inhabitants of Jamaica on Behalf of the College
of New Jersey,* which he published in several local papers in 1772. While
Witherspoon emphasizes Princeton's moral discipline, he states that it
has never been a religious seminary because students do not even cover
the basics of theology, and he stresses that his own experiences as an
"opposer of lordly domination and sacerdotal tyranny" have led him to
be a strong supporter of religious freedom (114). Witherspoon emphasizes his ties with Edinburgh and his "constant intercourse and great
intimacy with the members of the University of Glasgow." His contacts
with Glasgow are particularly important because Thomas Reid had been
teaching there since 1764. Witherspoon's description of the curriculum
shows that he had personally taken over the studies that were central
to the Scots' reforms: moral philosophy, modern history, and rhetoric
and criticism. He emphasizes the importance of English at several points
in the *Address*—in his introductory references to his own background,
in his discussions of the students' daily orations and the grammar school,
and in his concluding remarks on the need for more professors (105,
109, 111, 115). He also defends the college's efforts to spread "a Spirit

of Liberty" as testimony to its independence from "those in power" (112).

This "spirit of liberty" was criticized in the local papers by writers who questioned the propriety of having students speak on political issues: "The Students in their public Exhibitions have very often entered deeply into the Party Politics and Contentions of England both in former and latter Times, and in such Manner as to give the greatest Offence to many who were present" (rptd. *New Jersey Archives* 1st series 28: 353). These conservative critics wanted to return to classical studies because they were less controversial and better suited to youthful studies. As "A Friend of Impartiality" wrote in the *Pennsylvania Chronicle* of October 19, 1772, "Institutions of this sort I always understood were intended to enable our youth . . . to attain a competent acquaintance with classic lore . . . with the manners and customs and the philosophical tenets of antiquity." Instead, the writer heard commencement orations on "perplexing political topics" like the British Constitution and the American situation (rptd. *New Jersey Archives* 1st series 28: 317). These conservative responses to the political orientation of Witherspoon's reforms mark a basic conflict over the purpose of higher education. Those who sought a return to the classics wanted colleges to return to their traditional role of instilling the classical knowledge essential to a scholarly gentleman, while Witherspoon was more committed to the ideal of the college graduate as a public leader who was prepared to speak to the political problems of contemporary life.

This conflict focused on commencement because it was the occasion where college graduates were initiated into the educated community by demonstrating their mastery of the shared values and knowledge that defined that community. Thousands of people came to witness the commencement orations, debates, processions, and musical performances. Walsh calls the broadsides that announced the commencement orations "an intellectual challenge to the learned community by the graduating Bachelors" (5). Under Witherspoon, these challenges became less concerned with the traditional topics covered by a classical education and more concerned with the political issues of the day. As one can see from the newspaper articles and commencement broadsides from the period, Witherspoon's own commencement orations mirrored his developing political commitment. In 1768, he spoke on free trade, a controversial issue given the recent British restrictions. His speech was followed by orations on patriotism, genius, and the importance of defending civil liberties even to the death (rptd. *New Jersey Archives* 1st series 26: 285–88). In 1770, he gave an oration on the natural right to defend one's freedom against a king who acts against the law. Other speakers praised the recent "Non-Importation Agreement" as "a noble

Exertion of Self denial and public Spirit," recommended the "Utility of American Manufactures," and argued that the purpose of classical studies was to advance scientific knowledge (rptd. *New Jersey Archives* 1st series 27: 268–69).

Thus, Witherspoon soon after arriving at Princeton embraced the political controversies of the time as part of the concerns of higher education. While the increased attention to English alienated those who wanted to see higher education retain its conservative emphasis on the classics, others spoke for making the classics serve contemporary public life. By encouraging his students to speak to political issues, Witherspoon was following the traditional ideals of public leadership that his predecessors had established. Even before he actually became an important political leader, he kept himself and his students informed on current political controversies; he collected democratic pamphlets from soon after his arrival and kept them bound together in his library (Collins 1: 119). His students probably did not need much encouragement to become interested in politics, for the commencement speakers who praised American manufactures in 1770 stood dressed in the homespun clothes that they had all agreed to wear (rptd. *New Jersey Archives* 27: 209). In any case, under Witherspoon commencement exercises became important public occasions for students to demonstrate their ability to speak to the political issues of the day.

Rhetorical Theory and Practice in Eighteenth-Century America

At the commencement of 1783 Witherspoon's students were praising the political significance of rhetoric, while Hugh Blair at the same time in his courses at Edinburgh was largely ignoring contemporary political debate and relying entirely on classical models of political discourse (*Lectures on Rhetoric and Belles Lettres* 2: 46–73; see Miller). The differing attitudes are not surprising given the contexts. The Continental Congress was meeting at Princeton after having been driven out of Philadelphia, and Witherspoon's students addressed an audience that included seven signers of the Declaration of Independence, nine signers of the Articles of Confederation, eleven signers of the Constitution, and two future presidents (Norris 105). Faced with such an audience, Witherspoon's students would have been directly aware of the same general lesson that the political conflicts of the time impressed on aspiring students throughout America: Rhetoric was a political art of considerable public influence. The apolitical attitude of Scottish belletristic rhetoric reflected a different political context. No more telling comment on the insignificance of open debate in Scottish politics could be made than that by a Scottish member of Parliament who reflected on a long career of deal making and concluded that "I have heard many arguments which convinced my judgment, but never one which influenced my vote" (qtd. in Johnston 215). In Scotland, as in America, pamphlets and speeches often did influence public events, but the creation of a national political life in America made rhetoric far more politically and educationally significant. The increased educational emphasis on rhetoric was a direct response to the intensifying public debate, which created a need for leaders who could speak and write for the public. There are clear parallels between the rising public debate and the rise of English studies; for example, the number of American newspapers rose from twenty-six to forty-four in the decade preceding the Declaration of Independence, while the number of books on English—spellers, dictionaries, grammars, and rhetorics— grew from nine in 1769 to thirty-six by 1789 (Evans).

Such developments gave added significance to moral philosophy as well as rhetoric because the former provided an intellectual focus on public life, while the latter provided the skills necessary to speak to the public. From Scots like Hutcheson and from classical civic humanists like Cicero, Witherspoon and other American educational reformers adopted the basic assumption that humans are by nature social creatures who need an active public life to exercise their rational and moral faculties. From this assumption, the Scots had argued that moral philosophy—including jurisprudence, politics, ethics, and "oeconomicks"— covered the "commanding arts" of what an educated person should know (Hutcheson, *Short* 2). As we have seen, some of the same Scots who redefined the "commanding arts" of ethics and politics also pioneered the study of English rhetoric, composition, and literature at the college level. However, as has also been noted, the Scottish literati's desire for advancement in polite society led them to emphasize belletristic studies at the expense of political rhetoric, and this approach was reinforced by Hutcheson's discussions of political economy and civic ethics in the terms of aesthetics. While the Scots thus developed a political philosophy without a political voice, their educational philosophy did open up the curriculum to the study of public life, and in America, this opening came at a time when the educated classes were assuming new leadership roles in an increasingly literate and self-aware public, roles that made speaking in political forums more important than the polite taste of British high culture.

One can see how public leadership was actually changing by comparing Witherspoon's students with those of his predecessors. In the two decades before Witherspoon arrived at Princeton, 46.4 percent of the graduates entered the ministry (McLachlan xxi–ii). However, only 24.3 percent of Witherspoon's students became ministers (Maclean 357, 402–03), and between 1777 and 1794 only 13 percent of his students did so (Collins 2: 222). According to Sloan, the number of students entering the ministry declined at all American colleges, though not as severely as at Princeton (*Scottish Enlightenment* 131n). Witherspoon's students increasingly went on to become other kinds of leaders. Thirteen became college presidents, twenty officers in the revolutionary army, twenty-three judges, three Supreme Court justices, twenty-one senators, thirty-nine representatives, twelve governors, one vice-president (Aaron Burr), and one president (James Madison) (Norris 94). The major cause of this transition was the politicization of American society that resulted from the Revolution and the creation of a national state. However, the ministry was itself changing. In the colonial period a minister had held considerable cultural authority as the spokesman for the moral traditions of the community, but the Great Awakening had created divisions within the major churches that weakened their ability to minister to the expanding population. Increasing numbers of people began to grow up outside the established churches, particularly on the frontier; and in the cities, ministers' traditional authority was undermined by increasing social diversification. As a result, ministers were increasingly seen as contractual employees, and the social authority of the church was itself diminished (see Henretta 210; May 61).

At the same time that ministers were losing their traditional social authority, the conflict with Britain was creating a need for a new sort of social leader, a political leader who could address the increasingly literate population on the pressing issues of the day. According to Morgan, "In 1740 America's leading intellectuals were clergymen and thought about theology; in 1790 they were statesmen and thought about politics. . . . One may properly consider the American Revolution, as an intellectual movement, to mean the substitution of political for clerical leadership and of politics for religion as the most challenging area of human thought and endeavor" (11). In the last three decades of the eighteenth century, Americans created regional and national assemblies with the authority to regulate public life, business, and war. With the creation of a national political life came the institutionalization not just of political parties, but of political interests, interests defined by new ideologies as well as by traditional loyalties. While leadership roles like the ministry had called for graduates educated in the classics and theology, the role of politician called for individuals with a new awareness of political ideology and the skills to negotiate between conflicting political interests. John Witherspoon was one of the central figures in the transition from clerical to political leadership; he helped introduce the Scottish moral philosophy that was pivotal to that transition; and he taught one of the greatest practical theorists of the new political ideology, James Madison.

The basic ideals of Witherspoon's educational philosophy are perhaps best expressed in the graduation sermon that was first delivered in 1775. This sermon presents a civic vision that views an active public life as the completion of a Christian commitment. For Witherspoon, humanity is by nature social, and Christianity calls one to public service. Witherspoon's *Christian Magnanimity* is indebted to the Scottish moral philosophers who treated "benevolence" as the sympathetic feelings for others that lead us to an active public life. While Witherspoon distinguishes his own ideal from such "worldly" magnanimity, he presents a social ideal that is quite similiar, the ideal of the leader who forswears "sloth and ease" to work hard to accomplish great things (116, 118). Such industriousness instills personal virtue, protects the rights of all, and promotes the "interest and happiness of mankind" (120). In the pulpit and the classroom, Witherspoon would often preach and teach the basic theme that frugality, prudence, industriousness, and common sense promote both individual morality and public prosperity, a theme his Calvinist forebearers and his capitalist descendants would both have approved.

The time had come, however, for Witherspoon to start practicing the political theories he taught. As early as 1771, in *Ignorance of the British with Respect to America* Witherspoon expresses his commitment to America. From at least 1773, revolutionary feelings had become more and more pronounced at Princeton, and Witherspoon himself had become increasingly politically active. He was to become perhaps the most politically influential college educator in America, and he was certainly more directly involved in revolutionary politics than the presidents of the other American universities. Witherspoon's commitment to the American cause had developed into outright support for revolution by 1776, when he preached the *Dominion of Providence over the Passions of Men,* which is one of the most significant political statements made by a religious leader during the Revolution. For Witherspoon, the step from educator and minister to politician was easy to make because all three were simply different ways of exercising the public leadership he had sought to teach and preach.

Witherspoon as a Practicing Rhetorician

Witherspoon became an advocate of the public interest very early in the conflict with Britain. In 1768 and 1769, he made tours through the colonies that so impressed him with the relative prosperity, the safety and ease of travel, and the comparatively democratic political assemblies that he began to encourage Scottish emigration (Collins 2: 115–18). He was criticized in the Scottish press for being unpatriotic because such efforts sapped Britain's strength, and in 1771 he wrote a response, a letter for the *Scots Magazine,* which was not accepted and remained unpublished until included in his collected works. Witherspoon argues that one is "a friend to his country" by being a friend to its people, which in this case meant offering them the opportunity to escape their poverty by emigrating (4: 285). He implicitly rejects the accepted mercantilist belief that a country is made prosperous by keeping the public poor and thus industrious. He argued instead that emigration only threatens "landholders, who may run some risk of being obliged to lower their rents. But is this a liberal way of thinking, to say a man is an enemy to his country, while he promotes the happiness of the great body of the people with a small diminution of the interest of a handful?" (4: 286). In 1774 in *Thoughts on American Liberty,* Witherspoon moves toward thinking of the American public interest as distinct from the political interests of Britain. He recommends that the Continental Congress profess loyalty to the king but maintain a united front, pass the delayed nonimportation agreements, strengthen colonial militias, draw up a plan of union, and, most of all, take a stand "not only that we esteem the claim of the British parliament to be illegal and unconstitutional, but that we are firmly determined never to submit to it and do deliberately prefer war with all its horrors, and even extermination itself to slavery, rivetted on us and our posterity" (4: 298–99).

Such works made Witherspoon a well-known public figure. He was a leader of the Presbyterian Church from his first attendance at the reunified synod in 1769 (Collins 1: 123), and the speaking tours that he made through the colonies in his first years in America gave him wide recognition as a spokesman for Princeton and Presbyterianism, America's second largest church (Sweet 3). Only the Congregationalists were more numerous, but they were largely confined to New England. The Presbyterians were centered in New Jersey and Pennsylvania, but they were truly a national church with congregations spread throughout America. America's two largest churches shared a Calvinist tradition that made resistance to tyranny virtually a religious obligation, and Witherspoon helped to ensure that American Presbyterians remembered their political as well as their religious traditions. He headed the committee that wrote a pastoral letter to be read to all congregations on June 29, 1775, and that letter contains the same political proposals as *Thoughts on American Liberty,* including the very passage quoted above. The letter advises church members to respect the king but to support the Continental Congress then meeting in Philadelphia as the representatives of the united colonies. This letter casts ministers in the role of

"men and citizens" and has them offer specific political recommendations on how to approach the conflict, recommendations that changed
the role of the Presbyterian clergy from uncommitted observers to
active supporters of the revolution.

Witherspoon's career on both sides of the Atlantic offers many such
examples of how Presbyterianism supported political reform, but the
most significant example is *Dominion of Providence,* which was preached
on May 17, 1776. According to Trinterud, Witherspoon's sermon gave
"the enormous weight of his prestige to the bringing of politics into the
pulpit. Others had, of course, done it before, but they were lesser men
in influence than he" (249). Witherspoon states that the interests of
religious and political freedom are the same because "there is not a
single instance in history in which civil liberty was lost, and religious
liberty preserved entire." He also cites Cromwell and "the republican
opposition to monarchial usurpation during the civil wars" (140–41,
136). In line with the Commonwealth tradition, Witherspoon argues
that because humans are fallible, human authority is equally fallible: "I
do not refuse submission to their unjust claims because they are corrupt
or profligate . . . but because they are men, and therefore liable to all
the selfish bias inseparable from human nature" (141). While he thus
assumes the traditional Calvinist view that human nature is basically
flawed, he argues that Americans have an historic opportunity to create
a new political and moral order, for the cause of America is the "cause
of justice, of liberty, and of human nature" (140). Witherspoon and
many other revolutionary leaders felt that they were creating not just a
new nation, but a new national character based on a "public spirit" that
would bring "all ranks of men" together (142). In *An Address to the Natives
of Scotland residing in America,* which was published with *Dominion of
Providence,* Witherspoon argues that because America was being con-
sciously created, rather than simply resulting from the "caprices" of
kings, Americans had a unique opportunity to create a nation that
would realize the potential of the Commonwealth (*Works* 3: 54). In
"Upon the Confederation," Witherspoon argues that there had been
"great improvements, not only in human knowledge, but in human
nature," and thus Americans could create a government based on "that
enlarged system called the balance of power" that would remedy not
just the weaknesses of preceding constitutions but also some of the
weaknesses of the human constitution itself (151).

In both the *Address* and *Dominion of Providence* Witherspoon preaches
the social values that he sought to establish as part of the new national
character. He speaks in the same terms that he had used in his final
remarks to his graduating students at Princeton, terms like "frugality,"
"temperance," "moderation," and "decency." Witherspoon's comments

on "the public interest of religion" highlight the recurrent theme that individual morality and public prosperity depend upon a strong Protestant work ethic: "Habits of industry prevailing in a society not only increase its wealth as their immediate effect, but they prevent the introduction of many vices and are intimately connected with sobriety and good morals. . . . Industry, therefore, is a moral duty of the greatest moment, absolutely necessary to national prosperity, and the sure way of obtaining the blessing of God" (144, 146). For Witherspoon, frugality "stands in the most immediate connection both with virtuous industry and active public spirit" (146). Such statements show how Witherspoon's work ethic helped to translate the classical ideal of civic leadership into terms that justified business and industry, which were an anathema to traditional civic humanists like Aristotle.

Witherspoon spent most of his time in the years following the appearance of *Dominion of Providence* practicing rather than teaching rhetoric. Princeton was overrun by the British on November 29, 1776, and even when classes resumed the following year, Witherspoon was frequently absent (see Norris 92; Wertenbaker 57–62). Witherspoon gained considerable notoriety from *Dominion of Providence,* which went through at least nine editions in Philadelphia, London, and Glasgow and was reviewed in the *Monthly Review* in 1778 and in the *Scots Magazine* in 1777. The two Glasgow editions of *Dominion of Providence* and *An Address to the Natives of Scotland* included hostile commentary that identified Witherspoon as "a chief promoter of the American revolt." According to the "Advertisement" to the Glasgow editions, "the unhappy commotions in our American colonies" are due to "clerical influence: and none . . . had a greater share . . . than Dr Witherspoon" (ii). These comments provide contemporary testimony on the important role that clergymen were playing in arousing public support for the American cause, and the accompanying comment that Witherspoon's sermon "blends the most rebellious sentiments with the most sacred and important truths" suggests that the editor was uncomfortably aware of how easily traditional Calvinist assumptions could be put to such uses. With *Dominion of Providence* Witherspoon himself thus achieved international recognition as an influential spokesman for American interests. The sermon marks the beginning of the most important period of Witherspoon's public career. In May 1776, he joined the New Jersey provincial assembly, and from there he went on to the Continental Congress, where he served until 1782.

As head of what Pomfret has called the most radical delegation in the New Jersey Assembly, Witherspoon played an active part in removing the royal governor, William Franklin, and setting up an independent political body (253). When the Continental Congress wrote the Assembly recommending this course of action, the correspondence was sent to Witherspoon personally (see Collins 1: 208–09). Witherspoon's support was particularly vital because the middle colonies were far from the flashpoints of the conflict, and public feelings were more divided than in New England, as were political allegiances generally because of the greater social and economic heterogeneity. While the southern colonies were dominated by a landed aristocracy and the New England colonies lacked real political or cultural diversity, the middle colonies had a mixture of English and non-English speaking immigrants spread out over large plantations, trade centers, and middle-class small towns. This cultural and social diversity made the public negotiation of political and cultural values vitally important to the creation of a shared public identity. As Henretta discusses, the provincial assemblies of the middle colonies through "compromise and accommodation" built up a political system that gave "institutional legitimacy and an encompassing constitutional form to its cultural diversity." As a result, political factionalism "was perhaps more intense here than anywhere in the British empire" (115–16). The factional character of this environment was important for Witherspoon because he encountered political forums where public interests were not just managed, as they had been in Scotland, but created through public debates that demonstrated that political factions could be socially constructive and not just debilitating

As a member of the Continental Congress, Witherspoon became one of the fifty-six signatories to the Declaration of Independence, but his role in the actual passage of the Declaration is unclear. Conservatives in Congress used the arrival of Witherspoon and the New Jersey delegates on July 1, 1776, to argue that more time was needed because the colonies were not "ripe" for independence. Witherspoon, in a speech that prepared the way for the whole Congress to vote to consider the Declaration, apparently responded that the country was "not only ripe for the measure but in danger of becoming rotten for the want of it." While Collins accepts the reports of this oration, he argues convincingly against the popular legend that Witherspoon gave a later pivotal speech that decided the actual passage of the Declaration on July 4 (2: 218–21). This disputed speech, which is inscribed on the monuments to Witherspoon in Philadelphia and Washington, includes the famous remark that "there is a tide in the affairs of men—a nick of time. We perceive it now before us. To hesitate, is to consent to slavery."

We do not have to accept the secondhand accounts of this speech to recognize that Witherspoon played an important part in the creation of the United States. The correspondence that remains at Princeton and elsewhere includes letters to Franklin, Madison (who refers to him simply as "the Doctor"), Hamilton, Adams, and Richard Henry Lee (who made the motion for independence). While Witherspoon served on important Congressional committees in the areas of finance and foreign relations, the other members' accounts of him are sketchy, perhaps because he was a clergyman who was older than three-quarters of those who signed the Declaration and who spoke in a broad Scots accent that Adams found unintelligible at times (see Stohlman 143–47). Even though he might have had problems understanding Witherspoon's accent, Adams called him "as high a Son of Liberty, as any Man in America" (2: 112–13), and France's first minister to America viewed him as the "soul of his party" (Stohlman 132). Witherspoon's importance was recognized by loyalists as well. He was burned in effigy alongside Washington by Howe's army, and he was criticized by loyalists on both sides of the Atlantic, including some of his old opponents in the Moderate party (Maclean 395; Stohlman 108, 131).

Witherspoon's public career offers useful specific insights into how his rhetorical theory was reflected in his rhetorical practice. His speeches and essays are characterized by careful logical argumentation and a plain style. As Witherspoon himself noted to a visitor touring his home at Princeton, "no flowers in my garden, nor in my discourses either" (Collins 1: 148). In his rhetorical practice, Witherspoon typically draws on common experience for evidence and regularly expresses his distrust of abstract speculations and philosophical theories. On political questions he reasons from historical precedents, and on religious questions he stays close to the Bible. His speaking style was cool, even cold, and he labored with a nervous speech impediment all of his life. However, he was an effective speaker who wrote out and memorized important speeches and sermons, rather than reading them as many ministers did. According to Maclean, in Congress Witherspoon commonly waited for the appropriate moment to speak and then introduced his memorized speech by referring to what had just been said, thus giving his audience the impression that his carefully prepared remarks had come directly from the matter at hand (396). Witherspoon thus recognized the practical significance of the rhetorician's art of saying the right thing at the right time to speak to the immediate situation.

In the political rhetoric of Witherspoon and the other founders of the American republic, one can also see the influence of the Scottish moral philosophy that Witherspoon helped to introduce to American college classrooms. Garry Wills has argued that Jefferson's Declaration was decisively influenced by Scottish moral philosophy, but as Hamowy has shown, Wills tends to overstate his case for the Scots' influence. Nonetheless, the Scottish sources of Jefferson's development are intriguing. In addition to William Small (Jefferson's Scottish teacher) and such figures as Hume and Ferguson, Wills argues rather convincingly that Jefferson was indebted to Hutcheson, whose moral sense philosophy shaped Jefferson's views of human nature and human rights; to Kames, whom Jefferson read avidly from his youth and whose works he collected throughout his life; and to Reid, particularly his "egalitarian epistemology, his humble empiricism, and his communitarian morality" (*Inventing* 213, 192). According to Wills, Reid's common-sense philosophy was behind Jefferson's statement that the founding assumptions of the American republic were "self-evident" to all, and Wills gives particular emphasis to Jefferson's comment that the purpose of his writings was "to place before mankind the common sense of the subject" (*Inventing* 184, 190). The points of contact between Reid's common-sense philosophy and Jefferson are significant because historians have too often dismissed common-sense philosophy as conservative and close-minded without really examining its specific effects on the social history of ideas (See May and Berlin).

Madison's *Federalist* essays are particularly important for investigating the relationship between the political rhetoric of the American Revolution and the Scottish moral philosophy that Witherspoon helped introduce. These essays were intended to persuade literate Americans of the principles of the new form of government in order to create a shared understanding of the new public identity. In perhaps the most important essay, *Federalist* Number Ten, Madison redefines some of the basic assumptions of classical civic humanism and the Commonwealth tradition. Most important of all, Madison modifies the traditional distrust of factions by arguing that they can be socially constructive if they are regulated to control the inescapable competition of interests. He opens the essay by accepting the traditional assumption that factionalism is the greatest threat to popular government. However, Madison argues that the sources of faction are not merely unenlightened self-interest, but rather the liberty and diversity that naturally exist in any heterogeneous democratic society. For Madison, the common good does not transcend private interests, it arises from a careful regulation of them: "The regulation of these various and interfering interests forms the principal task of modern legislation, and involves the spirit of party and faction in the necessary and ordinary operations of the government" (*Federalist* 18).

Madison implicitly rejects the idea that an easy harmony will be achieved between conflicting private interests and the public good through enlightened feelings of benevolence, and he explicitly rejects the view that an enlightened leader speaking for the common good can mediate such conflicts: "It is in vain to say that enlightened statesmen will be able to adjust these clashing interests and render them all subservient to the public good" (*Federalist* 19). In place of the public leaders who civic humanists from Cicero to Hutcheson had idealized as an alternative to absolute authority, Madison seeks to establish a system of checks and balances that would not produce harmony but would regulate competition. To do this, he overturns the traditional assumption that a democratic government can only exist in a small homogeneous society that shared a mutual self-interest and argues instead that a large republic is actually superior because it solves the other basic problem of popular governments, the tyranny of a majority faction: "Extend the sphere, and you take in a greater variety of parties and interests; you make it less probable that a majority of the whole will have a common motive to invade the rights of citizens; or if such a common motive exists, it will be more difficult for all who feel it to discover their own strength and to act in unison with each other" (*Federalist* 20). By taking these positions, Madison adds a new realism to traditional civic philosophy. He recognizes that factions are a natural part of the political life of a heterogeneous public, and he replaces the ideal of the leader who will speak for the common good with a system of competing self-interests, the constitutional system of checks and balances that he helped to create and publicly defend.

The specific influences of Witherspoon on Madison are unclear. While an undergraduate, Madison heard Witherspoon's lectures on moral philosophy and rhetoric, which presented the unified social philosophy that will be discussed in the next section. In 1772 Madison returned to Princeton to pursue postgraduate studies in moral philosophy and theology (see Smylie). With Witherspoon, Madison read the sources that would shape his political philosophy: Aristotle, Cicero, Grotius, Pufendorf, Locke, Harrington, and Scottish moral philosophers and historians like Hutcheson, Hume, Smith, and Robertson. In Witherspoon's *Lectures on Moral Philosophy,* Madison was presented with a philosophy of governance that emphasized that competing interests should be "so balanced that when one draws to his own interest or inclination, there may be an over poise upon the whole" (203). Witherspoon was hardly original in such doctrines, but it was probably just his traditionalism that was most important about his influence on Madison. Witherspoon introduced Madison to a broad and diverse tradition, a tradition that included natural rights theorists, civic humanists, and a strong dose of Calvinism. Madison and Witherspon and the other public advocates of the American cause used the basic religious and political ideals of such traditions to persuade the American people that they were united by common values and should fight to defend their common interest. In his political rhetoric, Witherspoon himself drew on these beliefs to support his ideal of the hardworking and temperate public leader, an ideal that was central to his educational philosophy as well. This ideal personified the competitive ideology of the Protestant work ethic, and this same competitive ideology was enshrined in the system of competing interests balanced off against each other that his student helped to institutionalize.

Witherspoon's Lectures on Moral Philosophy

As Cohen discusses, it is generally agreed that "the Scottish common-sense philosophy introduced at the end of the eighteenth century at Princeton by President Witherspoon spread until it formed almost the sole basis of philosophic instruction" in America (258). Some scholars view common-sense philosophy as a conservative influence because it limited the "American mind" with an empirical epistemology and a political orthodoxy that upheld accepted social beliefs as authorized by human nature itself (Martin vii). To avoid reducing common-sense philosophers to convenient straw men, however, more attention must be paid to the actual educational and political reforms that common-sense philosophers helped to support. While Witherspoon was neither a radical nor a romantic, he was certainly not a reactionary either. His public career provides the context for his lectures on moral philosophy and rhetoric, and throughout that career he stood for protecting political rights and reforming the educational curriculum to make it more relevant to the needs of a wider section of society. As the culminating studies of the curriculum at Princeton, these lectures present his ideal of the broadly educated individual with the rhetorical, ethical, and political abilities needed to debate contemporary political issues in democratic forums. This educational philosophy is clearly an appealing alternative to the moribund classicism that it replaced and to the comparatively apolitical belletrism of Hugh Blair. To be fair in such comparisons, we should recognize that these are Witherspoon's lecture notes published posthumously without his revisions.

After first defending moral philosophy against clergy like Jonathan Edwards who viewed it as "infidelity reduced to a system," Witherspoon devotes three lectures to a Lockean description of human understanding, to which he adds the Scots' characteristic emphases on common sense and the moral sense. In lecture five, Witherspoon moves from epistemology and ethics to develop a political philosophy based on the premise that where we are not obligated by moral or political duties, we are free to do as we will. In lectures six through nine, he outlines our duties to God, our fellow man, and ourselves. In lecture ten, he discusses political rights and duties, and in lectures eleven, twelve, and thirteen, he addresses domestic, civil, and international relations. The final three

lectures are devoted to jurisprudence and a concluding "Recapitulation." At each point in the discussion, Witherspoon summarizes the
major positions, outlines their practical implications, and offers suggestions for further reading. He refers most often to Hutcheson (which he
spells "Hutchinson"), but at the end of the lectures he also cites Kames,
Ferguson, Smith, and Reid as well as sources from the natural rights
and civic humanist traditions, including Commonwealth writers like
Harrington. From beginning to end, the purpose of Witherspoon's
lectures is not to develop a new system of thought but to provide a
broad overview to his students to prepare them for the ethical and
political decisions that they would have to make in public life.

Witherspoon begins by drawing on Locke's empiricism and Hutcheson's theory of the moral sense to demonstrate the reasonableness of
human experience and the moral sensitivity of human nature. Like his
own teacher, Witherspoon had his students read Locke, and he adopts
Locke's basic view that the mind is comprised of the understanding,
will, and affections and that knowledge is derived from either sensation
or reflection (157, 159). Like the other common-sense philosophers,
Witherspoon reasserts the reliability of empirical evidence as the only
solid foundation for making inductive generalizations about human
experience (159). To support this position against Hume's skepticism,
Witherspoon later on refers to "some late writers of Scotland," who
have argued for "the dictates of common sense, which are either simple
perceptions, or seen with intuitive evidence. These are the foundation
of all reasoning, and without them, to reason is a word without meaning"
(173). Like these common-sense philosophers, Witherspoon thus quali-
fies Locke's empiricism by arguing that human nature is not simply a
tabula rasa before experience because we have certain natural rational
tendencies and moral sensitivities, including the commonsensical tendency to believe that we and the world exist and the moral sensitivity
to feel benevolently toward others. Witherspoon accepts Hutcheson's
general conception of the moral sense, particularly the idea that morality is a matter of placing a benevolent "public affection" above feelings
of "self interest." However, Witherspoon prefers the traditional term
"conscience," which he defines as a natural sensitivity to moral obligations bestowed by God (161). As in *Ecclesiastical Characteristics,* Witherspoon straightforwardly rejects Hutcheson's synthesis of morality and
aesthetics by concluding that while the aesthetic sense may be important
to "taste and criticism," it is of very little importance "in point of morals"
(161).

While he rejects the aestheticism of Hutcheson's moral sense, Witherspoon adopts Hutcheson's political philosophy almost without reservation. In the second chapter of book three of his *System of Moral*

Philosophy, Hutcheson covers the same issues that Witherspoon addresses in lecture twelve. Witherspoon finds the simple forms of government lacking and argues for a republic with a mixed system of governance that will have three essential features: the branches of government "must be so balanced that when every one draws to his own interest or inclination, there may be an over poise upon the whole"; each branch must be dependent on the others for its operation; and the basis of power must be property in order to insure that self-interest is collateral with an interest in the "public welfare" (203). These were precisely the points that Hutcheson had stressed, and they had been basic to Whig political thought since the Commonwealth writers had used them to justify the gentry's efforts to gain more power for Parliament against the king (see Robbins, "Hutcheson" 246).

While Witherspoon was thus indebted to Hutcheson, his debt is hardly to Hutcheson alone. Both Witherspoon and Hutcheson talk about "duties" and "public virtue," the characteristic concerns of civic humanists from Cicero to the Commonwealth writers. Like this tradition, they reason that since an active public life develops basic human virtues, our major duty to both the public and ourselves is to regulate self-interest in order to foster the higher moral potential that comes from disinterested political involvement. Following the natural rights tradition, Hutcheson and Witherspoon also emphasize the rights that the individual maintains through the social contract from the natural state. Such a state of independence from the community was inconceivable to civic humanists like Aristotle because they defined individuals as citizens and human nature itself as essentially social. According to Witherspoon, the social contract establishes the "principle that men are originally and by nature equal, and consequently free" (191). Through the social contract, governments are founded to protect the "public good" as well as the individual's rights to life, labor, liberty, opinion (religion in Princeton ms 9070.01: 96), association, and the presumption of innocence before the law (191, 189–90). Individuals also have the right to resist governments that do not serve these purposes (200). Witherspoon, like Hutcheson, thus combines traditions that stress the duties of the citizen and the rights of the individual to develop a civic ethics and a democratic politics.

While Witherspoon's political philosophy shares the limitations of the traditions he was working from, it is far broader than that embodied in the established classical curriculum. For example, at about the same time that Witherspoon was providing James Madison and his classmates with a survey of the ideas that would prove fundamental to the founding of the republic, Thomas Clap, the influential president of Yale, published *An Essay on the Nature and Foundations of Moral Virtue and Obliga-*

tion; Being a Short Introduction to the Study of Ethics; for the Use of the Students of Yale College (1765). The very title of Clap's work shows that he adhered to the more narrow view of moral philosophy that confined it to ethics and thus isolated it from the study of contemporary politics. Clap in fact maintains that ethics can only be studied in a religious context and explicitly rejects the rising concern for "Laws of Nature and Nations, or a System of *civil Laws,* generally obtaining among Mankind." Such concern for the good of "public Communities" is inappropriate because "no fallen Creature can become *truly virtuous*" (ii). Clap rejects theories of ethics based on "Self-Interest," "Benevolence," "moral taste," and other first principles, and while Clap mentions Hutcheson and other contemporary sources, he limits morality to religion because God is the "*sole* Foundation and Standard of all that Virtue, Goodness and Perfection which can exist in the Creature" (3).

Witherspoon has more in common with Scottish moral philosophers than he does with a traditionalist like Clap. Like them, Witherspoon put the study of contemporary social affairs at the top of the educational curriculum. His *Lectures on Moral Philosophy* is actually quite similiar to Adam Ferguson's *Institutes of Moral Philosophy For the Use of Students in the College of Edinburgh* (1769). Like Witherspoon, Ferguson turned his students' attention to the study of politics, natural law, and natural rights, and he stressed the central civic humanist ideal of an active political life. Witherspoon is historically important because he helped to institutionalize these concerns and ideals in America. While his lectures were not published during his lifetime, his students founded colleges and academies from New York to Tennessee, where they often read from their own worn copies of his lectures (see Come). Those who did not actually read from his lectures brought with them an educational philosophy that made moral philosophy the culminating study of a college education. As Witherspoon notes at the end of his lectures, moral philosophy's "importance is manifest from this circumstance, that it not only points out personal duty; but is related to the whole business of active life. The languages, and even mathematical and natural knowledge are but handmaids to this superior science" (229).

Witherspoon's Lectures on Eloquence

Witherspoon's *Lectures on Eloquence* share many of the fundamental concerns of his *Lectures on Moral Philosophy,* perhaps the most fundamental being the basic idea that liberty fulfilled "all the human powers," especially eloquence (203). These lectures were delivered along with the *Lectures on Moral Philosophy* to students in both their third and fourth years. The common concerns of these two sets of lectures led Guthrie to call the 1810 edition of *Lectures on Moral Philosophy and Eloquence* "the first complete American rhetoric" ("Rhetorical Theory in Colonial America" 56). Subsuming both under the term rhetoric is not entirely inappropriate because moral philosophy and rhetoric share a common tradition that reaches back to the classical figures who established them as integral concerns. From Aristotle and Cicero onwards, civic humanists have understood rhetoric to be a political art fundamental to the ideal of the citizen orator who could speak effectively and morally on issues of public importance, an ideal that made rhetoric, ethics, and politics closely related studies. Despite his specific debts to contemporary sources like Hutcheson, Witherspoon is most indebted to this broader tradition, for as Guthrie notes, Witherspoon draws largely on classical rhetoric interpreted "in the light of the philosophy of his own time" ("Rhetorical Theory in Colonial America" 56).

Despite Witherspoon's basic debts to classical rhetoric, Scottish sources were as broadly influential in eighteenth-century rhetoric as they were in moral philosophy. The *Lectures on Rhetoric and Belles Lettres* (1783) of Witherspoon's classmate Hugh Blair established the Scots' long dominance of college English studies when it was adopted at Brown in 1783, at Yale in 1785, at Harvard in 1788, and at virtually every American college by the turn of the century (Guthrie, "Rhetorical Theory in America 1635–1850" 61). Blair's *Lectures* and George Campbell's *Philosophy of Rhetoric* (1776) remained the standard sources of college English studies up until the Civil War. These texts became important at the same time that Thomas Reid and Dugald Stewart's common-sense philosophy became predominant in the study of moral philosophy (see Phillipson). However, the Scottish influence on American education that is often identified with these rhetoricians and moral philosophers actually predates them. The study of English at the college level actually began about the middle of the eighteenth century as part of a curriculum that was developing an unprecedented concern for contemporary life and letters, a development that was centered in the closely related studies of rhetoric and moral philosophy in the last two years. Witherspoon is part of the early Scottish influence that first helped to establish this curriculum. While he refers to "some late writers of Scotland" who have argued for "the dictates of common sense," his moral philosophy is influenced far more by Hutcheson than by Reid (3: 376), and his rhetoric is less belletristic and more politically oriented than that which Blair's work eventually instituted (see Halloran; Miller).

Witherspoon's *Lectures on Eloquence*, which were written in 1768, lack the polish that Blair gave his published lectures. What we get from Witherspoon is not a work revised for a reading public but a practical

course in rhetoric and composition. Witherspoon offers useful advice
on how to write and speak for public audiences and includes ample
references to the best classical and contemporary sources—Aristotle,
Cicero, Ward, Lawson, Fenelon, Lamy, Rollin, Kames, and Gerard.
Witherspoon covers many of the points that are still being taught in
contemporary composition classes—the thesis sentence, outlining, topic
sentences, and paragraphing. He also covers the basics of public speaking, particularly the need to say the right thing at exactly the right
moment. Such practical emphases reflect Witherspoon's own experience as a public speaker and writer, and it is as a practicing political
rhetorician, rather than a rhetorical theorist, that he is most significant.
Though Witherspoon shares some of Blair's and Campbell's basic assumptions, Witherspoon emphasized public politics, not belles lettres
or philosophies of human understanding. According to Howell, who
concludes his study with Witherspoon, he was "a gifted and admirable
teacher of the new rhetoric" whose lectures "brought the affairs of
their time into Witherspoon's classroom and made his students see that
eloquence was a part of the concern of mankind for liberty, national
welfare, the rule of law, and moral truth" (687).

In his opening lecture, Witherspoon defines his subject as "composition, taste, and criticism" (231), but he actually devotes the majority of
his lectures to composition. His first three lectures present "preliminary
discourses" on eloquence, "some general rules . . . to all sorts of writing,"
and "some general rules to form the taste and direct the conduct of a
student" (233, 236, 241). In lecture four, he outlines the seven parts of
the body of his lectures:

1. To treat of language in general—its qualities and powers, eloquent
speech, and its history and practice as an art [lectures four and five].
2. To consider oratory as divided into its three great kinds—the sublime,
simple, and mixed; their characters, their distinctions, their beauties, and their
uses [lectures six through ten].
3. To consider it as divided into its constituent parts— invention, disposition,
style, pronunciation and gesture [eleven and twelve].
4. To consider it as its object is different—information, demonstration,
persuasion, entertainment [lecture thirteen].
5. To consider it as its subject is different—the pulpit, the bar, and the
senate, or any deliberative assembly [fourteen and the first half of fifteen].
6. To consider the structure and parts of a particular discourse—their order,
connection, proportion, and ends [latter half of fifteen].
7. Recapitulation, and an inquiry into the principles of taste, or of beauty
and gracefulness, as applicable not only to oratory, but to all the other (commonly called) the fine arts [lecture sixteen]. (247–48)

In his first lecture, Witherspoon emphasizes that both nature and nurture are essential to the development of the complete orator, whom he describes in terms that echo the classical ideal of Cicero and Quintilian (234). However, Witherspoon does not limit his ideal of the effective public speaker and writer to political forums; he addresses all the major genres that his students would compose for public audiences, including scientific, historical, and literary writings. In the following two lectures, he advises his students to follow a five-point program to develop their general eloquence and taste: "Study and imitate the best examples," practice writing and speaking, read widely in all the "branches that are subordinate to the study of eloquence," "guard against . . . blemishes in writing and speaking," and "follow nature" (237, 239, 241, 244, 246). In these introductory lectures, Witherspoon establishes the distinction between "genius" and general good taste and eloquence. While the former is rare, people who are not absolutely lacking in native ability can master good taste and composition: "Persons of the middle capacity do also, perhaps generally, fill the most useful and important stations in human life. A very great genius is often like a very fine flower, to be wondered at, but of little service either for food or medicine" (236). Clearly evident in these comments is his guiding concern for an active public life and his Calvinist sense of what such a life required.

The strengths and limitations of Witherspoon's approach become even more evident when he turns to the nature of language in general and eloquence in particular in lectures four and five. In lecture three he concludes that "the grammar of every language is ultimately fixed by custom" (242), but like Campbell, Witherspoon soon shows a nostalgia for the idea that language could be purified and preserved against the errors of common usage (Campbell 169–203; see also Baugh and Cable 283). He devotes considerable attention to the "blemishes" that Americans must "guard against" in his *Lectures on Eloquence* and in his *Druid* essays, where he suggests that Americans should consider imitating the French Academy's efforts to regulate usage (*Works* 3: 495). Nonetheless, such proscriptions and prescriptions are peripheral to Witherspoon's interest in the public functions of language. He stresses the contemporary political functions of persuasive discourse and refers to controversial public orators to show that political rhetoric was as important among his enlightened contemporaries as it was in the classical period. Unlike Blair, who felt that tastes had changed since the heated oratory of the ancients, Witherspoon refers not just to classical examples of political oratory but also to William Pitt and George Whitefield, a politician and an evangelist who demonstrated the contemporary taste for heated debate (256).

In lectures six through ten, Witherspoon discusses the literary issues that are characteristic of the belletristic approach. As an example of primitive genius, Witherspoon cites the bardic verse of Ossian, the notorious forgery that Blair proudly enshrined as proof of the unrefined genius of ancient Scottish poetry. Like Blair, Witherspoon draws on Longinus and Burke for his concept of the sublime. According to Witherspoon, the sublime can be felt in "the voice of thunder, or penetration of lightning" or seen in "a wild uncultivated forest, a vast precipice, or steep cataract or waterfall," each of which is "supposed to be an object more august and striking than any ornaments produced by human skill" (259, 235). But one senses from the tone of such comments that he has limited interest in such suppositions and is more comfortable discussing such practical concerns as the mimetic nature of language, which he uses to evaluate the descriptive powers of poetry (237, 263). In any case, he does not linger over the poetic imagination but devotes the bulk of this section of his lectures to surveying the three major styles, identifying the diverse sorts of writing to which each is suited, and briefly discussing the tropes and figures. He also offers advice on "raising the passions" of an audience because he considers them to be fundamental to persuasive eloquence: "To move the passions of others so as to incline their choice or to alter their purpose is particularly the design of eloquence" (263).

While Witherspoon's utilitarian assumptions limited his appreciation of literature, these same assumptions underlay the practical strengths of his discussion of the composing process in lectures eleven and twelve. He accepts the traditional division of the composing process into invention, arrangement, style, and delivery; but like the other theorists that Howell classifies as "new" rhetoricians, Witherspoon rejects traditional aids to invention like the topics and commonplaces and argues instead that one will discover what needs to be said from experience and from the specifics of the issue at hand (280). This position reflects the influence of Locke and his preference for inductive investigations of experience over deductions from accepted truths. While Witherspoon concludes that invention is largely unteachable, he does offer a number of practical suggestions on the art of arrangement and development, which he calls "disposition or distribution" (281). He lays special emphasis on the need for a careful order as an aid to the audience's understanding and memory. His advice on how to use a thesis sentence to develop and organize a discourse is as useful today as it would have been for his own students (283), and his discussion of the principles of organization—including the recommendation that the divisions should be necessary, coordinate, exhastive, and clearly interrelated—could easily be found in a contemporary textbook on composition (284–85). Witherspoon even discusses the role of topic sentences in paragraph development (285).

Witherspoon's recognition that purpose is central to the rhetorician's art led him in lecture thirteen to offer a conceptualization of the aims of discourse that is among the most useful offered in the eighteenth century: "The ends a writer or speaker may be said to aim at are information, demonstration, persuasion, and entertainment" (290). He also recognizes that these are "frequently intermixed" and that "persuasion is also used in a sense that includes them all" (290). Under each of these general categories, he discusses a variety of scientific and literary genres. Information includes histories, fables, and letters; demonstration covers "scientific writing, whether essays, systems or controversy"; persuasion includes any discourse that "would bring the reader or hearer to determinate choice"; and entertainment refers largely to literature (291–94). While this conception of the purposes of discourse may seem simple, even commonsensical today, one must remember that through much of the nineteenth century college English studies were hindered by a pedagogy that emphasized the modes of development—narration, description, exposition, and argument—above the purposes that discourses were meant to accomplish (see Connors). Even today textbooks often mix the modes and aims of discourse in a way that reveals how purposeless college composition can be. Throughout the range of genres that he discusses, Witherspoon stresses his basic point that purpose is the controlling feature of any discourse, and when he offers advice on style and development, he relates these matters to the purpose that the genre is intended to serve (see 291). In this way, Witherspoon avoids the common problem of making terms like "perspicuity" into abstract prescriptions for a single correct style.

Witherspoon's career as a practicing rhetorician is most evident in lectures fourteen and fifteen, where he addresses the three forums that his students would face upon graduation. Like Blair, Witherspoon offers advice on how to speak and write for the pulpit, bar, and deliberative assemblies. Witherspoon's specific purpose is to "delineate the character of an accomplished minister, lawyer and senator" (295). He begins his discussion of these professions by stressing that no one can "make a truly distinquished figure in any of them without being well acquainted with literature and taste," with literature no doubt understood in the eighteenth-century sense of all learned writing (295). Witherspoon's discussion follows from this statement to stress not specific rhetorical skills but the moral and intellectual qualities that public leaders require. These lectures are perhaps the most significant of the entire course because they offer useful insights into the ideal of public service that Witherspoon sought to teach in his *Lectures on Moral Philosophy* and preach in his sermon on *Christian Magnanimity*. These lectures are also important because they specifically distinguish Witherspoon's perspective from the approach that Blair's *Lectures on Rhetoric and Belles Lettres* institutionalized.

Witherspoon begins with the public leader as minister and not surprisingly stresses the moral dimensions of such leadership. He emphasizes that the minister must negotiate between pleasing "persons of finer taste, who are too much attached to the outside of things and are immediately disgusted with every error against propriety," and the "poor ignorant creatures" who are also a part of the congregation (298, 297). He reminds his students that the gospel was first "preached to the poor. In this our blessed master was distinguished both from the heathen philosophers and Jewish teachers," who taught only the learned (297). If one remembers Witherspoon's own conflict with the Moderates over the rights of local congregations and his attacks on the ideal of the minister as the refined spokesman for the upper classes, one can see that he is not merely moralizing here but is speaking from his practical commitment to the belief that ministers must speak to and for all members of their congregations. To do this, the minister must above all have "a lively sense of religion upon his own heart" (295). This piety must be combined with "experimental knowledge," which is "superior to all other, and necessary to the perfection of every other kind" (296). In such comments as these, one can see him reasoning from a Lockean sense of "experimental" as *experiential* and an evangelical sense of the religious experience: "Experimental knowledge is the best sort in every branch, but it is necessary in divinity because religion is what cannot be truly understood unless it is felt" (296).

When Witherspoon addresses the "eloquence of the bar" in lecture fifteen, one can see how easily his Calvinist morality is translated into the practical sensibility needed for the law, which he praises as the "direct road to promotion and the way of obtaining the highest offices in the state" (301). Like the minister, the lawyer must be broadly educated and above all must possess "probity or real untainted integrity" (301). Lawyers must not "undertake a cause which they knew not to be just" because they must be a force for morality and can only be personally successful if they have an ethical reputation (301). From the practical value of integrity, he turns to the need for "assiduity and method in business" and praises the ideal of "order and punctuality," which keeps everything in its proper place and makes a lawyer as good as his word (302). The lawyer must also have "delicacy in his manners and deportment in general, and the conduct of his business in particular" (302). This sense of decorum includes a rhetorical sensitivity to the "propriety of time and place—what belongs to him that speaks, or to him or them that are spoken to," a rhetorical sensitivity that is exemplified by Cicero, according to Witherspoon (303). The lawyer must also have an "extensive knowledge in the arts and sciences, in history and in the laws," because history "points out the state of society and human affairs in every age" and law bestows a "knowledge of the great principles of equity and of natural and political law as applied in general" (303).

When Witherspoon turns to "promiscuous deliberative assemblies," his political theory and practice lead him to a far more positive view of the value of political rhetoric than that offered by Blair's belletristic perspective. Even in 1768 when Witherspoon first wrote these lectures, he realized that the study of political rhetoric would be important for his students because many would "have occasion to act in that sphere and to be members of the provincial assemblies" (304). He rejects the view that "circumstances have changed" since rhetoric reigned over classical politics because in contemporary assemblies people supposedly "come all prepared by private interest, and will vote just as they are engaged without regard to either eloquence or truth" (304). In thus phrasing the problem in terms of the public conflict among private interests, he draws on the central paradigm of Scottish social philosophy, and he reasons from this line of thought to conclude that since "human nature is always the same," persuasive eloquence must be as capable of mediating such conflicts as it was in the classical period (304). To prove his point, Witherspoon for the second time cites "Mr. Pitt, now Earl of Chatham," whose oratory was then shaping the politics of the British Empire, and George Whitefield, the fiery evangelist of the Great Awakening (304). The crucial difference between Blair and Witherspoon is that Witherspoon could endorse controversial public figures as models of eloquence, while Blair was advising his students that the educated refinement of contemporary audiences made such heated oratory a thing of the past. Just as Witherspoon's understanding of rhetoric owed much to his own political life, Blair's experience as a purveyor of church patronage led him to conclude that "ministerial influence" had reduced the importance of political debate, which is precisely the conclusion that Witherspoon refused to accept (Blair, *Lectures on Rhetoric and Belles Lettres* 2: 43).

Witherspoon next includes a succinct summary of the essentials of the classical ideal of the public orator. For a strong ethical appeal, the political leader must have "dignity of character and disinterestedness." Like the other two types of public leaders, the politician's practical wisdom comes from a "knowledge of the most liberal kind, that is the knowledge of men and manners, of history, and of human nature."

From this logical understanding of human nature in action in society, the political orator also learns how to exercise a "power over the passions" of his audience (305). These three requirements are of course the ethical, logical, and pathetic appeals that Aristotle had first defined as essential to the rhetorician's art, and like such classical civic humanists as Aristotle and Cicero, Witherspoon argues that these abilities are best instilled by a liberal arts education, particularly by the concerns of moral philosophy for political life and human nature. Following this line of thought, he concludes his discussion of political rhetoric by arguing that orators must have the ability to adjust their message to their audience and "to choose the proper time for exerting it" (305). This ability was known as *kairos* in classical rhetorical theory, and Witherspoon accepts the classical view that only actual practice in political assemblies can bestow such sensitivity to the rhetorical situation (305). His own rhetorical practice no doubt reinforced his appreciation of classical sources like Aristotle's *Rhetoric*, which was included in his library. Witherspoon's approach to classical rhetoric is clearly exemplified in the conclusion of lecture five. In his discussion of the basic parts of a speech or essay, as elsewhere, Witherspoon balances classical theory against his own experience and adopts what proves useful. In this case he argues that a simplified model of beginning, middle, and end is more useful than the more complicated model offered by Cicero, but Witherspoon nonetheless draws on Cicero for practical advice on each of the three parts of the simplified paradigm (305–9; see also Howell 683).

In his final lecture, Witherspoon draws on contemporary sources to present his students with a survey of the various perspectives on the concept of taste. Witherspoon mentions Hutcheson, Addison, Hogarth, Burke, and Gerard, as well as the belletrists' favorite classical source, Longinus. Witherspoon is not really interested in choosing among the conflicting views of whether taste is determined by the properties of aesthetic objects, based in some psychological faculty, or determined by the cultual values of a particular society. He shows his own utilitarian bias by reasoning that "whatever exercises our faculties, without fatiguing them, gives pleasure" (318), and he concludes his lectures by advising his students not to devote themselves too much to such trivial inquiries: "Carrying taste to a finical nicety in any one branch is a thing not only undesirable but contemptible, the reason of which may be easily seen: when a person applies his attention so much to a matter of no great moment, it occasions a necessary neglect of other things of much greater value. After you pass a certain point, attachment to a particular pursuit is useless, and then it proceeds to be hurtful, and at last contemptible" (318). In these final lines, Witherspoon advises his students that they should not pursue specialized studies in literature or any other specific field, but rather should aspire to be more generally useful to the educated public. Witherspoon's own career would have offered them a powerful example of how to do just that.

One could easily conclude from Witherspoon's concluding comments on the limited value of imaginative literature that Witherspoon and the other Scottish common-sense philosophers *did* try to place strict limits on "the American Mind," but what does one really gain from such abstract generalizations? Such convenient abstractions about the history of ideas offer little insight into Witherspoon's intellectual and political theory, nor do they even begin to explain how political and cultural attitudes were negotiated in social practice in the period. As Henretta discusses, "Taken together, the trinity of republicanism, Protestantism, and capitalism formed an interlocking web of ideas which defined the limits of social action and established the ideological and institutional framework within which the next generations of Americans would struggle to work out their individual lives" (222). To do justice either to the complexity of this ideological network or to the individuals who worked within and against it, more research needs to be done on how educated inquiry and public debate affected social life. Only then can the intellectual history of rhetorical theory and moral philosophy be understood as part of the social history of rhetorical practice. Witherspoon will inevitably become better known to us as we learn more about the social history of ideas in the eighteenth century.

A Note on the Texts

A checklist of the various editions of the pieces included in this collection appears at the end of this section. I have compared the two American editions of Witherspoon's *Works* (1800–1801 and 1802) with the first Scottish edition of his *Works* (1804) and with the American editions of the individual pieces included in this collection. The lack of significant textual variants among the editions of the individual works suggests that Witherspoon did not revise his writings in subsequent editions. The only exception that I found to this generalization is the *Ecclesiastical Characteristics,* to which he added an additional maxim in the third edition, the edition used as the copy text for the American editions of his *Works*. The Scottish edition of the *Works* is riddled with misprints, particularly in the Latin passages, which show that it was much less carefully prepared for the press. For these reasons, the "corrected" second American edition of the *Works* was chosen as the copy text for this collection.

Most of this collection consists of the *Lectures on Moral Philosophy* and *Lectures on Eloquence.* These works are Witherspoon's lecture notes posthumously edited and published by Ashbel Green, a student of Witherspoon's who went on to become president of Princeton. Green states that although the lectures "assume the form of regular discourses," Witherspoon viewed them "as little more than a syllabus or compend," and would "enlarge before a class at the times of recitation" (*Works* 3: 366). These enlargments are unfortunately not included in the students' notes that remain at Princeton. Collins's edition of the *Lectures on Moral Philosophy* observes all the variants from the students' notes that he consulted, and the differences are surprisingly minor. My own examination of the students' notes of the *Lectures on Moral Philosophy* and *Lectures on Eloquence* failed to uncover major departures from the published editions. One variant that did appear in several of the manuscripts, including Princeton mss AM 12800, was the substitution of the word "handmaids" for "hard words" in this sentence from the final "Recapitulation" in the *Lectures on Moral Philosophy:* "The languages, and even mathematical and natural knowledge, are but hard words to this superior science [moral philosophy]" (3: 470). The published version of this sentence is almost nonsensical, and the alternate phrasing is important because it more clearly expresses Witherspoon's belief that moral philosophy should be the "superior science," which in fact it was at Princeton under his leadership. Although Witherspoon's *Lectures* are often unpolished and even cryptic, they do present a more accurate picture of what was actually taught at the time than if they had been extensively revised for the reading public, as for example Blair's *Lectures on Rhetoric and Belles Lettres* were.

To increase the readibility of the *Lectures* and the other works included in this collection, I have modernized the spelling, punctuation, and typography. I have not changed the substance or structure of any sentences, but I have removed excessive and distracting punctuation. Witherspoon himself did not consider punctuation to be a very important part of composition. According to the *Lectures on Eloquence,* authors need not worry much about punctuation because it is little used in private writings and publishers will add what is needed in the writings they print (243–44). I have not sought to correct what we might think of as grammatical errors but merely to improve the readibility of the texts.

A Publication History of the Works in This Collection

All of the pieces included in this collection appear in the editions of Witherspoon's *Works:*

The Works of the Rev. John Witherspoon. 4 vols. Philadelphia: 1800–1801.
Subsequent editions: Philadelphia, 1802.

The Works of John Witherspoon, D.D. 9 vols. Edinburgh, 1804.
Subsequent editions: Edinburgh, 1815.

A checklist of Witherspoon's publications appears in Collins's biography of Witherspoon (2: 237–66). According to Collins and other available sources, the works included in this collection appeared individually in the following editions:

1. *Ecclesiastical Characteristics: or, the Arcana of Church Policy, being an Humble Attempt to open up the Mystery of Moderation. Wherein is shewn a plain and easy Way of attaining to the Character of a Moderate Man, as at present in Repute in the Church of Scotland.* Glasgow, 1753.
Subsequent editions:
"The Second Edition, Corrected and Enlarged." Glasgow, 1754.
"The Third Edition, Corrected and Enlarged." Glasgow, 1754.
According to the title page of the third edition, "The First Edition of the Characteristics was published in the beginning of October 1753; the Second, the middle of December following; and this Third, the end of May 1754." Collins speculates that there may have been a separate edition in December 1753, as the title page seems to suggest (see *Witherspoon* 2: 238). However, copies of such an edition have not been found, and it seems more likely that this note refers to December 1754. This edition contains "An Additional Maxim."
London, 1754.
Glasgow, 1755.
Edinburgh, 1763.
Rotterdam, n.d. [Collins believes it may have appeared in 1763.]
Philadelphia, 1767. [The title page states that this edition was "Re-Printed" from the London edition.]
Edinburgh, 1842.
Also included in:
Essays on Important Subjects . . . To which are added by the Publishers, Ecclesiastical Characteristics. 3 vols. London, 1765.
Subsequent editions:
Edinburgh, 1768.

Bungay, 1800.

Edinburgh, 1805.

Reprints of Scarce Tracts Connected with the Church of Scotland. Number
    1. *Ecclesiastical Characteristics.* Edinburgh, 1842.

2. *Address to the Inhabitants of Jamaica, and the West-India Islands, in Behalf
    of the College of New Jersey.* Philadelphia, 1772.

Also included in:

Pennsylvania Gazette. October 28, 1772.

New York Gazette. November 16, 1772.

Miscellaneous Works. Philadelphia, 1803.

*New Jersey Archives: Documents Relating to the Colonial, Revolutionary
    and Post-Revolutionary History of the State of New Jersey.* Vol. 27.
    Newark, 1907.

3. *Christian Magnanimity: A Sermon, Preached at Princeton, September,
    1775—the Sabbath preceeding the Annual Commencement; And again with
    Additions, September 23, 1787. To which is added an Address to the Senior
    Class, who were to receive the Degree of Bachelor of Arts.* Princeton, 1787.

Also included in:

Sermons by the Late John Witherspoon. . . . Edinburgh, 1798.

The Youth's Companion; or a Safe Guide to Eminence. Compiled by Ama-
    tor Virtutis. Andover, 1820.

4. *The Dominion of Providence over the Passions of Men. A Sermon preached
    at Princeton, on the 17th of May, 1776. Being the General Fast appointed
    by the Congress through the United Colonies To which is added, An Address
    to the Natives of Scotland residing in America.* Philadelphia, 1776.

Subsequent editions:

"The Second Edition, with Elucidating Remarks." "Philadelphia
    Printed: Glasgow Re-printed", 1777.

"The Third Edition, with Elucidating Remarks." Glasgow, 1777.

    The two Glasgow editions included hostile commentary on With-
    erspoon's support for the American cause.

Belfast, 1777.

London, 1778.

London, 1779.

    The London editions did not include the *Address to the Natives of
    Scotland,* which was printed separately.

Also included in:

Sermons by the late John Witherspoon. Edinburgh, 1798.

5. *Lectures on Moral Philosophy, and Eloquence.* Philadelphia, 1810.

*Lectures on Moral Philosophy . . . To which is added, but the same author,
    An Address to the Students of the Senior Class, and Letters on Education
    and Marriage.* Philadelphia, 1822.

Lectures on Moral Philosophy. Ed. Varnum Lansing Collins. Princeton, 1912.
Lectures on Moral Philosophy. Ed. Jack Scott. Newark, Delaware, 1982.

References

"Account of the Late Duke Gordon, M.A., including Anecdotes of the University of Edinburgh." *The Scots Magazine* 64 (1802): 18–32.

"Account of the Public Life and Character of the Late Dr. Erskine, of Edinburgh." *The Scots Magazine* 65 (1803): 75–82.

ADAMS, JOHN. *Diary and Autobiography of John Adams.* Ed. L. H. Butterfield. 4 vols. Cambridge, Mass.: The Belknap Press of Harvard UP, 1961.

ALY, BOWER. *The Rhetoric of Alexander Hamilton.* New York: Columbia UP, 1941.

BALDWIN, ALICE M. "Sowers of Sedition: The Political Theories of Some of the New Light Presbyterian Clergy of Virginia and North Carolina." *William and Mary Quarterly* 5 (1948): 52–76.

BAUGH, ALBERT C., and THOMAS CABLE. *A History of the English Language.* 3rd ed. Englewood Cliffs: Prentice, 1978.

BEATTIE, JAMES. "Lectures on 'A View of the Practical Part of the Stoics'; being an abstract of Cicero's first book *De Officiis with additional remarks.*" Marischal College, 1778. Edinburgh University Library mss.

BERLIN, JAMES A. *Writing Instruction in Nineteenth-Century American Colleges.* Carbondale: Southern Illinois UP, 1984.

BLAIR, HUGH. *Lectures on Rhetoric and Belles Lettres.* Ed. Harold F. Harding. 2 vols. Edinburgh, 1783. Carbondale: Southern Illinois UP, 1965.

BLAIR, SAMUEL. *An Account of the College of New Jersey.* Woodbridge, N.J., 1764.

BOHMAN, GEORGE V. "Rhetorical Practice in Colonial America." *History of Speech Education in America.* Ed. Karl R. Wallace. New York: Appleton, 1954. 60–79.

BOWER, ALEXANDER. *The History of the University of Edinburgh.* 2 vols. Edinburgh: Oliphant, Waugh and Innes, 1817.

BROCK, WILLIAM R. *Scotus Americanus: A Survey of the Sources for Links between Scotland and America in the Eighteenth Century.* Edinburgh: Edinburgh UP, 1982.

BRODERICK, FRANCIS L. "Pulpit, Physics, and Politics: The Curriculum of the College of New Jersey 1746–1794." *William and Mary Quarterly* 6 (1949): 50–51.

BUTTERFIELD, LYMAN H., ed. *John Witherspoon Comes to America.* Princeton: Princeton UP, 1953.

CAMPBELL, GEORGE. *The Philosophy of Rhetoric.* Edinburgh, 1776. Carbondale: Southern Illinois UP, 1963.

CARLYLE, ALEXANDER. *The Autobiography of Dr. Alexander Carlyle of Inveresk, 1722–1805.* Ed. John Hill. London & Edinburgh: T. N. Foulis, 1910.

CHEYNEY, EDWARD POLTS. *History of the University of Pennsylvania, 1740–1940.* Philadelphia: U of Pennsylvania P, 1940.

CLAP, THOMAS. *An Essay on the Nature and Foundation of Moral Virtue and Obligation; Being a Short Introduction to the Study of Ethics; for the Use of the Students of Yale College.* New Haven, 1765.

"Cliosophic Society Minutes." July 2, 1792–June 19, 1801. Princeton University Archives mss.

COHEN, MORRIS R. *American Thought.* Glencoe: Free Press, 1954.

COLLINS, VARNUM LANSING. *President Witherspoon.* 2 vols. Princeton: Princeton UP, 1925.

———, ed. *Lectures on Moral Philosophy.* John Witherspoon. Princeton: Princeton UP, 1922.

COME, DONALD ROBERT. "The Influence of Princeton in Higher Education in the South before 1825." *William and Mary Quarterly* 2 (1945): 359–96.

CONNORS, ROBERT J. "The Rise and Fall of the Modes of Discourse." *College Composition and Communication* 32 (1981): 444–55.

CRAIG, DAVID. *Scottish Literature and the Scottish People: 1680–1830.* London: Chatto & Windus, 1961.

DAVIES, SAMUEL. *Religion and Public Spirit.* New York, 1761.

DRUMMOND, GEORGE. "Rules of Conversation." In "Book of essays written by Students in the class of John Stevenson, Professor of Logic and Metaphysics, Edinburgh University, 1737–1750." University of Edinburgh mss.

EVANS, CHARLES. *American Bibliography.* 14 vols. New York: Peter Smith, 1903–59.

FECHNER, ROGER JEROME. "The Moral Philosophy of John Witherspoon and the Scottish-American Enlightenment." Diss. U of Iowa, 1974.

The Federalist Papers. Alexander Hamilton, James Madison, and John Jay. Ed. Roy P. Fairfield. 2nd ed. Baltimore: John Hopkins UP, 1981.

FERGUSON, ADAM. *Institutes of Moral Philosophy for the Use of Students in the College of Edinburgh.* 2nd ed. Edinburgh: A. Kincaid, W. Creech, and J. Bell, 1773.

FIERING, NORMAN. "Moral Philosophy in America, 1650–1750, and Its British Context." Diss. Columbia U, 1969.

FITHIAN, PHILIP V. "Letters & Exercises While at Princeton College,

1771–72." *Fithian Journal and Letters, 1767–1774.* Princeton University mss.

FORDYCE, DAVID. *Dialogues Concerning Education.* London, 1745.

———. "The Elements of Moral Philosophy." *The Preceptor.* . . . 6th ed. 2 vols. London, 1765.

GRANT, ALEXANDER. *The Story of the University of Edinburgh During Its First Three Hundred Years.* 2 vols. London: Longmans, Green, and Co., 1884.

GUDER, DARREL L. "The Story of Belles Lettres at Princeton: An Historical Investigation of the Expansion and Secularization of Curriculum at the College of New Jersey with Special Reference to the Curriculum of English Language and Letters." Diss. U of Hamburg, 1964.

GUTHRIE, WARREN. "The Development of Rhetorical Theory in America: The Dominance of the Rhetoric of Style 1635–1730." *Speech Monographs* 13 (1946): 14–22.

———. "The Development of Rhetorical Theory in America 1635–1850: II." *Speech Monographs* 14 (1947): 38–54.

———. "Rhetorical Theory in Colonial America." *History of Speech Education in America: Background Studies.* Ed. Karl R. Wallace. New York: Appleton, 1954. 48–59.

HALLORAN, MICHAEL S. "Rhetoric in the American College Curriculum: The Decline of Public Discourse." *Pretext* 3 (1982): 245–69.

HAMOWY, R. "Jefferson and the Scottish Enlightenment: A Critique of Garry Wills's *Inventing America: Jefferson's Declaration of Independence.*" *William and Mary Quarterly* 36 (1979): 503–23.

[HENDERSON, ROBERT]. "A Short Account of the University of Edinburgh, the Present Professors in it, and the Seven Parts of Learning taught by them." *Scots Magazine* 3 (August, 1741): 371–74.

HENRETTA, JAMES A. *The Evolution of American Society, 1700–1815.* Lexington: Heath, 1973.

HOOK A. *Scotland and America: A Study of Cultural Relations 1750–1835.* Glasgow: Blackie, 1975.

HOWELL, WILBUR SAMUEL. *Eighteenth-Century British Logic and Rhetoric.* Princeton: Princeton UP, 1971.

HUTCHESON, FRANCIS. *Short Introduction to Moral Philosophy in Three Books Containing the Elements of Ethics and the Law of Nature.* Glasgow: Robert Foulis, 1747.

———. *A System of Moral Philosophy; To Which is prefixed some account of the life, writings, and character of the author by William Leechman.* London: A. Millar, 1755.

JEFFERSON, THOMAS. *Autobiography.* New York: Capricorn Books, 1959.

JOHNSTON, THOMAS. *Working Classes in Scotland.* Glasgow: Forward Publishing Co., 1920.

KELLY, BROOKS MATHER. *Yale, A History.* New Haven: Yale, 1974.

LANDSMAN, NED C. *Scotland and Its First American Colony, 1683–1765.* Princeton: Princeton UP, 1985.

McALLISTER, JAMES L. "Francis Alison and John Witherspoon: Political Philosophers and Revolutionaries." *Journal of Presbyterian History* 54 (1976): 33–60.

McLACHLAN, JAMES. *Princetonians: 1748–1768.* Princeton: Princeton UP, 1976.

MACLEAN, JOHN. *History of the College of New Jersey: 1746–1854.* New York: Arno Press, 1969.

MARTIN, TERENCE. *The Instructed Vision.* Bloomington: Indiana UP, 1961.

MAY, HENRY F. *The Enlightenment in America.* Oxford: Oxford UP, 1976.

MILLER, THOMAS. P. "Blair, Witherspoon and the Rhetoric of Civic Humanism." *Scotland and America in the Age of Enlightenment.* Ed. Richard Sher and Jeffrey Smitten. Edinburgh: Edinburgh UP, 1990.

MORGAN, EDMUNDS. "The American Revolution Considered as an Intellectual Movement." *Paths of American Thought.* Ed. Arthur M. Schlesinger, Jr. and Morton White. Boston: Houghton, 1963. 11–33.

MORREN, NATHANIEL. *Annals of the General Assembly of the Church of Scotland, 1739–1766.* 2 vols. Edinburgh: John Johnstone, 1838–40.

MORRISON, SAMUEL ELIOT. *Harvard College in the Seventeenth Century.* Cambridge: Harvard UP, 1936.

———. *Three Centuries of Harvard, 1636–1936.* Cambridge: Belknap Press of Harvard UP, 1936.

New Jersey Archives: Documents Relating to the Colonial, Revolutionary and Post-Revolutionary History of the State of New Jersey. Newark: New Jersey Historical Society, 1880–1928.

NORRIS, EDWIN MARK. *The Story of Princeton.* Boston: Little, Brown, 1917.

NORTON, DAVID FATE. "Francis Hutcheson in America." *Studies in Voltaire and the Eighteenth Century* 154 (1976): 1547–68.

PHILLIPSON, NICHOLAS. "The Pursuit of Virtue in Scottish University Education: Dugald Stewart and Scottish Moral Philosophy in the Enlightenment." *Universities, Society, and the Future.* Ed. Nicholas Phillipson. Edinburgh: Edinburgh UP, 1983. 82–101.

POCOCK, J. G. A. *Virtue, Commerce, and History: Essays on Political Thought and History, Chiefly in the Eighteenth Century.* Cambridge: Cambridge UP, 1985.

POMFRET, JOHN E. *Colonial New Jersey, a History.* New York: Scribner's, 1973.

POTTER, DAVID. *Debating in the Colonial Chartered College.* New York: Bureau of Publications, Teachers College, Columbia University, 1944.

PRINGLE, J. "Lectures from Cicero." Edinburgh, 1741. Edinburgh University mss.

QUINCY, JOSIAH. *The History of Harvard University.* 2 vols. 1860. New York: Arno Press, 1977.

RICH, GEORGE EUGENE. "John Witherspoon: His Scottish Intellectual Background." Doctoral thesis. Syracuse University, 1964.

ROBBINS, CAROLINE. *The Eighteenth-Century Commonwealthman: Studies in the Transmission, Development and Circumstances of English Liberal Thought from the Restoration of Charles II until the War with the Thirteen Colonies.* Cambridge: Harvard UP, 1961.

———. " 'When It Is That Colonies May Turn Independent:' An Analysis of the Environment and Politics of Francis Hutcheson (1694–1746)." *William and Mary Quarterly* 11 (1954): 214–51.

ROBERTSON, WILLIAM, et al. "Reasons of Dissent from the Judgment and Resolution of the Commission, March 11, 1752. . . ." *Annals of the General Assembly of the Church of Scotland, 1739–1766.* Ed. Nathaniel Morren. 2 vols. Edinburgh: John Johnstone, 1838–1840. 1: 231–42.

RUDOLPH, FREDERICK. *The American College and University: A History.* New York: Vintage Books, 1962.

SCHMITZ, ROBERT MORRELL. *Hugh Blair.* Morningside Heights, N. Y.: King's Cross Press, 1948.

SCOTT, JACK, ed. *Lectures on Moral Philosophy.* John Witherspoon. Newark: Delaware UP, 1982.

SCOTT, WILLIAM ROBERT. *Francis Hutcheson, His Life, Teaching and Position in the History of Philosophy.* 1900. New York: A. M. Kelley, 1966.

SHAFTESBURY, ANTHONY ASHLEY COOPER (Earl of). *Characteristics of Men, Manners, Opinions, Times, etc.* 1711. Ed. John M. Robertson. 2 vols. Indianapolis: Bobbs-Merrill, 1964.

SHAW, JOHN STUART. *The Management of Scottish Society, 1707–1764: Power, Nobles, Lawyers, Edinburgh Agents and English Influences.* Edinburgh: John Donald, 1983.

SHER, RICHARD. *Church and University in the Scottish Enlightenment: The Moderate Literati of Edinburgh.* Edinburgh: Edinburgh UP, 1985.

SLOAN, DOUGLAS, ED. *The Great Awakening and American Education: A Documentary History.* New York: Teachers College Press, 1973.

———. *The Scottish Enlightenment and the American College Ideal.* New York: Teachers College Press, 1971.

SMITH, WILLIAM. *Some Thoughts on Education: With Reasons for Erecting a College in this Province. . . .* New York, 1752.

SMOUT, T. C. *A History of the Scottish People.* New York: Scribner's, 1969.

SMYLIE, JAMES H. "Madison and Witherspoon: Theological Roots of American Political Thought." *Princeton University Chronicle* 22 (Spring, 1961): 118–32.

SOMMERVILLE, THOMAS. *My Own Life and Times 1741–1814.* Edinburgh: Edmonton & Douglas, 1861.

STOHLMAN, MARTHA LOU LEMMON. *John Witherspoon: Parson, Politician, Patriot.* Philadelphia: Westminster, 1976.

SWEET, WILLIAM WARREN. *Religion in the Development of American Culture, 1765–1840.* New York: Scribner's, 1952.

TENNENT, GILBERT. *The Danger of an Unconverted Ministry.* 1740. Rptd. *The Colonial Idiom.* Ed. David Potter and Gordon L. Thomas. Carbondale: Southern Illinois UP, 1970. 469–87.

TENNENT, GILBERT, and SAMUEL DAVIES. "A General Account of the Rise and State of The College of New Jersey. . . ." 1742. Rptd. *The Great Awakening and American Education: A Documentary History.* Ed. Douglas Sloan. New York: Teachers Co.

THORP, WILLARD, et al. *The Princeton Graduate School: A History.* Princeton: Princeton UP, 1978.

TRINTERUD, LEONARD J. *The Form of an American Tradition: A Re-Examination of Colonial Presbyterianism.* Freeport, N.Y.: Books for Libraries Press, 1949.

WALSH, JAMES J. *Education of the Founding Fathers of the Republic.* New York: Fordham UP, 1935.

WERTENBAKER, THOMAS JEFFERSON. *Princeton, 1746–1896.* Princeton: Princeton, 1946.

WILLS, GARRY. *Explaining America: The Federalist.* Garden City, N.Y.: Doubleday, 1981.

———. *Inventing America: Jefferson's Declaration of Independence.* Garden City, N.Y.: Doubleday, 1978.

WITHERSPOON, JOHN. "Lectures on Moral Philosophy." [1771–72]. Princeton University Library mss SM 12800.

———. *Works.* 4 vols. Philadelphia: William W. Woodward, 1802.

WITHERSPOON, JOHN, et al. "Answers to the Reasons of Dissent." *Annals of the General Assembly of the Church of Scotland, 1739–1766.* Ed. Nathaniel Morren. 2 vols. Edinburgh: John Johnstone, 1838–40. 1: 243–60.

ECCLESIASTICAL CHARACTERISTICS

OR, THE ARCANA OF CHURCH POLICY

Being an humble attempt to open the mystery of moderation.
Wherein is shewn, a plain and easy way of attaining to the
character of a moderate man, as at present in repute
in the Church of Scotland.

Dedication To The Departed Ghost, Surviving Spirit,
of the late Reverend Mr.———, Minister in ———,

Worthy Sir,

During a great part of the time I spent in composing the following treatise, I was fully resolved to have sent it abroad by itself and not to have dedicated it to any person in the world; and indeed in a confined sense of the word *world,* you see I have still kept my resolution. The reason of this my intended purpose was that I find the right honorable the earl of Shaftesbury in an advertisement or ticket prefixed to his works hath expressed a contempt and disdain of all dedications, prefaces, or other discourses by way of forerunners to a book. This he seems to think a mean and cowardly way in an author of creeping into the world and begging the reception which he dares not claim.

Being satisfied, therefore, of the justness of this observation, and being also somewhat confident (as his lordship seems to have been) of the intrinsic worth of my performance, I intended to have come forth in this masterly manner.

But upon more mature deliberation, I discovered that the only objections against dedications were the self-diffidence just now mentioned and the suspicion of flattery for selfish ends, which is so contrary to disinterested benevolence; so that if I could frame a dedication which should be quite beyond the imputation of any of these two purposes, I should then wholly escape his lordship's censure.

57

This aim I think I have fallen nothing short of when I have dedicated this book to you, most illustrious SHADE! as my most malignant enemies cannot but grant that I could have no expectation of your encouraging me, either by buying my book, recommending it to others, or giving it away to the poor, nay, or even so much as for my translation to a better benefice in assembly or commission.

It startled me a little that this conduct might perhaps by evil disposed persons be represented as an approach to popery and resembling their worshipping of saints, but I hope that can scarcely be imputed to me in the present case since you never were esteemed a saint while you lived, nor ever thirsted after that title.

Another more material objection occurred to me, that a dedication to a dead man is either almost or altogether unprecedented. But I am not much concerned, though this method of proceeding should be thought bold and new, because this is the character which the incomparable Mr. ———— gives of his own essays upon the principles of morality and natural religion. Besides, I am not altogether destitute of authority; for the memorable dean Swift has used the freedom to dedicate his Tale of a Tub to Prince Posterity. I have also seen a satirical poem, called Sure Divino, dedicated with great solemnity to Prince (or rather I believe to King) Reason. If, therefore, one of these authors might dedicate a book to a faculty of the human mind and the other to an abstract idea, I hope it is no great presumption in me to dedicate mine to you, though "in statue mortuorum," especially as there is not a living man who hath so good a claim to the compliment of a treatise upon my subject.

But a more graveling difficulty than any of these kept me some time in suspense, viz. how to get the book presented to you, as I did not find in myself any inclination to depart this life in order to transport it. After much trouble, I was at length relieved by reflecting that Mr. Pope has assured us that the ghosts of departed ladies always haunt the places in which they delighted while they were alive; and therefore, from analogy, it is to be supposed that the same thing holds with regard to departed ministers. If this is the case, I look upon it as certain that your chief residence is in the assembly house at Edinburgh, where you have in your lifetime both given and received so much pleasure. For though I will not limit you in your unembodied state from making circuits through the country and visiting synods or presbyteries, particularly in the M———se and G————, where there are so many men after you own heart, yet, I dare say, you will not be absent from the assembly, nor any of the quarterly meetings of the commission which hath so often saved the church from impending dangers.

It is therefore my purpose to go to Edinburgh in May next when the assembly meets, of which I am a member, and there to lay before you my performance, hoping it will prove most delicious and savory to all your senses, to the names of which and the manner of their present operation I am wholly a stranger.

It is probable you have not been accustomed, these two or three years past, to hear your own praises celebrated; and therefore I shall no farther launch out into them than to say that there is not one branch of the character recommended in the following pages in which you were not eminent and that there never was one stone by you left unturned for promoting the good cause, —— That you may still sit upon the throne and, by your powerful, though invisible influence, make the interest of moderation prevail is the ardent wish and the pious prayer of,

Sir,
Your most obedient
and admiring Servant.

THE PREFACE

Gratitude obligeth me to acknowledge the kind reception which the world hath given to the following generous effort for the honor of our church. This shows either that panegyric is by no means so unacceptable to mankind in general, as some ill-natured authors insinuate, or that this of mine hath been executed with very uncommon skill. If this last should be the true solution, it would give me a double satisfaction. However, as the love of detraction in some persons is incurable, and as many have such ulcerated minds that there is no possibility of applying to them even in the softest and most friendly manner without offending them, to prevent the spreading of any such baleful influence, I think it proper to add a few things upon the structure of this performance, part of which should have accompanied the first edition if it had not pleased the publisher to print it without any communication from the author.

From the beginning I foresaw it would occur as an objection that I have not properly denominated that party in the church which I have chosen to celebrate by the words *moderation* and *moderate men*. It is alleged that for these two or three years past they have made little use of these words and have chosen rather to represent themselves as supporters of the constitution, as acting upon constitutional principles, as lovers of order, and enemies to confusion, etc., while at the very same time, the opposite party have taken up the title of *moderation* and pretend to be acting upon *moderated principles*. It is also hinted that the just severities which the times render necessary require a different phraseology.

In answer to this I observe that my treatise has really been a work of time (as, I hope, appears from its maturity), the most part of it having been composed above two years ago and before this change of language was introduced. It was originally intended only to exhibit a general view of the different parties in religion and learning among us, though it hath now admitted a very particular account of the latest and most recent differences in the church, chiefly because *the present* seems likely to be an *era* of some consequence, and to be big with some very great events as well as persons. Besides, I consider that this name of *moderate men* was much longer the designation of my friends than those lately invented; and as they do not even at present allow the claim of their enemies to that character, it is probable they intend to take it up again as soon as the designs now upon the anvil shall be completely executed. As to the name of *moderation* being inconsistent with a proper vigor in support of their own measures and wholesome severities against their enemies, it is an objection altogether frivolous, as appears from the following examples: A certain minister being asked the character of a friend of his who had come up to the assembly, and particularly whether or not he was a *moderate man,* answered, *O yes, fierce for moderation!*

I think it proper to inform the reader that one great reason of the uncommon choice of a patron to this work was an opinion I had long entertained, and in support of which I could allege very strong arguments from the sayings of some great men and philosophers, as well as the practice of a famous ancient nation with regard to their kings, that the true and proper time of ascertaining and fixing a man's character is when he has done his whole work, and that posterity hath as good a right to the possession and use of his fame after death as his contemporaries to his abilities during his life. At the same time, though the author had a particular hero in view, yet he chose to publish it without mentioning his name, or place of abode, or indeed any circumstance foreign to the character which might distinguish the person. The design of acting in this manner was that in case the world should universally agree to ascribe it to the same person he had in his eye, it might be such a justification of the truth of the character as very few modern dedications can boast of.

This invention I challenge as wholly my own and do hereby allow and recommend the use of it to all future authors, hoping it will change the fashion among writers of character and self-esteem from using no dedications at all to forming them upon a plan entirely new. Let them each keep his patron in his eye, draw his character as exactly and graphically as possible, and publish it without a name, or with this inscription *Detur dignissimo;* then if the world do universally ascribe it to the person intended, let his name be prefixed to the second edition; and it will be more true, and sterling, and acceptable praise than any hitherto found in that class of panegyrics. But if on the contrary the world shall ascribe it to a different person, let the author acquiesce in the determination, rejoice in so good an expedient for preventing a blunder, and make his court to his new patron, who will hardly refuse to admit him after so refined and delicate a compliment. I dare not recommend any thing like this method with respect to the books already printed because it would occasion so violent a controversy about the propriety of many dedications as could not be ended but by the sword, they being most of them addressed to great men, who having agreed upon this method of revenging gross affronts and terminating in the last resort all important disputes. Should any ask why I have not followed my own rule by now prefixing the name of my patron, they are to understand that for reasons known to myself I intend to defer it till the nineteenth or twentieth edition.

If any shall think fit to blame me for writing in so bold and assuming a way through the whole of my book, I answer I have chosen it on purpose as being the latest and most modern way of writing; and the success it has already met with is a demonstration of its propriety and beauty. The same thing also, to my great satisfaction, is a proof of the justice of a late author's scheme of Moral Philosophy, who has expelled *mortification, self-denial, humility,* and *silence* from among the number of the virtues and transferred them, as he expresseth himself, to the opposite column, that is to say the column of vices. This scheme, I dare say, will stand its ground; and, as a critic, I observe that it was probably the single circumstance just now mentioned that brought upon the author an adversary who, though possessed of many truly good qualities, had the misfortune to be always eminent for modesty and other bastard virtues of the same class.

There are some, I find, of the opinion that it was neither necessary nor useful for me to give so many examples of the conduct of the moderate in the illustration of the several maxims; and these eminent persons themselves seem to feel some pain from the exposing of their virtues to the public view. But is it not an established truth that example teaches better than precept? Is there anything more usual in moral writings than to illustrate other heroes of ancient times? And since the advantage of example is commonly said to be that it is a living law, or that it puts life into the precept, surely the best of all examples must be those of persons really and literally alive. Neither should such persons themselves be offended with this conduct since, as has been hinted above, mortification and self-denial are no more to be reckoned among the virtues but the vices.

However, I have the comfort to reflect that from the opposite opinions of those who have passed their judgment on this performance, I am in the middle, and consequently in the right; for there have been transmitted to me many noble instances of *moderation,* in expectation no doubt that they should be added to my collection. I thankfully acknowledge my obligations to these kind contributors but cannot make any use of their contributions at present, for it would at least double the bulk of the treatise, and thereby render it *less commodious for pocket-*

carriage. Further, I do assure them it was not through want of materials that a greater number of examples was not produced but from having duly weighed the proper proportion for a work of this extent; and to what hath been affixed with so much deliberation, I am resolved steadfastly to adhere.

It were indeed to be wished that every man was left to himself and allowed in peace and quietness to finish his own work his own way, for I have seldom observed these things called *hints and suggestions* to have any other effect than to perplex and mislead. An author's situation when persecuted with them seems to me to resemble that of a gentleman building a house or planning out a garden, who, if he harkens to the advice or attempts to gratify the taste of every visitor, will in all probability produce upon the whole a collection of inconsistencies, a system of deformity.

I am very sorry to be obliged thus to speak in obscurity by returning a public answer to private observations but cannot omit taking notice that it has been much wondered at that a certain very eminent person has been lost in the crowd of heroes without any particular of distinguishing compliment paid to himself. Now, this did not by any means flow from a want of respect and esteem, but from a distrust of my own abilities and a despair of being able to do justice to so illustrious a character. Neither indeed was there any great necessity (excepting mere compliment) of spreading his fame which hath already gone both far and wide. Besides, that his many and remarkable exploits, however strong and *pregnant* proofs they may be of benevolence and social affection, have some circumstances attending them which render them more proper subjects of discourse than writing. The glare would be rather too great for even the strong eyesight of this generation to endure when brought very near them. The sun is the most glorious of all objects in the firmament, and yet, though it were in the power of a painter to draw him in all his lustre, there would hardly be found a proper place for him in the largest palace in Great Britain.

The only other objection I shall take notice of is that in one respect I may be said to have drawn the picture larger than the life, in as much as I seem to suppose that all moderate men do in fact possess every one of the virtues which I have made to enter into the perfection of the character. This objection, though the one most insisted upon, is evidently both false and foolish. No reader of true discernment can imagine any such thing. If it were so, there would be no occasion for my book at all; on the contrary, the various maxims inserted in it and the various examples produced in illustration of them do show that there are different degrees of perfection even amongst the moderate themselves. They are a body, every member of which has neither the same abilities nor the same office. They are also a body most firmly united for mutual defence and support, so much, I confess, I intended to intimate; and that on account, they are entitled to a sort of community of goods and mutual participation of each other's excellencies. A head may very well boast of the beauty, elegance, and activity of the hands or the comely proportion and strength of the limbs belonging to it; and yet, though they are one body, it would be ridiculous to suppose that the head or hands are always in the dirt when they have the feet to carry them through it.

This metaphor of a body, however common, is one of the justest and most significative imaginable, out of which a very long allegory might be formed; but I shall prosecute it no farther at this time except to acknowledge that it convinces me of one real omission in my plan, viz., that what hath been just now hinted I ought to have inserted as a *thirteenth maxim* and illustrated it at large.[1] It would have been easy to show that the moderate are remarkable for the most perfect union and harmony and for a firm and steadfast adherence to each other in the prosecution of their designs. Neither is there any instance in which there is a stronger contrast or opposition between them and the orthodox, as manifestly appeared from the conduct of both parties in the General Assembly 1753. A friend of ours called the enemy upon that occasion *a parcel of conscientious fools;* had he then read the following maxims, which prove that they have as little *conscience* as *wisdom,* it is probable he would have bestowed on them their true and proper character.

ECCLESIASTICAL CHARACTERISTICS

Introduction

The reader will doubtless agree with me that moderation is an excellent thing, and particularly the noblest character of a churchman. It is also well known that as all churches have usually in them a moderate and a zealous, high-flying, wild party, so our church hath at present a certain party who glory in and fight for moderation, and who (it is to be hoped justly) appropriate to themselves wholly the character of moderate men. Neither is it a small presage of a glorious and blessed state of the church in its approaching periods that so many of our young men are smitten with the love of moderation, and generally burn with desire to appear in that noble and divine character.

1. This was done in the third edition.

This hath inspired me with the ambition and expectation of being helpful in training up as many as are desirous of it in this most useful of all sciences. For however perfectly it is known and however steadily practiced by many who are adepts, and notwithstanding there are some young men of pregnant parts who make a sudden surprising proficiency without much assistance, yet I have often observed that there are several persons who err in many instances from the right path, boggle at sundry particular steps of their leaders, and take a long time before they are thoroughly confirmed in their principles and practice. The same persons also, by an unstable conduct or by an imprudent or unreasonable discovery of their designs, have brought a reproach upon their party and been an obstruction to whatever work they had then in hand.

These bad effects, I humbly conceive, flow chiefly, if not only, from the want of a complete system of moderation containing all the principles of it and giving a distinct view of their mutual influence one upon another, as well as proving their reasonableness and showing by examples how they ought to be put in practice.

There is no work of this kind, to my knowledge, yet extant, which renders my present undertaking of it the more laudable and will, I hope, render it the more acceptable.

I must inform the reader that after I was fully convinced of the necessity of some such piece as what follows, but before I entered upon it myself, I earnestly entreated several of the most eminent men of the moderate stamp among us, those burning and shining lights of our church, who are and are esteemed to be our leaders, that some of them would set about it. However, they all devolved it upon me and made this satisfying excuse for themselves, that they were so busied in acting moderation, that they could not have time to write upon it. This soon led me to think what would become of many noble designs, and what advantage our discontented zealots might take if any of the expert steersmen of this ecclesiastical vessel of ours should retire from the helm but so long time as would be necessary to bring a work of such a nature to the perfection in strength, symmetry, and elegance that the reader will perceive even this of mine is arrived at.

I shall now proceed to the principal part of the work after I have informed the reader of the plan of it, which is briefly this, to enumerate distinctly and in their proper order and connection all the several maxims upon which moderate men conduct themselves, and forasmuch as the justice of many of them, being refined pieces of policy, is not very evident at first sight, I shall subjoin to each an illustration and confirmation of it from reason or experience or both. N.B. I shall make but very little use of Scripture because that is contrary to some of the maxims themselves, as will be seen in the sequel.

Maxim I

*All ecclesiastical persons of whatever rank, whether principals of
colleges, professors of divinity, ministers, or even probationers,
who are suspected of heresy are to be esteemed men of
great genius, vast learning, and uncommon worth and
are by all means to be supported and protected.*

ALL moderate men have a kind of fellow feeling with heresy, and as
soon as they hear of any one suspected, or in danger of being prosecuted
for it, zealously and unanimously rise up in his defense. This fact is
unquestionable. I never knew a moderate man in my life that did not
love and honor a heretic or that had not an implacable hatred at the
persons and characters of heresy-hunters, a name with which we have
thought proper to stigmatize these sons of Belial who begin and carry
on prosecutions against men for heresy in church-courts.

It is related of the apostle John, and an ugly story it is, that upon
going into a public bath and observing the heretic Cerinthus there
before him, he retired with the utmost precipitation lest the edifice
should fall and crush him when in company with such an enemy of the
truth. If the story be true, the apostle's conduct was ridiculous and wild;
but Dr. Middleton has shown that the story is not true; and indeed,
the known benevolence and charity of John's writings make it highly
probable. However, not to enter into that controversy whether it be true
or not, the conduct of all moderate men is directly opposite.

As to the justice of this maxim, many solid reasons may be given for
it. Compassion itself, which is one of the finest and most benevolent
feelings of the human heart, moves them to the relief of their distressed
brother. Another very plain reason may be given for it: Moderate men
are, by their very name and constitution, the reverse in all respects of
bigoted zealots. Now, it is well known that many of this last sort, both
clergy and common people, when they hear of a man suspected of
heresy conceive an aversion at him even before they know anything of
the case; nor after he is acquitted (as they are all of them commonly in
our church-courts) can they ever come to entertain a favorable opinion
of him. The reverse of this then is to be as early and as vigorous in his
defense as they are in his prosecution, and as implicit in our belief of
his orthodoxy as they are in their belief of his error.

I remember when I was discoursing once to this purpose, a certain
raw unexperienced person said he had always thought that, not moderation, but lukewarmness and indifference to truth was the reverse of
excessive zeal, and that moderation was situated in the middle betwixt
the two. To whom I answered, Young man you do not reflect that no

fierce man can be resisted but by one as fierce, nor overcome but by one fiercer than himself; if, therefore, nobody would oppose the zealots but such calm midsmen as you mention, in every such instance the balance of power must lean to their side, and the poor heretic must fall a sacrifice to the no small detriment of the cause of moderation, which by the by is commonly supported by the heretics in their stations, and therefore they deserve a grateful return.

This brings to my mind another reason for the maxim, viz. that heretics being so nearly related to the moderate men have a right to claim their protection out of friendship and personal regard. This serves a very noble end for it vindicates the Christian religion from the objection of some infidels, who affirm that it does not recommend private friendship; now moderate men, having all a very great regard to private friendship and personal connections, do by their practice, which is the most solid way, confute this slander.

I may add to these another argument for the great character of heretics, as asserted in the maxim, which I picked up from the preaching of a seceding minister. He told his hearers that when the devil looks out for an instrument to propagate error, he never makes choice of a weak silly man but one able and learned, as well knowing, I suppose, that though God can support his cause by any instrument whatever, yet he needs always the best and most sufficient he can get. Now, though I hope no man will reckon me of this fanatic's principles so far as to think the devil the source of error, yet the citation serves my purpose, as it shows that he himself was convinced of the ability and learning of heretics, and all the world knows that the testimony of an enemy is the strongest of all evidences upon a man's side.

I shall conclude this maxim with observing that such tenderness for heretics, however due from some, is yet in many of the moderate character an instance of the most heroic and generous friendship. It is quite disinterested, as they themselves run not the smallest hazard of ever being in the like circumstances. Heretics are commonly an honest sort of people, but with all their book learning, of no great stock of prudence or policy. They publish and assert whatever they believe upon all points without considering the reception it is like to meet with from those of opposite principles. They affront the public to its face, which Lord Shaftesbury tells us ought not to be done. On the other hand, men thorough-paced in moderation discover their principles only at such times and to such persons as are able to bear them. By this means they preserve themselves from heresy, and indeed they cannot possibly fall into it unless by mistake, in which case as soon as they are challenged (if it is like to be attended with any temporal inconveniency), they deny it, explain it away, or repent and ask pardon.

In all this they follow the noble example of Mr.———, who in the assembly debates upon Professor Simson's affair happening to say something that was challenged by one present as heresy, immediately replied, "Moderator, if that be heresy, I renounce it."

Maxim II

*When any man is charged with loose practices or tendencies
to immorality, he is to be screened and protected as much as
possible, especially if the faults laid to his charge be, as they
are incomparably well termed in a sermon preached by a hopeful
youth that made some noise lately, "good humored vices."*

THE reason upon which this maxim is founded may be taken from the reasons of the former, "mutatis mutandis"; there being scarcely any of them that does not hold equally in both cases. A libertine is a kind of practical heretic and is to be treated as such. Dr. Tillotson observes in one of his sermons that the worst of all heresies is a bad life; now, if instead of worst, which is an uncomely expression, you would read greatest in that passage, then a libertine is the greatest of all heretics and to be honored in proportion. Even the apostle Paul (who is very seldom of any use to us in our reasonings) seems to suppose that they are men of most knowledge who are most free and bold in their practice, and that they are only weak brethren who are filled with scruples. The weak man is restrained and confirmed by his narrow conscience, but the strong man believeth that he may EAT, and by parity of reason, DRINK all things.

In order to understand the nature of "good-humored vices," the reader may please to take notice that it is an observation of Lord Shaftesbury that "the best time for thinking upon religious subjects, is when a man is merry, and in good humor"; and so far is this observation drawn from nature that it is the time commonly chosen for that purpose by many who never heard of his lordship or his writings. Whatever, therefore, serves to promote merriment and heighten good humor must so far serve for the discovery of religious truth. But as there are many ways of making a person merry which narrow-minded people will call vice; from thence, in compliance with common language, arises the new compound "good-humored vices." It is not, however, so to be understood as if either the inventor of it or those who love and patronize him mean anything by it but what is, "in their apprehension," both innocent and laudable.

Let it also be observed that as gravity is almost a necessary conse-

quence of solitude, "good-humored vices" are certainly "social pleasures," and such as flow from and show benevolence; and this is an
affection for which our whole fraternity have the highest regard, insomuch that no surer mark can be taken of a man's being ONE OF US than
the frequent returns of this expression in his discourses or writings.

It will serve further for the support of this maxim that according to
modern discoveries, there is a great analogy between the "moral virtues," or, if you will, the "science of morals," and the "fine arts"; and it is
on account of this analogy that most of the present reigning expressions
upon the subject of morals are borrowed from the arts, as "beauty,
order, proportion, harmony, decency," etc. It is also established long
since and well known as a principle in the fine arts that a certain freedom
and boldness of manner is what chiefly constitutes grace and beauty.
Why then should not approbation be founded upon the same grounds
in both cases? Why should not a bold practice be as beautiful in real as
a bold hand is in imitated life, especially as all great geniuses have
actually laid claim to this as their peculiar privilege, not to be confined
to common forms, and that in opposition to the bulk of mankind, who
through want of taste, are not able to relish the finest performances in
any of the kinds?

I must not, however, omit taking notice to prevent mistakes of one
exception that must be made from this maxim; that is that when the
person to whose charge any faults are laid is reputed orthodox in his
principles, in the common acceptation of that word, or comes in by
orthodox influence, in that case they are all to be taken for granted as
true, and the evil of them set forth in the liveliest colors. In consequence
of this, he is to be prosecuted and torn to pieces on account of these
crimes. But if it so happen that he cannot be convicted upon a trial,
then it is best to make use of things as they really are, that is to express
suspicions, to give ingenious and dubious hints, and if possible, ruin
him without any trial at all. There was a noble example of this given a
few years ago in the case of a settlement in the bounds of a presbytery,
very many of whom are eminent in moderation. In that case, there were
several faults laid to the charge of the candidate; and yet, though he
himself very much insisted upon an inquiry into their truth and a
judgment upon their relevancy, the presbytery wisely refused to do
either the one or the other, but left them to have their own natural
weight in fame, rumor, and conversation.

The necessity of this exception is very evident: For in the supposed
case all the reasons for protection to the young man fail; to satisfy
himself of which, let the reader view these reasons as they are annexed
to the first maxim and save my book from the deformity of repetition.

Maxim III

*It is a necessary part of the character of a moderate man
never to speak of the Confession of Faith but with a sneer,
to give sly hints that he does not thoroughly believe it, and
to make the word orthodoxy a term of contempt and reproach.*

THE Confession of Faith, which we are now all laid under a disagreeable necessity to subscribe, was framed in times of hot religious zeal; and therefore it can hardly be supposed to contain anything agreeable to our sentiments in these cool and refreshing days of moderation. So true is this that I do not remember to have heard any moderated man speak well or recommend it in a sermon or private discourse in my time. And, indeed, nothing can be more ridiculous than to make a fixed standard for opinions, which change just as the fashions of clothes and dress. No complete system can be settled for all ages, except the maxims I am now compiling and illustrating, and their great perfection lies in their being ambulatory so that they may be applied differently with the change of times.

Upon this head some may be ready to object that if the Confession of Faith be built upon the sacred Scriptures, then, change what will, it cannot as the foundation upon which it rests remains always firm and the same. In answer to this, I beg leave to make a very new and therefore striking comparison: When a lady looks at a mirror, she sees herself in a certain attitude and dress, but in her native beauty and color; should her eye on a sudden be tinctured with the jaundice, she sees herself all yellow and spotted; yet the mirror remains the same faithful mirror still, and the alteration arises not from it but from the object that looks at it. I beg leave to make another comparison: When an old philosopher looked at the evening star, he beheld nothing but a little twinkling orb, round and regular like the rest; but when a modern views it with a telescope, he talks of phases, and horns, and mountains, and what not; now this arises not from any alteration in the star, but from his superior assistance in looking at it. The application of both these similitudes I leave to the reader.

But besides these general reasons, there is one very strong particular reason why moderate men cannot love the Confession of Faith: Moderation evidently implies a large share of charity, and consequently a good and favorable opinion of those that differ from our church; but a rigid adherence to the Confession of Faith, and high esteem of it, nearly borders upon or gives great suspicion of harsh opinions of those that differ from us, and does not experience rise up and ratify this observation? Who are the narrow-minded, bigoted, uncharitable persons among us? Who are the severe censurers of those that differ in judgment? Who are the damners of the adorable heathens, Socrates, Plato, Marcos Antonius, etc.? In fine, who are the persecutors of the inimitable heretics among ourselves? Who but the admirers of this antiquated composition, who pin their faith to other men's sleeves and will not endure one jot less or different belief from what their fathers had before them! It is therefore plain that the moderate man, who desires to enclose all intelligent beings in one benevolent embrace, must have an utter abhorrence at that vile hedge of distinction, the Confession of Faith.

I shall briefly mention a trifling objection to this part of our character—that by our subscription we sacrifice sincerity, the queen of virtues, to private gain and advantage. To which I answer in the first place that the objection proves too much, and therefore must be false and can prove nothing; for, allowing the justice of the objection, it would follow that a vast number, perhaps a majority, of the clergy of the church of England are villains; their printed sermons being, many of them, diametrically opposite to the articles which they subscribe. Now, as this supposition can never be admitted by any charitable man, the objection from whence it flows as a necessary consequence must fall to the ground.

But farther, what is there more insincere in our subscriptions than in these expressions of compliment and civility, which all acknowledge lawful, although they rarely express the meaning of the heart! The design is sufficiently understood in both cases, and our subscriptions have this advantage above forms of compliment, in point of honesty, that we are at a great deal of pains usually to persuade the world that we do not believe what we sign, whereas the complaisant gentleman is very seldom at any pains about the matter.

What is said might suffice in so clear a case, but I am here able to give a proof of the improvement of the age by communicating to the reader a new way of subscribing the Confession of Faith in a perfect consistency with sincerity, if that be thought of any consequence; it is taken from the method of attesting some of our gentlemen elders of the general assembly. Many insist that they ought to be attested and do attest them as qualified in all respects if the attestors are wholly ignorant about the matter because, in that case, there is no evidence to the contrary, and the presumption ought to lie on the favorable side. Now, as every new discovery should be applied to all the purposes for which it may be useful, let this method be adopted by the entrants into the ministry and applied to their subscription of the Confession of Faith. Nothing is more easy than for them to keep themselves wholly ignorant of what it contains, and then they may with a good conscience subscribe it as true because it ought to be so.

Maxim IV

A good preacher must not only have all the above and subsequent principles of moderation in him, as the source of everything that is good; but must, over and above, have the following special marks and signs of a talent for preaching. (1) His subjects must be confined to social duties. (2) He must recommend them only from rational considerations, viz. the beauty and comely proportions of virtue, and its advantages in the present life without any regard to a future state of more extended self-interest. (3) His authorities must be drawn from heathen writers, none, or as few as possible, from Scripture. (4) He must be very unacceptable to the common people.

THESE four marks of a good preacher, or rules for preaching well (for they serve equally for both purposes), I shall endeavor distinctly to illustrate and confirm that this important branch of my subject may be fully understood.

As to the first of these rules, that a preacher's subjects must be confined to "social duties," it is quite necessary in a moderate man because his moderation teaches him to avoid all the high flights of evangelic enthusiasm and the mysteries of grace which the common people are so fond of. It may be observed, nay, it is observed, that all of our stamp avoid the word grace as much as possible and have agreed to substitute the "moral virtues" in the room of the "graces of the spirit," which is the orthodox expression. And indeed it is not in this only, but in all other cases, that we endeavor to improve the phraseology and show that besides sentiment, even in language itself, we are far superior to and wiser than our fathers before us. I could show this by a great many examples, but that would be too tedious; and therefore only add to the one mentioned above that where an ancient orthodox man or even an old fashioned modern who thinks religion can never be amended either in matter or manner would have said "a great degree of sanctification," a man of moderation and politeness will say, "a high pitch of virtue." Now, as this is the case, it is plain a moderate preacher must confine his subjects to social duties chiefly and not insist on such passages of Scripture as will by the very repetition of them contaminate his style, and may perhaps diffuse a rank smell of orthodoxy through the whole of his discourse.

After all, I cannot refuse that it is still a more excellent way for those who have talents equal to the undertaking to seize an orthodox text, explain it quite away from its ordinary sense, and constrain it to speak the main parts of our own scheme. Thus a noble champion of ours chose once for his subject, Rom. 8:2, "For the law of the Spirit of life, in Christ Jesus, hath made me free from the law of sin and death," which he explained in this manner, "the law of the Spirit of life," that is, the moral sense, "in Christ Jesus," which is the sum of the Christian religion, etc. The advantage of this way is that it is tearing the weapons out of the hands of the orthodox and turning them against themselves. And it may perhaps in time have the effect to make our hearers affix our sense to their beloved Scriptures, or at least, which is the next thing, prevent them from being able to find any other. However, I must acknowledge that this way of doing is not for every man's management; and therefore I continue my advice to the generality still to adhere to the rule as first delivered.

The second rule will be easily confirmed, that duties are to be recommended only from "rational considerations." What can be imagined more foolish than to contradict this? If there be any thing in a sermon different from rational considerations, it must be irrational, that is to say, absurd. It is in this part of our scheme that we moderate men obtain a glorious triumph over our adversaries and despisers. Who but must smile when they hear the contemptible, vulgar, ignorant, hotheaded country elders, or silly women, led captive by them at their will saying they do not love this rational way of going to heaven!

But to explain this method a little further, the rational way of preaching is sometimes set in opposition to the pathetic way of raising the passions. This last is what we greatly disapprove of; there is something immoderate in the very idea of raising the passions; and therefore it is contrary to our character, nor was it ever known that a truly moderate man raised or moved any affection in his hearers, unless perhaps the affection of anger against himself. We leave that to your vehement bawlers, or your whining lamenters, who are continually telling "they will spend and be spent" for the salvation of their hearers, which Lord Shaftesbury elegantly derides by calling it "the heroic passion of saving souls." And let any unprejudiced person judge whether there is not something vastly great, something like an heroic fortitude in that man who can talk of future judgment, heaven and hell, with as much coolness and indifference as if it were a common matter. To say the truth, indeed, we do not often meddle with these alarming themes. However, as I observed upon the first mark of a good preacher, that it is glorious to rob the orthodox of a text and make it bend to our plan, so it is also an uncommon excellence to treat these subjects with calmness and to prove that we ought to do so. Thus a great proficient in our way, lately preaching upon Acts 24:25, where Paul made Felix to tremble by his discourse, proved from it that ministers ought not to raise the passions of their hearers. An ignorant observer would have thought that the passion of terror was raised in Felix to a great degree, and that he was little better than a Cambuslang convict. But mark the lucky expression our hero got hold of: "As he reasoned of righteousness," etc. as he reasoned, that is argued, and proved by rational considerations.

This example gives me a fine opportunity of making a kind of contrast and showing from fact the difference between an orthodox and a moderate preacher. I myself heard one of the first kind upon the text just now mentioned, and his first observation was that the apostle Paul was a faithful "reprover" speaking home to Felix: (1) of "righteousness" to convince him of any iniquity he had been guilty of in his government; (2) of "temperance," which he said should be translated "continence," and was probably intended as a reproof to him and Drusilla, who were living in adultery. His next and main observation was that Felix was "convicted," but "stifled" his convictions and delayed his repentance, saying, "Go thy way for this time; when I have a convenient reason, I will call for thee." Then followed a great deal of stuff, which I do not incline to transcribe; but it was just what the vulgar call experimental preaching, I suppose to distinguish it from rational.

But how contrary to this did our moderate friend? He first observed that St. Paul was a "moral," or a "legal preacher" discoursing of "righteousness" and "temperance" without a word of "faith"; and then, that he was a "reasoning preacher" who did not strive to raise people's passions but informed their judgment. I was indeed a little disappointed upon consulting the original to find that the word used, which is *dialego-menou*, signifies only "continuing his discourse" and so might be either in the "reasoning" or "pathetic" way; but I was satisfied by reflecting that the word evidently includes both, and so "reasoning" being the best, it is to be supposed the apostle preferred it.

Agreeably to this rule, Lord Shaftesbury, and after him a bright luminary in our own church, gives an advice to all moderate clergymen not to affect that idle title of "ambassadors" or "plenipotentiaries from heaven" so fondly claimed by zealots; and I take the liberty to suppose that the reason of the advice was the same in both, viz. "That under this character zealots put on an air of authority, and deliver their message with a pathos, to which they would otherwise have been strangers." His lordship indeed explodes the conceit sufficiently; he asks, "Gentlemen, where is your commission? how has it been conveyed? where are the letters patent? where the credentials?" with many more questions, easier for his lordship to ask than for SOME PERSONS to answer.

The third rule, viz. recommending "virtue" from the authority and examples of the heathens, is not only highly proper because they were very virtuous, but hath this manifest advantage attending it, that it is a proper way of reasoning to two quite opposite kinds of persons. One is such as are real Christians, who will be ashamed by the superior excellence of mere heathens, as they call them, and whom they so much despise. The other is our present living heathens, who pay no regard to the Christian religion at all, and therefore will only be moved by the authority of the persons they esteem. It is well known there are multitudes in our island who reckon Socrates and Plato to have been much greater men than any of the apostles, although (as the moderate preacher I mentioned lately told his hearers) the apostle Paul had an university education and was instructed in logic by professor Gamaliel. Therefore let religion be constantly and uniformly called "virtue," and let the heathen philosophers be set up as the great patterns and promoters of it. Upon this head, I must particularly recommend M. Antoninus by name because an eminent person of the moderate character says his meditations is the BEST book that ever was written for forming the heart.

But perhaps the last part of this third rule will be thought to need most illustration and defence, viz. that none at all "or very little use is to be made of Scripture." And really, to deal plainly, the great reason of this is that very few of the Scripture motives and arguments are of the moderate stamp; the most part of them are drawn from orthodox principles. For example, the apostle Paul cannot even say, "Husbands, love your wives," but his argument and example comes in these words, "as Christ also loved the church." The apostle John also speaks in a very mysterious way of union with Christ, and abiding in him in order to bring forth fruit, which is his way of speaking for a virtuous life. Now, let any indifferent person judge how this kind of expression and others of a like nature, such as mortifying the deeds of the body through the Spirit, would agree with the other parts of our discourses: They would be like opposite kinds of fluids which will not compound; they would be quite heterogeneous, which is against all the rules of fine writing and hinders it from being an uniform, beautiful, and comely whole. Horace, in his Art of Poetry, gives this as his very first observation, "Humano capiti cervicem pictor equinam / Jungere si velit," which my learned reader cannot fail both to remember and understand, and which I desire him to apply to this subject we are now upon. If it be said that sermons are not poems, and therefore not to be compounded by the rules of poetry, I answer it is a mistake; many of our sermons, especially those composed by the younger sort among us, are poems; at least they are full of poetical flights, which comes much to the same thing; not to

mention that the rule agrees equally to prose and poetry. How often
have I heard parts of Mr. Addison's Cato, Young's Night-Thoughts,
and diverse other poems in sermons? And, to say the truth, they were
none of the worst parts of them. However, I would offer my advice, as
that of a person of some experience, to all young preachers not to do
Dr. Young the honor of borrowing anything from him again because
he is a snarling, sullen, gloomy, melancholy mortal; cites a great deal of
scripture; and particularly because he has given a vile sneer at the
practice I am just now recommending in the following two lines of his
Universal Passion.

> When doctors Scripture for the classics quit,
> Polite apostates from God's grace to wit.

I have only another advice to give upon this head, and that is that
when our young preachers think proper to borrow from modern
printed poems, they would be pleased to transpose them a little, so to
speak, that they may not be too easily discerned by young gentlemen
who read the magazines. However, I am in great hopes we shall shortly
be quite above the necessity of borrowing from anybody, in order to
make our sermons poetry; there are some persons of genius among us
who can make very good poetry of their own, of which I could produce
some recent instances, but I do not think it at present expedient.

The fourth and last rule for a preacher is that he must be "very
unacceptable to the people." The *Spectator* I remember somewhere
says that most of the critics in Great Britain seem to act as if the first
rule of dramatic writing were "not to please." Now, what they make the
first rule of writing plays, I make the last rule for composing sermons,
not as being the least but the most important. It is indeed the grand
criterion, the most indispensable rule of all. Though one should pretend
to adhere to all the former rules and be wanting in this alone, he would
be no more than "a sounding brass, or a tinkling cymbal," pardon the
expression, the importance of the matter requires it. I shall put a case.
Suppose a man should have the approbation of the very best judges,
viz. those whose taste we ourselves allow to be good; if at the same time
he happens to be acceptable to the common people, it is a sign that he
must have some subtle refined fault which has escaped the observation
of the good judges aforesaid; for there is no man even of our own
fraternity so perfect and uniform in judging right as the common
people are in judging wrong.

I hope there is little need of assigning reasons for this great characteristic of the art of preaching; I suppose it will be allowed to be, if not
altogether, at least next to self-evident: All the several reasons that

have been given for the particular maxims of moderation concur in establishing this; for the people are all declared enemies of moderation in its principles and practice; and therefore if moderation be right, they must be wrong. There is a known story of a heathen orator, who, when the common people gave a shout of applause during his pronouncing an oration, immediately turned about to a friend, and asked him, what mistake he had committed. Now if an audience of vulgar heathens was allowed to be so infallibly wrong in their judgment, the same thing must hold, "a fortiori," in an audience of vulgar Christians.

From this it evidently follows that a popular preacher essentially signifies a bad preacher, and it is always so understood by us whenever we use the expression. If we but hear it reported of anyone that he is very popular among the lower sort, we are under no difficulty of giving his character without having heard him preach ourselves. In this case, fame is a certain guide to truth by being inverted; for we detest and despise him, precisely in the same proportion that the people admire him. On the other hand, the truly moderate man is not only above the applause of the multitude, but he glories in their hatred, and rejoices in himself in proportion as he has been so happy as to provoke and disoblige them. Of this I could give several notable examples, were it not that it must certainly offend their modesty, not only to praise them in print, but even to publish their highest virtues.

But now, upon the whole, as a great critic observes, that there is sometimes more beauty shown in a composition by receding from the rules of art when an important point is to be gained than by strictly adhering to them; so, all these rules notwithstanding, it shall be allowable for any moderate man upon an extraordinary emergency to break them for a good end: As for instance, he may speak even in Whitefield's style when his settlement has the misfortune to depend upon the people, which I have known done with good success. We are also well satisfied that Mr. T——r of Norwich and such like first-rate writers should make pompous collections of Scripture-texts as their truly laudable intention is, by altering Christianity, to reconcile it to moderation and common sense and to find out a meaning to words, which the writers of them, as living in the infancy of the church, had not discernment enough to intend.

To conclude this maxim it would be too formal for me, and too tedious to the reader, to enumerate all the objections that are by some raised against our way of preaching; I shall therefore mention but one and show it is false, hoping that the reader will suppose there is no more foundation for any of the rest. It is alleged there is no method in our discourses, but that they consist in random flights and general declamations. Nothing more untrue. The polite reader, or hearer, knows that there may be an excellent and regular method where there are no formal distinctions of firstly, secondly, and thirdly; but, to cut off all occasion of cavil, let the world hereby know that one of our most famous preachers chose once for his text John 11:29, and of that verse the following words, "He stinketh." He observed, we had there (or thereabouts) a description of the threefold state of a bad man: First, he sickened; secondly, he died; thirdly, he stank. This I take to have been an accuracy in point of method to which it will not be easy to find a parallel.

Maxim V

A minister must endeavor to acquire as great a degree of
politeness in his carriage and behavior and to catch as much of
the air and manner of a fine gentleman as possibly he can.

THIS is usually a distinguishing mark between the moderate and the orthodox, and how much we have the advantage in it is extremely obvious. Good manners is undoubtedly the most excellent of all accomplishments, and in some measure supplies the place of them all when they are wanting. And surely nothing can be more necessary to, or more ornamental and becoming in a minister: It gains him easy access into the world and frees him from that rigid severity which renders many of them so odious and detestable to the polite part of it. In former times, ministers were so monkish and recluse ordinarily, and so formal when they did happen to appear that all the jovial part of mankind, particularly rakes and libertines, shunned and fled from them or, when unavoidably thrown into their company, were constrained, and had no kind of confidence to repose in them; whereas now let a moderate, modern, well-bred minister go into promiscuous company, they stand in no manner of awe and will even swear with all imaginable liberty. This gives the minister an opportunity of understanding their character, and of perhaps sometimes reasoning in an easy and genteel manner against swearing. This, though indeed it seldom reforms them, yet it is as seldom taken amiss, which shows the counsel to have been administered with prudence.

How is it possible that a minister can understand wickedness unless he either practices it himself (but much of that will not yet pass in the world) or allows the wicked to be bold in his presence? To do otherwise would be to do in practice what I have known narrow-minded bigoted students do as to speculation, viz. avoid reading their adversaries' books because they were erroneous, whereas it is evident no error can be refuted till it be understood.

The setting of the different characters of ministers in immediate opposition will put this matter past all doubt, as the sun of truth rising upon the stars of error darkens and makes them to disappear. Some there are who may be easily known to be ministers by their very dress, their grave demure looks, and their confined precise conversation. How contemptible is this! But our truly accomplished clergy put off so entirely everything that is peculiar to their profession that were you to see them in the streets, meet with them at a visit, or spend an evening with them in a tavern, you would not once suspect them for men of that character. Agreeably to this, I remember an excellent thing said by a gentleman in commendation of a minister, that "he had nothing at all of the clergyman about him."

I shall have done with this maxim when I have given my advice as to the method of attaining to it, which is that students, probationers, and young clergymen while their bodies and minds are yet flexible should converse and keep company as much as may be with officers of the army under five and twenty, of whom there are no small number in the nation, and with young gentlemen of fortune, particularly such as by the early and happy death of their parents have come to their estates before they arrived at the years of majority. Scarce one of these but is a noble pattern to form upon, for they have had the opportunity of following nature, which is the all comprehensive rule of the ancients, and of acquiring a free manner of thinking, speaking, and acting without either the pedantry of learning or the stiffness contracted by a strict adherence to the maxims of worldly prudence.

After all, I believe I might have spared myself the trouble of inserting this maxim, the present rising generation being of themselves sufficiently disposed to observe it. This I reckon they have, either constitutionally, or perhaps have learned it from the inimitable Lord Shaftesbury, who in so lively a manner sets forth the evil of universities and recommends conversation with the polite Peripatetics as the only way of arriving at true knowledge.

Maxim VI

It is not only unnecessary for a moderate man to have much learning,
but he ought to be filled with a contempt of all kinds of learning
but one, which is to understand Leibnitz's scheme well, the chief parts
of which are so beautifully painted and so harmoniously sung by
Lord Shaftesbury, and which has been so well licked into
form and method by the late immortal Mr. H———n.

THIS maxim is necessary because without it the former could not be attained to. Much study is a great enemy to politeness in men, just as a great care of houshold affairs spoils the free careless air of a fine lady; and whether politeness is to be sacrificed to learning, let the impartial world judge. Besides the scheme which I have permitted the moderate man to study doth actually supersede the use of all other learning because it contains a knowledge of the whole and the good of the whole, more than which, I hope, will be allowed to be not only needless, but impossible.

This scheme excels in brevity, for it may be understood in a very short time, which, I suppose, prompted a certain clergyman to say that any student might get as much divinity as he would ever have occasion for in six weeks. It is also quite agreeable to the improvements that have been made in arts and sciences of late years, for everything is now more compendiously taught and more superficially understood than formerly, and yet as well and better to all the purposes of life. In the very mechanic arts, laborious diligence gives way to elegance and ease, as the lumpish, strong, old Gothic buildings, to more genteel, though slighter, modern ones. There have been schemes published for teaching children to read by way of diversion. Every year gives us a shorter method of learning some branch of knowledge. In short, in these last days the quintessence of everything has been extracted and is presented us, as it were, in little phials, so that we may come to all learning by one act of intuition. Agreeably to all this, have we not seen in fact many students of divinity brought up in hotbeds who have become speakers in general assemblies and strenuous supporters of a falling church before their beards were grown, to the perfect astonishment of an observing world?

I must also observe that there is a providential fitness of that scheme in another respect for the present age and time. When the fees of colleges and expense of boarding are raised, when the rate of living is quite altered, and when a spiteful landed interest and a heedless parliament have refused to grant any augmentation to our stipends, there is no other way that remains for us but to cheapen our education by taking less time to it and arriving at the point designed by a nearer cut. Then there will be no need at all for the critical study of the Scriptures, for reading large bodies of divinity, for an acquaintance with church history, or the writings of those poor creatures the Christian fathers; but all is absorbed into the good of the whole, of which I may say seriously and soberly what Dr. Tillotion says ironically of transubstantiation, that it is not only true, but it is all truth, and will not suffer any thing to be true but itself.

We find that moderate men have mostly, by constitution, too much spirit to submit to the drudgery of the kinds of learning above-mentioned, and despise all who do so. There is no controversy now about Arian, Arminian, Pelagian, or Socinian tenets, but only whether this good of-the-whole scheme holds. This shows, by the by, the injustice and malignity of those poor beings the Seceders, who cry out of erroneous doctrines in the church and assert that Arminianism is publicly taught by many. It is known that they mean by the moderate men when they speak so, and yet I will venture to affirm that there are not a few young men of that character who, if they were asked, could not tell what the five Arminian articles are, so little do they regard Arminianism. I myself, the reader will perceive, know the number of them; but whether I know any more about them or not, I shall preserve as a secret in my own mind. It will perhaps be objected against this maxim that the moderate party commonly set up on a pretence of being more learned than their adversaries, and are in fact thought to be very learned in their sermons by the vulgar, who for that reason hate them. Now, as to their pretending to be more learned than their adversaries, it is most just; for they have, as has been shown, got hold of the sum-total of learning, although they did not calculate it themselves. And as to their being thought learned in their sermons by the vulgar, it is sufficient for that purpose that they be unintelligible. Scattering a few phrases in their sermons, as harmony, order, porportion, taste, sense of beauty, balance of the affections, etc. will easily persuade the people that they are learned; and this persuasion is to all intents and purposes the same thing as if it were true. It is one of those deceitful feelings which Mr. H—— in his Essays has shown to be so beautiful and useful. These phrases they may easily get in books not above the size of an octavo, and if they incline to be very deep, they may get abundance of citations from the ancient heathen authors in Cudworth's intellectual system, and mostly translated to their hand.

I shall now subjoin a short catalogue of the most necessary and useful books, the thorough understanding of which will make a truly learned moderate man: Leibnitz's Theodicee, and his letters, Shaftesbury's Characteristics, Collins's Inquiry into Human Liberty, all Mr. H——n's pieces, Christianity as old as the Creation, D——n's Best Scheme, and H——'s Moral Essays.[2] The two last are Scots authors, and it is with

2. It hath been suggested to me that another author of our own country ought to have been added to the above catalogue, but I judged it improper for two reasons. One is that I do not find that author in so high esteem among the moderate as to deserve a place in so very nice and chosen a collection. But the other and principal reason is that the author here intended professeth himself a skeptic, the meaning of which, if I understand it right, is either that he does not believe there is any such thing as truth or that he himself is but seeking after truth and has not yet found it. Now this is by no means the case with the moderate, who are already in possession of the "ne plus ultra" of human knowledge. For though some of their doctrines are changeable by reason of the essential difference of persons, things, and times, yet during the period of any doctrine I have nowhere known stronger or severer dogmatists, as appears from their neglect of farther inquiry and

pleasure I can assure my countrymen, they are by far the most perfect of them all, carrying the consequence of the scheme to the most ravishing height. As to poetry, it will be sufficient to read "the Pleasures of the Imagination" and "the Tragedy of Agis," if it be published because in it dramatic poetry is carried to the summit of perfection, and it is believed by the author's friends that there never will be a tragedy published after it, unless by somebody who is delirious. But whether the knowledge of this effect and the compassion thence arising to future authors may not in a person of so much humility and self-denial and of so consummate and disinterested benevolence as that theatrical divine wholly prevent the publication, I cannot tell; and therefore must leave it to be brought forth by the midwife Occasion, from the womb of Time.[3]

But to give a still higher proof of my deep concern for the improvement and edification of ingenuous youth, I have taken the pains to extract very faithfully the sum and substance of the above library, and do here present it to the world under a name which is not without a meaning, though not intelligible to all, viz.

The Athenian Creed

I believe in the beauty and comely proportions of Dame Nature, and in almighty Fate, her only parent and guardian; for it hath been most graciously obliged (blessed be its name) to make us all very good.

I believe that the universe is a huge machine, wound up from everlasting by necessity, and consisting of an infinite number of links and chains, each in a progressive motion towards the zenith of perfection and meridian of glory; that I myself am a little glorious piece of clockwork, a wheel within a wheel, or rather a pendulum in this grand machine, swinging hither and thither by the different impulses of fate and destiny; that my soul (if I have any) is an imperceptible bundle of exceeding minute corpuscles, much smaller than the finest Holland sand; and that certain persons in a very eminent station are nothing else but a huge collection of necessary agents who can do nothing at all.

I believe that there is no ill in the universe, nor any such thing as virtue absolutely considered; that those things vulgarly called sins are only errors in the judgment, and soils to set off the beauty of Nature, or patches to adorn her face; that the whole race of intelligent beings, even the devils themselves (if there are any) shall finally be happy; so that Judas Iscariot is by this time a glorified saint, and it is good for him that he hath been born.

---

sovereign contempt of all opposers. In a certain university, about seven years ago (how it is now I cannot so certainly tell) if a man had spoken honorably of Dr. Samuel Clarke, it cannot be conceived with what derision he was treated by every boy of sixteen, who was wiser than to pay any regard to such a numskull, an enemy to the doctrine of necessity and wholly ignorant of the moral sense.

3. Agis, a tragedy, was published in the year 1758.

In fine, I believe in the divinity of L. S——, the saintship of Marcus Antoninus, the perspicuity and sublimity of A——e, and the perpetual duration of Mr. H——n's works, notwithstanding their present tendency to oblivion. Amen.

Maxim VII

A moderate man must endeavor, as much as he handsomely can, to put off any appearances of devotion, and avoid all unnecessary exercises of religious worship, whether public or private.

I fully intended upon this part of my subject to have been at some pains in showing the great indecency of a grave and apparently serious carriage or of introducing any religious subject of conversation into promiscuous company, but when I consider how successfully all visible religion was attacked, both by wits and preachers, immediately after the restoration of King Charles II; how constantly any disposition of this sort hath been borne down by all men of taste ever since that time, which is now near a whole century; and also how seldom any religious discourse is to be met with at this day, either among clergy or laity, I shall only rejoice in myself, and congratulate my reader, upon the purity of the times and proceed to the other part of the maxim.

Now, as to the public exercise of religious worship, although a certain measure of them is reasonable enough and though the office by which we have our bread obliges us to be often engaged in them, yet a truly moderate man without renouncing his calling has it in his power to pare off a great many superfluities with which the orthodox clergy are apt to overload religion and render it unpalatable to the polite world.

Being members of church-judicatures, and we hope the majority in most of them, the moderate party can discourage and stifle all motions for extraordinary fasts or thanksgivings, which experience has taught us serve only to promote idleness and discourage industry. Upon the day that Henry V fought at Agincourt, a solemn fast was kept in England for his success; and some historians are pleased to say that the prayers of the nation had some share in procuring the victory; but later histories have disproved this; and now it can be demonstrated upon paper that a fast day in Scotland loses 50,000 pounds to the nation, while nobody can make any calculation what it wins. For this reason, it was very refreshing to hear, as we did lately, that even in the most distant and northernly corners of this country, there is a set of clergy of an heroic spirit who are resolved to reform their people and beat them out of that unpolite and barbarous inclination, which many of them still retain, of hearing sermons.

With a view to the same good end, we can curtail our business at home, both as to the number and length of our pulpit performances. In our own families, though it would not perhaps yet be convenient to imitate the beau mondo so very quickly in discarding the worship of God altogether, yet we may by degrees sometimes omit it through hurry of business, at other times be dropping now and then at least some parts of it, and in gentlemen's families, take care to give discreet intimations that we do not incline to put them out of their ordinary way or occasion the least interruption to the mirth of the company.

Sometimes indeed it may happen by a concurrence of circumstances that one of us may at bedtime be unequally yoked with an orthodox brother who may propose a little unseasonable devotion between ourselves before we lie down to sleep, but there are twenty ways of throwing cold water upon such a motion; or, if it should be insisted upon, I could recommend a moderate way of complying with it from the example of one of our friends, who on a like occasion yielded so far that he stood up at the back of a chair and said, "O Lord, we thank thee for Mr. Bayle's Dictionary. Amen." This was so far from spoiling good company that it contributed wonderfully to promote social mirth and sweetened the young men in a most agreeable manner for their rest. Whatever is forced is unnatural and ought to be avoided, and therefore, what the Puritan said of square caps we may apply to many modes of devotion, "That he would not wear them, because his head was round."

The necessity of such a conduct cannot be denied when it is considered what effect the length and frequency of public devotion has had in driving most of the fashionable gentry from our churches altogether, and that even such of them as still vouchsafe their company sometimes are yet driven away from the sacrament of the Lord's Supper, where the service is expected to be more tedious and tiresome. Now, the only way to regain them to the church is to accommodate the worship, as much as may be, to their taste: The manner of doing which is so well known that I will not spend time in explaining it.

I confess there has been sometimes an ugly objection thrown up against this part of my argument, viz. that this desertion of public worship by those in high life seems in fact to be contemporary with, and to increase in a pretty exact proportion to, the attempts that have been and are made to suit it to their taste. It is alleged that they are led to such a conduct, not by the dictates of their reason, but by the depravation of their hearts, and therefore make use of the behavior of the clergy as an excuse and justification of their conduct. In answer to this objection, I shall not pretend to say what use gentlemen may sometimes make of our conduct, for I have known them often very preposterous in their judgment, condemning others for what they freely indulge in themselves, and no less unthankful, rendering evil for good. But still I say, there remains no strength in the objection to a man of moderate principles; for it plainly comes much to the same thing at last, whether the mountain comes to the mouse, or the mouse to the mountain. If I should meet a friend halfway that had got at a distance from me, though he should not move a foot, I am sure we should be nearer one another than if I had kept my place as well as he.

But whatever be in this, I must acknowledge that to be constantly whining and praying looks so extremely orthodox-like that I cannot help conceiving a prejudice at it for this very reason; and I doubt not but every moderate man will have the very same fellow feeling. In truth, a great abundance of devotion has such a tendency to inflame one with zeal that any man who would maintain his moderation had best keep out of the reach of such insnaring influence. Besides, it has been an old remark, and I begin to suspect there is some ground for it, that let one embrace what system of divinity he will, it is impossible to pray but according to the orthodox system. And whatever laudable pains had been taken by some of our friends to avoid this inconvenience, yet, from what I have observed in the most successful of them, I must own, I can at present see no other remedy but to deal as little that way as possible.

Maxim VIII

In church-settlements, which are the principal causes that come before ministers for judgment, the only thing to be regarded is who the patron and the great and noble heritors are for; the inclinations of the common people are to be utterly despised.

THAT this maxim is invariably observed by all moderate men is certain and may be attested by all that ever were present at a General Assembly of this national church. The case is not now as formerly, when presentations were held a grievance; for a presentation is "all in all" to a moderate man; and when there is no presentation, the greatness and nobility of the heritors are upon one side. I was witness once to a cause (which indeed unhappily miscarried), but there was a noble stand made for it by the moderate party because there was a lord upon the side of the minority, although he had no interest at all in the parish but a small bit of ground which he had got from a neighbor in order to run a dike straight. This appearance greatly rejoiced me as being a token to what perfection the spirit of moderation was arrived.

There are many reasons upon which this maxim is founded, as the implacable hatred we bear to the elders and common people and their constant wrong judgment, which has been illustrated above. As this is so very evident, I cannot pass it without expressing my grief and astonishment that so clear-sighted an author, and in all respects so agreeable to our sentiments, as Lord Shaftesbury should have said in his Essay on the *Freedom of Wit and Humor* that "it belongs to men of slavish principles to affect a superiority over the vulgar, and to despise the multitude." This hath made me doubt the truth of an assertion of Mr. G. L., one of our own disciples, "that perfection is attainable in this life"; for if ever anyone attained to perfection, surely Lord Shaftesbury was the man. But, to lessen the difficulty a little, it is probable he had something in his view quite different from settling of kirks when he wrote in this manner; for had he lived to our times and been an heritor in Scotland, I can hardly allow myself to think that ever he would have appeared on the side of the Christian people, though, without all question, he would have been chosen an elder and sent up "duly attested" to the General Assembly.

But to return the natural respect we owe to those in great and high stations claims from us the testimony of it required in the maxim. There is an original and essential difference between gentry and common people, which ought to be particularly kept up here. For this we have the authority of a certain worthy laird in the country, who always maintained upon his mind a sense of his dignity, not as a man, but as a gentleman. Of this disposition he gave the following laudable instance: Being a member of the kirk-session in his parish, the excise officer happened to come before them for fornication; and besides the ecclesiastical censure, it was thought proper to apply to the civil magistrate to get him fined according to law, but as the law appoints different fines for men in different stations, when some proposed he should be fined at the rate of a gentleman, the worshipful member above mentioned, though known to be very zealous against vice, strenuously opposed his having so much honor and gave the following excellent reason for it: "Since God Almighty has been pleased to make a distinction between gentlemen and other men, why should not we keep up this distinction in all cases?" And so he was fined only as a commoner.

Another thing strongly pleads for gentlemen having the chief hand in settling kirks, that nowadays very few of our principal gentry attend ordinances or receive any benefit by a minister after he is settled, unless perhaps talking of the news at a private visit or playing a game at backgammon; and therefore it is but fair that in lieu of the edification of the common people, they should have the honor or profit of conferring the benefice. I shall only further add that having no view of attending upon him ordinarily, they must be the best judges of his preaching gifts, as being most disinterested: For which reason nonresiding heritors, instead of deserving to be cut out altogether, as the stupid and undiscerning orthodox would have it, are by much to be preferred to those that reside.

The reader will easily perceive that I have here given much better reasons for this conduct than those commonly assigned, viz. the law in the case of patrons and the payment of the stipend in the case of heritors. For, as to the first of these, it is quite from the purpose; for the law maintains its own ground as far as it goes and is irresistible: The only question is, how we shall act as to what is left to us to determine? If the law hindered us to determine on any side we pleased, such causes never would be pleaded before us. As to the other, about the heritors paying the stipend, it is not just; for the whole nation pays it. The heritor gets his lands with that burden upon them sat first; and when one buys land from another, he never pays for the stipend: So that really an heritor is never a penny the poorer of the stipend, except that happening commonly to see the money first, he may perhaps be sorry that anybody should get it but himself. However, though these reasons be not sufficient at bottom, I deny not but it may be very proper to assign them to such as are ignorant enough to yield to them, or who have so squeamish stomachs as not to be able to digest the solid reasons upon which I have grounded my maxim. It is with the mind as with the body: It must be fed with such things as it is able to bear, and as will best agree with its frame and constitution.

Maxim IX

While a settlement is carrying on, the candidate against whom
there is a strong opposition from the people must be looked upon
and everywhere declared to be a person of great worth and
remarkable abilities, provided always that if ever the same person
after he is settled be at pains and succeed in gaining
the people's affection, he shall then fall as much below the
ordinary standard in his character as before he was raised above it.

BOTH parts of this maxim will appear very reasonable to all that see with our eyes. The people being against a man is a certain sign of his being a good preacher, as has been formerly proved; it is also a pretty sure sign of his being of moderate principles, "which make the comers there unto perfect"; and these two things are sufficient to justify us in raising his character. It is indeed often absolutely necessary when a process is in agitation that it may help him out with a scanty concurrence and have an influence upon the church courts, which are composed of a mixed multitude. Nor is it easy to conceive how excellent and well invented a weapon this is, the giving a man an extraordinary and high character. It necessarily imprints a kind of veneration of him on the minds of his judges and hath this peculiar advantage that there is no parrying of it; for whatever some few of different principles may think, they dare not plainly contradict it. Every man has it in his power to speak well of one another, but nobody must take the liberty to speak ill of a man in a public court, unless he can also venture to give him a libel. Many a time have I heard young men highly extolled in church courts when their settlement was in dependence who in strict truth were but middling kind of men, and some of them very heavy, who afterwards proved no small encumbrance upon the moderate body.

As to the other part of the maxim, taking away their character for ability when they apostatize to orthodoxy, this will be easily accounted for if it be remembered how they came by it. It was freely given them, and therefore it may be taken away at pleasure: It was given to bring them in as an additional strength to the moderate interest, and therefore, when they forsake that interest, it is but just to deprive them of it. If any shall object that this is not agreeable to the strict rules of veracity, I desire it may be remembered that the present fashionable scheme of moral philosophy is much improved in comparison of that which prevailed some time ago. Virtue does not now consist in "acting agreeably to the nature of things," as Dr. Clarke affirms, nor in "acting according to truth," which an old schoolmaster, one Woollaston, once wrote a book to prove, but in "the good of the whole"; and therefore an illustrious and noble end sanctifies the means of attaining it. Our sentiments in this respect are described by an anonymous poet, who I believe meant no good to us; however, it points out the character pretty plainly thus:

> To second him rose surly Peter,
> An angry bigot for good-nature:
> That truth should valued be by measure,
> And weight, he thought;
> That inch of truth, in courtesy,
> To span of interest should give way?
> And pound of gain, for ounce of lie,
> Is cheaply bought.

If it be further objected, that still this only satisfies ourselves, whereas in the case in hand it is necessary to satisfy the world. As to this, we can freely say that the man was good, but now he is bad; and that is no contradiction, for though the Confession of Faith maintains the infalli-

ble perseverance of the saints in grace, yet we never affirmed the necessary perseverance of men in moderation, these two things being entirely
distinct the one from the other. Some of our friends do fall away now
and then: Our strength ordinarily consists in young men; for there are
several who in old age through the decay of their faculties begin to
incline a little to orthodoxy, and then we term them not "old men" but
"old wives." However, there are also some who not only persevere but
gloriously improve in moderation to the latest old age, and to their
dying day; of which number was the late Rev. Mr. J. R. in K., whose
name I have thought proper to record in this immortal work that it may
be had in everlasting remembrance.

Maxim X

*WHENEVER we have got a settlement decided over the belly perhaps of
the whole people in the parish by a majority in the General Assembly,
the victory should be improved by appointing some of the
orthodox opposers of the settlement to execute it, especially
those of them that pretend to have a scruple of conscience at
having an active hand in any such settlement.*

THEY do not deserve a victory who know not how to push it or to
improve the advantage they have gained. A sentence of the General
Assembly, even as of any other court, signifies nothing if it be not
executed. To rest satisfied with the victory we have gained by the bare
decision would indeed be yielding it back again and losing in fact what
we gained in appearance. This is self-evident. But the next point is who
shall be employed in executing it: those who appointed, or those who
pretend a scruple of conscience at doing what appears to their disordered intellects to be what they call sinful? Now, as to this, allow me
only to ask a few plain questions. Is not every society divided into the
governing and the governed, the masters and the servants? What is the
subject of any debate in the Assembly that ends in a vote but to determine who is the one and who is the other? When once a vote has made
us masters, does not the same vote make the minority servants? And do
I need to ask further if there is any piece of drudgery to be performed
who it belongs to, the masters or the servants? Apply this then to the
case in hand: Who would hazard his own life in fording a river if he
had a servant to try the depth of it before him? Who would choose to
go to a pulpit under a shower of stones from an enraged populace if
he had others under his authority whom he could send upon the same
ungracious errand?

Now, the usefulness of this conduct is very evident; for it is plain they will either obey or disobey. If the first is the case, then we shall have the honor of bringing them, and they themselves the profit and advantage of being brought, into the hatred and abhorrence of the common people, in commendation of which state enough has been said already. If they disobey, they must be deposed and cast out as incorrigible to make way for those that are better than themselves. This will be to the advantage of the church, for young men, "caeteris paribis," are much better than old.

As this method or purging the church of corrupt members is likely to be a prevailing measure in our day, I shall endeavor to support it by a few but these demonstrative arguments, in most of which, indeed, I shall have little more than the honor of recording the sentiments and reasoning of some eminent men that were members of the two last General Assemblies.

In the first place it is certain that the command of a proper authority is sufficient to make any action not only innocent and lawful, but perfectly right, and strictly obligatory; insomuch that if an executioner should be commanded to hang his father or son for praying to God or reading his Bible, nay if one of Jesus Christ's disciples had happened to have been a Roman soldier and should have been commanded to crucify his master, he should have betrayed the most egregious ignorance of the Christian religion had he made the least difficulty in executing such orders.

It is to no purpose here to object the immutability of moral laws and the supreme authority of God, for if obedience to human authority be one of his laws, as it plainly is, then all his other laws must be submitted to such alterations and suspensions as our superiors think proper. The apostles do indeed sometimes speak of "obeying God rather than man," but we can explain this as easily as we do another text: In the third chapter of the Romans, which seems to teach that "we should not do evil that good may come;" for as in the one case whatever promotes good cannot be evil, so in the other if human authority be once duly interposed, it is obeying God to comply with whatever is enjoined thereby; and therefore it is impossible that ever there can an interference happen. Besides, some allowance must, no doubt, be made for the difference of times and disadvantages which all the ancient writers lay under, the late fine improvements in the science of morals not having then been excogitated. But I can assure the reader the principle which I have laid down is now the doctrine of this church, wherein both divines and lawyers who are members of our Assemblies are entirely agreed and will not suffer anybody to call it in question. And what an obvious beauty has moral virtue gained from the delicate and skillful hands that have lately been employed in dressing her ladyship! She was once stiff and rigid, like ice or cold iron; now she is yielding as water, and, like iron hot from the furnace, can easily be beaten into what shape you please. And here I must say I think it some pity that so fine a genius as Grotius did not flourish somewhat later, or that the moral sense was not started a little earlier, and so that great man preserved from falling into so great a blunder as maintaining that "even military authority may be resisted; and that a case may be given, when a soldier ought to disobey orders"; for now it is a settled point that even ecclesiastical authority (which, if there were any difference, I allow ought rather to be the milder of the two) is sufficient to bear down before it what were called the "eternal," no less, and "immutable laws of morality"; and by divine authority, "is paramount to divine authority itself."

I shall only observe two very plain and clear advantages in this principle, whereby it will appear how happy it is that the church hath fallen so entirely in with it and proceeds so uniformly upon it.

The first is that in case of necessity, an action which no body would choose perhaps to take the weight of upon them may yet be done without the least hazard of anybody's being called to account for it in the other world. If the doer of an action were to be the judge of its lawfulness, he might be damned perhaps for doing it in case it were found to be wrong; but upon this principle of implicit obedience to his superiors, there is no repelling his defense: It was not his province to judge whether it was lawful or unlawful; and the Assembly or Commission who gave the order, being bodies politic, are by that time all dissolved and appear only in the capacity of individuals.

The other advantage is this: if the supreme court of any kind were allowed to be the only proper judge of the lawfulness of its own appointments, it would be impossible in the nature of things that ever there could be a separation in the church or a rebellion in the state. The justness of this consequence is so evident that I shall not spend any time in illustrating it but heartily wish the principle from which it flows were universally embraced.

In the second place, the disobedient brethren have but one pretense for their conduct, which is groundless, viz. a "scruple of conscience"; as to which, hear Dr. Goodman, a noble English writer: "A tender conscience is nothing else but an ignorant and uninstructed mind; or a sickly, melancholy, and superstitious understanding." I could easily show that there is no such thing as a real scruple of conscience: The lawyers in the General Assembly, who are men of as great penetration as any in the land, have most of them plainly declared that they do not conceive it possible. A certain learned gentleman of this court hath assured us that taking away ministers' stipends would enlighten their conscience. The renowned author of Hudibras is known to be of the same opinion; from which two authorities I will endeavor to amend Dr. Goodman's definition: for a "tender, conscience is not an ignorant mind," but a "full stomach." This accounts for appearances better, and particularly for the epithet of tender commonly given to it, as all physicians are agreed that a wound upon a full stomach is very dangerous. Having thus rooted up the very foundation of this pretense, it is needless to go through the several particulars insisted upon by the disobedient as straitening to them; and therefore I shall but in a word mention one of them. They pretend it is a profane farce to confer in a solemn manner the care of the souls of a certain people, when nothing is really conferred but a legal title to a benefice, as also, that the candidate cannot conscientiously answer several of the questions commonly put on those occasions. But is it not extremely strange that anybody can be so dull as not to regard these questions in their only true and proper light, as a necessary piece of formality, without which a charge of horning for the stipends could not be raised? And as to the other part of the objection, whether it be not much more a mock ceremony to ordain a man to a congregation when a title to the benefice cannot be conferred, I shall leave the reader to determine as if the case were his own.

The third principle upon which our conduct is founded is of such undoubted variety that the bare mentioning of it is sufficient to convince all the world how little it stands in need of any proof; accordingly no moderate man views it in any other light than as an axiom, or self-evident truth, namely, that if any excuse for disobedience were once admitted, or any indulgence granted to these tender-conscienced inferiors, there would be an end of all government in an instant; neither commands nor obedience could proceed one step further, but every individual instrument of power in that fatal society, astonished at the monstrous phenomenon, would stare at one another; all the wheels of the political machine would stop at once, nay would split into ten thousand pieces; every relation and connection of their parts would be instantly dissolved, and the beautiful whole would rush into a wild chaos of anarchy and confusion. The reader will easily believe I am too wise to offer a proof of an axiom or self-evident truth; however, I think it but fair to inform him that such is the nature of paper and ink that they have not the power of doing it all the justice, even in narration, of which it is capable elsewhere.[4] Whoever has heard the demonstrative tone, or

4. I desire that this general assertion may not be misunderstood as if I intended a reflection upon some late discoveries in moral philosophy, for though an axiom, or self-evident truth, cannot be proved, yet a great genius, who can do anything, may take a view of these same axioms, dignify and adorn them by writing an essay round about each of them, and prove that they ought to be called Feelings. This is greatly to the advantage of the commonwealth of learning, as experience hath shown.

beheld the infallible air and gesture of certainty with which it has been asserted by an Assembly orator, would be ashamed that he ever stood in need to be put in mind of it; for my own part, I am so entirely influenced by it that if the most faithful, diligent, and useful servant should in the humblest manner represent to me that he had a scruple about executing any of my orders and beg to be excused, suppose from shaving me on Sunday morning, and I should unfortunately be so far off my guard as for once to indulge him, I would immediately dissolve my whole family and never more think of lodging with a living soul under the same happy roof.

Against this principle, however, some have presumed to object particular instances in Scripture history of such excuses being actually admitted without any apparent dissolution of the constitution, such as Gideon's passing from his order to his son to kill the two princes of Midian and slaying them himself, and that of Saul, who when his guards refused to fall upon the priests committed that affair to another without any farther noise. Now, not to mention the difficulty of arguing from facts of an ancient date, cited only by one author, and that very curtly, I humbly conceive these instances produced make directly against the objection; for it appears to me very evident that the kingdom was taken from Saul and given to David for this very reason, he being unfit to govern by thus allowing his authority to be trampled upon. Nor will it be easy to assign any different reason why none of the posterity of Gideon were ever permitted to rule Israel. There are some later instances of that sort nearer home thrown up by shallow politicians, as that of the hangman at Ayr who refused to execute the Whigs in King Charles II's time, and that which happened a few years ago among ourselves when the civil government overlooked the disobedience of a set of refractory clergymen who refused to read the act of parliament against the murderers of Captain Porteous. In the first of these cases, the judges acted in a laudable manner; for they deprived the man of his benefice; and for the crime of his disobedience, I am persuaded he died childless, for I have never heard of any of his posterity in that part of the country. In the other case, I confess the government was much to be blamed and have long been of opinion that their detestable lenity at that time was the cause of the late rebellion which followed so soon after it. It is to be hoped they will take warning for the time to come, for I am persuaded one other instance of the same kind would effectually set the Pretender upon the throne of Britain.

The last principle which I shall mention, and which with the rest I am sure is abundantly sufficient to support the maxim laid down for our conduct, is that the best method of conviction, and of all others the most proper for a church court, is that of authority supported in its highest rigor by censures which may be felt by men of the dullest capacities, as deposition and suspension from benefice as well as office. If the goodness of an argument or the excellency of a method is to be measured by the frequency of recourse that is had to it, I think none can dispute precedency with this. It must be allowed to be of all others the most Christian method; it reigned over the whole church without a rival for many ages; and though protestants for a while pretended to find fault with it in the hands of their enemies, yet, which of them all when they became able to make use of it have not tried it in their turn? And whether we consider the majority by whose hands this weapon is to be wielded or the minority upon whom the weight of it must fall, it will plainly appear to be admirably suited to the present times. As the beasts of burden who fall to be driven by this method, they are known to be such dull and lifeless animals (as they are most of them past the vigor of youth) that no other argument can make any impression upon them. However a horse might be managed who is a generous creature, nobody could think of another method to make an ass move but constantly to belabor its sides. There cannot be a clearer evidence of the dullness and stupidity of these obstinate beings we have to do with than the expense of rhetoric that has been thrown away upon them to persuade them of a thing as clear as the sun, viz. that if they had any conscience they would depose themselves and yield their place to more pliable successors. They even pretend conscience here again and tell us they are placed in a station which they dare not desert unless they be thrust out of it. Now, let the reader judge how incapable of persuasion one must be to find difficulty in so plain a case; and therefore how necessary it is that a more effectual method should be tried.

On the other hand, the majority in Assemblies and Commissions seems at present to be peculiarly adapted to such a method of conviction as I have mentioned. One part of our strength lies in the laity who attend our judicatures; these, as they possess no benefice in the church, they are out of the reach of this sort of censure, and therefore are only capable of inflicting, but not of suffering it; and as they are not much accustomed to solving cases of conscience, what other method can occur to them when things of this nature are thrown in their way than the more gentleman-like method for which Alexander the Great is so justly celebrated, viz. cutting the troublesome knot, which they would find tedious and difficult to untie? The rest of our side consists in clergy of the youngest sort, who, as they are imitators of the manners of gentlemen, may be supposed to act with the same spirit in public judgment. Though they can give flourishes of rhetoric enough; nay, though of one of them in particular I may literally say,

——He cannot ope
His mouth, but out there flies a trope;

Yet as for logic, it is well known this part of education is fallen into great contempt; and it is not to be expected that such brisk and lively spirits who have always hated everything that looked scholastic-like can bear to be tied down to the strict methods of argumentation. But though we were greater masters in this method of conviction, yet our blood may be easily supposed too warm for anything that is so slow, and at best so uncertain in its success. No, we are now the majority, and our power as a late acquisition is the more agreeable for being new; we must taste the sweets of authority, which can only be by compelling our inferiors to obey us. If our sentences are executed, it is the same thing to the new incumbent, the same thing to the church in general, and the same thing to us, whether the executors are willing or unwilling; for, as to that whole matter of conscience about which so much noise is made, I have already related our sentiments; from whence it is evident that such nonsense, as laying a violent temptation in men's way to act against the light of their own mind, is nothing but words without a meaning. And as to the expression of that apostle Paul about church power, which he uses over and over again, that it is "for edification, and not for destruction," it is no secret that there is a various reading; and if once we had "for destruction and not for edification" established as the true reading, which if we were dealers in criticism might perhaps be easily done, we would not only get rid of this troublesome text, but make an acquisition of it on our side of the question to the confusion of our greatest enemies.

Maxim XI

*The character which moderate men give their adversaries of
the orthodox party must always be that of "knaves" or "fools," and,
as occasion serves, the same person (if it will pass) may be
represented as a "knave" at one time and as a "fool" at another.*

THE justness of this proceeding may be easily made to appear. The principles of moderation being so very evident to reason, it is a demonstration that none but unreasonable men can resist their influence; and therefore we cannot suppose that such as are against us can be so from conscience. Besides, setting aside the superior intrinsic excellence of the one set of principles above the other, there are much stronger carnal motives, to speak in their own style, to act in their way than in ours; and therefore there is great ground to conclude that they act from hypocrisy, but not so of us. They please the people; we please, at least endeavor to please, those of high rank. Now there are many remarkable advantages they gain by pleasing the people, whereas it is evident "ex post facto" that we gain nothing by pleasing the gentry; for they never trampled upon us so much as of late and have entirely defeated our application to parliament for augmentation of stipend. So far are we from being in any respect the better of the gentry that we have really great reason to complain of them, for when we have endeavored to ingratiate ourselves with them by softness and complaisance and by going considerable lengths with them in their freedom, they oftentimes most ungenerously despise us but the more; nay, many of them have first taught us to live at a high rate, and then refuse to give us anything to keep it up. Now, as we men of reason could not but foresee this, it is plain nothing but the most disinterested virtue could lead us to act as we have done. Whereas, on the other hand, the orthodox have gained and do possess the esteem of the common people, and so, it is plain they could have no other view in their conduct but to attain it. However, to show our charity, we allow there are some on their side who are indifferently honest; but these are men of very weak intellectuals, as is evident from their not thinking as we do.

The other part of the maxim is abundantly reasonable, but not so easily put in practice, viz. representing the same individual person sometimes as a knave and sometimes as a fool. This affair is sometimes unluckily managed when it is incautiously attempted. In order to its being done successfully, therefore let the following rules be observed.

First, let a man be represented as a knave and a hypocrite to one sort of people in the world, and let him be represented as a fool, not to the same, but to another sort: Let the first be chiefly your better sort of people, particularly those among them that hate much profession of religion and are apt to call all strictness hypocrisy; the other, it is plain, must be the simple and credulous.

The second rule is that, if possible, there should be different persons employed in spreading these different calumnies of the same man. By this apparent consistency in everyone's opinion with itself, they will be the more easily maintained and be the less liable to discovery, and thus, as the several wheels of a watch, by opposite means, conspire in promoting the good of the whole. The principle upon which these two rules are founded is that probability ought to be studied in every falsehood we would have believed, which principle is laid down and finely illustrated in the Art of Political Lying, said to be written by one Dr. Arbuthnot.

It will not, I hope, be reckoned wandering from my subject when I observe that the very same principle of studying probability is to be applied to the celebration of the characters of our friends as well as the defamation of our enemies. These two designs indeed have a very strong connection, and do mutually support and promote one another. Praising one character is, by necessary and manifest consequence, a defamation of its opposite; and, in some cases, which may easily be conceived, it is the most eligible and the most effectual way of doing it. I have been present at a conversation where the chief intention of one of the speakers and what he had most at heart was to ruin the character and reputation of a certain person who happened to be mentioned with his hearers; but he could not well know whether they were able to bear a large quantity of unmixed reproach; he chose the wiser and safer method of celebrating another character and drawing it with all his art in such a manner as the strongest opposition possible might appear in some of its circumstances to that of the person intended to be wounded by reflection.

But in this, as in the former case, great judgment and prudence must be used; nothing must be said, the contrary of which is or may be easily known to be true; and particularly all the antiquated orthodox phrases in giving a minister's character are to be religiously avoided. The necessity of this direction will best appear from an example: Suppose I should say of Momus, he was a youth of early and continues to be a man of eminent piety walking with God and spending many hours every day in secret devotion; has a deep and strong sense upon his mind of the worth and value of time and lays it out wholly in fitting others and himself for eternity; has so sacred a regard for truth that he never tells a lie, even in jest; has a most humble deportment and is perfectly free from that prevailing fault of triumphing over the weak or shamefaced by raillery or impudence; has been frequently heard to express his displeasure at all lenity of carriage and frothy unprofitable discourse in persons of the sacred characters; and as he was always himself remarkable for a purity of conversation, so he cannot allow the most distant allusion to obscenity to pass without a reproof; in short, his whole behavior commands both the reverence and love of all who have the happiness of his acquaintance. I say, if I should draw the character of Momus in this manner, as some authors do those of the Puritan clergy about a hundred years ago, it is probable he would give me no thanks; and indeed, he would owe me none; for it would have much more the air of a satire than of a panegyric.

It is, however, possible to draw a character of the same person which shall have some truth, and much probability in it, and which, as being the character of a modern, shall be much more in the modern commendatory style. He is a man of a most sprightly and lively fancy, of an inexhaustible fund of wit and humor where he pleases to display it, though the iniquity of the times has in some measure checked its indulgence. He is, nothwithstanding the grimness of his countenance, entirely free from any sourness or moroseness of temper so that in his conversation a man may enjoy all manner of ease and freedom. He is a most genteel and elegant preacher and poet and, to my knowledge, a man of a warm and good heart.[5]

Maxim XII

As to the world in general, a moderate man is to have great charity for atheists and deists in principle and for persons that are loose and vicious in their practice, but none at all for those that have a high profession of religion and a great pretense to strictness in their walk and conversation.

THIS maxim seems to be pretty strongly laid, and yet, upon a strict inquiry, it will be found that we follow it very exactly. That we have charity for the first-mentioned sort of persons is evident, for we endeavor to accommodate ourselves to them and draw as near them as possibly we can, insisting upon nothing in our sermons but what may be said to be a part, or an improvement, of the law of nature. And as to our having no charity for the other sort, it is as evident; witness the odious idea we have affixed to the name of a "professor" (unless when it is meant of a professor in a college) and witness our ironical way of speaking when we say of a man he has a "grave sanctified air." Nay, even holiness and godliness are seldom taken by us in a very good sense: When we say "One of the holy brethren" or "A good godly lady," they would mistake us very much that would think we had a high opinion of any of these persons.

This our conduct a certain young man of the orthodox side reflected very severely upon, as he thought in a sermon which he afterwards printed in words to this purpose:

They can indeed talk very fluently of universal benevolence, and a charitable candid disposition—but their charity is confined to those who favor their opinions, or perhaps are indifferent about religion altogether; while the least appear-

5. This expression, "a man of a good heart," is much in fashion among the moderate, and of great significance and beauty; but it is only to be used in speaking to persons of some degree of taste; for I knew a particular instance in which it disobliged the person it was intended to gain.

ance of serious devotion, or fervent zeal for God, is enough to forfeit it. Indeed this charity is as mysterious as the faith of the most bigoted Catholic; it is equally full of contradictions; and seems resolved to found itself, not upon evidence, but upon the want of it. Where everything has the worst appearance, there they will believe well; but where the outward conduct is blameless, they candidly suspect that nothing but hypocrisy lies at the bottom.

But, with the leave of this smart youth, what he says of us is very true, and we maintain it to be right: for the very meaning of charity is to believe without evidence; it is not charity at all to believe good of a man when we see it, but when we do not see it. It is with charity in sentiment, as with charity in supplying the wants of the needy: We do not give alms to the rich but to the poor. In like manner, when there are all outward appearances of goodness, it requires no charity to believe well of the persons; but when there are none at all, or perhaps very many to the contrary, then I will maintain it is charity, and charity in its perfection, to believe well of them. Some object to this, "Well, since it is your will, have charity for them; but have charity also for such as are apparently good." Oh, the stupid world, and slow of heart to conceive! Is it not evident to a demonstration that if the appearance of wickedness be the foundation of charity, the appearance of goodness, which is its opposite, must be the foundation of a quite contrary judgment, viz. suspecting, or rather believing ill of them? If any still insist, that if not charity, yet justice should incline us to believe well of them, as I have seemingly confessed? I answer that we have no occasion for justice if we have charity; for charity is more than justice, even as the whole is more than a part: but though I have supposed, "argumentandi gratia," that justice requires this, yet it is not my sentiment; for the persons meant, being usually great enemies to us, are thereby cut off from any claim in justice to our good opinion; and being also, as has been proved, improper objects of charity, it remains that we should hate them with perfect hatred, as in fact we do.

Maxim XIII

ALL moderate men are joined together in the strictest bond of union,
and do never fail to support and defend one another to the utmost,
be the cause they are engaged in what it will.

THIS maxim I do not insert so much for the instruction of the ignorant, as for the perfection of my own plan and the honor of the whole body;

for I have hardly ever known it fail in any instance whatever. And as this character belongs without controversy to all the moderated, so it belongs to them by an exclusive privilege; for they do most loudly complain of and load with most opprobrious epithets any of the orthodox who attempt to imitate them in it, as has been sometimes known. Nothing indeed can be more just and reasonable than these complaints, for such conduct in the orthodox is a plain desertion of their own principles, a robbery and invasion of the property of others. Conscience, upon which they pretend to act, is of all things the most stiff and inflexible and cannot by any art be molded into another shape than that which it naturally bears, whereas the whole principles of moderation are most gentle and ductile, and may be applied to almost all purposes imaginable.

If any through an envious infidelity entertain a doubt of the truth asserted in the maxim, they are referred for satisfaction to the history of the proceedings of this church for these twenty years past, which I take to have been the true reforming period, and are hereby defied to produce an instance in which any moderate man, wise or unwise, old or young, grave or sprightly, failed to concur in supporting one of his own side whatever was his cause, active or passive, a project for advancement, or the danger of a prosecution. Let but one of us start a scheme in which he may find his account or become candidate for an office, the whole upon the first impulse, as the concordant strings of a musical instrument, answer to the touch, return and reverberate the sound. If Momus unwarily makes a sally into the territories of "good-humoured vice" and is unhappily betrayed by those who ought not to have been trusted, how powerfully is he upheld by the gravest of the party, and the uncharitable malevolent enemy stung and destroyed like the bear in the fable, for disturbing the hive of industrious bees? Nay, as a yet stronger instance (being more against nature), I could show in the records of a certain presbytery declarations signed by the most moderate hands, and yet containing as high and ranting expressions in favor of the rights of the Christian people as ever were used by the most orthodox writer because, by a wonderful concurrence of circumstances, they served at that time to promote the settlement of a moderate man.

Every eye must immediately perceive the beauty and excellence of this part of our character. What more amiable than union? Or what more necessary to the support of any society? And what more hateful and horrid than discord and division? Is it not also by this very means that we have obtained the victory and do still preserve our superiority over the orthodox party? They are wholly ignorant of the laws of society, as they have been lately well explained by some of our brethren in print, and know not that all who enter into it give up their rights as individuals and are bound "to follow what they disapprove," to see with the eyes, and act for the interest of the whole body.

It must be no small commendation of such conduct that in so doing we either follow or are followed by the most eminent and illustrious characters in this nation. It is probable there may be several controverted elections tried before the parliament in a short time, and I dare say any wise man will foretell their issue in each case much more certainly from the character of the person than from the merits of the cause. And it is with some pleasure I observe that whoever began this practice first, we have carried it to the greatest perfection: for amongst us the characters of men have been openly pleaded in defense of their cause, which if I am not mistaken hath hardly ever been done in any civil court.

How admirably does this principle fall in with the scheme of philosophy upon which the present generation is formed! It illustrates the truth of Mr. H——n's doctrine that virtue is founded upon instinct and affection, and not upon reason; that benevolence is its source, support, and perfection; and that all the particular rules of conduct are to be suspended when they seem to interfere with the general good. In short, it shows that the moderate are a transcript in miniature, and do most distinctly exhibit the order, proportion, and unity of design in the universal system.

Time would fail me if I should go through all the excellencies of this crowning maxim, and therefore I shall only further observe that it excels all the known principles of action for clearness and perspicuity. In order to determine which side to choose in a disputed question, it requires no long discussions of reason, no critical inquiry into the truth of controverted facts, but only some knowledge of the characters of men, a study much more agreeable, as well as more common, than that of books. To speak more properly, it requires no study at all of any kind; for, as to the gross or general tendency of a character, common fame communicates the impression and seldom or never deceives us. This is probably the reason that the maxim, as has been observed at the beginning of the illustration, is constantly and unerringly followed by the moderate of every age and condition, on which account I give as my opinion that it be added to the number of the feelings which are at present so much upon the growing hand.

Thus I have laid down and illustrated these excellent maxims, not without labor and expense of thought, and, I think, carried them so far as to make a complete system for the education and accomplishment of a moderate clergyman, for his guidance in public judgment, and his direction as to a private practice. And now, courteous reader, as a traveler after having gone through the different parts of a country ascends some eminence to review the whole, let us stand still and rejoice over the happy state of our motherchurch of Scotland, in which moderation so greatly prevails; and let us rejoice in hope of what improvements she may yet arrive at by adhering to these maxims now digested into such admirable form and order. O what noble, sublime, and impenetrable sermons shall now be preached! What victories and triumphs shall be obtained over the stupid populace by forced settlements, which never have such a beautiful and orderly form as when finished by soldiers marching in comely array with shining arms, a perfect image of the church militant! And what perfectly virtuous and sinless lives shall be led by these clergy, who with steady eye regard the good of this vast whole, which never yet went wrong! There is nothing indeed that any way tarnishes the beauty of this prospect but the miscarriage of the augmentation scheme, over which I could now lament in elegiac strains, but that my hope is not yet quite extinct; for who can tell whether, when we shall have brought moderation to perfection, when we shall have driven away the whole common people to the seceders, who alone are fit for them, and captivated the hearts of the gentry to a love of our solitary temples, they may not be pleased to allow us more stipends because we shall have nothing to do but spend them?

I would now propose that the next ensuing General Assembly would appoint (what indeed I might not without some reason expect, whether they appoint it or not) that all the professors of divinity in the nation shall lecture one day every week upon this system of moderation that our youth may be trained up from their infancy in a taste for it. This, I am sure, will be much more profitable than any of the antiquated systems of divinity, as Pictet or Turretine; nay, I am persuaded it is more exactly calculated for the present times than even the more modern authors, Epictetus and Marcus Antoninus, which last in Mr. Foulis's translation hath by many young divines in their first year, been mistaken for *Markii Medulla Theologiae*.

If this my treatise shall meet with the success and acceptance that it justly deserves, it is my intention to offer to the public a still more minute and particular delineation of the moderate character, either in another book of a different form from this, or perhaps in a second edition of the same, which shall in that case be the text and to which I will add large explanatory notes, containing much private history and referring to many particular facts in order to render it the more grateful, as well as the more instructing to the reader. I have also by me the "stamina vitae" of many useful and edifying treatises, which shall be produced in due time as the muses shall give assistance, such as, The art of making a flourished sermon with very little matter by a proper mixture of similies and by repeating every paragraph over again in the form of a soliloquy, One resolution of all cases of conscience from the good of the whole scheme, The horrid sin and danger of ministers spending too much time in catechizing and visiting in country parishes I do not make any mention of towns to avoid giving offense, as also lest it should prove true what I have heard, that the practice is scarcely known in any of our great towns, in which case my reasonings would look like beating the air. These with many others I am with assiduous care purchasing materials for completing, by observation and conversation, that our church may go on in a progressive motion toward the zenith of perfection and meridian of glory.

I shall now shut up this work by acquainting the reader with a secret, which perhaps he would not otherwise advert to, viz. that I enjoy the pleasure of having done a thing seemingly quite impracticable. I have given the moderate, and those who desire to be instructed in the science, a complete view of the maxims and principles of moderation without at the same time prostituting or giving them up to the possession of every common reader. Perhaps some will ask how I imagine I have effected this? I answer that I have so framed the whole of my book that it is really intelligible only to persons duly qualified, and to every such person it is transparent as the springwater. I have given only moderate reasons for moderate principles so that however strongly they may convince some, viz. those of our kidney, others they will be so far from convincing that they will be thought to operate a quite contrary way. I have managed this so carefully that I could venture to lay a wager of all that I am worth that this treatise shall be taken by very many to be the work of an orthodox pen and to be intended as a banter upon moderate men and their way. They will be tempted to laugh at us, whom they will imagine to be exposed by this revelation of our mysteries; but how ingeniously are they deceived? For, by that very means, every properly prejudiced mind is furnished with a complete system upon which to form his sentiments and regulate his conduct.

ADDRESS

To the
Inhabitants of Jamaica,
and Other West India Islands,
in Behalf of
the College of New Jersey

Gentlemen,

IT is unneccessary to begin this address by a labored encomium on learning in general, or the importance of public seminaries for the instruction of youth. Their use in every country, their necessity in a new or rising country, and particularly the influence of science in giving a proper direction and full force to industry or enterprise are indeed so manifest that they are either admitted by all, or the exceptions are so few as to be wholly unworthy of regard.

In a more private view, the importance of education is little less evident. It promotes virtue and happiness, as well as arts and industry. On this, as on the former, it is unnecessary to enlarge; only suffer me to make a remark, not quite so common, that if there is any just comparison on this subject, the children of persons in the higher ranks of life, and especially of those who by their own activity and diligence rise to opulence, have of all others the greatest need of an early, prudent, and well-conducted education. The wealth to which they are born becomes often a dangerous temptation, and the station in which they enter upon life requires such duties as those of the finest talents can scarcely be supposed capable of, unless they have been improved and cultivated with the utmost care. Experience shows the use of a liberal education in both these views. It is generally a preservative from vice of a certain class by giving easy access to more refined pleasures and inspiring the mind with an abhorrence of low riot and contempt for brutal conversation. It is also of acknowledged necessity to those who do not wish to live for themselves alone, but would apply their talents to the service of the public and the good of mankind. Education is therefore of equal

103

importance in order either to enjoy life with dignity and elegance, or employ it to the benefit of society in offices of power or trust.

But leaving these general topics, or rather taking it for granted that everything of this kind is by intelligent persons, especially parents, both believed and felt, I proceed to inform the public that it is intended to solicit benefactions from the wealthy and generous in behalf of a college of considerable standing founded at Nassau Hall in Princeton, New Jersey. In order to this it is necessary for me: (1) to show the great advantage it will be to the inhabitants of the West Indies to have it in their power to send their children to approved places of education on the continent of America, instead of being obliged to send them over for the very elements of science to South or North Britain; (2) to point out the situation and advantages of the College of New Jersey in particular. And as I was never a lover either of florid discourse or ostentatious promises, I shall endeavor to handle these two points with all possible simplicity, and with that reserve and decency which are so necessary where comparison in some respects cannot be avoided.

On the first of these points, let it be observed that places of education on the continent of America are much nearer to the West Indies than those in Great Britain, and yet sufficiently distant to remove the temptation of running home and lurking in idleness. This is a circumstance, which other things being supposed equal is by no means inconsiderable. Parents may hear much oftener from and of their children and may even visit them, as is known to have been the case here, with no great loss of time for business and to the advantage of their own health. They may also much more speedily and certainly be informed whether they are profiting and have justice done them or not, and remove or continue them at pleasure. The distance indeed is, if I mistake not, well proportioned in all respects. It is such as to allow of the advantages just now mentioned, and yet so great as to favor the behaviour and instruction of the youth. I have observed in the course of four years experience that those who came from the greatest distance have in general behaved with most regularity. Being removed from their relations, it becomes necessary for them to support a character, as they find themselves treated by their companions, teachers, and indeed all other persons, according to their behavior. This is so true that if parents are obliged to place their children out of their own families, an hundred miles distance is better than twenty, and so of every other proportion till we come to the hurtful extreme.

Let it be further observed, that the climate of the continent of North America is certainly much more healthy in itself, and probably also more suited to the constitutions of those who have been born in the West Indies, than that of Great Britain. Health is the foundation of every earthly blessing, and absolutely necessary both to the receiving instruction in youth and being able in riper years to apply it to its proper use. Parental tenderness will make everyone feel the importance of this to his own children. And whether the observation itself is just or not, I leave to be decided by the judgment of all who have been in both countries and the information they will readily give to those who have not.

Having touched on these circumstances, let us try to make the comparison as to the substance of the education itself. Here, I am sensible it behooves me to write with the utmost circumspection to avoid giving offense, and that to some this will appear at first sight altogether impossible. I am however not without the greatest hopes that I shall be able fully to prove the proposition I have laid down without giving any just ground of offense to persons of reflection and candor. No man can have a higher opinion of, and not many have a more thorough acquaintance with, the means of education at present in Great Britain than the author of this address, who was born in the neighborhood of Edinburgh, educated in it, and spent the greatest part of his after life in constant intercourse and great intimacy with the members of the University of Glasgow. He therefore says it both with pleasure and gratitude that any young gentlemen who is strictly sober in his behavior and who applies with steadiness and diligence has all possible advantages, particularly in North Britain with which he is best acquainted, for improving himself in classic literature, in every branch of science, and especially in the justly valued knowledge of the force and propriety of the English language, and in true taste, including all that is usually comprehended under the general expression of the belles lettres. Nay, further, he admits and affirms, that any gentleman of fortune who would give the last and highest polish to the education of a young man of promising parts would do well to send him after his principles are fixed and his judgment a little matured for a year or two to some of the universities of Great Britain. But notwithstanding these concessions, if they may be so called, it is hoped it will appear that it would be much more to the advantage of the gentlemen of the West Indies to give their children their grammar school and college education, at least to their first degree in the arts, in an American seminary, if conducted by persons of ability and integrity, than to send them to Great Britain; and that for two important reasons, first, the better to secure their instruction, and secondly, for the preservation of their morals.

1. For the greater security of their instruction. The colleges in Britain have by no means that forcible motive that we have, not only to teach those who are willing to learn, but to see that everyone be obliged to study and actually learn in proportion to his capacity. These old

foundations have stood so many ages, have had their character so long established, and are indeed so well known to be filled with men of the greatest ability, that they do not so much as feel any injury in point of reputation from one or more coming out of college almost as ignorant as they went in. The truth is, I do not think they ought to lose any character by it. Everyone knows that it is owing to the idleness or profligacy of the boy and not the insufficiency of the master. When the numbers of one class are from an hundred to an hundred and thirty or perhaps more, and when they do not live in college, how is it possible the master can keep them to their private studies, or even with any certainty discern whether they study diligently or not. A good professor is easily and speedily distinguished by his own performances, by the esteem, attachment, and progress of the diligent, but very little, if at all, hurt by the ignorance of the negligent. I write these things to vast numbers who know them as well as I do, and I could easily produce gentlemen in America who have freely and generously confessed themselves to be unhappy proofs of their truth. Let not anybody say I reflect upon the teachers for not using discipline to oblige them to apply. The numbers are so great that to try and judge every neglect would take more time than they have for their whole work. To this may be added that it may very often happen that the persons to whose charge boys in early life are sent from the West Indies, either are not themselves judges or from their situation and business have few opportunities of knowing whether they profit or not.

On the other hand, the young seminaries in America have their character constantly at stake for their diligence, as one or two untaught coming out from us affects us in the most sensible manner. As to the College of New Jersey in particular, we have seen the importance of this in so strong a light that whereas before we had half-yearly, we now have quarterly examinations carried on with the utmost strictness when all who are found deficient are degraded to the inferior class. So impartially have these trials been conducted that nothing is more usual than for those who suspect themselves, especially if their relations are near, to pretend sickness and avoid the examinations that they may afterward fall back without the dishonor of a sentence. Further, all the scholars with us as soon as they put on the gown are obliged to lodge in college and must of necessity be in their chamber in study hours, nor is it in the least difficult to discover whether they apply carefully or not. The teachers also live in college so that they have every possible advantage, not only for assisting the diligent but stimulating the slothful.

2. The second reason for preferring an American education is that their morals may be more effectually preserved. This, by all virtuous and judicious parents, will be held to a point of the last consequence.

The danger they run of contracting vicious habits by being sent to Britain has been often complained of, and therefore, I suppose, is matter of experience. If so, it will not be difficult to assign the causes of it, which may be safely mentioned because they carry no imputation upon the schools or colleges to which they are sent. They generally are, and are always supposed to be, of great wealth. The very name of a West Indian has come to imply in it great opulence. Now it is well known that in all the great towns in Britain a set of profligate boys, and sometimes artful persons farther advanced in life, attach themselves to such as are well supplied with money, impose upon their youth and simplicity, gratify them in every irregular desire, and lead them both into idleness and vice. There are also in every considerable place in Great Britain, but especially the principal cities where the colleges are fixed, a constant succession and variety of intoxicating diversions, such as balls, concerts, plays, races, and others. These, whatever may be pleaded for some of them in a certain measure for those further advanced, everybody must acknowledge are highly pernicious to youth in the first stages of their education. The temptation becomes so much the stronger, and indeed almost irresistible, when an acquaintance with these things is considered as fashionable life and necessary to the accomplishment of a man of breeding. Is it to be supposed that young persons of great fortune when they can be immediate partakers will wait with patience for the proper time when they may be permitted to view with caution such scenes of dissipation? On the contrary it may be expected that they will give into them with all the impetuosity and rashness of youth, and, when their parents expect them to return well stored with classic learning and philosophy, they may find them only well acquainted with the laws of the turf or gaming table and expert in the use of the reigning phrases of those honorable arts.

What provision is made for preserving and improving the morals of the scholars with us I leave it till I come to speak of the constitution and situation of the College of New Jersey. But before I dismiss this part of the subject I must just repeat that the two reasons I have given against a British education do and were intended only to conclude against sending boys in early life. At that time they are incapable of reaping the advantages chiefly to be valued in a British education. These are not only hearing and being able to judge of the public performances of men of letters, in the pulpit, at the bar, and in parliament; but being introduced to the acquaintance and enjoying the conversation of men of eminence. This is a favor that would not be granted to boys, and if granted could be of no service, but contributes in the highest degree to the delight and instruction of those of riper years. Experience seems greatly to confirm this, for as many boys have left some of the best schools in Britain with little classic knowledge though supported at great expence, so those who received their first education in this country and went home to finish it have seldom returned without great and real improvement.

In addition to these arguments in behalf of American colleges, drawn from the instruction and morals of the youth who are sent to them, I cannot help mentioning one other which must have great weight in a view somewhat different. These colleges must necessarily in time produce a number of young men proper to undertake the office of private tutors in gentlemen's families. There are some who prefer a private to a public education at any rate, especially in the very first stages, and some find it necessary, as not being able to support the expense of sending their children so early and keeping them so long from home. Now all who know the situation of things in Britain must be sensible how difficult it is to get young men of capacity or expectation to leave their native country in order to undertake the instruction of gentlemen's children. In this office there is little prospect of increase of fortune to balance the risk of going to a new and dangerous, or supposed dangerous, climate. But those who are born and educated in America will not only increase the number of such teachers, but they will have no such hideous apprehensions of going to any part of the continent or islands. Whatever is done, therefore, to raise and support proper seminaries in America will in time be followed by this great and general benefit, which I have been assured is very much needed in many or most of the West India islands.

I will now proceed to speak a little of the Constitution and Advantages of the College of New Jersey in particular.

About twenty-four years ago, several gentlemen and ministers in this province, by the friendship and patronage of Jonathan Belcher, Esq., then governor, obtained a very ample royal charter incorporating them under the title of Trustees of the College of New Jersey and giving them the same privileges and powers that are given to the "two English Universities, or any other University or College in Great-Britain." They, although only possessed of a naked charter, without any public encouragement, immediately began the instruction and very soon after, by their own activity and zeal and the benevolence of others who had the highest opinion of their integrity, raised a noble building called Nassau Hall at Princeton, New Jersey. This they chose to do though it wasted their capital, as their great intention was to make effectual provision, not only for the careful instruction, but for the regular government of the youth. There all the scholars are lodged, and also boarded, except when they have express license to board out in the president's house or elsewhere.

The regular course of instruction is in four classes exactly after the manner and bearing the names of the classes in the English universities: freshman, sophomore, junior, and senior. In the first year, they read Latin and Greek, with the Roman and Grecian antiquities, and rhetoric. In the second continuing the study of the languages, they learn a complete system of geography, with the use of the globes, the first principles of philosophy, and the elements of mathematical knowledge. The third, though the languages are not wholly omitted, is chiefly employed in mathematics and natural philosophy. And the senior year is employed in reading the higher classics, proceeding in the mathematics and natural philosophy, and going through a course of moral philosophy. In addition to these, the president gives lectures to the juniors and seniors, which consequently every student hears twice over in his course, first upon chronology and history, and afterwards upon composition and criticism. He has also taught the French language last winter, and it will continue to be taught to those who desire to learn it.

During the whole course of their studies, the three younger classes, two every evening formerly, and now three because of their increased number, pronounce an oration on a stage erected for that purpose in the hall immediately after prayers, that they may learn by early habit presence of mind and proper pronunciation and gesture in public speaking. This excellent practice, which has been kept up almost from the first foundation of the college, has had the most admirable effects. The senior scholars every five or six weeks pronounce orations of their own composition, to which all persons of any note in the neighborhood are invited or admitted.

The college is now furnished with all the most important helps to instruction. The library contains a very large collection of valuable books. The lessons of astronomy are given upon the orrery, lately invented and constructed by David Rittenhouse, Esq. which is reckoned by the best judges the most excellent in its kind of any ever yet produced; and when what is commissioned and now upon its way is added to what the college already possesses, the apparatus for mathematics and natural philosophy will be equal, if not superior, to any on the continent.

As we have never yet been obliged to omit or alter it for want of scholars, there is a fixed annual commencement on the last Wednesday of September, when, after a variety of public exercises always attended by a vast concourse of the politest company from the different parts of this province and the cities of New York and Philadelphia, the students whose senior year is expiring are admitted to the degree of Bachelors of Arts; the Bachelors of three years standing to the degrees of Masters; and such other higher degrees granted as are either regularly claimed or the trustees think fit to bestow upon those who have distinguished themselves by their literary productions, or their appearances in public life.

On the day preceding the commencement last year, there was (and it will be continued every year hereafter) a public exhibition and voluntary contention for prizes open for every member of college. These were first, second, and third prizes on each of the following subjects: (1) reading the English language with propriety and grace, and being able to answer all questions on its orthography and grammar; (2) reading the Latin and Greek languages in the same manner, with particular attention to true quantity; (3) speaking Latin; (4) Latin versions; (5) pronouncing English orations. The preference was determined by ballot, and all present permitted to vote who were graduates of this or any other college.

As to the government of the college, no correction by stripes is permitted. Such as cannot be governed by reason and the principles of honor and shame are reckoned unfit for residence in a college. The collegiate censures are (1) private admonition by the president, professor, or tutor; (2) before the faculty; (3) before the whole class to which the offender belongs; (4) and the last and highest, before all the members of college assembled in the hall. And, to preserve the weight and dignity of these censures, it has been an established practice that the last or highest censure, viz. public admonition, shall never be repeated upon the same person. If it has been thought necessary to inflict it upon anyone, and if this does not preserve him from falling into such gross irregularities a second time, it is understood that expulsion is immediately to follow.

Through the narrowness of the funds, the government and instruction has hitherto been carried on by a president and three tutors. At last commencement, the trustees chose a professor of mathematics and intend as their funds are raised to have a greater number of professorships and carry their plan to as great perfection as possible.

The above relates wholly to what is properly the college; but there is also at the same place, established under the particular direction and patronage of the president, a grammar school where boys are instructed in the Latin and Greek languages with the utmost care and on the plan of the most approved teachers in Great Britain. It is now so large as to have two masters for the languages and one for writing and arithmetic, and as some are sent with a design only to learn the Latin, Greek, and French languages, arithmetic, geography, and the practical branches of the mathematics without going through a full college course, such scholars are permitted to attend the instruction of the classes in whatever coincides with their plan. It is also now resolved at the request of several gentlemen to have an English master after next vacation for teaching the English language regularly and grammatically, and for perfecting by English exercises those whose previous instruction may have been defective or erroneous.

I have thus laid before the public a concise account of the constitution of the college of New Jersey and must now earnestly recommend it to the assistance and patronage of men of liberal and ingenuous minds. I am sensible that nothing is more difficult than to write in behalf of what the writer himself has so great a part in conducting, so as neither to fail in doing justice to the subject, nor exceed in improper or arrogant professions. And yet to employ others to write for us, who may have some pretense as indifferent persons, to embellish our characters is liable to still greater suspicion. The very best security one can give to the public for decency and truth is to write openly in his own person that he may be under a necessity to answer for it if it is liable to challenge.

This is the method I have determined to follow, and that I may neither offend the delicacy of my friends, nor provoke the resentment of my enemies, I will endeavor humbly to recommend this college to the attention and esteem of men of penetration and candor, chiefly from such circumstances as have little or no relation to the personal characters of those now employed but are essential to its situation and constitution, and therefore must be supposed to have not only the most powerful, but the most lasting effect. The circumstances to which I would entreat the attention of impartial persons are the following.

1. The College of New Jersey is altogether independent. It hath received no favor from government but the charter, by the particular friendship of a person now deceased. It owes nothing but to the benefactions of a public so diffusive that it cannot produce particular dependence or operate by partial influence. From this circumstance it must be free from two great evils and derive the like number of solid advantages. There is no fear of being obliged to choose teachers upon ministerial recommendation or in compliance with the overbearing weight of family interest. On the contrary, the trustees are naturally led and in a manner forced to found their choice upon the characters of the persons and the hope of public approbation. At the same time those concerned in the instruction and government of the college are as far removed as the state of human nature will admit from any temptation to a fawning, cringing spirit and mean servility in the hope of court favor or promotion.

In consequence of this, it may naturally be expected, and we find by experience that hitherto in fact, the spirit of liberty has breathed high and strong in all the members. I would not be understood to say that a seminary of learning ought to enter deeply into political contention; far less would I meanly court favor by professing myself a violent partisan in any present disputes. But surely a constitution which naturally tends to produce a spirit of liberty and independence, even though this should sometimes need to be reined in by prudence and moderation, is infinitely preferable to the dead and vapid state of one whose very existence depends upon the nod of those in power. Another great advantage arising from this is the obligation we are under to recommend ourselves by diligence and fidelity to the public. Having no particular prop to lean to on one side, we are obliged to stand upright and firm by leaning equally on all. We are so far from having our fund so complete as of itself to support the necessary expense that the greater part of our annual income arises from the payments of the scholars, which we acknowledge with gratitude have been for these several years continually increasing.

2. This leads me to observe that it ought to be no inconsiderable recommendation of this college to those at a distance that it has the esteem and approbation of those who are nearest it and know it best. The number of undergraduates, or proper members of college, is near four times that any college on the continent to the southward of New England, and probably greater than that of all the rest put together. This we are at liberty to affirm has in no degree arisen from pompous descriptions or repeated recommendations in the public papers. We do not mean to blame the laudable attempts of others to do themselves justice. We have been often found fault with and perhaps are to blame for neglect in this particular. It is only mentioned to give full force to the argument just now used, and the fact is certainly true. I do not remember that the name of the College of New Jersey has been above once or twice mentioned in the newspapers for three years, except in a bare recital of the acts of the annual commencements. The present address arises from necessity, not choice; for had not a more private application been found impracticable, the press had probably never been employed.

3. It may not be amiss to observe on this subject that the great utility of this seminary has been felt over an extensive country. Many of the clergy, episcopal and presbyterian, in the different colonies received their education here, whose exemplary behavior and other merit we suffer to speak for themselves. We are also willing that the public should attend to the characters and appearance of those gentlemen in the law and medical departments who were brought up at Nassau Hall and are now in the cities of New York and Philadelphia, and perhaps the greatest number of their pupils received their instruction here. We are not afraid, but even wish that our claim should be decided by the conduct of those in general who have come out from us, which is one of the most conclusive arguments; for a tree is known by its fruits. It is at the

same time an argument of the most fair and generous kind; for it is left to be determined by mankind at their leisure; and if the appeal be not in our favor, it must be unspeakably injurious.

4. The place where the college is built is most happily chosen for the health, the studies and the morals of the scholars. All these were particularly attended to when the spot was pitched upon. Princeton is on a rising ground, from whence there is an easy gradual descent for many miles on all quarters, except the north and northwest, from whence at the distance of one mile it is sheltered by a range of hills covered with woods. It has a most beautiful appearance, and in fact has been found one of the healthiest places, as it is situated in the middle of one of the most healthful countries on the whole continent. It is upon the great post road almost equally distant from New York and Philadelphia, so as to be a center of intelligence and have an easy conveyance of everything necessary, and yet to be wholly free from the many temptations in every great city, both to the neglect of study and the practice of vice. The truth is it is to this happy circumstance, so wisely attended to by the first trustees, that we owe our being enabled to keep up the discipline of the college with so great regularity and so little difficulty. We do not wish to take any honor in this respect to ourselves. Doubtless the masters of every college will do their best in this respect. But it is not in the power of those who are in great cities to keep the discipline with equal strictness, where boys have so many temptations to do evil and can so easily and effectually conceal it after it is done. With us, they live all in college under the inspection of their masters; and the village is so small that any irregularity is immediately and certainly discovered, and therefore easily corrected.

It has sometimes happened through rivalship or malice that our discipline has been censured as too severe and rigorous. This reproach I always hear, not with patience only, but with pleasure. In the mouth of an adversary, it is a clear confession that the government is strict and regular. While we avail ourselves of this, we prove that the accusation of oppressive rigor is wholly without foundation from the number of scholars and the infrequency of public censures, but above all from the warm and almost enthusiastic attachment of those who have finished their course. Could their esteem and friendship be expected in return for an austere and rigorous confinement, out of which they had escaped as birds out of the snare of the fowler? We admit that it is insupportable to the idle and profligate; for either they will not bear with us, or we will not bear with them; but from those who have applied to their studies, and reached the honors of college, we have almost without exception found the most sincere, active, and zealous friendship.

5. This college was founded and hath been conducted upon the most

catholic principles. The charter recites as one of its grounds, "That every religious denomination may have free and equal liberty and advantage of education in the said college, any different sentiments in religion notwithstanding." Accordingly there are now and have been from the beginning, scholars of various denominations from the most distant colonies, as well as West India islands; and they must necessarily confess that they never met with the least uneasiness or disrespect on this account. Our great advantage on this subject is the harmony of the board of trustees, and the perfect union in sentiment among all the teachers, both with the trustees and with one another. On this account, there is neither inclination nor occasion to meddle with any controversy whatever. The author of this address confesses that he was long accustomed to the order and dignity of an established church, but a church which hath no contempt or detestation of those who are differently organized. And, as he hath ever been in that church an opposer of lordly domination and sacerdotal tyranny, so he is a passionate admirer of the equal and impartial support of every religious denomination which prevails in the northern colonies and is perfect in Pennsylvania and the Jerseys to the unspeakable advantage of those happy and well-constituted governments.

With respect to the College of New Jersey, every question about forms of church government is so entirely excluded, that though I have seen one set of scholars begin and finish their course, if they know nothing more of religious controversy than what they learned here, they have that science wholly to begin. This is altogether owing to the union of sentiment mentioned above; for, if you place as teachers in a college persons of repugnant religious principles, they must have more wisdom and self-denial than usually fall to the lot of humanity if the whole society is not divided into parties and marshaled under names if the changes are not frequent; and, when they take place they will be as well known as any event that can happen in such a society. On the contrary, there is so little occasion with us to canvass this matter at all that, though no doubt accident must discover it as to the greatest number, yet some have left the college as to whom I am wholly uncertain at this hour to what denomination they belong. It has been and shall be our care to use every means in our power to make them good men and good scholars, and, if this is the case, I shall hear of their future character and usefulness with unfeigned satisfaction under every name by which a real protestant can be distinguished.

Having already experienced the generosity of the public in many parts of the continent of America, I cannot but hope that the gentlemen of the islands will not refuse their assistance, according to their abilities, in order to carry this seminary to a far greater degree of perfection than any to which it has yet arrived. The express purpose to which the benefactions now requested will be applied is the establishment of new professorships, which will render the institution not only more complete in itself, but less burthensome to those who have undertaken the important trust. The whole branches of mathematics and natural philosophy are now taught by one professor; and the president is obliged to teach divinity and moral philosophy, as well as chronology, history, and rhetoric, besides the superintendance and government of the whole. The short lives of the former presidents have been by many attributed to their excessive labors, which, it is hoped, will be an argument with the humane and generous to lend their help in promoting so noble a design.

I am, gentlemen,
Your most obedient,
Humble servant,
JOHN WITHERSPOON

Nassau Hall, at Princeton, New Jersey, March 21, 1772

CHRISTIAN
MAGNANIMITY

Preached at Princeton, September, 1775,
the Sabbath preceding the Annual Commencement;
and again with Additions, September 23, 1787.

That you would walk worthy of God, who hath called you into his kingdom and glory.

—1 Thess. 2:12

THE PRESENT state was intended to be, and I think must by every person of reflection be admitted to be, a continual trial of the faith and constancy of a Christian. It is therefore a duty we owe to others in general, but in a special manner the elder to the younger, to give them faithful warning of the temptations and dangers to which they must of necessity be exposed if they mean to walk in the paths of piety and virtue. It hath often occurred to me in meditating on this subject that as false money is most dangerous when it is likest to the true, so those principles and that character which approach the nearest to true religion, if notwithstanding they are essentially different from it, will be most ready to impose on an uncautious and unsuspecting mind. Therefore, if there is such a thing as a worldly virtue, a system of principles and duty dictated by the spirit of the world and the standard of appprobation or blame with the men of the world, and if this is at bottom essentially different from and sometimes directly opposed to the spirit of the gospel, it must be of all others the most dangerous temptation to persons of a liberal education and an ingenious turn of mind.

This, if I am not mistaken, is really the case. There are some branches of true religion which are universally approved, and which impiety itself cannot speak against, such as truth and integrity in speech, honesty in dealing, humanity and compassion to persons in distress. But there are other particulars in which the worldly virtue and the Christian virtue seem to be different things. Of these I shall select one as an example,

116

viz. spirit, dignity, or greatness of mind. This seems to be entirely of the worldly cast: It holds a very high place in the esteem of all worldly men; the boldest pretensions are often made to it by those who treat religion with neglect and religious persons with disdain or defiance. It is also a virtue of a very dazzling appearance, ready to captivate the mind, and particularly to make a deep impression on young persons when they first enter into life. At the same time, the gospel seems to stand directly opposed to it. The humility of the creature, the abasement and contrition of the sinner, the dependance and self-denial of the believer, and above all, the shame and reproach of the cross itself seem to conspire in obliging us to renounce it.

What shall we say then, my brethren? Shall we say that magnanimity is no virtue at all, and that no such excellence belongs to human nature? Or shall we admit that there is beauty and excellence in it—confessing at the same time that it does not belong to religion, and only say that though we want this, we have many other and better qualities in its place? To this I can never agree, for every real excellence is consistent with every other, nay every real excellence is adorned and illustrated by every other. Vices may be inconsistent with each other, but virtues never can. And, therefore, as magnanimity is an amiable and noble quality—one of the greatest ornaments of our nature, so I affirm that it belongs only to true and undefiled religion and that every appearance of the one without the other is not only defective but false.

The Holy Scriptures, it is true, do chiefly insist upon what is proper to humble our pride, and to bring us to a just apprehension of our character and state. This was wise and just because of that corruption and misery into which we are fallen, the contrary would have been unjust. It is evidently more necessary in the present state of human nature to restrain pride than to kindle ambition. But as the scripture points out our original dignity and the true glory of our nature, so every true penitent is there taught to aspire after the noblest character and to entertain the most exalted hopes. In the passage which I have chosen as the subject of my discourse, you see the Apostle exhorts the Thessalonians to walk suitably to the dignity of their character and the importance of their privileges, which is a short but just description of true and genuine greatness of mind.

My single purpose from these words at this time is to explain and recommend magnanimity as a christian virtue, and I wish to do it in such a manner as neither to weaken its lustre nor admit any degree of that corrupt mixture by which it is often counterfeited and greatly debased. Some infidels have in terms affirmed that Christianity has banished magnanimity and by its precepts of meekness, humility, and passive submission to injury has destroyed that nobleness of sentiment which rendered the ancients so illustrious and gives so much majesty and dignity to the histories of Greece and Rome. In opposition to this, I hope to be able to show that real greatness is inseparable from sincere piety and that any defect in the one must necessarily be a discernible blemish in the other. With this view, I will first give you the principles of magnanimity in general as a natural quality; secondly, I will show what is necessary to give it real value as a moral virtue; thirdly, show that it shines with the most perfect brightness as a Christian grace; and afterwards improve the subject by a practical application of what may be said for your instruction and direction.

First, then, let me state the principles of magnanimity in general as a natural quality. I think it must be admitted that as there is a real difference between bodies as to size and bulk, as well as other sensible qualities, so there is a real character of greatness or meanness applicable to the mind distinct from its other qualities or powers. It is, however, I apprehend a simple impression which cannot be explained or further analyzed, but may easily be felt, and is best illustrated by its effects. These may be summed up in the following particulars: To magnanimity it belongeth to attempt, (1) great and difficult things; (2) to aspire after great and valuable possessions; (3) to encounter dangers with resolution; (4) to struggle against difficulties with perseverance; and (5) to bear sufferings with fortitude and patience.

1. It belongs to magnanimity to attempt great and difficult things. Those who from a love of sloth and ease neglect the exercise or improvement of their powers and those who apply them with ever so great assiduity and attention to things mean or of small consequence are plainly destitute of this quality. We perceive a meanness and want of spirit in this respect when particular persons fall below their rank in life, or when, as is too frequently the case in any rank, they fall below human nature itself. When a prince or other person of the first order and importance in human life busies himself in nothing but the most trifling amusements or arts of little value, we call it mean; and when any man endowed with rational powers loses them through neglect or destroys them by the most groveling sensuality, we say he is acting below himself. The contrary of this, therefore, or the vigorous exertion of all our powers, and particularly the application of them to things of moment and difficulty, is real magnanimity.

2. It belongs to magnanimity to aspire after great and valuable possessions. It is more difficult properly to illustrate this as a branch of magnanimity because of its frequent perversion, which will be afterwards explained. It seems however to be necessarily included in the general character. A great mind has great capacities of enjoyment as well as action. And as there is a difference between the blessing in our view,

both in point of dignity and extent, such a man will not be easily satisfied
or put up with what is either mean or scanty while he can acquire and
possess a better and more extensive portion. The large and increasing
desires of the human mind have often been made an argument for the
dignity of our nature, and our having been made for something that is
great and excellent.

3. It belongs to magnanimity to encounter dangers with resolution.
This is inseparable from and constitutes a leading part of the character.
Even the most excellent and valuable services to mankind if they are
attended with no difficulty at all or meet with no opposition, though
they retain the character of utility, yet for want of this circumstance,
they lose that of greatness. Courage is always considered as a great
quality; it has had the admiration, or rather adoration, of mankind in
every age. Many when they speak of magnanimity mean nothing else
but courage, and when they speak of meanness have little other idea
but that of timidity. Neither is there, I think, any human weakness that
is more the object of contempt and disdain than cowardice, which when
applied to life in general is commonly called pusillanimity.

4. It belongs to greatness to struggle against difficulties with steadiness and perseverance. Perseverance is nothing else but continued and
inflexible courage. We see some persons who show the greatest activity
and boldness for a season, but time and opposition weaken their force
and seem, if I may speak so, to exhaust their courage as if they wasted
the power by exertion. Perseverance, therefore, is necessary to greatness. Few things are more contrary to this character than fickleness and
unsteadiness. We commonly join together the characters of weak and
changeable.

5. In the last place, it belongs to greatness to bear sufferings with
fortitude and patience. This is a kindred quality to the former and is
necesary to complete the character of magnanimity. Such is the state of
human things that suffering is in one way or another wholly unavoidable. It often happens that difficulties cannot be removed or enemies
cannot be conquered, and then it is the last effort of greatness of mind
to bear the weight of the one, or the cruelty of the other, with firmness
and patience. This virtue has always been of the greatest reputation. It
is a well known saying of a heathen philosopher that a great man
suffering with invincible patience under a weight of misfortunes is a
sight which even the gods must behold with admiration.

Having thus pointed out the principles, or rather enumerated the
chief effects of magnanimity as a natural quality, let us now in the
second place consider what is necessary to give it real value as a moral
virtue. This is of the utmost importance, and must appear so to all who
will consider the subject with attention. That I may set the matter in as

clear a light as possible, observe that to render magnanimity a valuable quality it must further have the following characters.

1. The object of our desires must be just as well as great. Some of the noblest powers of the human mind have often been exerted in invading the right instead of promoting the interest and happiness of mankind. As the history of the world is little else than the history of human guilt, so many of the most illustrious names transmitted down to us have been those of the most active and successful destroyers of their fellow creatures. There may be, and there have been in such persons, many or most of the ingredients of natural greatness of mind; but these have only served to make the characters in the eye of reason more hideous and detestable.

2. Our desires ought to be governed by wisdom and prudence, as well as justice. If any person either forms difficult projects or aspires after great possessions and in prosecution of his purposes exerts ever so much courage, fortitude, and patience, yet, if these designs are less useful or these possessions less valuable than others to which he might have applied the same talents, it cannot deserve the name of true magnanimity. If any person, for example, forms a resolution of exerting his skill in such feats or performances as have nothing or very little valuable in them but that they are difficult and uncommon, I think no man will pretend that he has any title to the character of greatness of mind, otherwise a rope-dancer might be a hero; or if any person should spend a whole life in the most unwearied application to the single purpose of accumulating wealth, however vast his desires, or however astonishing his success, his merit would be very small. Nay, we must be sensible that he has lost many opportunities of doing signal service to mankind and of acquiring more valuable and durable enjoyments, while in pursuit of this, which after all will disappoint his hopes.

3. The principle of action must be honorable as well as the achievements illustrious. If a person does things ever so extraordinary in their nature, overcomes the greatest difficulties, or braves the most formidable dangers merely to make his name famous, we must at once perceive how much it detracts even from his name itself. This is not the language of religion only; it is the language of reason and the dictate of the human heart. An insatiable thirst for praise is so far from being amiable that it is hateful or contemptible. I am sensible that a thirst for fame is not only apparent in, but seems to have been confessed by many of the most distinguished heroes of antiquity; but as it certainly does abate in a good degree the luster of their good actions, so the indulgence that is given them upon this head is wholly owing to the disadvantages they lay under in a state of heathenism and their ignorance of a better and nobler principle. "Nothing," says an eminent author, "can be great, the

contempt of which is great"; and therefore, if a contempt of riches, a neglect of fame, and a readiness to sacrifice both to duty and usefulness is one of the most glorious characters we can conceive, it is plain that not the deeds, but the principles is the evidence, and not the head nor the hands of man, but the heart is the seat of genuine greatness.

4. In the last place in order to real greatness, every attempt must be possible and rational, perhaps probable. Nothing is more common than to find persons under the pretence of great and illustious designs prosecuting what is not of any value when obtained, and at the same time scarcely possible, and no way probable to be obtained at all. This is declining altogether from the line of greatness and going into the path of extravagance. Again, should any man undertake what he was altogether unable to perform, however excellent the design were in itself, we would not dignify it even with the name of ambition; he would acquire and deserve the character, not of greatness, but of folly or madness.

On the whole, it is plain that these moral principles must enter into the composition of true greatness and that, when they are wanting, the natural characters mentioned before degenerate into vice and assume the names of pride, ambition, temerity, ferocity and obstinacy.

This leads me, in the third place, to show, not only that there is nothing in real religion contrary to magnanimity, but that there, and there only it appears in its beauty and perfection. Let me briefly run over and apply to religion the above-mentioned ingredients of magnanimity.

1. It is to attempt great and difficult things. Religion calls us to the greatest and most noble attempts, whether in a private or public view. In a private view, it calls us to resist and subdue every corrupt and sinful passion, however strongly the indulgence is solicited by the tempting object or recommended by the artful seducer. The importance and difficulty of this struggle appear not only from the holy scriptures, but from the experience and testimony of mankind in every age. What cautions are given by Solomon upon this subject? "He that is slow to anger, is better than the mighty, and he that ruleth his spirit, than he that taketh a city." The wisest heathens have inculcated the necessity of self-government and the danger of surrounding temptation by many instructive images. But why should I extend this part of the subject? How few are successful in this attempt? This alone is a sufficient proof that it is great and difficult, and every person exercised to godliness will be abundantly sensible of it from the state of his own heart.

In a public view, every good man is called to live and act for the glory of God and the good of others. Here he has as extensive a scene of activity as he can possibly desire. He is not indeed permitted to glory or to build an altar to his own vanity, but he is both permitted and obliged to exert his talents, to improve his time, to employ his substance, and to hazard his life in his Maker's service or his country's cause. Nor am I able to conceive any character more truly great than that of one, whatever be his station or profession, who is devoted to the public good under the immediate order of Providence. He does not seek the bubble reputation in the deadly breach, but he complains of no difficulty, and refuses no service, if he thinks he carries the commission of the King of kings.

2. The truly pious man aspires after the greatest and most valuable possessions. He despises, indeed, the uncertain and the unsatisfying enjoyments of time. His desires after present enjoyments are subjected to the will of God. He has given them up without reserve, yet his heavenly Father knoweth that he hath need of these things, and therefore he both asks and hopes to receive what is suitable and necessary, and believes that a little that a just man hath is better than the riches of many wicked. But the glorious object of the Christian's ambition is the inheritance incorruptible and undefiled, and that fadeth not away. The honorable relation he stands in to God as his adopted child in Christ Jesus inclines and authorizes him to hope for this purchased possession and enables him to look down with becoming indifference on all the glory of this transitory world. Let the rich man glory in his riches and the wise man glory in his wisdom; he only glories in this, that he knoweth the Lord and shall be with him forever.

3. True piety encounters the greatest dangers with resolution. The fear of God is the only effectual means to deliver us from the fear of man. Experience has abundantly shown that the servants of Christ have adhered to his cause and make profession of his name in opposition to all the terrors which infernal policy could present to them and all the sufferings with which the most savage inhumanity could afflict them. But as this belongs to the case of persecution for conscience sake, which by the peculiar kindness of Providence is exceedingly rare among us, it is proper to observe that every Christian has frequent opportunities of manifesting a holy resolution in encountering the reproach and derision of worldly men for adhering to his duty. And when we consider how hard it is to bear reproach and scorn, called in scripture the *trial of cruel mockings*, there will appear to be no small measure of dignity and heroism in him who can calmly submit to it from every quarter rather than depart from his duty. There are not a few who are apt to boast of their spirit and resolution, who are yet unable to bear reproach and meanly make the sentiments of others and the caprice of fashion the rule of duty in place of the clear dictates of conscience and the word of God. How contemptible is this compared to the conduct of that man who seeks no fame but by honest means, and fears no reproach for

honest actions but contents himself with a silent and believing regard to him who sees in secret, and who shall at last bring every work into judgment.

4. True piety perseveres with constancy in opposition to continual trial. This is indeed what distinguishes the Christian warfare from that of every other. It continues through life, and the last enemy to be overcome is death. In all the conflicts between men on earth, the issue may be speedily expected, and the reward immediately bestowed. But in religion, it is only he who shall endure to the end that shall be saved. This adds greatly to the difficulty and seems to show not only the excellence and beauty, but the real dignity and magnanimity of the Christian character.

5. In the last place, true piety endures suffering with patience and fortitude. If we reflect upon the number of suffering martyrs whose testimonies are upon record, we shall see with what calmness and composure, with what undaunted firmness, and sometimes with what exultation and triumph they have gone to a scaffold, or been tied to a stake. Can any person, think you, who hath gone to the field of battle in quest of glory, or who hath braved the danger of the seas in quest of wealth or power be once compared with those who have cheerfully given up the precious life or submitted their bodies to the torture to keep their consciences undefiled? But, my brethren, Christian patience is much more frequently tried in another manner. The believer has made an unreserved surrender of himself and his all to the disposal of Providence: His faithfulness to this promise is brought almost every day to the trial. For the Christian then to suffer reproach without rendering evil for evil or railing for railing, to be submissive under the loss of substance, and say with Job, Job 1:21, "Naked came I out of my mother's womb, and naked shall I return thither: the Lord gave, and the Lord hath taken away; blessed be the name of the Lord." To yield up relations, and to say with David, 2 Sam. 12:23, "I shall go to him but he shall not return to me." To look forward to approaching death, and say with the apostle Paul, 2 Tim. 4:6, "I am now ready to be offered, and the time of my departure is at hand." This is magnanimity indeed; this is the most solid glory to which any child of Adam can possibly attain. I proceed in the last place to make some practical improvement of what hath been said.

1. You may learn from what hath been said that whenever honor differs from conscience, it is a treacherous guide; wherever spirit and dignity of mind, as a worldly virtue, differs from true religion, and even from the simplicity of the gospel, it is false and spurious. The gospel, it is true, will not suffer men to seek revenge or to delight in it. It will humble them in the sight of God and make them self-denied in the

presence of men, yet it will constrain them not to refuse any duty to the one, or any useful service to the other. It will not suffer them to be ambitious of higher places of honor and trust, but it will make them active and zealous in the duties of that place in which they already are. It will not suffer them to resent injuries and gratify revenge, but it will make them withstand a king upon his throne if he presume to interfere in the matters of their God. What is there here that is not noble?

After all, the testimony in favor of true piety is universal, if carefully attended to. Everyone must acknowledge that ostentation and love of praise, and whatever is contrary to the self-denial of the gospel, tarnish the beauty of the greatest actions. Courage and modesty, merit and humility, majesty and condescension appear with ten-fold glory when they are united; it is impossible to separate them; to divide is to destroy them. They are like light and shade in a picture, which are necessary to each other, and which by their union constitute the beauty and augment the lustre of the piece. So true is this that the highest polish that any person can receive in commerce with the world is to have an apparent disposition to prefer the interest of others to his own, to guard against every degree of offence, and to be always ready to oblige. I have often been pleased with that observation of a foreigner of high rank, that worldly politeness is only an imperfect imitation of Christian charity; it is nothing else but a studied appearance of that deference to the judgment and attention to the interest of others which a true Christian hath as the rule of his duty and the disposition of his heart.[1]

2. Suffer me to observe that as Christian magnanimity is more excellent than that of the world, it is also more practicable and, in fact, more universal. Worldly magnanimity is what always requires such talents as do not fall to the lot of many and such opportunities for its exercise as seldom occur. The road to heroism is not open to every man. But that magnanimity which is the fruit of true religion, being indeed the product of divine grace, is a virtue of the heart and may be attained by persons of mean talents and narrow possessions and in the very lowest stations of human life. In fact, there have been and are daily examples of it in every rank. We see the heroic fortitude of the martyrs as manifest in those of early years and the weaker sex, as in any other; and whoever will visit the solitary walks of life may find in the lowest stations humility, thankfulness, patience under affliction, and submission to Providence, such as would do honor to the most approved virtue and the most enlightened mind. To despise riches and restrain the motions of envy and impatience in a needy state is perhaps as truly noble as to improve them wisely in a higher.

1. The prince of Conti.

Thus the honor which is chiefly desirable is equally open to the rich and to the poor, to the learned and to the unlearned, to the wise and to the unwise, as it cometh from God, who is no respecter of persons. One of the best and happiest effects of serious reflection is to bring us in a great measure all upon a level; as, indeed, in one most important respect, the magistrate with his robes, the scholar with his learning, and the day laborer that stands unnoticed are all upon the same footing—for we must all appear before the judgment seat of Christ.

The Dominion of Providence Over the Passions of Men

Preached at Princeton on the 17th of May, 1776, being the general fast appointed by the Congress through the United Colonies. Dedicated to the Hon. John Hancock, Esq., president of the Congress of the United States of America.

Surely the Wrath of Man shall praise thee; the remainder of Wrath shalt thou restrain.

—Psalm 76:10

THERE IS not a greater evidence either of the reality or the power of religion than a firm belief of God's universal presence and a constant attention to the influence and operation of his providence. It is by this means that the Christian may be said in the emphatical scripture language, "to walk with God, and to endure as seeing him who is invisible."

The doctrine of divine providence is very full and complete in the sacred oracles. It extends not only to things which we may think of great moment, and therefore worthy of notice, but to things the most indifferent and inconsiderable: "Are not two sparrows sold for a farthing," says our Lord, "and one of them falleth not to the ground without your heavenly Father"; nay, "the very hairs of your head are all numbered." It extends not only to things beneficial and salutary, or to the direction and assistance of those who are the servants of the living God, but to things seemingly most hurtful and destructive and to persons the most refractory and disobedient. He overrules all his creatures, and all their actions. Thus we are told that "fire, hail, snow, vapor, and stormy wind, fulfill his word" in the course of nature; and even so the most impetuous and disorderly passions of men that are under no restraint from themselves are yet perfectly subject to the dominion of Jehovah. They carry his commission, they obey his orders, they are limited and restrained by his authority, and they conspire with everything else in promoting his glory. There is the greater need to take notice of this that men are not generally sufficienctly aware of the distinction between the law of God and his purpose; they are apt to suppose that as the temper of the sinner is contrary to the one, so the outrages of the sinner are able to defeat the other, than which nothing can be more false. The truth is plainly asserted and nobly expressed by the psalmist in the text, "Surely the wrath of man shall praise thee; the remainder of wrath shalt thou restrain."

This psalm was evidently composed as a song of praise for some signal victory obtained, which was at the same time a remarkable deliverance from threatening danger. The author was one or other of the later prophets, and the occasion probably the unsuccessful assault of Jerusalem by the army of Sennacherib king of Assyria in the days of Hezekiah. Great was the insolence and boasting of his generals and servants against the city of the living God, as may be seen in the thirty-sixth chapter of Isaiah. Yet it pleased God to destroy their enemies, and by his own immediate interposition to grant them deliverance. Therefore the Psalmist says in the fifth and sixth verses of the psalm, "The stout-hearted are spoiled, they have slept their sleep. None of the men of might have found their hands. At thy rebuke, O God of Jacob! both the chariot and the horse are cast into a deep sleep." After a few more remarks to the same purpose, he draws the inference, or makes the reflection in the text, "Surely the wrath of man shall praise thee; the remainder of wrath shalt thou restrain," which may be paraphrased thus, the fury and injustice of oppressors shall bring in a tribute of praise to thee; the influence of thy righteous providence shall be clearly discerned; the countenance and support thou wilt give to thine own people shall be gloriously illustrated; thou shalt set the bounds which the boldest cannot pass.

I am sensible, my brethren, that the time and occasion of this psalm may seem to be in one respect ill suited to the interesting circumstances of this country at present. It was composed after the victory was obtained; whereas we are now but putting on the harness and entering upon an important contest, the length of which it is impossible to foresee, and the issue of which it will perhaps be thought presumption to foretell. But as the truth with respect to God's moral government is the same and unchangeable; as the issue in the case of Sennacherib's invasion did but lead the prophet to acknowledge it, our duty and interest conspire in calling upon us to improve it. And I have chosen to insist upon it on this day of solemn humiliation, as it will probably help us to a clear and explicit view of what should be the chief subject of our prayers and endeavors, as well as the great object of our hope and trust in our present situation.

The truth, then, asserted in this text, which I propose to illustrate and improve, is that all the disorderly passions of men, whether exposing the innocent to private injury or whether they are the arrows of divine judgment in public calamity, shall in the end be to the praise of God; or, to apply it more particularly to the present state of the American colonies and the plague of war, the ambition of mistaken princes, the cunning and cruelty of oppressive and corrupt ministers, and even the inhumanity of brutal soldiers, however dreadful, shall finally promote the glory of God, and in the meantime while the storm continues, his mercy and kindness shall appear in prescribing bounds to their rage and fury.

In discoursing on this subject, it is my intention, through the assistance of divine grace, (1) to point out to you in some particulars how the wrath of man praises God; (2) to apply these principles to our present situation, by inferences of truth for your instruction and comfort and by suitable exhortations to duty in the important crisis.

In the first place, I am to point out to you in some particulars how the wrath of man praises God. I say in some instances because it is far from being in my power either to mention or explain the whole. There is an unsearchable depth in the divine counsels which it is impossible for us to penetrate. It is the duty of every good man to place the most unlimited confidence in divine wisdom and to believe that those measures of providence that are most unintelligible to him are yet planned with the same skill and directed to the same great purposes as others, the reason and tendency of which he can explain in the clearest manner. But where revelation and experience enables us to discover the wisdom, equity, or mercy of divine providence, nothing can be more delightful or profitable to a serious mind, and therefore I beg your attention to the following remarks.

1. In the first place, the wrath of man praises God as it is an example and illustration of divine truth and clearly points out the corruption of our nature, which is the foundation stone of the doctrine of redemption. Nothing can be more absolutely necessary to true religion than a clear and full conviction of the sinfulness or our nature and state. Without this there can be neither repentance in the sinner, nor humility in the believer. Without this all that is said in scripture of the wisdom and mercy of God in providing a Saviour is without force and without meaning. Justly does our Saviour say, "The whole have no need of a physician, but those that are sick. I came not to call the righteous, but sinners to repentance." Those who are not sensible that they are sinners

will treat every exhortation to repentance and every offer of mercy with disdain or defiance.

But where can we have a more affecting view of the corruption of our nature than in the wrath of man when exerting itself in oppression, cruelty, and blood? It must be owned, indeed, that this truth is abundantly manifest in times of the greatest tranquility. Others may, if they please, treat the corruption of our nature as a chimera; for my part, I see it everywhere, and I feel it every day. All the disorders in human society, and the greatest part even of the unhappiness we are exposed to, arises from the envy, malice, covetousness, and other lusts of man. If we and all about us were just what we ought to be in all respects, we should not need to go any further for heaven, for it would be upon earth. But war and violence present a spectacle still more awful. How affecting is it to think that the lust of domination should so rarely be satisfied with their own possessions and acquisitions, or even with the benefit that would arise from mutual service, but should look upon the happiness and tranquility of others as an obstruction to their own? That, as if the great law of nature were not enough, "Dust thou art, and to dust thou shalt return," they should be so furiously set for the destruction of each other? It is shocking to think since the first murder of Abel by his brother Cain what havoc has been made of man by man in every age. What is it that fills the pages of history but the wars and contentions of princes and empires? What vast numbers has lawless ambition brought into the field and delivered as a prey to the destructive sword?

If we dwell a little upon the circumstances, they become deeply affecting. The mother bears a child with pain, rears him by the laborious attendance of many years; yet in the prime of life, in the vigor of health and bloom of beauty, in a moment he is cut down by the dreadful instruments of death. "Every battle of the warrior is with confused noise and garments rolled in blood," but the horror of the scene is not confined to the field of slaughter. Few go there unrelated, or fall unlamented; in every hostile encounter, what must be the impression upon the relations of the deceased? The bodies of the dead can only be seen, or the cries of the dying heard for a single day, but many days shall not put an end to the mourning of a parent for a beloved son, the joy and support of his age, or of the widow and helpless offspring for a father taken away in the fullness of health and vigor.

But if this may be justly said of all wars between man and man, what shall we be able to say that is suitable to the abhorred scene of civil war between citizen and citizen? How deeply affecting is it that those who are the same in complexion, the same in blood, in language, and in religion, should notwithstanding butcher one another with unrelenting rage, and glory in the deed? That men should lay waste the fields of their fellow subjects with whose provision they themselves had been often fed, and consume with devouring fire those houses in which they had often found a hospitable shelter.

These things are apt to overcome a weak mind with fear or overwhelm it with sorrow, and in the greatest number are apt to excite the highest indignation and kindle up a spirit of revenge. If this last has no other tendency than to direct and invigorate the measures of self-defense, I do not take upon me to blame it; on the contrary, I call it necessary and laudable.

But what I mean at this time to prove by the preceding reflections and wish to impress on your minds is the depravity of our nature. James 4:1, "From whence come wars and fighting among you? Come they not hence even from your lusts that war in your members?" Men of lax and corrupt principles take great delight in speaking to the praise of human nature and extolling its dignity without distinguishing what it was, at its first creation, from what it is in its present fallen state. These fine speculations are very grateful to a worldly mind. They are also much more pernicious to uncautious and unthinking youth than even the temptations to a dissolute and sensual life, against which they are fortified by the dictates of natural conscience and a sense of public shame. But I appeal from these visionary reasonings to the history of all ages and the inflexible testimony of daily experience. These will tell us what men have been in their practice, and from thence you may judge what they are by nature while unrenewed. If I am not mistaken, a cool and candid attention either to the past history or present state of the world, but above all to the ravages of lawless power, ought to humble us in the dust. It should at once lead us to acknowlege the just view given us in scripture of our lost state, to desire the happy influence of renewing grace each for ourselves, and to long for the dominion of righteousness and peace when "men shall beat their swords into plow-shares, and their spears into pruning hooks; when nation shall not lift up sword against nation, neither shall they learn war any more" (Mic. 4:3).[1]

1. I cannot help embracing this opportunity of making a remark or two upon a virulent reflection thrown out against this doctrine, in a well known pamphlet, *Common Sense*. The author of that work expresses himself thus: "If the first king of any country was by election, that likewise establishes a precedent for the next; for to say that the right of all future generations is taken away, by the act of the first electors, in their choice not only of a king, but of a family of kings forever, hath no parallel in or out of Scripture, but the doctrine of original sin, which supposes the free will of all men lost in Adam; and from such comparison, and it will admit of no other, hereditary succession can derive no glory. For as in Adam all sinned, and as in the first electors all men obeyed; as in the one all mankind were subject to Satan, and in the other to sovereignty; as our innocence was lost in the first, and our authority in the last; and as both disable us from reassuming some former state and privilege, it unanswerably follows that original sin and hereditary

2. The wrath of man praiseth God, as it is the instrument in his hand for bringing sinners to repentance and for the correction and improvement of his own children. Whatever be the nature of the affliction with which he visits either persons, families, or nations, whatever be the disposition or intention of those whose malice he employs as a scourge; the design on his part is to rebuke men for iniquity, to bring them to repentance, and to promote their holiness and peace. The salutary nature and sanctifying influence of affliction in general is often taken notice of in scripture, both as making a part of the purpose of God and the experience of his saints. Heb. 12:2, "Now, no affliction for the present seemeth to be joyous, but grievous: Nevertheless, afterwards it yieldeth the peaceable fruit of righteousness unto them which are exercised thereby." But what we are particularly led to observe by the subject of this discourse is that the wrath of man, or the violence of the oppressor that praiseth God in this respect, has a peculiar tendency to alarm the secure conscience to convince and humble the obstinate sinner. This is plain from the nature of the thing and from the testimony of experience. Public calamities, particularly the destroying sword, is so awful that it cannot but have a powerful influence in leading men to

---

succession are parallels. Dishonorable rank! Inglorious connection! Yet the most subtle sophist cannot produce a just simile" (*Common Sense*, page 11, Bradfords' edition). Without the shadow of reasoning, he is pleased to represent the doctrine of original sin as an object of contempt or abhorrence. I beg leave to demur a little to the candor, the prudence, and the justice of this proceeding.

Was it modest or candid for a person without name or character to talk in this supercilious manner of a doctrine that has been espoused and defended by many of the greatest and best men that the world ever saw, and makes an essential part of the established creeds and confessions of all the Protestant churches without exception? I thought the grand modern plea had been freedom of sentiment and charitable thoughts of one another. Are so many of us then beyond the reach of this gentleman's charity? I do assure him that such presumption and self-confidence are no recommendation to me, either of his character or sentiments.

Was it prudent, when he was pleading a public cause, to speak in such opprobrious terms of a doctrine which he knew, or ought to have known, was believed and professed by, I suppose, a great majority of very different denominations. Is this gentleman ignorant of human nature, as well as an enemy to the Christian faith? Are men so little tenacious of their religious sentiments, whether true or false? The prophet thought otherwise, who said, "Hath a nation changed their gods which yet are no gods?" Was it the way to obtain the favor of the public to despise what they hold sacred? Or shall we suppose this author so astonishingly ignorant as to think that all men now whose favor is worth asking have given up the doctrine of the New Testament? If he does, he is greatly mistaken.

In fine, I ask, where was the justice of this proceeding? Is there so little to be said for the doctrine of original sin that it is not to be refuted but despised? Is the state of the world such as to render this doctrine not only false but incredible? Has the fruit been of such a quality as to exclude all doubts of the goodness of the tree? On the contrary, I cannot help being of opinion that such has been the visible state of the world in every age as cannot be accounted for on any other principles than what we learn from the word of God, that the imagination of the heart of man is only evil from his youth, and that continually (Gen. 6:5; 8:21).

consider the presence and the power of God. It threatens them not only
in themselves, but touches them in all that is dear to them, whether
relations or possessions. The prophet Isaiah says, Is. 26:8, 9. "Yea, in
the way of thy judgments, O Lord, have we waited for thee—for when
thy judgments are in the earth, the inhabitants of the world will learn
righteousness." He considers it as the most powerful means of alarming
the secure and subduing the obstinate. Is. 26:2, "Lord when thy hand
is lifted up, they will not see, but they shall see and be ashamed for their
envy at the people, yea the fire of thine enemies shall devour them." It
is also sometimes represented as a symptom of a hopeless and irrecover-
able state when public judgments have no effect. Thus says the prophet
Jeremiah, Jer. 5:3. "O Lord, are not thine eyes upon the truth? Thou
hast stricken them, but they have not grieved; thou hast consumed
them, but they have refused to receive correction: they have made their
faces harder than a rock, they have refused to return." We can easily
see in the history of the children of Israel, how severe strokes brought
them to submission and penitence. Ps. 78:34, 35, "When he slew them,
then they sought him, and they returned and inquired early after God,
and they remembered that God was their rock, and the high God their
redeemer."

Both nations in general and private persons are apt to grow remiss
and lax in a time of prosperity and seeming security, but when their
earthly comforts are endangered or withdrawn, it lays them under a
kind of necessity to seek for something better in their place. Men must
have comfort from one quarter or another. When earthly things are in
a pleasing and promising condition, too many are apt to find their rest
and be satisfied with them as their only portion. But when the vanity
and passing nature of all created comfort is discovered, they are compelled to look for something more durable as well as valuable. What
therefore can be more to the praise of God than that when a whole
people have forgotten their resting place, when they have abused their
privileges and despised their mercies, they should by distress and suffering be made to harken to the rod and return to their duty?

There is an inexpressible depth and variety in the judgments of God,
as in all his other works; but we may lay down this as a certain principle
that if there were no sin, there could be no suffering. Therefore they
are certainly for the correction of sin, or for the trial, illustration, and
perfecting of the grace and virtue of his own people. We are not to
suppose that those who suffer most, or who suffer soonest, are therefore
more criminal than others. Our Saviour himself thought it necessary to
give a caution against this rash conclusion, as we are informed by the
evangelist Luke, Luke 13:1. "There were present at that season some
that told him of the Galileans, whose blood Pilate had mingled with

their sacrifices. And Jesus answering said unto them, suppose ye that these Galileans were sinners above all the Galileans, because they suffered such things? I tell you nay, but except ye repent, ye shall all likewise perish." I suppose we may say with sufficient warrant that it often happens that those for whom God hath designs of the greatest mercy are first brought to the trial that they may enjoy in due time the salutary effect of the unpalatable medicine.

I must also take leave to observe, and I hope no pious humble sufferer will be unwilling to make the application, that there is often a discernible mixture of sovereignty and righteousness in providential dispensations. It is the prerogative of God to do what he will with his own, but he often displays his justice itself by throwing into the furnace those who, though they may not be visibly worse than others, may yet have more to answer for, as having been favored with more distinguished privileges, both civil and sacred. It is impossible for us to make a just and full comparision of the character either of persons or nations, and it would be extremely foolish for any to attempt it, either for increasing their own security or impeaching the justice of the Supreme Ruler. Let us therefore neither forget the truth, nor go beyond it. "His mercy fills the earth." He is also "known by the judgment which he executeth." The wrath of man in its most tempestuous rage fulfills his will and finally promotes the good of his chosen.

3. The wrath of man praiseth God, as he sets bounds to it or restrains it by his providence, and sometimes makes it evidently a means of promoting and illustrating his glory.

There is no part of divine providence in which a greater beauty and majesty appears than when the Almighty Ruler turns the counsels of wicked men into confusion and makes them militate against themselves. If the psalmist may be thought to have had a view in this text to the truths illustrated in the two former observations, there is no doubt at all that he had a particular view to this, as he says in the latter part of the verse, "the remainder of wrath shalt thou restrain." The scripture abounds with instances in which the designs of oppressors were either wholly disappointed or in execution fell far short of the malice of their intention, and in some they turned out to the honor and happiness of the persons or the people whom they were intended to destroy. We have an instance of the first of these in the history to which my text relates.[2] We have also an instance in Esther, in which the most mischievous designs of Haman, the Son of Hammedatha the Agagite, against Mordecai the Jew and the nation from which he sprung turned out at

2. The matter is fully stated and reasoned upon by the prophet Isaiah, ch. 10, from the 5th to the 49th verse.

last to his own destruction, the honor of Mordecai, and the salvation and peace of his people.

From the New Testament I will make choice of that memorable event on which the salvation of believers in every age rests as its foundation, the death and sufferings of the Son of God. This the great adversary and all his agents and instruments prosecuted with unrelenting rage. When they had blackened him with slander, when they scourged him with shame, when they had condemned him in judgment and nailed him to the cross, how could they help esteeming their victory complete? But oh the unsearchable wisdom of God! They were but perfecting the great design laid for the salvation of sinners. Our blessed Redeemer by his death finished his work, overcame principalities and powers, and made a show of them openly, triumphing over them in this cross. With how much justice do the apostles and their company offer this doxology to God,

They lift up their voice with one accord, and said, Lord thou art God which hast made heaven and earth, and the sea, and all that in them is; Who by the mouth of thy servant David hast said, Why did the Heathen rage, and the people imagine vain things? The kings of the earth stood up, and the rulers were gathered together against the Lord, and against his Christ. For of a truth, against thy holy Child Jesus, whom thou hast anointed, both Herod and Pontius Pilate, with the Gentiles, and the people of Israel were gathered together, for to do whatsoever thy hand and thy counsel determined before to be done. (Acts 4:24, 28)

In all after ages, in conformity to this, the deepest laid contrivances of the prince of darkness have turned out to the confusion of their author; and I know not but considering his malice and pride, this perpetual disappointment and the superiority of divine wisdom may be one great source of his suffering and torment. The cross hath still been the banner of truth under which it hath been carried through the world. Persecution has been but as the furnace to the gold, to purge it of its dross, to manifest its purity, and increase its lustre. It was taken notice of very early that the blood of the martyrs was the seed of Christianity; the more abundantly it was shed, the more plentifully did the harvest grow.

So certain has this appeared that the most violent infidels both of early and later ages have endeavored to account for it, and have observed that there is a spirit of obstinacy in man which inclines him to resist violence, and that severity doth but increase opposition, be the cause what it will. They suppose that persecution is equally proper to propagate truth and error. This though in part true will by no means generally hold. Such an apprehension, however, gave occasion to a glorious triumph of divine providence of an opposite kind, which I must shortly relate to you. One of the Roman emperors, Julian, surnamed the apostate, perceiving how impossible it was to suppress the gospel by violence, endeavored to extinguish it by neglect and scorn. He left the Christians unmolested for some time, but gave all manner of encouragement to those of opposite principles, and particularly to the Jews, out of hatred to the Christians; and that he might bring public disgrace upon the Galileans, as he affected to style them, he encouraged the Jews to rebuild the temple of Jerusalem and visibly refute the prophecy of Christ that it should lie under perpetual desolation. But this profane attempt was so signally frustrated that it served as much as any one circumstance to spread the glory of our Redeemer and establish the faith of his saints. It is affirmed by some ancient authors, particularly by Ammianus Marcellinus, a heathen historian, that fire came out of the earth and consumed the workmen when laying the foundation. But in whatever way it was prevented, it is beyond all controversy from the concurring testimony of heathens and Christians that little or no progress was ever made in it, and that in a short time, it was entirely defeated.

It is proper here to observe that at the time of the Reformation when religion began to revive, nothing contributed more to facilitate its reception and increase its progress than the violence of its persecutors. Their cruelty and the patience of the sufferers naturally disposed men to examine and weigh the cause to which they adhered with so much constancy and resolution. At the same time also, when they were persecuted in one city, they fled to another and carried the discoveries of Popish fraud to every part of the world. It was by some of those who were persecuted in Germany that the light of the Reformation was brought so early into Britain.

The power of divine providence appears with the most distinguished lustre when small and inconsiderable circumstances and sometimes the weather and seasons have defeated the most formidable armaments and frustrated the best concerted expeditions. Near two hundred years ago, the monarchy of Spain was in the height of its power and glory and determined to crush the interest of the Reformation. They sent out a powerful armament against Britain giving it ostentatiously, and in my opinion profanely, the name of the Invincible Armada. But it pleased God so entirely to discomfit it by tempests that a small part of it returned home, though no British force had been opposed to it at all.

We have a remarkable instance of the influence of small circumstances in providence in the English history. The two most remarkable persons in the civil wars had earnestly desired to withdraw themselves from the contentions of the times, Mr. Hampden and Oliver Cromwell. They had actually taken their passage in a ship for New England when by an arbitrary order of council they were compelled to remain at home. The consequence of this was that one of them was the soul of the republican opposition to monarchical usurpation during the civil wars, and the other in the course of that contest was the great instrument of bringing the tyrant to the block.

The only other historical remark I am to make is that the violent persecution which many eminent Christians met with in England from their brethren, who called themselves Protestants, drove them in great numbers to a distant part of the world where the light of the gospel and true religion were unknown. Some of the American settlements, particularly those in New England, were chiefly made by them; and as they carried the knowledge of Christ to the dark places of the earth, so they continue themselves in as great a degree of purity, of faith, and strictness of practice, or rather a greater than is to be found in any protestant church now in the world. Does not the wrath of man in this instance praise God? Was not the accuser of the brethren who stirs up their enemies thus taken in his own craftiness, and his kingdom shaken by the very means which he employed to establish it.[3] I proceed now to the second general head, which was to apply the principles illustrated above to our present situation, by inferences of truth for your instruction and comfort and by suitable exhortations to duty in this important crisis. And,

1. In the first place, I would take the opportunity on this occasion and from this subject to press every hearer to a sincere concern for his own soul's salvation. There are times when the mind may be expected to be more awake to divine truth, and the conscience more open to the arrows of conviction than at others. A season of public judgment is of this kind, as appears from what has been already said. That curiosity and attention at least are raised in some degree is plain from the unusual throng of this assembly. Can you have a clearer view of the sinfulness of your nature than when the rod of the oppressor is lifted up, and when you see men putting on the habit of the warrior and collecting on every hand the weapons of hostility and instruments of death? I do not blame your ardor in preparing for the resolute defense of your temporal rights. But consider, I beseech you, the truly infinite importance of the

3. Lest this should be thought a temporizing compliment to the people of New England, who have been the first sufferers in the present contest and have set so noble an example of invincible fortitude in withstanding the violence of oppression, I think it proper to observe that the whole paragraph is copied from a sermon on Psal. 74:22, prepared and preached in Scotland, in the month of August, 1758.

salvation of your souls. Is it of much moment whether you and your children shall be rich or poor, at liberty or in bonds? Is it of much moment whether this beautiful country shall increase in fruitfulness from year to year being cultivated by active industry and possessed by independent freemen, or the scanty produce of the neglected fields shall be eaten up by hungry publicans while the timid owner trembles at the tax gatherer's approach? And is it of less moment my brethren whether you shall be the heirs of glory or the heirs of hell? Is your state on earth for a few fleeting years of so much moment? And is it of less moment what shall be your state through endless ages? Have you assembled together willingly to hear what shall be said on public affairs and to join in imploring the blessing of God on the counsels and arms of the united colonies, and can you be unconcerned what shall become of you forever when all the monuments of human greatness shall be laid in ashes, for "the earth itself and all the works that are therein shall be burnt up."

Wherefore my beloved hearers as the ministry of reconciliation is committed to me, I beseech you in the most earnest manner to attend to "the things that belong to your peace before they are hid from your eyes." How soon and in what manner a seal shall be set upon the character and state of every person here present it is impossible to know, for he who only can know does not think proper to reveal it. But you may rest assured that there is no time more suitable, and there is none so safe, as that which is present, since it is wholly uncertain whether any other shall be yours. Those who shall first fall in battle have not many more warnings to receive. There are some few daring and hardened sinners who despise eternity itself and set their Maker at defiance, but the far greater number by staving off their convictions to a more convenient season have been taken unprepared, and thus eternally lost. I would therefore earnestly press the apostle's exhortation, 2 Cor. 6:1, 2. "We then, as workers together with him, beseech you also, that ye receive not the grace of God in vain: For he saith, I have heard thee in a time accepted, and in the day of salvation have I succoured thee: Behold, now is the accepted time; behold, now is the day of salvation."

Suffer me to beseech you, or rather to give you warning, not to rest satisfied with a form of godliness, denying the power thereof. There can be no true religion till there be a discovery of your lost state by nature and practice and an unfeigned acceptance of Christ Jesus as he is offered in the gospel. Unhappy they who either despise his mercy or are ashamed of his cross! Believe it, "There is no salvation in any other. There is no other name under heaven given amongst men by which we must be saved." Unless you are united to him by a lively faith, not the resentment of a haughty monarch, but the sword of divine justice hangs over you, and the fulness of divine vengeance shall speedily overtake you. I do not speak this only to the heaven daring profligate or groveling sensualist but to every insensible secure sinner, to all those however decent and orderly in their civil deportment who live to themselves and have their part and portion in this life, in fine to all who are yet in a state of nature, for "except a man be born again, he cannot see the kingdom of God." The fear of man may make you hide your profanity: prudence and experience may make you abhor intemperance and riot; as you advance in life, one vice may supplant another and hold its place; but nothing less than the sovereign grace of God can produce a saving change of heart and temper or fit you for his immediate presence.

2. From what has been said upon this subject, you may see what ground there is to give praise to God for his favors already bestowed on us respecting the public cause. It would be a criminal inattention not to observe the singular interposition of Providence hitherto in behalf of the American colonies. It is however impossibe for me in a single discourse, as well as improper at this time, to go through every step of our past transactions; I must therefore content myself with a few remarks. How many discoveries have been made of the designs of enemies in Britain and among ourselves in a manner as unexpected to us as to them and in such season as to prevent their effect? What surprising success has attended our encounters in almost every instance? Has not the boasted discipline of regular and veteran soldiers been turned into confusion and dismay before the new and maiden courage of freemen in defense of their property and right? In what great mercy has blood been spared on the side of this injured country? Some important victories in the south have been gained with so little loss that enemies will probably think it has been dissembled, as many even of ourselves thought till time rendered it undeniable. But these were comparatively of small moment. The signal advantage we have gained by the evacuation of Boston, and the shameful flight of the the army and navy of Britain, was brought about without the loss of a man. To all this we may add that the counsels of our enemies have been visibly confounded so that I believe I may say with truth that there is hardly any step which they have taken, but it has operated strongly against themselves and been more in our favor than if they had followed a contrary course.

While we give praise to God the supreme disposer of all events for his interposition in our behalf, let us guard against the dangerous error of trusting in or boasting of an *arm of flesh*. I could earnestly wish that while our arms are crowned with success, we might content ourselves with a modest ascription of it to the power of the Highest. It has given me great uneasiness to read some ostentatious, vaunting expressions in our newspapers, though happily I think much restrained of late. Let us not return to them again. If I am not mistaken, not only the holy scriptures in general and the truths of the glorious gospel in particular, but the whole course of providence seem intended to abase the pride of man and lay the vainglorious in the dust. How many instances does history furnish us with of those who after exulting over and despising their enemies were signally and shamefully defeated.[4] The truth is, I believe, the remark may be applied universally, and we may say that through the whole frame of nature and the whole system of human life that which promises most, performs the least. The flowers of finest color seldom have the sweetest fragrance. The trees of quickest growth or fairest form are seldom of the greatest value or duration. Deep waters move with least noise. Men who think most are seldom talkative. And I think it holds as much in war as in anything that every boaster is a coward.

Pardon me, my brethren, for insisting so much upon this, which may seem but an immaterial circumstance. It is my opinion of very great moment. I look upon ostentation and confidence to be a sort of outrage upon Providence, and when it becomes general and infuses itself into the spirit of a people, it is a forerunner of destruction. How does Goliath, the champion armed in a most formidable manner, express his disdain of David the strippling with his sling and his stone, I Sam. 14:42, 43, 44, 45. "And when the Philistine looked about and saw David, he disdained him: for he was but a youth, and ruddy, and of a fair countenance. And the Philistine said unto David, Am I a dog, that thou comest to me with staves? And the Philistine cursed David by his gods, and the Philistine said to David, come to me, and I will give thy flesh unto the fowls of the air, and to the beasts of the field." But how just and modest the reply? Then "said David to the Philistine, thou comest to me with a sword and with a spear, and with a shield, but I come unto thee in the name of the Lord of hosts, the God of the armies of Israel, whom thou hast defied." I was well pleased with a remark of this kind thirty years ago in a pamphlet,[5] in which it was observed that there was a great deal of profane ostentation in the names given to ships of war, as the *Victory*, the *Valient*, the *Thunderer*, the *Dreadnought*, the *Terrible*, the *Firebrand*, the *Furnace*, the *Lightning*, the *Infernal*, and many more of the same kind. This the author considered as a symptom of the

---

4. There is no story better known in British history than that the officers of the French army the night preceding the battle of Agincourt played at dice for English prisoners before they took them, and the next day were taken by them.

5. Britain's Remembrancer.

national character and manners very unfavorable and not likely to obtain the blessing of the God of Heaven.[6]

3. From what has been said you may learn what encouragement you have to put your trust in God and hope for his asistance in the present important conflict. He is the Lord of hosts, great in might, and strong in battle. Whoever hath his countenance and approbation shall have the best at last. I do not mean to speak prophetically, but agreeably to the analogy of faith and the principles of God's moral government. Some have observed that true religion and in her train dominion, riches, literature, and arts have taken their course in a slow and gradual manner from east to west since the earth was settled after the flood, and from thence forebode the future glory of America. I leave this as a matter rather of conjecture than certainty, but observe that if your cause is just, if your principles are pure, and if your conduct is prudent, you need not fear the multitude of opposing hosts.

If your cause is just, you may look with confidence to the Lord and entreat him to plead it as his own. You are all my witnesses that this is the first time of my introducing any political subject into the pulpit. At this season however, it is not only lawful but necessary, and I willingly embrace the opportunity of declaring my opinion without any hesitation that the cause in which America is now in arms is the cause of justice, of liberty, and of human nature. So far as we have hitherto proceeded, I am satisfied that the confederacy of the colonies has not been the effect of pride, resentment, or sedition, but of a deep and general conviction that our civil and religious liberties, and consequently in a great measure the temporal and eternal happiness of us and our posterity, depended on the issue. The knowledge of God and his truths have from the beginning of the world been chiefly, if not entirely, confined to those parts of the earth where some degree of liberty and political justice were to be seen; and great were the difficulties with which they had to struggle from the imperfection of human society and the unjust decisions of usurped authority. There is not a single instance in history

---

6. I am sensible that one or two of these were ships taken from the French, which brought their names with them. But the greatest number had their names imposed in England, and I cannot help observing that the *Victory,* often celebrated as the finest ship ever built in Britain, was lost in the night without a storm by some unknown accident, and about twelve hundred persons, many of them of the first families in the nation, were buried with it in the deep. I do not mean to infer anything from this but that we ought to live under the practical persuasion of what no man will doctrinally deny, that there is no warring with the elements or him who directs their force, that he is able to write disappointment on the wisest human schemes, and by the word of his power to frustrate the efforts of the greatest monarch upon earth.

in which civil liberty was lost, and religious liberty preserved entire. If therefore we yield up our temporal property, we at the same time deliver the conscience into bondage.

You shall not, my brethren, hear from me in the pulpit what you have never heard from me in conversation, I mean railing at the king personally, or even his ministers and the Parliament, and people of Britain as so many barbarous savages. Many of their actions have probably been worse than their intentions. That they should desire unlimited dominion if they can obtain or preserve it is neither new nor wonderful. I do not refuse submission to their unjust claims because they are corrupt or profligate, although probably many of them are so, but because they are men, and therefore liable to all the selfish bias inseparable from human nature. I call this claim unjust, of making laws to bind us in all cases whatsoever, because they are separated from us, independent of us, and have an interest in opposing us. Would any man who could prevent it give up his estate, person, and family to the disposal of his neighbor, although he had liberty to choose the wisest and the best master? Surely not. This is the true and proper hinge of the controversy between Great Britain and America. It is however to be added that such is their distance from us that a wise and prudent administration of our affairs is as impossible as the claim of authority is unjust. Such is and must be their ignorance of the state of things here, so much time must elapse before an error can be seen and remedied, and so much injustice and partiality must be expected from the arts and misrepresentation of interested persons, that for these colonies to depend wholly upon the legislature of Great Britain would be like many other oppressive connections, injury to the master and ruin to the slave.

The management of the war itself on their part would furnish new proof of this, if any were needful. Is it not manifest with what absurdity and impropriety they have conducted their own designs? We had nothing so much to fear as dissension, and they have by wanton and unnecessary cruelty forced us into union. At the same time to let us see what we have to expect and what would be the fatal consequence of unlimited submission, they have uniformly called those acts *lenity*, which filled this whole continent with resentment and horror. The ineffable disdain expressed by our fellow subject in saying "that he would not harken to America, till she was at his feet" has armed more men and inspired more deadly rage than could have been done by laying waste a whole province with fire and sword. Again we wanted not numbers but time, and they sent over handful after handful till we were ready to oppose a multitude greater than they have to send. In fine, if there was one place stronger than the rest and more able and willing to resist, there they made the attack, and left the others till they were dully informed, completely incensed, and fully furnished with every instrument of war.

I mention these things, my brethren, not only as grounds of confidence in God, who can easily overthrow the wisdom of the wise, but as decisive proofs of the impossibility of these great and growing states being safe and happy when every part of their internal polity is dependent on Great Britian. If on account of their distance and ignorance of our situation they could not conduct their own quarrel with propriety for one year, how can they give direction and vigor to every department of our civil constitutions from age to age? There are fixed bounds to every human thing. When the branches of a tree grow very large and weighty, they fall off from the trunk. The sharpest sword will not pierce when it cannot reach. And there is a certain distance from the seat of government where an attempt to rule will either produce tyranny and helpless subjection, or provoke resistance and effect a separation.

I have said, if your principles are pure—the meaning of this is if your present opposition to the claims of the British ministry does not arise from a seditious and turbulent spirit or a wanton contempt of legal authority, from a blind and factious attachment to particular persons or parties, or from a selfish rapacious disposition and a desire to turn public confusion to private profit, but from a concern for the interest of your country and the safety of yourselves and your posterity. On this subject I cannot help observing that though it would be a miracle if there were not many selfish persons among us, and discoveries now and then made of mean and interested transactions, yet they have been comparatively inconsiderable both in number and effect. In general, there has been so great a degree of public spirit that we have much more reason to be thankful for its vigor and prevalence than to wonder at the few appearances of dishonesty or disaffection. It would be very uncandid to ascribe the universal ardor that has prevailed among all ranks of men and the spirited exertions in the most distant colonies to anything else than public spirit. Nor was there ever perhaps in history so general a commotion from which religious differences have been so entirely excluded. Nothing of this kind has as yet been heard, except of late in the absurd but malicious and detestable attempts of our few remaining enemies to introduce them. At the same time I must also for the honor of this country observe that though government in the ancient forms has been so long unhinged, and in some colonies not sufficient care taken to substitute another in its place; yet has there been by common consent a much greater degree of order and public peace than men of reflection and experience foretold or expected. From all these circumstances I conclude favorably of the principles of the friends of liberty and do earnestly exhort you to adopt and act upon those which have been described, and resist the influence of every other.

Once more, if to the justice of your cause, and the purity of your principles, you add prudence in your conduct, there will be the greatest reason to hope, by the blessing of God, for prosperity and success. By prudence in conducting this important struggle, I have chiefly in view union, firmness, and patience. Everybody must perceive the absolute necessity of union. It is indeed in everybody's mouth, and therefore instead of attempting to convince you of its importance, I will only caution you against the usual causes of division. If persons of every rank, instead of implicitly complying with the orders of those whom they themselves have chosen to direct, will need judge every measure over again when it comes to be put in execution; if different classes of men intermix their little private views or clashing interest with public affairs and marshal into parties, the merchant against the landholder, and the landholder against the merchant; if local provincial pride and jealousy arise, and you allow yourselves to speak with contempt of the courage, character, manners, or even language of particular places, you are doing a greater injury to the common cause than you are aware of. If such practices are admitted among us, I shall look upon it as one of the most dangerous symptoms, and if they become general, a presage of approaching ruin.

By firmness and patience, I mean a resolute adherence to your duty, and laying your account with many difficulties, as well as occasional disappointments. In a former part of this discourse, I have cautioned you against ostentation and vain glory. Be pleased farther to observe that extremes often beget one another, the same persons who exult extravagantly on success are generally most liable to despondent timidity on every little inconsiderable defeat. Men of this character are the bane and corruption of every society or party to which they belong, but they are especially the ruin of an army if suffered to continue in it. Remember the vicissitude of human things and the usual course of providence. How often has a just cause been reduced to the lowest ebb, and yet when firmly adhered to, has become finally triumphant. I speak this now while the affairs of the colonies are in so prosperous a state lest this propriety itself should render you less able to bear unexpected misfortunes; the sum of the whole is that the blessing of God is only to be looked for by those who are not wanting in the discharge of their own duty. I would neither have you to trust in an arm of flesh, nor sit with folded hands and expect that miracles should be wrought in your defense; this is a sin which is in Scripture styled tempting God. In opposition to it, I would exhort you as Joab did the host of Israel, who, though he does not appear to have had a spotless character throughout, certainly in this instance spoke like a prudent general and a pious man: 2 Sam. 10: 12, "Be of good courage, and let us behave ourselves valiantly for our people and for the cities of our God, and let the Lord do that which is good in his sight."

I shall now conclude this discourse by some exhortations to duty, founded upon the truths which have been illustrated above, and suited to the interesting state of this country at the present time.

1. Suffer me to recommend to you an attention to the public interest of religion, or in other words, zeal for the glory of God and the good of others. I have already endeavored to exhort sinners to repentance; what I have here in view is to point out to you the concern which every good man ought to take in the national character and manners, and the means which he ought to use for promoting public virtue; and bearing down impiety and vice. This is a matter of the utmost moment, and which ought to be well understood, both in its nature and principles. Nothing is more certain than that a general profligacy and corruption of manners make a people ripe for destruction. A good form of government may hold the rotten materials together for some time, but beyond a certain pitch, even the best constitution will be ineffectual, and slavery must ensue. On the other hand, when the manners of a nation are pure, when true religion and internal priciples maintain their vigour, the attemps of the most powerful enemies to oppress them are commonly baffled and disappointed. This will be found equally certain, whether we consider the great principles of God's moral government or the operation and influence of natural causes.

What follows from this? That he is the best friend to American liberty who is most sincere and active in promoting true and undefiled religion, and who sets himself with the greatest firmness to bear down profanity and immorality of every kind. Whoever is an avowed enemy to God, I scruple not to call him an enemy to his country. Do not suppose, my brethren, that I mean to recommend a furious and angry zeal for the circumstantials of religion, or the contentions of one sect with another about their peculiar distinctions. I do not wish you to oppose anybody's religion, but everybody's wickedness. Perhaps there are few surer marks of the reality of religion than when a man feels himself more joined in spirit to a true holy person of a different denomination, than to an irregular liver of his own. It is therefore your duty in this important and critical season to exert yourselves, everyone in his proper sphere, to stem the tide of prevailing vice, to promote the knowledge of God, the reverence of his name and worship, and obedience to his laws.

Perhaps you will ask what it is that you are called to do for this purpose farther than your own personal duty? I answer this itself when taken in its proper extent is not a little. The nature and obligation of visible religion is, I am afraid, little understood and less attended to.

Many, from a real or pretended fear of the imputation of hypocrisy, banish from their conversation and carriage every appearance of respect and submission to the living God. What a weakness and meanness of spirit does it discover for a man to be ashamed in the presence of his fellow sinners, to profess that reverence to almighty God which he inwardly feels; the truth is, he makes himself truly liable to the accusation which he means to avoid. It is as genuine and perhaps a more culpable hypocrisy to appear to have less religion than you really have than to appear to have more. This false shame is a more extensive evil than is commonly apprehended. We contribute constantly, though insensibly, to form each others character and manners; and therefore, the usefulness of a strictly holy and conscientious deportment is not confined to the possessor, but spreads its happy influence to all that are within its reach. I need scarcely add that in proportion as men are distinguished by understanding, literature, age, rank, office, wealth, or any other circumstance, their example will be useful on the one hand, or pernicious on the other.

But I cannot content myself with barely recommending a silent example. There is a dignity in virtue which is entitled to authority, and ought to claim it. In many cases it is the duty of a good man by open reproof and opposition to wage war with profaneness. There is a scripture precept delivered in very singular terms to which I beg your attention: "Thou shalt not hate thy brother in thy heart, but shalt in any wise rebuke him, and not suffer sin upon him." How prone are many to represent reproof as flowing from ill nature and surliness of temper? The Spirit of God, on the contrary, considers it as the effect of inward hatred, or want of genuine love, to forebear reproof when it is necessary or may be useful. I am sensible there may in some cases be a restraint from prudence agreeably to that caution of our Saviour, "Cast not your pearls before swine, lest they trample them under their feet, and turn again and rent you." Of this every man must judge as well as he can for himself, but certainly, either by open reproof or expressive silence or speedy departure from such society, we ought to guard against being partakers of other men's sins.

To this let me add that if all men are bound in some degree, certain classes of men are under peculiar obligations to the discharge of this duty. Magistrates, ministers, parents, heads of families, and those whom age has rendered venerable are called to use their authority and influence for the glory of God and the good of others. Bad men themselves discover an inward conviction of this, for they are often liberal in their reproaches of persons of grave characters or religious profession if they bear with patience the profanity of others. Instead of enlarging on the duty of men in authority in general, I must particularly recommend this matter to those who have the command of soldiers enlisted for the defense of their country. The cause is sacred, and the champions for it ought to be holy. Nothing is more grieving to the heart of a good man than to hear from those who are going to the field the horrid sound of cursing and blasphemy; it cools the ardor of his prayers, as well as abates his confidence and hope in God. Many more circumstances affect me in such a case than I can enlarge upon, or indeed easily enumerate at present; the glory of God, the interest of the deluded sinner, going like a devoted victim and imprecating vengeance on his own head, as well as the cause itself committed to his care. We have sometimes taken the liberty to forebode the downfall of the British empire from the corruption and degeneracy of the people. Unhappily the British soldiers have been distinguished among all the nations in Europe for the most shocking profanity. Shall we then pretend to emulate them in this infernal distinction, or rob them of the horrid privilege? God forbid. Let the officers of the army in every degree remember that as military subjection, while it lasts, is the most complete of any, it is in their power greatly to restrain, if not wholly to banish, this flagrant enormity.

2. I exhort all who are not called to go into the field to apply themselves with the utmost diligence to works of industry. It is in your power by this mean not only to supply the necessities, but to add to the strength of your country. Habits of industry prevailing in a society not only increase its wealth as their immediate effect, but they prevent the introduction of many vices and are intimately connected with sobriety and good morals. Idleness is the mother or nurse of almost every vice; and want, which is its inseparable companion, urges men on to the most abandoned and destructive courses. Industry, therefore, is a moral duty of the greatest moment, absolutely necessary to national prosperity, and the sure way of obtaining the blessing of God. I would also observe that in this, as in every other part of God's government, obedience to his will is as much a natural mean as a meritorious cause of the advantage we wish to reap from it. Industry brings up a firm and hardy race. He who is inured to the labor of the field is prepared for the fatigues of a campaign. The active farmer who rises with the dawn and follows his team or plow must in the end be an overmatch for those effeminate and delicate soldiers who are nursed in the lap of self-indulgence and whose greatest exertion is in the important preparation for and tedious attendance on a masquerade or midnight ball.

3. In the last place, suffer me to recommend to you frugality in your families and every other article of expense. This the state of things among us renders absolutely necessary, and it stands in the most immediate connection both with virtuous industry and active public spirit.

Temperance in meals and moderation and decency in dress, furniture, and equipage have, I think, generally been characteristics of a distinguished patriot. And when the same spirit pervades a people in general, they are fit for every duty and able to encounter the most formidable enemy. The general subject of the preceding discourse has been the wrath of man praising God. If the unjust oppression of your enemies, which withholds from you many of the usual articles of luxury and magnificence, shall contribute to make you clothe yourselves and your children with the works of your own hands and cover your tables with the salutary productions of your own soil, it will be a new illustration of the same truth, and a real happiness to yourselves and your country.

I could wish to have every good thing done from the purest principles and the noblest views. Consider, therefore, that the Christian character, particularly the self-denial of the gospel, should extend to your whole deportment. In the early times of Christianity when adult converts were admitted to baptism, they were asked among other questions, do you renounce the world, its shows, its pomp, and its vanities? I do. The form of this is still preserved in the administration of baptism, where we renounce the devil, the world, and the flesh. This certainly implies not only abstaining from acts of gross intemperance and excess, but a humility of carriage, a restraint and moderation in all your desires. The same thing, as it is suitable to your Christian profession, is also necessary to make you truly independent in yourselves, and to feed the source of liberality and charity to others, or to the public. The riotous and wasteful liver, whose craving appetites make him constantly needy, is and must be subject to many masters, according to the saying of Solomon, "The borrower is servant to the lender." But the frugal and moderate person, who guides his affairs with descretion, is able to assist in public counsels by a free and unbiased judgment, to supply the wants of his poor brethren, and sometimes by his estate and substance to give important aid to a sinking country.

Upon the whole, I beseech you to make a wise improvement of the present threatening aspect of public affairs, and to remember that your duty to God, to your country, to your families, and to yourselves is the same. True religion is nothing else but an inward temper and outward conduct suited to your state and circumstances in providence at any time. And as peace with God and conformity to him adds to the sweetness of created comforts while we possess them, so in times of difficulty and trial, it is in the man of piety and inward principle that we may expect to find the uncorrupted patriot, the useful citizen, and the invincible soldier. God grant that in America true religion and civil liberty may be inseparable and that the unjust attempts to destroy the one, may in the issue tend to the support and establishment of both.

PART OF A SPEECH IN CONGRESS, UPON THE CONFEDERATION

THE ABSOLUTE necessity of union to the vigor and success of those measures on which we are already entered is felt and confessed by every one of us without exception; so far, indeed, that those who have expressed their fears or suspicions of the existing confederacy proving abortive have yet agreed in saying that there must and shall be a confederacy for the purposes of and till the finishing of this war. So far it is well, and so far it is pleasing to hear them express their sentiments. But I entreat gentlemen calmly to consider how far the giving up all hopes of a lasting confederacy among these states for their future security and improvement will have an effect upon the stability and efficacy of even the temporary confederacy, which all acknowledge to be necessary? I am fully persuaded that when it ceases to be generally known that the delegates of the provinces consider a lasting union as impracticable, it will greatly derange the minds of the people and weaken their hands in defense of their country, which they have now undertaken with so much alacrity and spirit. I confess it would to me greatly diminish the glory and importance of the struggle, whether considered as for the rights of mankind in general, or for the prosperity and happiness of this continent in future times.

It would quite depreciate the object of hope, as well as place it at a greater distance. For what would it signify to risk our possessions and shed our blood to set ourselves free from the encroachments and oppression of Great Britain—with a certainty as soon as peace was settled with them of a more lasting war, a more unnatural, more bloody, and much more hopeless war, among the colonies themselves? Some of us consider ourselves as acting for posterity at present, having little expectation of living to see all things fully settled and the good consequences of liberty taking effect. But how much more uncertain the hope of seeing the internal contests of the colonies settled upon a lasting and equitable footing?

One of the greatest dangers I have always considered the colonies as exposed to at present is treachery among themselves, augmented by bribery and corruption from our enemies. But what force would be added to the arguments of seducers if they could say with truth that it was of no consequence whether we succeeded against Great Britain or not; for we must, in the end, be subjected, the greatest part of us, to the power of one or more of the strongest or largest of the American states? And here I would apply the argument which we have so often used against Great Britain—that in all history we see that the slaves of freemen and the subject states of republics have been of all others the most grievously oppressed. I do not think the records of time can produce an instance of slaves treated with so much barbarity as the Helots by the Lacedaemonians, who were the most illustrious champions for liberty in all Greece; or of provinces more plundered and spoiled than the states conquered by the Romans for one hundred years before Caesar's dictatorship. The reason is plain: there are many great men in free states. There were many consular gentlemen in that great republic, who all considered themselves as greater than kings, and must have kingly fortunes, which they had no other way of acquiring but by governments of provinces, which lasted generally but one year and seldom more than two.

In what I have already said, or may say, or any cases I may state, I hope every gentlemen will do me the justice to believe that I have not the most distant view to particular persons or societies, and mean only to reason from the usual course of things and the prejudices inseparable from men as such. And can we help saying that there will be a much greater degree, not only of the corruption of particular persons, but the defection of particular provinces from the present confederacy, if they consider our success itself as only a prelude to a contest of a more dreadful nature, and indeed much more properly a civil war than that which now often obtains a name? Must not small colonies in particular be in danger of saying we must secure ourselves? If the colonies are independent states, separate and disunited, after this war, we may be sure of coming off by the worse. We are in no condition to contend with several of them. Our trade in general, and our trade with them, must be upon such terms as they shall be pleased to prescribe. What will be the consequence of this? Will they not be ready to prefer putting themselves under the protection of Great Britain, France, or Holland, rather than submit to the tyranny of their neighbors, who were lately their equals? Nor would it be at all impossible that they should enter into such rash engagements as would prove their own destruction from a mixture of apprehended necessity and real resentment.

Perhaps it may be thought that breaking off the confederacy and leaving it unfinished after we have entered upon it will be only postponing the duty to some future period? Alas, nothing can exceed the absurdity of that supposition. Does not all history cry out that a common danger is the great and only effectual means of settling difficulties and composing differences. Have we not experienced its efficacy in producing such a degree of union through these colonies as nobody would have prophesied and hardly would have expected?

If therefore at present, when the danger is yet imminent, when it is so far from being over that it is but coming to its height, we shall find it impossible to agree upon the terms of this confederacy; what madness is it to suppose that there ever will be a time, or that circumstances will so change as to make it even probable that it will be done at an after season? Will not the very same difficulties that are in our way be in the way of those who shall come after us? Is it possible that they should be ignorant of them, or inattentive to them? Will they not have the same jealousies of each other, the same attachment to local prejudices and particular interest? So certain is this that I look upon it as on the repentance of a sinner—every day's delay, though it adds to the necessity, yet augments the difficulty and takes from the inclination.

There is one thing that has been thrown out by which some seem to persuade themselves of and others to be more indifferent about the success of a confederacy—that from the nature of men, it is to be expected that a time must come when it will be dissolved and broken in pieces. I am none of those who either deny or conceal the depravity of human nature, till it is purified by the light of truth and renewed by the Spirit of the living God. Yet I apprehend there is not force in the reasoning at all. Shall we establish nothing good because we know it cannot be eternal? Shall we live without government because every constitution has its old age and its period? Because we know that we shall die, shall we take no pains to preserve or lengthen out life? Far from it, sir: it only requires the more watchful attention to settle government upon the best principles and in the wisest manner that it may last as long as the nature of things will admit.

But I beg leave to say something more, though with some risk that it will be thought visionary and romantic. I do expect, Mr. President, a progress, as in every other human art, so in the order and perfection of human society, greater than we have yet seen; and why should we be wanting to ourselves in urging it forward? It is certain, I think, that human science and religion have kept company together and greatly assisted each other's progress in the world. I do not say that intellectual and moral qualities are in the same proportion in particular persons; but they have a great and friendly influence upon one another in societies and larger bodies.

There have been great improvements, not only in human knowledge, but in human nature, the progress of which can be easily traced in history. Everybody is able to look back to the time in Europe when the liberal sentiments that now prevail upon the right of conscience would have been looked upon as absurd. It is but little above two hundred years since that enlarged system called the balance of power took place; and I maintain that it is a greater step from the former disunited and hostile situation of kingdoms and states to their present condition than it would be from their present condition to a state of more perfect and lasting union. It is not impossible that in future times all the states on one quarter of the globe may see it proper by some plan of union to perpetuate security and peace, and sure I am, a well planned confederacy among the states of America may hand down the blessings of peace and public order to many generations. The union of the seven provinces of the Low Countries has never yet been broken, and they are of very different degrees of strength and wealth. Neither have the cantons of Switzerland ever broken among themselves, though there are some of them Protestants and some of them papists by public establishment. Not only so, but these confederacies are seldom engaged in a war with other nations. Wars are generally between monarchs of single states that are large. A confederation of itself keeps war at a distance from the bodies of which it is composed.

For all these reasons, sir, I humbly apprehend that every argument from honor, interest, safety, and necessity conspire in pressing us to a confederacy; and if it be seriously attempted, I hope by the blessing of God upon our endeavors, it will be happily accomplished. . . .

Lectures on
Moral Philosophy

Lecture I

Moral philosophy is that branch of science which treats of the principles
and laws of duty or morals. It is called *philosophy*, because it is an inquiry
into the nature and grounds of moral obligation by reason, as distinct
from revelation.

Hence arises a question, is it lawful, and is it safe or useful to separate
moral philosophy from religion? It will be said it is either the same or
different from revealed truth; if the same, unnecessary—if different,
false and dangerous.

An author of New England, says moral philosophy is just reducing
infidelity to a system. But however specious the objections, they will be
found at bottom not solid. If the Scripture is true, the discoveries of
reason cannot be contrary to it; and therefore, it has nothing to fear
from that quarter. And as we are certain it can do no evil, so there is a
probability that it may do much good. There may be an illustration and
confirmation of the inspired writings, from reason and observation,
which will greatly add to their beauty and force.

The noble and eminent improvements in natural philosophy which
have been made since the end of the last century have been far from
hurting the interest of religion; on the contrary, they have greatly
promoted it. Why should it not be the same with moral philosophy,
which is indeed nothing else but the knowledge of human nature? It is
true that infidels do commonly proceed upon pretended principles of
reason. But as it is impossible to hinder them from reasoning on this
subject, the best way is to meet them upon their own ground and to
show from reason itself the fallacy of their principles. I do not know
anything that serves more for the support of religion than to see from
the different and opposite systems of philosophers that there is nothing
certain in their schemes but what is coincident with the word of God.

Some there are, and perhaps more in the present than any former
age, who deny the law of nature and say that all such sentiments as have

been usually ascribed to the law of nature are from revelation and tradition.

We must distinguish here between the light of nature and the law of nature. By the first is to be understood what we can or do discover by our own powers without revelation or tradition; by the second, that which, when discovered, can be made appear to be agreeable to reason and nature.

There have been some very shrewd and able writers of late, viz. Dr. Willson of New Castle and Mr. Ricalton of Scotland, who have written against the light of nature showing that the first principles of knowledge are taken from information. That nothing can be supposed more rude and ignorant, than man without instruction. That when men have been brought up so, they have scarcely been superior to brutes. It is very difficult to be precise upon this subject and to distinguish the discoveries of reason from the exercise of it. Yet I think, admitting all or the greatest part of what such contend for, we may notwithstanding consider how far anything is consonant to reason, or may be proven by reason; though perhaps reason if left to itself would never have discovered it.

Dr. Clark was one of the greatest champions for the law of nature, but it is only since his time that the shrewd opposers of it have appeared. The Hutchinsonians (so called from Hutchinson of England) insist that not only all moral, but also all natural knowledge comes from revelation, the true system of the world, true chronology, all human arts, etc. In this, as is usual with most other classes of men, they carry their nostrum to extravagance. I am of the opinion that the whole Scripture is perfectly agreeable to sound philosophy, yet it was never intended to teach us everything. The political law of the Jews contains many noble principles of equity and excellent examples to future lawgivers, yet it was so local and peculiar that certainly it was never intended to be immutable and universal.

It would be more just and useful to say that all simple and original discoveries have been the production of Providence, and not the invention of man. On the whole, it seems reasonable to make moral philosophy, in the sense above explained, a subject of study. And indeed let men think what they will of it, they ought to acquaint themselves with it. They must know what it is, if they mean even to show that it is false.

The Division of the Subject

Moral philosophy is divided into two great branches, ethics and politics; to this some add jurisprudence, though this may be considered as a part of politics.

Ethics relate to personal duties, politics to the constitution, government, and rights of societies, and jurisprudence to the administration of justice in constituted states.

It seems a point agreed upon that the principles of duty and obligation must be drawn from the nature of man. That is to say, if we can discover how his Maker formed him, or for what he intended him, that certainly is what he ought to be.

The knowledge of human nature, however, is either perplexed and difficult of itself, or hath been made so by the manner in which writers in all ages have treated it. Perhaps this circumstance itself is a strong presumption of the truth of the Scripture doctrine of the depravity and corruption of our nature. Supposing this depravity, it must be one great cause of difficulty and confusion in giving an account of human nature as the work of God.

This I take to be indeed the case with the greatest part of our moral and theological knowledge.

Those who deny this depravity will be apt to plead for everything or for many things as dictates of nature which are in reality propensities of nature in its present state, but at the same time the fruit and evidence of its departure from its original purity. It is by the remaining power of natural conscience that we must endeavor to detect and oppose these errors.

(1) We may consider man very generally in his species as distinct from and superior to the other creatures, and what it is in which the difference truly consists; (2) as an individual, what are the parts which constitute his nature.

Philosophers have generally attempted to assign the precise distinction between men and the other animals, but when endeavoring to bring it to one peculiar incommunicable characteristic, they have generally contradicted one another and sometimes disputed with violence and rendered the thing more uncertain.

The difficulty of fixing upon a precise criterion only serves to show that in man we have an example of what we see also everywhere else, viz. a beautiful and insensible gradation from one thing to another so that the highest of the inferior is, as it were, connected and blended with the lowest of the superior class. Birds and beasts are connected by some species, so that you will find it hard to say whether they belong to the one or the other. So indeed it is in the whole vegetable as well as animal kingdom. (1) Some say men are distinguished from brutes by reason, and certainly this, either in kind or degree, is the most honorable of our distinctions. (2) Others say that many brutes give strong signs of reason, as dogs, horses and elephants, but that man is distinguished by memory and foresight; but I apprehend that these are upon the same footing with reason. If there are some glimmerings of reason in the brute creation, there are also manifest proofs of memory and some of foresight. (3) Some have thought it proper to distinguish man from the inferior creatures by the use of speech, no other creatures having an articulate language. Here again we are obliged to acknowledge that our distinction is chiefly the excellence and fullness of articulate discourse; for brutes have certainly the art of making one another understand many things by sound. (4) Some have said that man is not completely distinguished by any of these, but by a sense of religion. And I think it must be admitted that of piety or a sense of a Supreme Being, there is not any trace to be seen in the inferior creatures. The stories handed about by weak-minded persons, or retailed by credulous authors, of respect in them to churches or sacred persons are to be disdained as wholly fabulous and visionary. (5) There have been some who have said that man is distinguished from the brutes by a sense of *ridicule*.

The whole creation (says a certain author) is grave except man; no one laughs but himself. There is something whimsical in fixing upon this as the criterion, and it does not seem to set us in a very respectable light. Perhaps it is not improper to smile upon the occasion and to say that if this sentiment is embraced, we shall be obliged to confess kindred with the apes, who are certainly themselves possessed of a risible faculty, as well as qualified to excite laughter in us. On the whole there seems no necessity of fixing upon some one criterion to the exclusion of others.

There is a great and apparent distinction between man and the inferior animals, not only in the beauty of his form, which the poet takes notice of *Os homini sublime dedit*, etc., but also in reason, memory, reflection, and the knowledge of God and a future state.

A general distinction, which deserves particularly to be taken notice of in moral disquisitions, is that man is evidently made to be guided and protected from dangers and supplied with what is useful more by reason, and brutes more by instinct.

It is not very easy and perhaps not necessary to explain instinct. It is something previous to reason and choice. When we say the birds build their nests by instinct and man builds his habitation by reflection, experience, or instruction, we understand the thing well enough; but if we attempt to give a logical definition of either the one or the other, it will immediately be assaulted by a thousand arguments.

Though man is evidently governed by something else than instinct, he also has several instinctive propensities, some of them independent of and some of them intermixed with his moral dispositions. Of the first kind are hunger, thirst, and some others; of the last is the *storge* or parental tenderness towards offspring.

On instinct we shall only say farther that it leads more immediately to the appointment of the Creator and, whether in man or in other creatures, operates more early and more uniformly than reason.

Lecture II

CONSIDERING man as an individual, we discover the most obvious and remarkable circumstances of his nature, that he is a compound of body and spirit. I take this for granted here because we are only explaining the nature of man. When we come to his sentiments and principles of action, it will be more proper to take notice of the spirituality and immortality of the soul and how they are proved.

The body and spirit have a great reciprocal influence one upon another. The body on the temper and disposition of the soul, and the soul on the state and habit of the body. The body is properly the minister of the soul, the means of conveying preceptions to it, but nothing without it.

It is needless to enlarge upon the structure of the body; this is sufficiently known to all except we descend to anatomical exactness, and then, like all the other parts of nature, it shows the infinite wisdom of the Creator. With regard to morals, the influence of the body in a certain view may be very great in enslaving men to appetite, and yet there does not seem any such connection with morals as to require a particular description. I think there is little reason to doubt that there are great and essential differences between man and man as to the spirit and its proper powers, but it seems plain that such are the laws of union between the body and spirit that many faculties are weakened and some rendered altogether incapable of exercise merely by an alteration of the state of the body. Memory is frequently lost and judgment weakened by old age and disease. Sometimes, by a confusion of the brain in a fall, the judgment is wholly disordered. The instinctive appetites of hunger and thirst seem to reside directly in the body, and the soul to have little more than a passive perception. Some passions, particularly fear and rage, seem also to have their seat in the body, immediately producing a certain modification of the blood and spirits. This indeed is perhaps the case in some degree with all passions: whenever they are indulged, they give a modification to the blood and spirits which make them easily rekindled, but there are none which do so instantaneously arise from the body and prevent deliberation, will, and choice, as these now named. To consider the evil passions to which we are liable, we may say those that depend most upon the body are fear, anger, voluptuousness, and those that depend least upon it are ambition, envy, covetousness.

The faculties of the mind are commonly divided into these three kinds, the understanding, the will, and the affections; though perhaps it is proper to observe that these are not three qualities wholly distinct, as if they were three different beings, but different ways of exerting the same simple principle. It is the soul or mind that understands, wills, or is affected with pleasure and pain. The understanding seems to have truth for its object, the discovering things as they really are in themselves and in their relations one to another. It has been disputed whether good be in any degree the object of the understanding. On the one hand it seems as if truth and that only belonged to the understanding because we can easily suppose persons of equal intellectual powers and opposite moral characters. Nay, we can suppose malignity joined to a high degree of understanding, and virtue or true goodness to a much lower. On the other hand, the choice made by the will seems to have the judgment or deliberation of the understanding as its very foundation. How can this be, it will be said, if the understanding has nothing to do with good or evil. A considerable opposition of sentiments among philosophers has arisen from this question. Dr. Clark and some others make understanding or reason the immediate principle of virtue. Shaftesbury, Hutchinson, and others make affection the principle of it. Perhaps neither the one nor the other is wholly right. Probably both are necessary.

The connection between truth and goodness, between the understanding and the heart, is a subject of great moment, but also of great difficulty. I think we may say with certainty that infinite perfection, intellectual and moral, are united and inseparable in the Supreme Being. There is not however in inferior natures an exact proportion between the one and the other, yet I apprehend that truth naturally and necessarily promotes goodness, and falsehood the contrary; but as the influence is reciprocal, malignity of disposition, even with the greatest natural powers, blinds the understanding and prevents the perception of truth itself.

Of the will it is usual to enumerate four acts: desire, aversion, joy, and sorrow. The two last Hutchinson says are superfluous, in which he seems to be right. All the acts of the will may be reduced to the two great heads of desire and aversion, or in other words, choosing and refusing.

The affections are called also passions because often excited by external objects. In as far as they differ from a calm deliberate decision of the judgment or determination of the will, they may be called strong propensitities implanted in our nature, which of themselves contribute not a little to bias the judgment or incline the will.

The affections cannot be better understood than by observing the difference between a calm deliberate general inclination, whether of the selfish or benevolent kind, and particular violent inclinations. Every man deliberately wishes his own happiness, but this differs considerably from a passionate attachment to particular gratification, as a love of riches, honors, pleasures. A good man will have a deliberate fixed desire of the welfare of mankind, but this differs from the love of children, relations, friends, country.

The passions are very numerous and may be greatly diversified because everything, however modified, that is the object of desire or aversion may grow by accident or indulgence to such a size as to be called, and deserve to be called, a passion. Accordingly we express ourselves thus in the English language, a passion for horses, dogs, play, etc.

However all the passions may be ranged under the two great heads of love and hated. To the first belong esteem, admiration, goodwill, and every species of approbation, delight, and desire; to the other, all kinds of aversion, and ways of expressing it, envy, malice, rage, revenge to whatever objects they may be directed.

Hope and fear, joy and sorrow, though frequently ranked among the passions seem rather to be states or modifications of the mind attending the exercise of every passion according as its object is probable or improbable, possessed or lost.

Jealousy seems to be a passion of a middle nature, which it is not easy to say whether it should be ranked under the head of love or hatred. It is often said of jealousy between the sexes that it springs from love, yet it seems plainly impossible that it can have place wtihout forming an ill opinion of its object, at least in some degree. The same thing may be said of jealousy and suspicion in friendship.

The passions may be ranged in two classes in a different way, viz. as they are selfish or benevolent, public or private. There will be great occasion to consider this distinction afterwards in explaining the nature of virtue and the motives that lead to it. What is observed now is only to illustrate our nature as it really is. There is a great and real distinction between passions, selfish and benevolent. The first point directly and immediately at our own interest in the gratification; the others point immmediately at the happiness of others. Of the first kind is the love of fame, power, property, pleasure. And of the second is family and domestic affection, friendship and patriotism. It is to no purpose to say that ultimately it is to please ourselves or because we feel a satisfaction in seeking the good of others; for it is certain that the direct object in view in many cases is to promote the happiness of others; and for this many have been willing to sacrifice everything, even life itself.

After this brief survey of human nature in one light or in one point of view, which may be called its capacity, it will be necessary to return back and take a survey of the way in which we become acquainted with the objects about which we are to be conversant, or upon which the above faculties are to be exercised.

On this it is proper to observe in general that there are but two ways in which we come to the knowledge of things, viz., first, sensation, second, reflection.

The first of these must be divided again into two parts, external and internal.

External arises from the immediate impression of objects from without. The external senses in number are five: seeing, hearing, feeling, tasting, and smelling.

In these are observable the impression itself, or the sensation we feel and the supposition inseparable from it that it is produced by an external object. That our senses are to be trusted in the information they give us seems to me a first principle because they are the foundation of all our after reasonings. The few exceptions of accidental irregularity in the senses can found no just objection to this, as there are so many plain and obvious ways of discovering and correcting it.

The reality of the material system I think may be easily established, except upon such principles as are subversive of all certainty and lead to universal skepticism; and persons who would maintain such principles do not deserve to be reasoned with because they do not pretend to communicate knowledge but to take all knowledge from us.

The Immaterialists say that we are conscious of nothing but the impression or feeling of our own mind, but they do not observe that the impression itself implies and supposes something external that communicates it and cannot be separated from that supposition. Sometimes such reasoners tell us that we cannot show the substance separate from its sensible qualities; no more can any man show me a sensible quality separate from a particular subject. If any man will show me whiteness without showing me anything that is white, or roundness without any thing that is round, I will show him the substance without either color or shape.

Immaterialism takes away the distinction between truth and falsehood. I have an idea of a house or tree in a certain place, and I call this true; that is I am of the opinion there is really a house or tree in that place. Again, I form an idea of a house or tree as what may be in that place; I ask what is the difference if after all you tell me there is neither tree, house, nor place anywhere existing. An advocate for that system says that truth consists in the liveliness of the idea, than which nothing can be more manifestly false. I can form as distinct an idea of anything that is not as anything that is when it is absent from my sight. I have a much more lively idea of Jupiter and Juno and many of their actions from Homer and Virgil, though I do not believe that any of them ever existed, than I have of many things that I know happened within these few months.

The truth is the immaterial system is a wild and ridiculous attempt to unsettle the principles of common sense by metaphysical reasoning, which can hardly produce anything but contempt in the generality of persons who hear it, and which I verily believe never produced conviction even on the persons who pretend to espouse it.

Lecture III

INTERNAL sensation is what Mr. Hutchinson calls the finer powers of perception. It takes its rise from external objects, but by abstraction considers something farther that merely the sensible qualities—

1. Thus with respect to many objects, there is a sense of beauty in the appearance, structure, or composition which is altogether distinct from mere color, shape, and extension. How then is this beauty perceived? It enters by the eye, but it is perceived and relished by what may be well enough called an internal sense, quality, or capacity of the mind.

2. There is a sense of pleasure in imitation, whence the arts of painting, sculpture, and poetry are often called the imitative arts. It is easy to see that the imitation itself gives the pleasure, for we receive much pleasure from a lively description of what would be painful to behold.

3. A sense of harmony.

4. A sense of order or proportion.

Perhaps after all the whole of these senses may be considered as belonging to one class, and to be the particulars which either singly, or by the union of several of them, or of the whole produce what is called the pleasures of the imagination. If so, we may extend these senses to everything that enters into the principles of beauty and gracefulness— order, proportion, simplicity, intricacy, uniformity, variety—especially as these principles have anything in common that is equally applicable to all the fine arts, painting, statuary, architecture, music, poetry, and oratory.

The various theories upon the principles of beauty, or what it is that properly constitutes it, are of much importance on the subject of taste and criticism, but of very little in point of morals. Whether it be a simple perception that cannot be analysed, or a *Je ne sais quoi,* as the French call it, that cannot be discovered, it is the same thing to our present purpose, since it cannot be denied that there is a perception of beauty and that this is very different from the mere color or dimensions of the object. This beauty extends to the form and shape of visible or to the grace and motion of living objects, indeed to all works of art and productions of genius.

These are called the reflex senses sometimes, and it is of moment to observe both that they really belong to our nature and that they are very different from the grosser perceptions of external sense.

It must also be observed that several distinguished writers have added as an internal sense that of morality, a sense and perception of moral excellence and our obligation to conform ourselves to it in our conduct.

Though there is no occasion to join Mr. Hutchinson or any other in their opposition to such as make reason the principle of virtuous conduct, yet I think it must be admitted that a sense of moral good and evil is as real a principle of our nature as either the gross external or reflex senses, and as truly distinct from both as they are from each other.

This moral sense is precisely the same thing with what in scripture and common language we call conscience. It is the law which our Maker has written upon our hearts, and both intimates and enforces duty previous to all reasoning. The opposers of innate ideas and of the law of nature are unwilling to admit the reality of a moral sense, yet their objections are wholly frivolous. The necessity of education and information to the production and exercise of the reflex senses or powers of the imagination is every whit as great as to the application of the moral sense. If therefore anyone should say, as is often done by Mr. Locke, if there are any innate principles what are they? Enumerate them to me; if they are essential to man, they must be in every man; let me take any artless clown and examine him and see if he can tell me what they are. I would say, if the principles of taste are natural they must be universal. Let me try the clown then, and see whether he will agree with us, either in discovering the beauty of a poem or picture, or being able to assign the reasons of his approbation.

There are two senses which are not easily reducible to any of the two kinds of internal senses, and yet certainly belong to our nature. They are allied to one another—a sense of ridicule and a sense of honor and shame. A sense of the ridiculous is something peculiar, for though it be admitted that everything that is ridiculous is at the same time unreasonable and absurd, yet it is as certain the terms are not convertible, for anything that is absurd is not ridiculous. There are a hundred false-hoods in mathematics and other sciences that do not tempt anybody to laugh.

Shaftesbury has through his whole writings endeavored to establish this principle that ridicule is the test of truth, but the falsehood of that opinion appears from the above remark, for there is something really distinct from reasoning in ridicule. It seems to be putting imagination in the place of reason (see Brown's Essays on the Characteristics).

A sense of honor and shame seems in a certain view to subject us to the opinions of others as they depend upon the sentiments of our fellow creatures. Yet, perhaps we may consider this sentiment as intended to be an assistant or guard to virtue by making us apprehend reproach from others for what is in itself worthy of blame. This sense is very strong and powerful in its effects, whether it be guided by true or false principles.

After this survey of human nature, let us consider how we derive either the nature or obligation of duty from it.

One way is to consider what indications we have from our nature of the way that leads to the truest happiness. This must be done by a careful attention to the several classes of perceptions and affections to see which of them are most excellent, delightful, or desirable.

They will then soon appear to be of three great classes, as mentioned above, easily distinguishable from one another and gradually rising above one another:

1. The gratification of the external senses. This affords some plea-sure. We are led to desire what is pleasing and to avoid what is disgustful to them.

2. The finer powers of perception give a delight which is evidently more excellent, and which we must necessarily pronounce more noble. Poetry, painting, music, etc., the exertion of genius, and exercise of the mental powers in general give a pleasure, though not so tumultuous, much more refined, and which does not so soon satiate.

3. Superior to both these is a sense of moral excellence and a pleasure arising from doing what is dictated by the moral sense.

It must doubtless by admitted that this representation is agreeable to truth, and that to those who would calmly and fairly weigh the delight of moral action, it must appear superior to any other gratification, being most noble, pure and durable. Therefore we might conclude that it is to be preferred before all other sources of pleasure, that they are to give way to it when opposite, and to be no otherwise embraced than in subserviency to it.

But though we cannot say there is anything false in this theory, there are certainly very essential defects. As for example, it wholly confounds or leaves entirely undistinguished acting virtuously from seeking happiness, so that promoting our own happiness will in that case be the essence or definition of virtue, and a view to our own interest will be the sole and complete obligation to virtue. Now there is good ground to believe not only that reason teaches us, but that the moral sense dictates to us something more on both heads, viz. that there are disinterested affections that point directly at the good of others, and that these are so far from meriting to be excluded from the notion of virtue altogether that they rather seem to claim a preference to the selfish affections. I know the friends of the scheme of self-interest have a way of coloring or solving this. They say men only approve and delight in benevolent affections as pleasing and delightful to themselves. But this is not satisfying, for it seems to weaken the force of public affection very much to refer it all to self interest, and when nature seems to be carrying you out of yourself by strong instinctive propensities or implanted affections to turn the current and direction of these into the stream of self-interest, in which experience tells us we are most apt to run to a vicious excess.

Besides it is affirmed, and I think with good reason, that the moral sense carries a good deal more in it than merely an approbation of a certain class of actions as beautiful, praiseworthy or delightful, and therefore finding our interest in them as the most noble gratification. The moral sense implies also a sense of obligation, that such and such things are right and others wrong, that we are bound in duty to do the one, and that our conduct is hateful, blameable, and deserving of punishment if we do the contrary; and there is also in the moral sense or conscience an apprehension or belief that reward and punishment will follow according as we shall act in the one way or in the other.

It is so far from being true that there is no more in virtuous action than a superior degree of beauty or a more noble pleasure, that indeed the beauty and sweetness of virtuous action arises from this very circumstance—that it is a compliance with duty or supposed obligation. Take away this, and the beauty vanishes as well as the pleasure. Why is it more pleasant to do a just or charitable action than to satisfy my palate with delightful meat, or to walk in a beautiful garden, or read an exquisite poem? Only because I feel myself under an obligation to do it, as a thing useful and important in itself. It is not duty because pleasing, but pleasing because duty. The same thing may be said of beauty and approbation. I do not approve of the conduct of a plain, honest, industrious, pious man because it is more beautiful than that of an idle profligate, but I say it is more beautiful and amiable because he keeps within the bounds of duty. I see a higher species of beauty in moral action, but it arises from a sense of obligation. It may be said that my interest and duty are the same, because they are inseparable and the one arises from the other; but there is a real distinction and priority of order. A thing is not my duty because it is my interest, but it is a wise appointment of nature that I shall forfeit my interest if I neglect my duty.

Several other remarks might be made to confirm this. When any person has by experience found that in seeking pleasure he embraced a less pleasing enjoyment in place of one more delightful, he may be sensible of mistake or misfortune, but he has nothing at all of the feeling of blame of self-condemnation; but when he hath done an immoral action, he has an inward remorse and feels that he has broken a law and that he ought to have done otherwise.

Lecture IV

THIS therefore lays us under the necessity of searching a little further for the principle of moral action. In order to do this with the greater accuracy and give you a view of the chief controversies on this subject, observe that there are really three questions upon it which must be inquired into and distinguished. I am sensible they are so intimately connected that they are sometimes necessarily intermixed, but at others, not distinguishing leads into error. The questions relate to (1) the nature of virtue, (2) the foundation of virtue, (3) the obligation of virtue.

When we inquire into the nature of virtue, we do enough when we point out what it is or show how we may come to the knowledge of every particular duty and be able to distinguish it from the opposite vice. When we speak of the foundation of virtue, we ask or answer the question, why is it so? Why is this course of action preferable to the contrary? What is its excellence? When we speak of the obligation of virtue, we ask by what law we are bound, or from what principles we ought to be obedient to the precepts which it contains or prescribes.

After speaking something to each of these, to the controversies that have been raised upon them and the propriety or importance of entering far into these controversies or a particular decision of them, I shall proceed to a detail of the moral laws of the several branches of duty according to the division first laid down.

As to the nature of virtue or what it is or, in other words, what is the rule by which I must try every disputed practice—that I may keep clear of the next question, you may observe that upon all the systems they must have recourse to one or more of the following, viz. conscience, reason, experience. All who found virtue upon affection, particularly Hutchinson, Shaftesbury, and their followers, make the moral sense the rule of duty and very often attempt to exclude the use of reason on this subject. These authors seem also to make benevolence and public affection the standard of virtue in distinction from all private and selfish passions.

Doctor Clark and most English writers of the last age make reason the standard of virtue, particularly as opposed to inward sentiment or affection. They have this to say particularly in support of their opinion that reason does in fact often control and alter sentiment, whereas sentiment cannot alter the clear decision of reason. Suppose my heart dictates to me anything to be my duty, as for example to have compassion on a person detected in the commission of crimes; yet if upon cool reflection I perceive that suffering him to go unpunished will be hurtful to the community, I counteract the sentiment from the deductions of reason.

Again, some take in the aid of experience, and chiefly act upon it. All particularly who are upon the selfish scheme find it necessary to make experience the guide to show them what things are really conducive to happiness and what not.

We shall proceed to consider the opinions upon the nature of virtue, the chief of which are as follows.

1. Some say that virtue consists in acting agreeable to the nature and reason of things, and that we are to abstract from all affection, public and private, in determining any question upon it (Clark).

2. Some say that benevolence or public affection is virtue and that a regard to the good of the whole is the standard of virtue. What is most remarkable in this scheme is that it makes the sense of obligation in particular instances give way to a supposed greater good (Hutchinson).

3. One author (Woolston, *Religion of Nature Delineated*) makes truth the foundation of virtue, and he reduces the good or evil of any action to the truth or falsehood of a proposition. This opinion differs not in substance but in words only from Dr. Clark's.

4. Others place virtue in self-love and make a well regulated self-love the standard and foundation of it. This scheme is best defended by Dr. Campbell of St. Andrews.

5. Some of late have made sympathy the standard of virtue, particularly Smith in his *Theory of Moral Sentiments*. He says we have a certain feeling by which we sympathize and, as he calls it, go along with what appears to be right. This is but a new phraseology for the moral sense.

6. David Hume has a scheme of morals that is peculiar to himself. He makes everything that is *agreeable* and *useful* virtuous, and vice versa, by which he entirely annihilates the difference between natural and moral qualities, making health, strength, cleanliness, as really virtues as integrity and truth.

7. We have an opinion published in this country that virtue consists in the love of being as such (Edwards).

Several of these authors do easily and naturally incorporate piety with their system, particularly Clark, Hutchinson, Campbell, and Edwards.

And there are some who begin by establishing natural religion, and then found virtue upon piety. This amounts to the same thing in substance, for reasoners upon the nature of virtue only mean to show what the Author of nature has pointed out as duty. And after natural religion is established on general proofs, it will remain to point out what are its laws, which, not taking in revelation, must bring us back to consider our own nature and the rational deductions from it.

The opinions on the foundation of virtue may be summed up in the four following: (1) the will of God; (2) the reason and nature of things; (3) the public interest; (4) private interest.

(1) The will of God. By this is not meant what was mentioned above, that the intimations of the divine will point out what is our duty, but that the reason of the difference between virtue and vice is to be sought nowhere else than in the good pleasure of God, that there is not intrinsic excellence in any thing but as he commands or forbids it. They pretend that if it were otherwise there would be something above the Supreme Being, something in the nature of things that would lay him under the law of necessity or fate. But notwithstanding the difficulty of our forming clear conceptions on this subject, it seems very harsh and unreasonable to say that the difference between virtue and vice is no other than the divine will. This would be taking away the moral character even of God himself. It would not have any meaning then to say he is infinitely holy and infinitely perfect. But probably those who have asserted this did not mean any more than that the divine will is so perfect and excellent that all virtue is reduced to conformity to it—and that we ought not to judge of good and evil by any other rule. This is as true as that the divine conduct is the standard of wisdom.

(2) Some found it in the reason and nature of things. This may be said to be true, but not sufficiently precise and explicit. Those who embrace this principle succeed best in their reasoning when endeavoring to show that there is an essential difference between virtue and vice. But when they attempt to show wherein this difference doth or can consist, other than public or private happiness, they speak with very little meaning.

(3) Public happiness. This opinion is that the foundation of virtue, or that which makes the distinction between it and vice, is its tendency to promote the general good, so that utility at bottom is the principle of virtue, even with the great patrons of disinterested affection.

(4) Private happiness. Those who choose to place the foundation of

virtue here would have us to consider no other excellence in it than what immediately conduces to our own gratification.

Upon these opinions I would observe that there is something true in every one of them, but that they may be easily pushed to an error by excess.

The nature and will of God is so perfect as to be the true standard of all excellence, natural and moral; and if we are sure of what he is or commands, it would be presumption and folly to reason against it or put our views of fitness in the room of his pleasure; but to say that God, by his will, might have made the same temper and conduct virtuous and excellent which we now call vicious seems to unhinge all our notions of the supreme excellence even of God himself.

Again, there seems to be in the nature of things an intrinsic excellence in moral worth and an indelible impression of it upon the conscience distinct from producing or receiving happiness, and yet we cannot easily illustrate its excellence but by comparing one kind of happiness with another.

Again, promoting the public or general good seems to be so nearly connected with virtue that we must necessarily suppose that universal virtue could be of universal utility. Yet there are two excesses to which this has sometimes led: one the fatalist and necessitarian schemes to which there are so many objections, and the other the making the general good the ultimate practical rule to every particular person so that he may violate particular obligations with a view to a more general benefit.

Once more it is certain that virtue is as really connected with private as with public happiness, and yet to make the interest of the agent the only foundation of it seems so to narrow the mind and to be so destructive to the public and generous affections as to produce the most hurtful effects.

If I were to lay down a few propositions on the foundation of virtue, as a philosopher, they should be the following:

1. From reason, contemplation, sentiment, and tradition, the Being and infinite perfection and excellence of God may be deduced; and therefore what he is and commands is virtue and duty. Whatever he has implanted in uncorrupted nature as a principle is to be received as his will. Propensities resisted and contradicted by the inward principle of conscience are to considered as inherent or contracted vice.

2. True virtue certainly promotes the general good, and this may be made use of as an argument in doubtful cases to determine whether a particular principle is right or wrong, but to make the good of the whole our immediate principle of action is putting ourselves in God's place and actually superseding the necessity and use of the particular principles of

duty which he hath impressed upon the conscience. As to the whole, I believe the universe is faultless and perfect, but I am unwilling to say it is the best possible system because I am not able to understand such an argument and because it seems to me absurd that infinite perfection should exhaust or limit itself by a created production.

3. There is in the nature of things a difference between virtue and vice, and however much virtue and happiness are connected by the divine law and in the event of things, we are made so as to feel towards them and conceive of them as distinct. We have the simple perceptions of duty and interest.

4. Private and public interest may be promoted by the same means, but they are distinct views; they should be made to assist and not destroy each other.

The result of the whole is that we ought to take the rule of duty from conscience enlightened by reason, experience, and every way by which we can be supposed to learn the will of our Maker and his intention in creating us such as we are. And we ought to believe that it is as deeply founded as the nature of God himself, being a transcript of his moral excellence, and that it is productive of the greatest good.

Lecture V

IT remains only that we speak of the obligation of virtue, or what is the law that binds us to the performance and from what motives or principles we ought to follow its dictates.

The sentiments upon this subject differ, as men have different views of the nature and foundation of virtue, yet they may be reduced within narrower bounds.

The obligation of virtue may be easily reduced to two general kinds, duty and interest. The first, if real, implies that we are under some law or subject to some superior to whom we are accountable. The other only implies that nature points it out to us as our own greatest happiness, and that there is no other reason why we ought to obey.

Now I think it is very plain that there is more in the obligation of virtue than merely our greatest happiness. The moral sentiment itself implies that it is duty independent of happiness. This produces remorse and disapprobation, as having done what is blameable and of ill desert. We have two ideas very distinct when we see a man mistaking his own interest and not obtaining so much happiness as he might, and when we see him breaking through every moral obligation. In the first case we consider him as only accountable to himself; in the second we consider him as accountable to some superior and to the public. This sense of duty is the primary notion of law and of rights, taken in their most extensive signification as including everything we think we are entitled to expect from others, and the neglect or violation of which we consider as wrong, unjust, vicious, and therefore blameable. It is also affirmed with great apparent reason by many, particularly Butler in his Analogy and his sermons, that we have a natural feeling of ill desert and merited punishment in vice. The patrons of these selfish ideas alone are those who confine the obligation of virtue to happiness.

But of those who are or would be thought of the opposite sentiment, there are some who differ very considerably from others. Some who profess great opposition to the selfish scheme declare also great aversion to founding the obligation of virtue in any degree on the will of a superior, or looking for any sanction of punishment to corroborate the moral laws. This they especially treat with contempt when it is supposed to be from the deity. Shaftesbury speaks with great bitterness against taking into view a future state of what he calls more extended self-interest. He says men should love virtue for its own sake without regard to reward or punishment. In this he has been followed by many reasoners, as far as their regard to religion would permit them.

If however we attend to the dictates of conscience, we shall find evidently a sense of duty, of self-approbation and remorse, which plainly shows us to be under a law and that law to have a sanction: what else is the meaning of the fear and terror and apprehension of guilty persons? *Quorum mentes si recludantur* etc. says Cicero.

Nor is this all, but we have all certainly a natural sense of dependence. The belief of a divine being is certainly either innate and necessary or has been handed down from the first man and can now be well supported by the clearest reason. And our relation to him not only lays the foundation of many moral sentiments and duties, but completes the idea of morality and law by subjecting us to him and teaching us to conceive of him, not only as our Maker, preserver and benefactor, but as our righteous governor and supreme judge. As the being and perfections of God are irrefrangibly established, the obligation of duty must ultimately rest here.

It ought not to be forgotten that the belief or apprehension of a future state of rewards and punishments has been as universal as the belief of a deity, and seems inseparable from it, and therefore must be considered as the sanction of the moral law. Shaftesbury inveighs severally against this, as making man virtuous from a mercenary view; but there are two ways in which we may consider this matter, and in either light his objections have little force. (1) We may consider the primary obligations of virtue as founded upon a sense of its own excellence, joined with a sense of duty and dependance on the Supreme

Being, and rewards and punishments as a secondary motive, which is found in fact to be absolutely necessary to restrain or reclaim men from vice and impiety. (2) Or we may consider that by the light of nature, as well as by revelation, the future reward of virtue is considered as a state of perfect virtue, and the happiness is represented as arising from this circumstance. Here there is nothing at all of a mercenary principle but only an expectation that true goodness, which is here in a state of imperfection and liable to much opposition, shall then be improved to the highest degree and put beyond any possibility of change.

We may add to these obligations the manifest tendency of a virtuous conduct to promote even our present happiness: this in ordinary cases it does and, when joined with the steady hope of futurity, does in all cases produce a happiness superior to what can be enjoyed in the practice of vice. Yet perhaps the stoics of old, who denied pain to be any evil and made the wise man superior to all the vicissitudes of fortune, carried things to a romantic and extravagant height. And so do some persons in modern times, who setting aside the consideration of a future state teach that virtue is its own reward. There are many situations in which, if you deprive a good man of the hope of future happiness, his state seems very undesirable. On the contrary, sometimes the worst of men enjoy prosperity and success to a great degree, nor do they seem to have any such remorse as to be an adequate punishment of their crimes. If any should insist that a good man has always some comfort from within, and a bad man a self-disapprobation and inward disquiet suited to their character, I would say that this arises from the expectation of a future state, and a hope on the one side and fear on the other of their condition there.

Those who declaim so highly of virtue being its own reward in this life take away one of the most considerable arguments which from the dawn of philosophy has always been made use of as a proof of a future state, viz. the unequal distribution of good and evil in this life. Besides they do not seem to view the state of bad men properly. When they talk of remorse of conscience as a sufficient punishment, they forget that this is seldom to a high degree but in the case of some gross crimes. Cruelty and murder, frequent acts of gross injustice are sometimes followed with deep horror of conscience; and a course of intemperance or lust is often attended with such dismal effects upon the body, fame, and fortune that those who survive it a few years are a melancholy spectacle and a burden to themselves and others. But it would be very loose morality to suppose none to be bad men but those who were under the habitual condemnation of conscience. On the contrary, the far greater part are blinded in the understandings, as well as corrupt in their practice. They deceive themselves and are at peace. Ignorance and inattention keep the multitude at peace. And false principles often produce self-justification and ill-founded peace, even in atrocious crimes. Even common robbers are sometimes found to justify themselves, and say I must live, I have a right to my share of provision as well as that proud fellow who rolls in his chariot.

The result of the whole is that the obligation to virtue ought to take in all the following particulars: A sense of its own intrinsic excellence, of its happy consequences in the present life, a sense of duty and subjection to the Supreme Being, and a hope of future happiness and fear of future misery from his decision.

Having considered the reasonings on the nature, foundation, and obligation of virtue, I now proceed to a more particular detail of the moral laws and shall take them under the three heads formerly mentioned, ethics, politics, and jurisprudence.

Lecture VI

As to the first, we must begin with what is usually called the states of man, or the several lights or relation in which he may be considered as laying a foundation for duty. These states may be divided into two kinds: (1) natural; (2) adventitious.

The natural states may be enumerated thus: (1) his state with regard to God, or natural relation to him; (2) to his fellow-creatures; (3) solitude or society; (4) peace or war. Perhaps we may add to these (5) his outward provision, plenty or want.

These are called natural states because they are necessary and universal. All men and at all times are related to God. They were made by him and live by his providence. We must also necessarily know our fellow creatures and their state to be similar to ours in this respect and many others. A man must at all times be independent or connected with society, at peace with others or at war, well provided or in want.

The other states are called adventitious because they are the effect of choice and the fruit of industry, as marriage, family, master and servant; particular voluntary societies, callings or professions; characters or abilities natural and acquired; offices in a constituted society; property; and many particular modifications of each of these.

In prosecuting the subject farther and giving an analysis of the moral duties founded upon these states, I shall first take notice of our relation to God, with the proofs of his being and perfections, and then consider the moral laws under three heads: our duty to God, to our neighbor, and to ourselves.

First, our duty to God. To this place I have reserved what was to be said upon the proof of the being of God, the great foundation of all natural religion, without which the moral sense would be weak and insufficient.

The proofs of the being of God are generally divided into two kinds: (1) *a priori;* (2) *a posteriori.* The first is, properly speaking, metaphysical reasoning downward from the first principles of science or truth and inferring by just consequence the being and perfections of God. Clark's *Demonstration* (if there be anything that should be called *a priori,* and if this is a conclusive method of reasoning) is as complete as anything ever published, perhaps he has carried the principle as far as it will go.

This way of arguing begins by establishing our own existence from consciousness. That we are not necessarily existent, therefore, must have a cause; that something must have existed from all eternity, or nothing ever could have existed; that this being must exist by an internal necessity of nature; that what exists necessarily must exist alike everywhere, must be perfect, act everywhere, be independent, omnipotent, omniscient, infinitely good, just, true—because as all these are evidently perfections or excellencies, that which exists by a necessity of nature must be possessed of every perfection. And the contrary of these virtues, implying weakness or insufficiency, cannot be found in the infinite being.

The other medium of proof, commonly called *a posteriori,* begins with contemplating the universe in all its parts; observing that it contains many irresistible proofs that it could not be eternal, could not be without a cause; that this cause must be intelligent; and from the astonishing greatness, the wonderful adjustment and complication of things, concludes that we can set no bounds to the perfection of the Maker because we can never exhaust the power, intelligence, and benignity that we see in his works. In this way of arguing we deduce the moral perfections of the deity from the faint resemblances of them that we see in ourselves. As we necessarily conceive justice, goodness, truth, etc. to be perfections or excellencies, we are warranted by the plainest reason to ascribe them to the divine being in an infinite degree.

There is perhaps at bottom no difference between these ways of reasoning because they must in some degree rest upon a common principle, viz. that everything that exists must have a cause. This is equally necessary to both the chains of reasoning and must itself be taken for an original sentiment of nature, or an impression necessarily made upon us from all that we see and are conversant with. About this and some other ideas great stir has been made by some infidel writers, particularly David Hume, who seems to have industriously endeavored to shake the certainty of our belief upon cause and effect, upon personal identity and the idea of power. It is easy to raise metaphysical subtleties and confound the understanding on such subjects. In opposition to this, some late writers have advanced with great apparent reason that there are certain first principles or dictates of common sense which are either simple perceptions or seen with intuitive evidence. These are the foundation of all reasoning, and without them to reason is a word without meaning. They can no more be proved than you can prove an axiom in mathematical science. These authors of Scotland have lately produced and supported this opinion to resolve at once all the refinements and metaphysical objections of some infidel writers.

There is a different sort of argument often made use of or brought in aid of the others for the being of God, viz. the consent of all nations and the universal prevalence of that belief. I know not whether we must say that this argument rests also upon the principle that nothing can exist without a cause, or upon the plan just now mentioned. If it is an universal dictate of our nature, we must take it as true immediately without further examination.

An author I formerly mentioned has set this argument in a peculiar light (Dr. Wilson of Newcastle). He says that we receive all our knowledge, as philosophers admit, by sensation and reflection. Now, from all that we see, and all the reflection and abstraction upon it we are capable of, he affirms it is impossible we could ever form the idea of a spirit or a future state. They have, however, been early and universal, and therefore must have been communicated at first and handed down by information and instruction from age to age. So that unless upon the supposition of the existence of God and his imparting the knowledge of himself to men, it is impossible that any idea of him could ever have entered into the human mind. There is something ingenious and a good deal of probability in this way of reasoning.

As to the nature of God, the first thing to be observed is the unity of God. This is sufficiently established upon the reasonings both *a priori* and *posteriori*. If these reasonings are just for the being of God, they are strictly conclusive for the unity of God. There is a necessity for the existence of one Supreme Being, the first cause, but not necessity for more; nay, one supreme independent being does not admit any more. And when we view the harmony, order, and unity of design in the created system, we must be led to the belief of the unity of God.

Perhaps it may be thought an objection to this (especially if we lay any stress on the universal sentiments of mankind) that all nations have been so prone to the belief and worship of a plurality of gods. But this argument is rather specious than solid, as however prone men were to worship local inferior deities, they seem to have considered them only as intermediate divinities and intercessors between them and the supreme God.

The perfections of God may be divided into two kinds, *natural* and *moral.*

1. The natural perfections of God are spirituality, immensity, wisdom, and power.

We call these natural perfections because they can be easily distinguished, and in idea at least separated from goodness of disposition. It is highly probable indeed that supreme excellence, natural and moral, must always reside in the same subject and are truly inseparable; yet we distinguish them not only because the ideas are distinct, but because they are by no means in proportion to one another in inferior natures. Great powers of mind and perfection of body are often joined to malignity of disposition. It is not so however in God, for as his natural perfections are founded on reason, so his moral excellence is evidently founded in the moral sense or conscience which he has implanted in us.

Spirituality is what we may call the *very nature* of God. It must be admitted that we cannot at present form any complete or adequate idea of a spirit. And some, as you have heard formerly, insist that without revelation we could never have acquired the idea of it that we have. Yet there are many who have reasoned in a very strong and seemingly conclusive manner to show that mind or intelligence must be a substance altogether distinct from matter. That all the known properties of matter are incapable of producing thought, as being wholly of a different kind, that matter as such and universally is inert and divisible, thought or intelligence active and uncompounded (see the best reasoning on this subject in Baxter's Immateriality of the Soul).

Immensity in the Divine Being is that by which he is everywhere and equally present. Metaphysicians, however, differ greatly upon this subject. The Cartesians will not admit that place is at all applicable to spirits. They say it is an idea wholly arising from extension, which is one of the peculiar and essential qualities of matter. The Newtonians, however, who make so much use of the idea of infinite space, consider place as essential to all substance, spirit as well as matter. The difficulties are great on both sides. It is hard to conceive of spirit at all, separating from it the qualities of matter, and after we have attempted to do so, it seems to be bringing them back to talk of place. And yet it seems not only hard but impossible to conceive of any real being without suppposing it in some place, and particularly upon the immensity of the Deity, it seems to be putting created spirits too much on a level with the infinite spirit to deny his immensity. It is I think certain they are either confined to a place, or so limited in their operations as is no way so well expressed as by saying we are here and nowhere else. And in this sense both parties must admit the divine immensity—that his agency is equal, universal, and irresistible.

Wisdom is another natural attribute of God implying infinite knowledge—that all things in all their relations, all things existing, and all things possible are the objects of the divine knowledge. Wisdom is usually considered as respecting some end to be attained, and it implies the clear discovery of the best and most effectual means of attaining it.

Power is the being able to do all things without limit or restraint. The omnipotence of God is always considered as an essential perfection and seems to arise immediately from creation and providence. It is common to say that God can do all things except such as imply a contradiction—such as to make a thing to be and not to be at the same time; but this is unnecessary and foolish in the way of an exception, for such things are not the objects of power at all. They are mere absurdities in our conception, and indeed we may say of our own creation. All things are possible with God—nothing can withstand his power.

Lecture VII

SECOND, the moral perfections of God are holiness, justice, truth, goodness, and mercy.

Holiness is sometimes taken in a general and comprehensive sense as being the aggregate, implying the preference of all moral excellence; yet it is sometimes used, and that both in the scripture revelation and by heathen writers, as a peculiar attribute. In this limited sense it is extremely difficult to define or explain. Holiness is that character of God to which veneration, or the most profound reverence in us, is the correspondent affection. It is sometimes also expressed by purity, and when we go to form an idea of it, perhaps we can scarce say anything better than that it is his being removed at an infinite distance from the grossness of material indulgence.

Justice is an invariable determination to render to all their due. Justice seems to be founded on the strong and unalterable perception we have of right and wrong, good and evil, and particularly that the one deserves reward and the other punishment. The internal sanction, or the external and providential sanction of natural laws, point out to us the justice of God. The chief thing that merits attention upon this subject is the controversy about what is called the vindictive justice of God. That is to say, is there in God, or have we a natural sense of the propriety of, a disposition to inflict punishment independently of the consequences, viz. the reformation of the offender or the example of others. This loose moralists often declaim against. Yet it seems plain that the sense in our minds of good and ill desert makes guilt the proper object of punishment simply in itself. This may have a relation to general order and the good of the whole, which however is out of our reach.

The truth of God is one of his perfections greatly insisted upon in Scripture and an essential part of natural religion. It is inseparable from infinite perfection, for any departure from truth must be considered as arising from weakness or necessity. What end could be served to a self-sufficient and all sufficient being by falsehood or deception?

Goodness in God is a disposition to communicate happiness to others. This is easily understood. The creation is a proof of it—natural and moral evil no just objection to it because of the preponderancy of happiness.

Mercy, as distinguished from goodness or benignity, is his being of a placable nature—ready to forgive the guilty or to remit deserved punishment. It has been disputed how far mercy or placability is discoverable by reason. It is not mercy or forgiveness unless it would have been just at the same time to have punished. There are but two ways by which men from reason may infer the attribute of mercy to belong to the Deity: (1) because we ourselves are sensible of this disposition and see in it a peculiar beauty; (2) from the forebearance of Providence that sinners are not immediately overtaken with punishment but have space given them to repent. Yet as all the conclusions drawn from these principles nust be vague and general, the expectations of the guilty founded upon them must be very uncertain. We must conclude, therefore, that however stable a foundation there is for the other attributes of God in nature and reason, the way in which, and the terms on which, he will show mercy can be learned from Revelation only.

Having considered the being and perfections of God, we proceed to our duty to him. This may be considered in two views, as general and special.

1. By the first I understand our duty to obey him and submit to him in all things. This you see includes every branch of moral duty to our neighbor and ourselves, as well as to God, and so the particular parts of it will be considered afterwards. But in this place, considering every good action as an act of obedience to God, we will a little attend to the divine sovereignity and the foundation of it.

In speaking of the foundation of virtue, I took in a sense of dependence and subjection to God. But as men are not to be deterred from bold inquiries, a further question is raised by some: what is properly the foundation of the divine dominion? (1) Some found it directly upon Omnipotence. It is impossible to resist his power. This seems to lay us under a necessity, rather than to convince us of duty. We ought however to think and speak of this subject with reverence, and certainly omnipotence seems to oblige us to actual, if it should not bring us to willing, obedience. It is somewhat remarkable that in the book of Job, composed on purpose to resolve some difficulties in Providence, where God is brought in as speaking himself out of the whirlwind, he makes use of no other argument than his tremendous majesty and irresistible power. Yet to rest the matter wholly upon this seems much the same as founding virtue on mere will. Therefore, (2) some found the divine dominion on his infinite excellence; they say it is the law of reason that the wisest should rule, and therefore that infinite perfection is entitled to universal sway. Even this, taken separate and alone, does not seem wholly to satisfy the mind. If one person is wiser than another, it seems reasonable that the other should learn of him and imitate him; but it scarcely seems a sufficient reason that the first should have absolute authority. But perhaps the weakness of the argument taken in this view may arise from the inconsiderable difference between man and man, when compared to the superiority of universal and unchangeable perfection. (3) Some found it upon creation. They say that God has an absolute property in all his creatures; he may therefore do what he will with his own. This no doubt goes a good way and carries considerable force with it to the mind, the rather that, as you will afterwards see, it is something similar to this in us that lays the foundation of our most perfect rights, viz. that the product of our own industry is properly at our own disposal.

As upon the foundation of virtue I thought it necessary to unite the principles of different writers, so upon this subject I think that all the three particulars mentioned ought to be admitted as the grounds of the divine dominion: omnipotence, infinite excellence, and the original production and continual preservation of all creatures.

2. Our duty to God may be considered more specially as it points out the duties we owe immediately to himself. These may be divided into internal and external.

First, the internal are all included under the three following, love, fear, and truth.

The love of God, which is the first and great duty both of natural and revealed religion, may be explained in a larger and more popular or in a more specific and stricter way.

In the first, love may be resolved into the four following acts: (1) esteem, (2) gratitude, (3) benevolence, (4) desire.

These four will be found inseparable from true love, and it is pretty much in the same order that the acts succeed one another. Love is founded on esteem, on the real or supposed good qualities of the object. You can no more love that which you despise than that which you hate.

Gratitude is also inseparable from it, to have a lively sense of favors received and to esteem them for the sake of the person from whom they came. Benevolence or rejoicing in the happiness and wishing well to the object. And lastly, a desire of a place in his esteem. Whatever we love, we desire to possess, as far as it is suited to our faculties.

The stricter and more precise method of considering the love of God is to divide it into two branches, benevolence and desire. And indeed our affection to God seems to be capable of the same division as our affection to our fellow creatures, benevolent and selfish. I think it undeniable that there is a disinterested love of God, which terminates directly upon himself without any immediate view to our own happiness—as well as a discovery of our great interest in his favor.

The second great duty to God is fear, but here we must carefully distinguish this affection from one which bears the name and is different from it—at least in a moral view it is altogether opposite. Dutiful fear is what may be otherwise called veneration and has for its object the infinity of the divine perfection in general, but particularly his majesty and greatness. The other is merely a fear of evil or punishment from him: these are called sometimes a filial and a servile fear. The first increases, as men improve in moral excellence, and the other is destroyed. Perfect love casteth out fear. Perhaps however opposite, as they have the same name they may be said to be the same natural affection, only as it takes place in innocent or holy and in guilty creatures. The same majesty of God, which produces veneration in the upright, produces horror and apprehension of punishment in the guilty.

The third great duty is trust. This is a continual dependence on God for everything we need, together with an approbation of and absolute resignation to his providence.

2. Second, the external duties to God I shall briefly pass over being only all proper and natural expressions of the internal sentiments.

It may be proper however to take notice in general of the worship due to God that whether we consider the nature of things or the universal practice of mankind in all ages, worship, and that not only private but public and social worship, is a duty of natural religion.

Some of the enemies of revealed religion have spoken with great virulence against this, as unreasonable and even dishonorable to the Divine Being. The substance of what they say is this, that as it would be no part of the character of an eminent and good man to desire and take pleasure in others praising him and recounting his good qualities, so it is absurd to suppose that the Supreme Being is pleased with incense, sacrifices, and praises. But it ought to be observed that he does not require these acts and exercises as any gratification to himself, but as in themselves just and necessary and suited to the relation we stand in to him and useful for forming our temper and universal practice. We ought also to remember that we must not immediately and without discrimination reason from what would be praise and blameworthy among men to what would be just or unjust in God because the circumstances are very different. Besides, though for any man to desire the applause of his fellow creatures or be pleased with adulation would be a mean and contemptible character because indeed there is such unspeakable imperfection in the best of men, yet when any duty or sentiment is fully and manifestly due from man to man, there is nothing improper or dishonorable in requiring or expecting it. Thus a parent requires respect and submission from his children, a master from his servants; and though the injury is merely personal, he thinks himself entitled to punish every expression of contempt or disregard. Again, every man who has bestowed signal favors upon another expects to see evidence of a grateful and sensible mind, and severely condemns every sentiment or action that indicates a contrary disposition.

On the whole then we see that if the worship of God be what is due from us to him, in consequence of the relation we stand in to him, it is proper and necessary that he should require it. To honor God is to honor supreme excellence, for him not to expect and demand it would be to deny himself.

One other difficulty I shall touch upon a little. It respects the duty of prayer, and the objections lie equally against it on the footing of natural religion and revealed. The objections are two. (1) Why does God, who perfectly knows all our wants, require and expect prayer before he will supply them? To this I would answer that he supplies great multitudes of our wants without our asking it, and as to his requiring the duty of prayer, I say the same thing as of worship in general: it is reasonable and necessary to express, and to increase upon our minds, a sense of dependence and thereby lay us under an obligation of properly improving what we receive. (2) The other obligation is with regard to the force or efficacy of prayer. Why, it is said, should we pray when the whole system of divine providence is fixed and unalterable? Can we possibly suppose that God will change his purposes from a regard to our cries or tears? To this some answer no, otherwise than as before, that without having any effect on the event, it has only an effect upon our minds in bringing us to a right temper. Dr. Leechman of Glasgow in his discourse on prayer makes no other answer to this difficulty. But I think to rest it here, and admit that it has no influence in the way of causality upon the event, would in a great measure break the force and fervency of prayer. I would therefore say further that prayer has a real efficacy on the event, and just as much as any other second cause. The objection arises from going beyond our depth, and reasoning from the unchangeable purpose of God to human actions, which is always unjust and fallacious. However unable we may be to explain it, notwithstanding the fixed plan of Providence, there is a real influence of second causes both natural and moral, and I apprehend the connection between cause and effect is similar in both cases. If it is fixed from eternity that there shall be a plentiful crop upon a certain field, I know that nothing whatsoever can prevent it, if otherwise, the efforts of the whole creation cannot produce it; yet I know as certainly that, hypothetically, if it is not ploughed and sown, there will be no grain upon it, and that if it be properly manured and dressed, it will probably be fruitful. Thus in moral matters, prayer has as real an influence in procuring the blessing as ploughing and sowing has in procuring the crop, and it is as consistent with the established order of nature and the certainty of events in the one case, as in the other; for this reason the stoical fate of old, was call the *ignava ratio* of the stoics, as they sometimes made use of the above fallacious reasoning.

Lecture VIII

WE come now to our duty to man. This may be reduced to a short sum by ascending to its principle. Love to others, sincere and active, is the sum of our duty.

Benevolence, I formerly observed, ought not to be considered as the whole of virtue, but it certainly is the principle and sum of that branch of duty which regards others.

We may distinguish between (1) particular kind affections, and (2) a calm and deliberate goodwill to all. The particular kind affections, as to family, friends, country, seem to be implanted by nature to strengthen the general principle; for it is only or chiefly by doing good to those we are particularly related to that we can promote the general happiness.

Particular kind affections should be restrained and directed by a calm goodwill to all. Wherever our attachments to private persons prevent a greater good, they become irregular and excessive.

Some think that a calm and settled goodwill to others is an improvement of the particular affections and arises from the more narrow to the more extensive, from family, friends, country, to all our fellow creatures. But it seems more reasonable to say that the general affection is a dictate of our conscience of a superior kind. If it were only an increase and extension of the private affection, it would grow more weak as the distance from ourselves increased, whereas in fact the more enlarged affections are intended to be more powerful than the confined.

When we are speaking of kind affections, it will not be improper to observe that some unbelievers have objected against the gospel that it does not recommend private friendship and the love of our country. But if fairly considered, as the Scripture both by example and precept recommends all particular affections, so it is to its honor that it sets the love of mankind above them every one, and by so much insisting on the forgiveness of injuries and love of enemies, it has carried benevolence to its greatest perfection. The parable of the Samaritan in answer to the question who is my neighbor is one of the greatest beauties in moral painting anywhere to be seen.

The love of our country to be sure is a noble and enlarged affection, and those who have sacrificed private case and family relations to it have become illustrious; yet the love of mankind is still greatly superior. Sometimes attachment to country appears in a littleness of mind, thinking all other nations inferior and foolishly believing that knowledge, virtue, and valor are all confined to themselves. As the Romans long ago made the *Punica fides* to mean deceit, so there are not wanting among us those who think that all the French are interested, treacherous, and cowardly.

On the great law of love to others, I shall only say further that it ought to have for its object their greatest and best interest, and therefore implies wishing and doing them good in soul and body.

It is necessary now to descend to the application of this principle to particular duties, and to examine what are the rights or claims that one man has upon another. Rights and obligations are correlative terms. Whatever others have a just right or title to claim from me, that is my duty, or what I am obliged to do to them.

Right in general may be reduced, as to its source, to the supreme law of moral duty; for whatever men are in duty obliged to do, that they have a claim to, and other men are considered as under an obligations to permit them. Again, as our own happiness is a lawful object or end, we are supposed to have each a right to prosecute this; but as our prosecutions may interfere, we limit each other's rights, and a man is said to have a right or power to promote his own happiness only by those means which are not in themselves criminal or injurious to others.

Rights may be divided or classed in several different ways, an attention to all of which is of use on this subject. Rights may be 1. natural or acquired. Natural rights are such as are essential to man, and universal; acquired are those that are the fruits of industry, the effects of accident or conquest. A man has a natural right to act for his own preservation, and to defend himself from injury, but not a natural right to domineer, to riches (comparatively speaking), or to any particular office in a constituted state.

2. Rights are considered as perfect and imperfect. Those are called

perfect rights which can be clearly ascertained in their circumstances, and which we may make use of force to obtain when they are denied us. Imperfect rights are such as we may demand and others ought to give us, yet we have no title to compel them. Self-preservation is a perfect right, but to have a grateful return for a favor is not a perfect right.

All the duties of justice are founded on the perfect rights; those of mercy generally on the imperfect rights.

The violation of an imperfect right is often as great an act of immorality as that of a perfect right. It is often as immoral, or more so, to refuse to supply the necessitous, or to do it too sparingly, as to commit a small injury against a man's person or fortune. Yet the last is the breach of a perfect right, and the other of an imperfect.

Human laws reach only in ordinary cases to the perfect rights. Sometimes imperfect rights by being carried far become perfect, as humanity and gentleness in a parent to a child may be so grossly violated as to warrant the interposition of human authority.

3. Rights are alienable and unalienable. The first we may, according to justice and prudence, surrender or give up by our own act; the others we may not. A man may give away his own goods, lands, money. There are several things which he cannot give away, as a right over his own knowledge, thoughts, etc. Others, which he ought not, as a right to judge for himself in all matters of religion, his right to self-preservation, provision, etc. Some say that liberty is unalienable and that those who have even given it away may lawfully resume it.

The distinction between rights as alienable and unalienable is very different from that of natural and acquired. Many of the rights which are strictly natural and universal may be alienated in a state of society for the good of the whole, as well as of private persons; as for example the right of self-defense, this is in a great measure given up in a state of civil government into the hands of the public; and the right of doing justice to ourselves or to others in matters of property is wholly given up.

4. Rights may be considered as they differ with regard to their object. (1) Rights we have over our own persons and actions. This class is called liberty. (2) Rights over things or goods which belong to us. This is called property. (3) Rights over the persons and actions of other men. This is called authority. (4) Rights in the things which are the property of others, which are of several sorts.

When we come to the second great division of moral philosophy, politics, the above distinctions will be more fully explained; at present it is sufficient to point at them in order to show what are the great lines of duty from man to man.

Our duty to others, therefore, may be all comprehended in these two particulars, justice and mercy.

Justice consists in giving or permitting others to enjoy whatever they have a perfect right to—and making such a use of our own rights as not to encroach upon the rights of others. There is one writer, David Hume, who has derided the duty of justice, resolving it wholly into power and conveniency, and has affirmed that property is common, than which nothing can be more contrary to reason; for if there is anything clear as a dictate of reason, it is that there are many rights which men severally possess which others ought not to violate. The foundation of property in goods, I will afterwards show you, is plainly laid in the social state.

Another virtue which this author ridicules is chastity. This however will be found to be included in justice, and to be found in the sentiments of all nations, and to have the clearest foundation both in nature and public utility.

Mercy is the other great branch of our duty to man, and is the exercise of the benevolent principle in general, and of the several particular kind affections. Its acts, generally speaking, belong to the class of imperfect rights, which are strongly binding upon the conscience and absolutely necessary to the subsistence of human society, yet such as cannot be enforced with rigor and precision by human laws.

Mercy may be generally explained by a readiness to do all the good offices to others that they stand in need of and are in our power, unless they are opposed to some perfect right, or an imperfect one of greater moment.

Lecture IX

THE third class of moral duties is what contains our duty to ourselves.

This branch of duty is as real and as much founded in the moral principle as any of the former. Conscience as clearly testifies the evil of neglecting it, and vicious conduct in this respect does generally lead us directly not only to misery, but to shame.

We may, I think, divide our duties to ourselves into two heads, which will be both distinct and comprehensive: (1) self-government, (2) self-interest.

1. The first of these is to keep our thoughts, desires, and affections in due moderation. If it be asked what is due moderation, I answer it may be discovered three ways. When the indulgence interferes with our duty (1) to God, (2) to ourselves, and, (3) to our neighbor.

When our thoughts or desires are such as to be contrary to the love, fear, or trust we owe to God, then they are to be restrained and brought into subjection. Thus are generated the virtues of *humility contentment, patience,* and such as are allied to them.

When our thoughts and inward temper are such as to be any way injurious to others, they must be governed and restrained; hence arises the obligation to guard against all the immoral passions, which will produce meekness and composure of spirit.

And when we have got but a little experience, we shall speedily find that an excessive indulgence of any passion—love, hatred, anger, fear—discomposes us exceedingly and is an evil instead of a blessing. We shall therefore perceive the necessity of continence, self-denial, fortitude, restraint, and moderation in everything how good soever.

2. The other general branch of duty to ourselves may be called self-interest. This, taking in natural religion, includes our relation to the Divine Being, and attending particularly to that of procuring his favor. Therefore it is a prime part of our duty to ourselves to guard against anything that may be hurtful to our moral character or religious hopes.

We ought to be active and diligent in acquiring everything necessary for life and comfort. Most of our duties to ourselves resemble the duties of justice and mercy to others. If there are certain offices due to them, and if they have rights and claims in consequence of their state and relations, the same is the case with ourselves. We are therefore to take all proper methods to preserve and acquire the goods both of mind and body—to acquire knowledge, to preserve health, reputation, possessions.

The whole must be kept within some limits; chiefly we must guard against interfering with the rights of others.

It will be proper before concluding this part of the subject to take notice of the opinions of the ancients, particularly their enumeration of what are called the cardinal virtues.

Their cardinal virtues were *justice, temperance, prudence,* and *fortitude.* Justice included the whole of our duty to our neighbor. Humanity or benevolence you see is kept out of view, though a virtue of the first class; but all its exercises are with them ranked under the head of justice; temperance was by them considered as much more extensive than being moderate in the use of meats and drink, to which the English word is chiefly confined. The *Egkrateia* of the Greeks signified not only abstinence in meats and drink, but continence or purity and a moderation of all our desires of whatever kind, of fame and riches, as well as pleasures. Prudence, even in the way they generally explain it, seems scarcely to be a moral, or so much as a natural quality. Prudence they say is taking the wisest course to obtain some good end. Placing this among the cardinal virtues will show how matters stood among them. Great parts or talents were in high esteem. They did not very fully distinguish between a good man and a great man. Prudence seems rather an embellishment of an illustrious character, than a moral virtue. Another reason why prudence seems to have held such a place among the ancients was that their chief foundation for virtue was interest, or what will produce happiness. The inquiry upon this subject was what is the *summum bonum*. Now to this, prudence is very necessary. Agreeably to all this, they commonly called the virtuous man the *wise man,* and he was always a hero.

Fortitude is easily understood and may be considered in two lights, as active and passive, which gives the two great virtues of patience and valor.

One of the most remarkable qualities in morals among the ancients was the debate upon the Stoical position that pain is no evil, nor pleasure any good. This arises from comparing external things with the temper of the mind, when it appears without doubt that the latter is of much more consequence to happiness than the former. They used to reason thus: outward possessions when bestowed upon a bad man make him no better but worse, and finally more miserable. How then can these be goods in themselves which become good or evil according to the state of him that uses them. They were therefore called the things indifferent. There was something strained and extravagant in some of their writings, and perhaps ostentatious, yet a great deal of true and just reasoning. The most beautiful piece of antiquity in the moral way, is the Tablature of Cebes.

Let us now recapitulate what we have gone through, and then add some observations or corollaries on the morality of actions. We have considered,

1. The nature of man.
2. The nature, foundation, and obligation of virtue.
3. Have given a sort of general analysis of the moral laws as pointing out our duty to God, to our neighbor, and ourselves.

We must now consider all morality in general as conformity to a law. We have seen above whence this law is collected, and derives its authority. Men may differ, not only as to the foundation but as to the import or meaning of the law in some particulars, but it is always supposed that the law exists.

The morality of actions may be considered in two different lights, but these very nearly related to each other: (1) as they are ranked and disposed of by the law itself; (2) in the conformity or opposition of the actions to the law.

Under the first view an action is either commanded, forbidden or permitted.

Commanded duties oblige absolutely, and as casuists used to say, *semper non vero ad semper,* that is to say they are obligatory upon all persons at the seasons that are proper for them, but not upon every person at every time because then there could be but one moral duty. All men are obliged to worship God, but this only at certain times, other duties have also their place and season.

Prohibitions oblige *semper et ad semper,* all persons at all times. We must not lie; this obliges every man at every moment because no time or circumstances can make it lawful.

On permission we may observe several things.

1. There is (as some say) a two-fold permission, the one full and absolute, which not only gives us a right to certain things with impunity but implies a positive approbation of the legislator, and the other implies only that the action is left at large, being neither commanded nor forbidden.

2. Permission in natural laws always implies the approbation of the legislator, and whatever is done in consequence of it is innocently done, for God and conscience do not permit or pass uncondemned any bad action.

3. It is otherwise in human laws; if they leave any action open, it may be done with impunity, and yet by no means with approbation. I may have a right by human laws to say things in a covered or couched manner, which yet may carry in them the highest degree of malignity.

4. The truth is when we consider the morality of action in a strict or proper manner, the whole class of permitted actions vanishes. They become by their intention and application either good or bad.

Considering actions in their conformity to the laws, a distinction arises similar to the former, into *good* or just, *bad,* and indifferent.

A good action must be wholly conformable to the law in its substance, and in all its circumstances. It is not enough that it be materially good, the time must be proper and the intention laudable.

A bad action is that which, either in substance or in any circumstance, is contrary to the law.

In consequence of this, strictly and properly speaking all truly good or just actions are equally so, arising from a perfect conformity to the law, as all straight lines are equally straight, but all bad actions are not equally bad, as lines may be bent in a different degree from the straight direction.

Indifferent actions, if there are any truly such, are those that are permitted, and neither commanded nor forbidden by the law; but when we consider the spirit and principles of true morality, we shall find no actions wholly indifferent because we are under an obligation to promote the happiness of ourselves and others, to which every action may be applied immediately or remotely; and subjection to the Divine Will may make part of our design in doing or forebearing anything whatever.

In estimating the morality of actions several circumstances must be considered: (1) the good done; (2) the principle from which it flows—self-interest of the contracted kind, benevolence, or hope of reward; (3) the hindrances or opposition that must be surmounted, as interest, inclination, difficulty. An objection seems to arise from this, not easily solved. If an action is the more virtuous the more opposition, internal and external, that is overcome, then the longer a man has had the habit of virtue and the more completely it is formed, the less merit in his actions. It seems also to take away all moral excellence from the Deity, who cannot be supposed to have the least opposition to encounter, either from within or without. This objection cannot be easily removed but by saying that the opposition is in no other respect an evidence of the good moral temper but as it shows the strength of that inclination that overcomes it, and therefore, when a moral habit is so strong as to overcome and annihilate all opposition, it is so much the more excellent.

An action good in itself may be made criminal by an evil intention.

But no action, in itself evil, can be made lawful or laudable by a good intention.

A man is obliged to follow the dictates of conscience, yet a mistaken conscience does not wholly absolve from guilt because he ought to have been at more pains to obtain information.

An action is not virtuous in proportion to its opposite being vicious. It is no high degree of virtue to love our offspring or provide for a family, but to neglect either is exceedingly vicious.

One phenomenon in human nature nearly connected with the moral feelings has been particularly considered by some writers, viz. that there is such a disposition in the generality of men to crowd to see objects of distress, as an extraordinary public execution. What is the desire that prompts to it? Is the sight of misery a pleasant feeling? Some resolve it merely into curiousity, which they consider as a natural and original impression. But there seems to be something in it different from novelty. Others say it arises from benevolence and is an exercise of compassion, and that we have a strong natural impulse to the affection of pity and really feel a pleasure in indulging it. But though every well-disposed mind is highly susceptible of pity, at least of all the benevolence and help that pity suggests when the object presents itself, we can scarcely say that the feeling is pleasant or that we have a desire after such objects in order to the gratification.

They who reason on the selfish scheme, as usual, resolve all into private interest; they say we delight to see objects of distress because it gives us a secret satisfaction in reflecting upon our own different situation. I believe there is such a satisfaction in narrow and contracted minds, but to those tolerably disposed it has an opposite effect; it makes them rather consider the calamities which they themselves are subject to, than those from which they are free.

Perhaps it would be best to take more than one principle to account for this effect: curiosity must make a part, and probably humanity and compassion also contribute to it. It seems to be thought some little alleviation to the sufferer's misery when others pity him, yet prudent persons knowing how unavailing this pity is often choose to be absent.

Sympathy is a particular affection in aid of benevolence, yet like all other private affections, when it is not moderated, it prevents its own effect: one deeply affected with the view of an object of distress is often thereby incapacitated to assist him.

Another question is sometimes subjoined to the above, why men have pleasure in seeing tragedy, which is a striking representation of a melancholy catastrophe. As far as the subject differs from comedy, it may be accounted for on the same principles with the desire to see objects of distress; but one powerful principle leads both to comedy and tragedy—a pleasure in the imitative arts. An exact portrait of any object whatever gives the highest pleasure, even though the object itself were originally terrible or disgusting.

We see plainly that an indulgence of the pleasure given by a fine performance is what crowds the theatre. Unhappily, to give greater pleasure to a corrupt mind, they often invent such scenes and conduct the matter so as to make the stage the greatest enemy to virtue and good morals.

Lecture X
Of Politics

POLITICS contain the principles of social union and the rules of duty in a state of society. This is but another and more complete view of the same things, drawn out more fully and applied to particular cases. Political law is the authority of any society stamped upon moral duty.

The first thing to be considered in order to see upon what principles society is formed is that state immediately previous to the social state. This is called the state of nature; violent and unnecessary controversies have been made on that subject. Some have denied that any such thing ever existed, that since there were men, they have always been in a social state. And to be sure, this is so far true that in no example or fact could it ever last long. Yet it is impossible to consider society as a voluntary union of particular persons without supposing those persons in a state somewhat different before this union took place: there are rights therefore belonging to a state of nature different from those of a social state.

And distinct societies or states independent are at this moment in a state of nature, or natural liberty, with regard to each other.

Another famous question has been: Is the state of nature a state of war or peace? Hobbes, an author of considerable note but of very illiberal sentiments in politics, is a strenuous advocate for a state of nature being a state of war. Hutchinson and Shaftesbury plead strongly that a state of nature is a state of society. However opposite and hostile their opinions seem to be with regard to each other, it seems no hard matter to reconcile them. That the principles of our nature lead to society—that our happiness and the improvement of our powers are only to be had in society—is of the most undoubted certainty, and that in our nature, as it is the work of God, there is a real goodwill and benevolence to others. But on the other hand, that our nature as it is now when free and independent is prone to injury, and consequently to war, is equally manifest, and that in a state of natural liberty there is no other way but force for preserving security and repelling injury. The inconveniences of the natural state are very many.

One class of the above-mentioned writers say that nature prompts to society, and the other, that necessity and interest obliges to it. Both are equally true.

Supposing then the state of natural liberty antecedent to society to be a reality, let us consider the perfect and imperfect rights belonging to that state that we may see more distinctly how and why they differ in a social state.

The perfect rights in a state of natural liberty are (1) a right to life; (2) a right to employ his faculties and industry for his own use; (3) a right to things that are common and necessary, as air, water, earth; (4) a right to personal liberty; (5) a power over his own life not to throw it away unnecessarily but for a good reason; (6) a right of private judgment in matters of opinion; (7) a right to associate, if he so incline, with any person or persons whom he can persuade (not force)—under this is contained the right to marriage; (8) a right to character, that is to say, innocence (not fame). It is easy to perceive that all these rights belong to a state of natural liberty, and that it would be unjust and unequal for any individual to hinder or abridge another in any one of them without consent or unless it be in just retaliation for injury received.

The imperfect natural rights are very numerous, but they are nearly the same in a state of nature as in a state of society, as gratitude, compassion, mutual good offices—if they will be no injury to the person performing them. Indeed they must be the same in a natural and in a social state because the very definition of an imperfect right is such as you cannot use force to obtain. Now, what you ought not to use force to obtain in a state of natural liberty, human laws in a well constituted state will not give you.

Society I would define to be an association or compact of any number of persons to deliver up or abridge some part of their natural rights in order to have the strength of the united body to protect the remaining and to bestow others.

Hobbes and some other writers of the former age treat with great contempt this which is generally called the social compact. He insists that monarchy is the law of nature. Few are of his sentiments now, at least in Britain, yet it is proper to trace them to the foundation.

It is to be admitted that society began first insensibly by families, and almost necessarily. Hence parental authority was the first law, and perhaps it extended for two or three generations in the early ages. Though the patrons of monarchy use this as an argument, it does not favor their scheme: this which they call the patriarchal government could not extend far; or supposing it could, there would be but one rightful king in all the earth, the lineal descendant of Adam's eldest son, not to mention that the very order of succession in hereditary right has never been uniform and is but of late settled in the European nations.

The truth is, though man for wise reasons afterwards to be noticed continues longer in a family dependance than other animals, yet in time he becomes *sui juris,* and when their numbers are increased, when they either continue together or remove and form distinct societies, it is plain that there must be supposed an expressed or implied contract.

Some say there is no trace or record of any such contract in the beginning of any society. But this is no argument at all, for things inseparable from and essential to any state commonly take place so insensibly that their beginning is not observed.

When persons believe themselves upon the whole rather oppressed than protected in any society, they think they are at liberty either to rebel against it or fly from it, which plainly implies that their being subject to it arose from a tacit consent.

Besides in migrations and planting of colonies in all ages, we see evident traces of an original contract and consent taken to the principles of union.

From this view of society as a voluntary compact results this principle, that men are originally and by nature equal, and consequently free.

Liberty either cannot or ought not to be given up in the social state: the end of the union should be the protection of liberty, as far as it is a blessing. The definition of liberty in a constituted government will be afterwards explained.

Some observe that few nations or societies in the world have had their constitutions formed on the principles of liberty: perhaps not one-twentieth of the states that have been established since the beginning of the world have been settled upon principles altogether favorable to liberty. This is no just argument against natural liberty and the rights of mankind, for it is certain that the public good has always been the real aim of the people in general in forming and entering into any society. It has also constantly been at least the professed aim of legislators. Therefore the principle seems to have been admitted, only they have failed or been disappointed in practice by mistake or deceit. Though perhaps not one-twentieth part of mankind have any tolerable skill in the fine arts, it does not follow that there are no such arts, or that the principles of them are not founded in nature.

Reason teaches natural liberty, and common utility recommends it. Some nations have seen this more clearly than others, or have more happily found the means of establishing it.

Here perhaps we should consider a little the question whether it is lawful to make men or to keep them slaves without their consent. This will fall afterwards to be considered more fully; in the meantime, observe that in every state there must be some superior and others inferior, and it is hard to fix the degree of subjection that may fall to the lot of particular persons. Men may become slaves, or their persons and labor be put wholly in the power of others by consent. They may also sometimes in a constituted state be made slaves by force as a punishment for the commission of crimes. But it is certainly unlawful to make inroads upon others, unprovoked, and take away their liberty by no better right than superior power.

It has sometimes been doubted whether it is lawful to take away the liberty of others for life, even on account of crimes committed. There can be no strong reason given against this except that which is supposed to operate in Great Britain against making malefactors slaves, that it would be unfavorable to rational liberty to see any rank of men in chains. But setting this aside, it seems plain that if men may forfeit their lives to the society, they may also forfeit their liberty, which is a less precious blessing. It seems also more agreeable both to equity and public utility to punish some sort of crimes with hard labor than death. Imprisonment for life has been admitted and practiced by all nations. Some have pleaded for making slaves of the barbarous nations, that they are actually brought into a more eligible state and have more of the comforts of life than they would have had in their own country. This argument may alleviate, but does not justify the practice. It cannot be called a more eligible state if less agreeable to themselves.

Upon the whole, there are many unlawful ways of making slaves, but also some that are lawful; and the practice seems to be countenanced in the law of Moses, where rules are laid down for their treatment, and an estimation of injuries done to them different from that of free men. I do not think there lies any necessity on those who found men in a state of slavery to make them free to their own ruin. But it is very doubtful whether any original cause of servitude can be defended but legal punishment for the commission of crimes. Humanity in the manner of treating them is manifestly a dictate of reason and nature, and I think also of private and public utility as much as of either.

The next step in opening the principles of the social state is to consider the foundation, establishment and extent of property. Some begin this by considering the property of man in general in the inferior creatures. Has he any right to use the lower irrational animals for labour, or food, or both?

It is needless to refine too much upon this subject. To use them for labor seems evidently lawful, as they are inferior, with strength fitted for it, and strength which they could not employ for the improvement and cultivation of the earth without the direction of man. They seem to be to man somehow as the body to the mind. They help to produce food for themselves and so increase their number and receive much more sensual pleasure sharing in all respects with their masters the fruit of their toil.

To use them for food is thus argued to be lawful. If suffered all to live, they would become too numerous and could not be sustained, so that death to many of them in a much worse way must be the certain consequence. Further, nature seems to dictate the use of them for food in the plainest manner, for they are food for one another in a regular gradation, the insect to the birds and fishes, many of them to the beasts, and the smaller to the greater, or the tamer to the more rapacious of every order.

If we take tradition or revelation for our guide, the matter is plain that God made man lord of the works of his hands and put under him all the other creatures. Only it appears that the grant of animal food was made no earlier than to Noah after the flood.

Let us next consider the establishment of private property. Private property is every particular person's having a confessed and exclusive right to a certain portion of the goods which serve for the support and convenciency of life.

In a very imperfect state of society, community of goods may subsist in a great degree, and indeed its subsisting is one of the surest signs of an imperfect state of society. Some attempts have been made in civilized states to introduce it, but without any considerable effect except in Sparta, the constitution of which was very singular. In small voluntary societies, especially of the religious kind, it may be established and will continue so long as the morals of the society are pure. But in civil society fully formed, especially if the state is at all extensive or intended to be so, private property is essentially necessary and founded upon the reason of things and public utility. The reasons of it are:

1. Without private property no laws would be sufficient to compel universal industry. There never was such a purity of manners and zeal for the public in the individuals of a great body but that many would be idle and slothful and maintain themselves upon the labor of others.

2. There is no reason to expect in the present state of human nature that there would be a just and equal distribution to everyone according to his necessity, nor any room for distinction according to merit.

3. There would be no place for the exercise of some of the noblest affections of the human mind, as charity, compassion, beneficence, etc.

4. Little or no incitement to the active virtues—labor, ingenuity, bravery, patience, etc.

Some have laid down schemes for making property common, as Sir Thomas Moore in his *Utopia;* but in general they are chimerical and impracticable. There is no instance in fact where any state that made a figure in the social life had their goods wholly in common. Sparta had the most of it, but it was a very small state and limited in its views; besides there was something so singular in the whole constitution of the Spartan government that its subsisting so long remains a phenomenon for politicians and reasoners yet to account for.

Supposing private property to be essential, or at least useful in the social state, the next question is how does this property take its rise or by what ways is it acquired?

The original ways of acquiring property may be reduced to these two: (1) prior occupation; (2) our own industry.

As to the first of these, it may be analysed thus. Of the things that lay in common for the use of man, I have a right to take what is convenient for me, and after I have taken it, nobody can have a better right, nor consequently any title to take it from me.

But many questions difficult to be resolved arise from the application of this principle. How far does this right extend? Must I take only what is sufficient for the present moment, or may I provide for future necessities and enjoyment. In vacant lands must I take only what I and my present followers can sufficiently occupy, or may I touch a continent and call it mine, though I shall not be able to fill it in many ages. I answer common utility must be the rule in all these cases, and anything more particular must be reserved till we come to the law of nations.

Some say that the water in large bays and rivers ought to be common to all because it is inexhaustible, and one's using it cannot waste or spoil it for the use of others. But the security of societies will point out the measure of property that must be in all those things.

The extent or object of property contains three particulars:

1. A right to the fullest use. Whatever is a person's property, he has a right to do with it as he pleases, with this single exception, if it may be called so, that he may not use it to the injury of others. Full property has no other exception, unless you call this an exception, that if any man would wantonly destroy the fruits of the earth or his habitation, in that case though they were his own people would hinder him, as supposing him to be mad and deprive him not only of that liberty but of all others.

2. Property implies a right of exclusion. We may hinder others from any way intermeddling with what is our property. This seems essential to the idea. Giving a full right to one implies that others have none.

3. It implies a power to alienate. That is to say, a right of alteration, commutation, donation during life, and disposal at death. Thus property is said to be perpetual. There are certain things called by *Civilians Res nullius,* such as temples, public edifices, gates and walls of cities, etc. Temples used to be said to be given to God, and in the laws of civilized states attention is paid to this circumstance. But as to the property or use, the case of them and of all the other things mentioned is very clear. They are under the inspection of the magistrate, or such persons as represent the community, and are by them kept for common use.

Lecture XI

IN the social life in general we may consider (1) domestic, (2) civil society.

The first of these we must consider as implying and made up of several relations, the chief of which are (1) the relation of marriage; (2) that of parents and children; (3) that of master and servant.

In marriage we ought to observe that though all creatures may be said to be propagated in a way in a great degree similar, yet there is something peculiarly distinguished, dignified and solemn in marriage among men. This distinction is necessary, and founded in reason and nature.

Human creatures at their birth are in a state weaker and more helpless than any other animals. They also arrive much more slowly at maturity and need by far most assistance and cultivation. Therefore a particular union of the parents is absolutely necessary, and that upon such powerful principles as will secure their common care. Marriage is a relation expressly founded upon this necessity and must be so conducted as to ascertain the property of the offspring and to promise the most assiduous, prudent, and extensive care.

This is the foundation of marriage drawn from the public good. But we ought also to observe that man is manifestly superior in dignity to the other animals, and it was intended that all his enjoyments, and even his indulgence of instinctive propensities, should be of a more exalted and rational kind than theirs. Therefore the propensity of the sexes to one another is not only reined in by modesty, but is so ordered as to require that reason and friendship and some of the noblest affections should have place. And it is certain that they have, if not a more violent, at least a more lasting and uniform influence in the married state than sensual desire.

It is further observed by moral writers that though beauty and personal attraction may be considered as the first motives, yet these are always supposed to be indications of something excellent in the temper within. So that even love of beauty in man is an attachment to moral excellence. Let a person attend with seriousness, and he will find that the utmost perfection of form in an idiot, or one thoroughly known to be of a very bad temper, is really no object of desire. Though in those who are little known, it is apt to prejudice the ignorant and unwary to judge favorably of the person.

The particulars which reason and nature point out relating to the marriage contract are as follow:

1. That it be between one man and one woman. Polygamy is condemned by nature, for it is found that the males born are to the females as 13 to 12, or as some say as 20 to 19, the overplus being to supply the greater waste of the male part of the species by war and dangerous occupations, hard labor, and traveling by land and sea.

2. The fundamental and essential part of the contract is fidelity and

chastity. This must immediately appear to be essential to the purpose of the union. Some writers say that this is especially binding upon the woman in order to ascertain the offspring, but everybody must see the absurdity of any distinction because the contract would neither be equal nor likely to be steadily observed if it were not mutual. Besides, as a late author has well observed, if chastity be a female virtue, how can men be unchaste without infringing upon it?

3. The contract should be for life, otherwise it would be short, uncertain, and mutual love and industry greatly weakened.

4. If superiority and authority be given to the man, it should be used with so much gentleness and love as to make it a state of as great equality as possible. Hutchinson and some other writers say there should be no superiority, and that their property being common, should not be alienated by the one without the other. Others think that perfect equality of power in two persons is not consistent with order and the common interest and therefore give authority to the man, and the laws of most nations give the man the disposal of property, with the reservation of particular rights to the woman.

Some heathen writers gave the man power of life and death over the woman, a thing evidently barbarous and unjust.

5. Marriages are sometimes dissolved by divorces, which our law permits only on three accounts—adultery, willful and obstinate desertion, and incapacity. The first two of these founded on the New Testament, and the last on reason, being not so properly a dissolution of a marriage as a declaration that it was void from the beginning and never took place.

Some writers of moral philosophy add as causes of divorce contrariety of temper, incurable diseases, and such as would infect the offspring. But none of them seem of sufficient moment. The first would be an evident temptation to causeless and wanton separations, and all the three may be guarded against by previous caution.

Hutchinson observes that in all nations marrying in near degrees of consanguinity or affinity has been avoided and abhorred, and he adds that the natural and general abhorrence of it has been greater than reason seems to dictate. Hence it has been conjectured to have been early tradition or revelation, and men have exercised their invention in finding out the true reason or ground of the prohibition.

One reason assigned is because if marriage were lawful to near relations, their frequent intercourse would be a strong temptation to uncleanness.

Another, that if permitted, it would frequently confound or invert the duties of relations by setting some above others whom they formerly used to obey.

A third reason, and perhaps the best, is that abstaining from blood relations in this voluntary contract extends the social ties and produces a greater number of family relations.

Whatever be the moral reason, it seems to have a strong sanction in nature; for it is observed that marriage between near relations, especially if repeated, greatly weakens the human race.

As to the extent of this prohibition, it has been various in different nations, but the most prevailing has been to forbid all within three degrees. The degrees are reckoned by the steps of descent between the parties and the common parent. Parent and child is the first, child and child the second, child and grandchild, the third, and two grandchildren or first cousins the fourth—when it becomes lawful.

Relation of Parents and Children

The first thing to be observed is that this relation is distinguished by the strongest instinct of parental affection. This seems necessary, as the education of children is a duty requiring so much time, care and expense, which nothing but the most rooted affection would submit to.

The rights of the parent may be summed up in these two: (1) authority, which requires subjection in the children; (2) a right to a grateful return in due time from the children. The first is a perfect right, as far as it extends, but must be limited.

Some nations have given parents the power of life and death over their children, and Hobbes insists that children are the goods and absolute property of their parents and that they may alienate them and fell them either for a time or for life. But both these seem ill founded because they are contrary to the end of this right, viz. instruction and protection. Parental right seems in most cases to be limited by the advantage of the children.

Children are no doubt to judge for themselves in matters of religion when they come to years, though the parents are under the strongest obligation to instruct them carefully to the best of their judgment. Those who insist that to leave them their judgment free they ought not to be taught any principles ought to consider that their scheme is impracticable and absurd. If the parents do not instruct them, they will imbibe prejudices and contract habits, perhaps of the worst kind, from others.

Children in most nations are considered as having a right exclusive of their parents to property given them by others.

Many nations have given the parents a right to dispose of their children in marriage, but this seems to be carrying parental authority too far if it be made absolute because it puts in the power of the parent to dispose of what is most essential to their happiness through the whole of their future life. Yet it seems very contrary to reason and nature that children in early life should dispose of themselves in marriage without consulting their parents.

Since we have denied the power of life and death to parents, it will be asked what is the sanction of their authority? I answer, moderate correction in early life, and as the very highest punishment, expulsion from their family or a forfeiture of the privileges which they despise.

As to the right to a grateful return, it is an imperfect right, but of the strongest kind: sometimes the civil authority interposes and obliges children to maintain their aged parents.

To the disgrace of human nature it is often observed that parental affection is much stronger than filial duty. We must indeed acknowledge the wisdom of Providence in making the instinctive impulse stronger in parents towards their children, than in children towards their parents because the first is more necessary than the other to the public good; yet when we consider both as improved into a virtuous disposition by reason and a sense of duty, there seems to be every whit as much baseness in filial ingratitude as in want of natural affection.

Relation of Master and Servant

This relation is first generated by the difference which God has permitted to take place between man and man. Some are superior to others in mental powers and intellectual improvement, some by the great increase of their property through their own or their predecessors industry, and some make it their choice, finding they cannot live otherwise better, to let out their labor to others for hire.

Let us shortly consider (1) how far this subjection extends; (2) the duties on each side.

As to the first it seems to be only that the master has a right to the labors and ingenuity of the servant for a limited time or at most for life. He can have no right either to take away life or to make it insupportable by excessive labor. The servant therefore retains all his other natural rights.

The practice of ancient nations of making their prisoners of war slaves was altogether unjust and barbarous, for though we could suppose that those who were the causes of an unjust war deserved to be made slaves, yet this could not be the case of all who fought on their side, besides the doing so in one instance would authorize the doing it in any other, and those who fought in defense of their country when unjustly invaded might be taken as well as others. The practice was also impolitic, as slaves never are so good or faithful servants as those who become so for a limited time by consent.

Lecture XII
Of Civil Society

CIVIL society is distinguished from domestic in the union of a number of families in one state for their mutual benefit.

We have before affirmed that society always supposes an expressed or implied contract or agreement. Let us now see what this agreement necessarily implies: (1) the consent of every individual to live in, and be a member of that society; (2) a consent to some particular plan of government; (3) a mutual agreement betweeen the subjects and rulers: of subjection on the one hand, of protection on the other. These are all implied in the union of every society, and they complete the whole.

Any objections that may be raised against this are easily solved, e.g., though every individual has not given an actual consent, yet his determination to live with any society implies it. Again, if it be asked how children come to be members of a society, it is answered they receive the benefits and partake of the rights of the society during the whole time of their education, and as they come to the use of reason, they both claim the privilege and acquiese in the duty of citizens. And if they find anything insupportable in their condition, they may alter it at their pleasure.

Have then all subjects a right when they see fit to remove from the society in which they are? I answer that in all ordinary cases they ought to have, at least in time of peace. Perhaps it may be affirmed with justice that they who have enjoyed the privileges of any society in time of peace, if war or danger to the public should arise, they may be hindered from emigrating at that time and compelled to contribute their share in what is necessary to the common defense.

Whatever is the form of government in any society, the members may be divided into two classes, the *rulers* and the *ruled,* the magistrates and subjects.

The rights of rulers may be divided into essential and accidental: the essential such as in general must be vested in rulers of every society, the accidental such as may be given to the rulers in some societies, but not in others.

The essential rights of rulers are what require most to be enumerated, and these again by some good writers are divided into greater and lesser essentials.

Of the first kind are (1) legislation; (2) taxation for the public expence; (3) jurisdiction, or the administration of justice; (4) representation, or appearing and acting in name of the whole in all transactions with adjacent independent states, chiefly for the purposes of making war or peace.

The less essential rights of rulers are many, and they are called less essential because they may be more varied than the others, such as coining of money, possessing or managing public edifices, conferring honors on officers, etc.

The rights of subjects in a social state cannot be enumerated, but they may be all summed up in *protection,* that is to say those who have surrendered part of their natural rights expect the strength of the public arm to defend and improve what remains.

It has been often said that government is carried on by rewards and punishments, but it ought to be observed that the only reward that a state can be supposed to bestow upon good subjects in general is protection and defense. Some few who have distinguished themselves in the public service may be distinguished by particular rewards, but to reward the whole is impossible because the reward must be levied from those very persons to whom it is to be given.

After what has been said on the foundation of society, viz. consent, perhaps it may be necessary to mention two exceptions.

1. It is said by some with apparent reason that a few persons if accidentally armed with power may constrain a large ignorant rabble to submit to laws which will be for their good. This I would admit in some cases, when there is an evident madness and disorder in the multitude and when there is a moral certainty that they will afterwards be pleased with the violence done them. But in general it is but a bad maxim that we may force people for their good. All lovers of power will be disposed to think that even a violent use of it is for the public good.

2. Though people have actually consented to any form of government, if they have been essentially deceived in the nature and operation of the laws, if they are found to be pernicious and destructive of the ends of the union, they may certainly break up the society, recall their obligation, and resettle the whole upon a better footing.

Of the Different Forms of Government

As soon as men began to consider and compare forms of government, they divided them into three general and simple kinds: (1) monarchy, (2) aristocracy, (3) democracy. These are called simple because they are clearly distinguishable from each other in their nature and effects. The ancients generally divided the forms of government in this manner because most of their governments were of one or other of these kinds with very little mixture.

Monarchy is when the supreme power is vested in a single person. Mr. Hutchinson says monarchy may be either absolute or limited, but this is an inaccuracy, for limited monarchy is one of the mixed kinds of government.

But monarchy may be either temporary or for life. The Roman dictators were absolute for a time, and so long as they continued, the government was purely monarchical, all other powers being dormant.

Monarchy may also be either hereditary or elective.

Aristocracy is that form of government in which the supreme power is lodged with a small number of nobles. This is capable of the same variations as monarchy, and it may be either temporary or perpetual, hereditary or elective, with this difference that a temporary or elective aristocracy always put some power in the hands of the people. The most complete aristocracy is when the ruling party have the power or cooptation within themselves and can fill up as they please the vacancies made by deaths or resignation.

Democracy is when the supreme power is left in the multitude. But as in large governments the people in a collective body cannot well meet together, nor could they transact business with any convenience if they did, they may meet by representatives chosen either by the whole or by particular districts.

From those simple forms are generated many complex forms; two of them may be compounded together, either in equal or in different proportions, or all these may be united, as in the British government.

After pointing out the simple forms of government, it will be proper to make some general observations upon government and apply them to the various forms to show whether any of them is preferable to the other and the advantages and defects of each in particular.

1. There are four things that seem to be requisite in a system of government, and every form is good in proportion as it possesses or attains them: (1) wisdom to plan proper measures for the public good; (2) fidelty to have nothing but the public interest in view; (3) secrecy, expedition, and dispatch in carrying measures into execution; and (4) unity and concord, or that one branch of the government may not impede or be a hindrance to another.

Monarchy has plainly the advantage in unity, secrecy, and expedition. Many cannot so easily nor so speedily agree upon proper measures, nor can they expect to keep their designs secret; therefore say some, if a man could be found wise enough and just enough for the charge, monarchy would be the best form of government. Accordingly we find that in the command of a ship, fleet, or army, one person is commonly intrusted with supreme power; but this does not apply to states for many reasons. No man can be found who has either skill sufficient, or if he had, could give attention to the whole departments of a great empire. Besides, in hereditary monarchies there is no security at all for either wisdom or goodness, and an elective monarchy, though it may seem to promise ability, has been always found in experience worse than the other because there is no reason to expect that an elected monarch will have the public good at heart, he will probably mind only private or family interest.

Aristocracy has the advantage of all the others for *wisdom* in deliberations; that is to say, a number of persons of the first rank must be supposed by their consultations to be able to discover the public interest. But it has very little or no prospect of fidelity or union. The most ambitious projects and the most violent and implacable factions often prevail in such states.

Democracy has the advantage of both the others for fidelity; the multitude collectively always are true in intention to the interest of the public because it is their own. They are the public. But at the same time it has very little advantage for wisdom, or union, and none at all for secrecy and expedition. Besides, the multitude are exceeding apt to be deceived by demagogues and ambitious persons. They are very apt to trust a man who serves them well with such power as that he is able to make them serve him.

If the true notion of liberty is the prevalence of law and order and the security of individuals, none of the simple forms are favorable to it.

Monarchy everyone knows is but another name for tyranny, where the arbitrary will of one capricious man disposes of the lives and properties of all ranks.

Aristocracy always makes vassals of the inferior ranks, who have no hand in government; and the great commonly rule with greater severity than absolute monarchs. A monarch is at such a distance from most of his subjects that he does them little injury, but the lord of a petty seigniory is a rigorous taskmaster to his unhappy dependants. The jealousy with which the members of an aristocratical state defend their own privileges is no security at all for humanity and easy treatment to their inferiors, for example, the Spartans in their treatment of the Helots, and the barons in all the feudal governments in their treatment of their vassals.

Pure democracy cannot subsist long, nor be carried far into the departments of state, it is very subject to caprice and the madness of popular rage. They are also very apt to choose a favorite and vest him with such power as overthrows their own liberty, for example, Athens and Rome.

Hence it appears that every good form of government must be complex so that the one principle may check the other. It is of consequence to have as much virtue among the particular members of a community as possible, but it is folly to expect that a state should be upheld by integrity in all who have a share in managing it. They must be so balanced that when everyone draws to his own interest or inclination, there may be an over poise upon the whole.

2. The second observation upon the forms of government is that where there is a balance of different bodies, as in all mixed forms, there must be always some *nexus imperii,* something to make one of them necessary to the other. If this is not the case, they will not only draw different ways, but will often separate altogether from each other. In order to produce this *nexus,* some of the great essential rights of rulers must be divided and distributed among the different branches of the legislature. For example in the British government, the king has the power of making war and peace, but the Parliament has the levying and distribution of money, which is a sufficient restraint.

3. The third observation is that the ruling part of any state must always have considerable property, chiefly of lands. The reason is property has such an invariable influence that whoever possesses property must have power. Property in a state is also some security for fidelty because interest then is concerned in the public welfare.

For this reason, did men in every state live entirely by agriculture, an agrarian law would be necessary to liberty because if a vast proportion of property came into a few hands, they would soon take all power to themselves. But trade and commerce supersede the necessity of this because the great and sudden fortunes accumulated by trade cause a rotation of property.

4. In a well-formed state the subjects should not be too numerous, nor too few. If very numerous, the principles of government cannot exert their force over the whole. The Roman Empire fell by its own weight. If the subjects are too few, they are not sufficient to supress internal insurrections or repel attacks from without.

5. It is frequently observed that in every government there is a supreme irresistible power lodged somewhere, in king, senate, or people. To this power is the final appeal in all questions. Beyond this we cannot go. How far does this authority extend? We answer as far as authority in a social state can extend; it is not accountable to any other tribunal; and it is supposed in the social compact that we have agreed

to submit to its decision. There is however an exception; if the supreme power wherever lodged come to be exercised in a manifestly tyrannical manner, the subjects may certainly if in their power resist and overthrow it. But this is only when it becomes manifestly more advantageous to unsettle the government altogether than to submit to tyranny. This resistance to the supreme power however is subverting the society altogether, and is not to be attempted till the government is so corrupt as that anarchy and the uncertainty of a new settlement is preferable to the continuance as it is.

This doctrine of resistance even to the supreme power is essentially connected with what has been said on the social contract and the consent necessary to political union. If it be asked who must judge when the government may be resisted, I answer the subjects in general, everyone for himself. This may seem to be making them both judge and party, but there is no remedy. It would be denying the privilege altogether to make the oppressive ruler the judge.

It is easy to see that the meaning of this is not that any little mistake of the rulers of any society will justify resistance. We must obey and submit to them always till the corruption becomes intolerable, for to say that we might resist legal authority every time we judged it to be wrong would be inconsistent with a state of society and to the very first idea of subjection.

The once famous controversy on passive obedience and nonresistance seems now in our country to be pretty much over; what the advocates for submission used to say was that to teach the lawfulness of resisting a government in any instance and to make the rebel the judge is subversive of all order and must subject a state to perpetual sedition. To which I answer, to refuse this inherent right in every man is to establish injustice and tyranny and leave every good subject without help, as a tame prey to the ambition and rapacity of others. No doubt men may abuse the privilege, yet this does not make it void. Besides it is not till a whole people rise that resistance has any effect, and it is not easy to suppose that a whole people would rise against their governors, unless when they have really received very great provocation. Whereas on the other hand, nothing is more natural than for rulers to grasp at power, and their situation enables them to do it successfully by slow and insensible encroachments. In experience there are many instances of rulers becoming tyrants, but comparatively very few of causeless and premature rebellions. There are occasional and partial insurrections in every government. These are easily raised by interested persons, but the great majority continues to support order.

6. Dominion, it is plain from all that has been said, can be acquired justly only one way, viz. by consent. There are two other ways

commonly mentioned, both of which are defective, inheritance and conquest. Hereditary power, which originally rose from consent and is supposed to be founded upon the continuance of consent (as that of the hereditary power in a limited monarchy), is as lawful as any; but when they pretend such a right from nature is independent of the people, it is absurd. That which is called the right of conquest ought to be exploded altogether. We shall see by and by what is the right of a conqueror in a just war. It was his right before, and he obtains possession of it by conquest. But to found any claim merely on conquest is not a right, but robbery.

Upon the whole, I will conclude with a few remarks upon the spirit and tendency of different forms of government.

1. Monarchical government has a tendency to politeness and elegance of manners, and generally to luxury. The submission and obsequiousness practiced at the court of a monarch diffuses itself through the whole state.

2. Aristocracy narrows the mind exceedingly, and indeed cannot long subsist in a large state. A small aristocracy, however, may subsist as a form of government as long as any method or longer.

3. Democracy tends to plainness and freedom of speech, and sometimes to a savage and indecent ferocity. Democracy is the nurse of eloquence because when the multitude have the power, persuasion is the only way to govern them.

Let us now ask this short question, what is the value and advantage of civil liberty?

Is it necessary to virtue? This cannot be supposed. A virtous mind and virtuous conduct is possible, and perhaps equally possible, in every form of government.

Is it necessary to personal private happiness? It may seems so. We see the subjects of arbitrary governments however not only happy, but very often they have a greater attachment to their form of government than those of free states have to theirs. And if contentment be necessary to happiness, there is commonly more impatience and discontent in a free state than in any other. The tyranny even of an absolute monarch does not affect with personal injury any of his subjects but a few, and chiefly those who make it their choice to be near him. Perhaps in free governments the law and the mob do more mischief to private property than is done in any absolute monarchy.

What then is the advantage of civil liberty? I suppose it chiefly consists in its tendency to put in motion all the human powers. Therefore it promotes industry, and in this respect happiness; produces every latent quality; and improves the human mind. Liberty is the nurse of riches, literature, and heroism.

Lecture XIII
Of the Law of Nature and Nations

THE next thing in order is to treat of what is called the law of nature and nations. It has been before observed that separate and independent states are with regard to one another in a state of natural liberty, or as man to man before the commencement of civil society. On this several questions arise. (1) Is there any such law? (2) What is the law? (3) What is its sanction, or how is it to be enforced?

That there is such a law is plain from the reasons that show the obligation which one man lies under to another. If there are natural rights of men, there are natural rights of nations. Bodies politic in this view do not differ in the least from individuals. Therefore as before, reason, conscience and common utility show that there is a law of nature and nations.

The question what it is must be considered in the same manner. I am not able to recollect any perfect or imperfect right that can belong to one man as distinguished from another, but what belongs to nations, save that there is usually less occasion for the imperfect rights. If we read over the perfect rights in a state of natural liberty, we shall see they all apply to nations.

It will also appear that the imperfect rights apply, but the occasions of exerting them are much more rare. For example, it is more rare to see a nation in a state of general indigence so as to require a supply. Yet this sometimes happens. It did so in the case of Portugal, at the time of the great earthquake at Lisbon. And the other nations of Europe lent them assistance. It is also from this priciple that ships of different nations meeting at sea will do acts of humanity to one another. Sometimes also there are national favors that deserve national gratitude. But this is seldom merited and, I believe, still seldomer paid.

As to the sanction of the law of nature and nations, it is no other than a general sense of duty and such a sense of common utility as makes men fear that if they notoriously break these laws, reproach and infamy among all nations will be the effect, and probably resentment and indignation by common consent.

The violation of the natural rights of mankind being a transgression of the law of nature, and between nations as in a state of natural liberty there being no method or redress but force, the law of nature and nations has as its chief or only object the manner of making war and peace.

In war it is proper to consider distinctly (1) the causes for which a just war may be carried on; (2) the time of commencing; (3) the duration; (4) the means by which it may be carried on.

(1) As to the first, the causes of commencing war are according to the principles above laid down, the violation of any perfect right—as taking away the property of the other state or the lives of its subjects, or restraining them in their industry, or hindering them in the use of things common, etc. There is only one perfect right, the violation of which does not seem to be a cause of war; I mean that by which we have a right to character. National calumny is scarcely a cause of war because it cannot be frequent or of great effect. The violation of imperfect rights cannot usually be a cause of war between nations, yet a case may be supposed in which even these would be a just cause of war. Suppose a ship of any nation should go into a port of another in the greatest distress, and not only the people in general but the governing part of the society should deny them all assistance. This would be an act of such notorious inhumanity and of such evil example that it may justify national resentment, and yet even here I think there should first be a demand of justice upon the offending persons before vengeance should be taken upon the state.

These are the just and legitimate causes of making war. Some add to them that when a nation is seen to put itself in such a situation as to defense, or as to the means of annoying others, that it seems to threaten hostilities, then we are not obliged to wait till it has committed actual injury but may put it in a state of incapacity; but there is no other truth in this but what is founded upon the other; for the preservation of our property implies that if others take such measures as are not to be accounted for but upon the supposition of an intention of wronging me, it is often easier and safer to prevent and disarm the robber than to suffer him to commit the violence, and then to strip him and rob him of his prey.

One thing more is to be added, that every nation has a right to join which it pleases of two contending parties. This is easily resolved into the general principles, for the injured party may be supposed to go to war in defense of some perfect right, and the cause being just, the imperfect right of humanity, as well as general and common utility, calls for assistance to the oppressed. So that if we have a right to associate with any nation, we may be entitled to protect their property and rights.

(2) As to the time of commencing war, it seems to be no way contrary to natural law to say it is at any time the injured party pleases after having received an injury; but accident or utility, or a desire in each party to manifest the equity of their cause, has introduced universally the custom of declaring war. This begun very early and, though not of absolute right, having been generally introduced must be continued, though there is often more of form than of substance in it; for nations do often begin both attack and defense before declaration, as well as

make all the necessary preparation for striking the most effectual blow. The meaning of a declaration of war seems to be to call upon the injured party to prevent it by reparation—likewise to manifest to all other states the justice of the cause.

(3) The duration of a war should be according to natural equity, till the injury be completely redressed and reasonable security given against future attacks; therefore the practice, too common, of continuing a war for the acquisition of empire is to be condemned. Because one state has done some injury to another, it seems quite unreasonable that they should not only repair the injury, but subvert and ruin the offending state altogether; this would be unreasonable between man and man if one had wronged another, not only to repair the wrong, but to take all the rest that he had and reduce his family to beggary. It is even more unreasonable in states because the offenders in states are not to be supposed to be the whole people, but only the rulers or perhaps only some individuals.

Perhaps it may be asked what is *reasonable* security against future injury. I answer, between equal independent nations, solemn treaties ought to be considered as security, but if faith has been often broken, perhaps something more may be required. The mutual complaints of nations against each other for breach of faith makes conquerors often demand such a degree of security as puts the conquered altogether in their power.

(4) As to the legitimate means of carrying on the war, in general it may be said in one word, by force or open violence. It is admitted on all hands that this force may be used against the person and goods, not only of the rulers, but of every member of the hostile state. This may seem hard, that innocent subjects of the state should suffer for the folly and indiscretion of the rulers or of other members of the same state, but it is unavoidable. The whole individuals that compose a state are considered but as one body; it would be impossible for an enemy to distinguish the guilty from the innocent; and when men submit to a government, they risk their own possessions on the same bottom with the whole in return for the benefits of society.

Open violence may be said to have no bounds, and therefore every method that can be invented and the most deadly weapons of annoyance may seem to be permitted. But from what has been said above, and upon the principles of general equity, all acts of cruelty and inhumanity are to be blamed, and all severity that has not an immediate effect in weakening the national strength of the enemy is certainly inhumanity— such as killing prisoners whom you can keep safely, killing women and children, burning and destroying everything that could be of use in life.

The use of poisoned weapons has been also generally condemned—the poisoning of springs or provisions.

To the honor of modern times, and very probably I think to the honor of Christianity, there is much more humanity in the way of carrying on war than formerly.

To aim particularly at the life of a leader or person of chief note seems to have nothing in it unjust or improper because the more important the life, it does more toward the finishing of the war; but what many seem to admit, the bribing of his own people to assassinate him privately, I cannot think honorable or fair.

A question is often moved in morals, how far it is lawful to deceive an enemy, especially if we hold the general and universal obligation of truth. To this it may be answered in the first place that we may certainly with great justice conceal our own designs from an enemy—as indeed we may generally from friends by silence and guarding against every circumstance that may betray them. Neither do I think there is anything at all blameworthy in a general of an army using ambiguous signs, as feigned marches of a part or the whole, putting up lights or such things, because after a declaration of war he does not pretend to give information to his enemy of his motions; nay it is expected on both sides that they will do the best they can to overreach one another in point of prudence. Yet I can scarce think it right to employ people to go to the enemy and, professing to be sincere, tell direct falsehoods and deceive them by that false intelligence.

It is the custom of all to send spies to discover the enemy's designs, and also to bribe some of the enemies themselves to discover the designs of their leaders. The last of which is, I think, at least of a doubtful nature, or rather unjust. Though sending spies is by all approved, yet (what may seem a little unaccountable) such spies are always punished with instant death by the opposite side when detected. The reason probably is that pretending friendship they have a right to consider them as traitors, or as they are in an act of hostility, they kill them, as they would do an enemy in battle when in their power.

These circumstances apply to all war in general, but there is a distinction of wars by civilians into two kinds, *solemn* and *civil*. The first includes all wars between states formerly independent, the other internal insurrections of a part of one government against another.

There has generally been a great difference in the behavior of the opposite parties in these different wars. In solemn wars there is a presumption of integrity in the plurality on both sides; each believes his own cause to be just. On this account they are to be treated with the more humanity. In civil wars the insurgents are considered as making unjust resistance to the ruling part of the society, and therefore guilty of the greatest crimes against society. Therefore they are often treated with great rigor, and when taken in battle, reserved to solemn trial and public execution. There is some reason for this in many cases, when it is indeed an unreasonable or unprovoked insurrection of disorderly citizens; but there are many cases in which the pretenses on both sides are so plausible that the war should be in all respects considered as solemn.

It should be observed, notwithstanding the hostile disposition, there are occasions, both in a treaty for peace and during the continuance of the war, when enemies are under the strongest obligations to sincerity in their behavior to each other—when proposals are made for accomodating the differences, for a suspension of arms, for an exchange of prisoners, or anything similar.

It is worthwhile to inquire whether the greatest honor and candor in war, with a strict adherence to all the laws above laid down, would give any party a great advantage who should take the liberty of transgressing them—as for example, who should use poisoned weapons, should send people to tell false stories, should bribe subjects to assassinate a hostile prince. I answer that they would have no advantage at all, but probably the contrary. There is something powerful in magnanimity which subdues the hearts of enemies, nay, sometimes terrifies them, and particularly inspires a general's army with invincible courage. Besides these, sinister arts are not so terrible as may be imagined: telling false news is as easily discovered as any trick whatsoever.

Prudence and integrity have no need of any assistance from fraud: acts even of generosity, from enemy to enemy, are often as useful as any acts of hostility. There was something very handsome in the Roman general who refused to avail himself of the treachery of a schoolmaster, as well as whimsical in the way in which he punished the traitor.

Of Making Peace

As already hinted, all proposals tending to this purpose ought to be made with the utmost sincerity. Of all deceits in war the most infamous is that of making treaty, or seeking a conference, only to take advantage of the security of one party to destroy him—by assassination or by breaking a truce to fight with advantage.

The terms of peace ought to be agreeable to the end of making war. Damages should be repaired and security given against future injury.

We have often said that nation to nation is as man to man in a state of natural liberty; therefore treaties of peace between nations should in general proceed upon the same principles as private contracts between man and man. There is however an exception: that contracts between individuals are (at least by law) always void when they are the effect of constraint upon one side. Now this must not hold in treaties between nations because it would always furnish a pretext for breaking them. On the side of the conquered, a treaty is always in a great degree the effect of necessity.

It is generally, however, laid down in most authors as a principle that the terms imposed and submitted to may be sometimes so rigorous and oppressive as to justify the injured party in revolting when they are able. This seems to me to be very lax in point of morals. It would be better I think to say that the people who made the treaty should not recede from it. Their posterity, however, at some distance cannot be supposed bound to unjust servitude by the deeds of their fathers.

Let us conclude this subject by a few remarks on the situation of neutral states.

1. Every state has a right when others are contending to remain neuter and assist neither party.

2. They have a right to all their former privileges with both the contending parties—may carry on their traffic with both, and may show all the usual marks of friendship to both. Only it has been generally agreed upon that they are not to trade with any of them in certain articles supposed to be of consequence in carrying on war, particularly provisions and arms.

3. Neutral powers should keep their harbors alike open to both for common refreshment and as an asylum to fly to. And it is held necessary that the contending powers must not carry on their quarrel nor exercise any hostilities within the territories of a neutral state.

4. Neutral states may purchase moveable goods from any of the contending parties which have been taken from the other. But not so with respect to lands or forts because if the other party are able, they will retake their possessions.

5. Deeds of a violent possessor are held to be valid, that is to say, if a conqueror prevails for a time, and levies tribute from any country and afterwards the rightful possessor prevails, it would be unjust to demand the tribute again because the true owner was not able to give protection to the subjects and what was paid was lost through his weakness. The same thing may be said of a dependant state: if it owes any money and service to a supreme state, and an enemy exact it by force, the proper creditor cannot justly demand it again.

On the whole, those things that have been generally received as the law of nature and nations are founded on the principles of equity, and when well observed, do greatly promote general utility.

Lecture XIV
Jurisprudence

JURISPRUDENCE is the method of enacting and administering civil laws in any constitution.

We cannot propose to go through a system of civil laws, and therefore what I have in view is to make some preliminary remarks and then to point out the *object* of civil laws and the manner of their operation.

1. The first preliminary remark is that a constitution is excellent when the spirit of the civil laws is such as to have a tendency to prevent offenses and make men good, as much as to punish them when they do evil.

This is necessary in some measure, for when the general disposition of a people is against the laws, they cannot long subsist, even by a strict and rigorous execution on the part of the rulers. There is however more of this in some constitutions that in others. Solon and Xenophon, as well as Lycurgus, seem to have formed their plan very much with this view to direct the manners of the people in the first place, which will always make the observation of particular laws easy.

But how shall the magistrate manage this matter, or what can be done by law to make the people of any state virtuous? If, as we have seen above, virtue and piety are inseparably connected, then to promote true religion is the best and most effectual way of making a virtuous and regular people. Love to God and love to man is the substance of religion; when these prevail, civil laws will have little to do.

But this leads to a very important disquisition, how far the magistrate ought to interfere in matters of religion. Religious sentiments are very various, and we have given it as one of the perfect rights in natural liberty, and which ought not to be alienated even in society, that everyone should judge for himself in matters of religion.

What the magistrate may do on this subject seems to be confined to the three following particulars.

(1) The magistrate (or ruling part of any society) ought to encourage piety by his own example, and by endeavoring to make it an object of public esteem. Whenever the general opinion is in favor of anything, it will have many followers. Magistrates may promote and encourage men of piety and virtue, and they may discountenance those whom it would be improper to punish.

(2) The magistrate ought to defend the rights of conscience and tolerate all in their religious sentiments that are not injurious to their neighbors. In the ancient heathen states there was less occasion for this because in the system of polytheism the different gods and rites were not supposed to be opposite, but coordinate and consistent; but when

there is believed to be but one God, the sentiments about his nature and worship will often be considered as essentially repugnant one to another.

The pretense of infidels that persecution only belongs to the Christian religion is absurd, for the Christian was the first religion that was persecuted, and it was the necessary consequence of saying that the gods of the heathens were no gods.

At present as things are situated one of the most important duties of the magistracy is to protect the rights of conscience.

It is commonly said, however, that in case any sect holds tenets subversive of society and inconsistent with the right of others that they ought not to be tolerated. On this footing popery is not tolerated in Great Britain because they profess entire subjection to a foreign power, the see of Rome, and therefore must be in opposition to the proper interest of their own state, and because violence or persecution for religion is a part of their religion, which makes their prosperity threaten ruin to others, as well as the principle imputed to them, which they deny, that faith is not to be kept with heretics. But however just this may be in a way of reasoning, we ought in general to guard against persecution on a religious account as much as possible because such as hold absurd tenets are seldom dangerous. Perhaps they are never dangerous, but when they are oppressed. Papists are tolerated in Holland without danger to liberty. And though not properly tolerated, they are now connived at in Britain.

In ancient times, in great states the censorial power was found necessary to their continuance, which inspected the manners of men. It seems probable that supporting the religious sects in modern times answers this end, for the particular discipline of each sect is intended for the correction of manners.

(3) The magistrate may enact laws for the punishment of acts of profanity and impiety. The different sentiments of men and religion ought not by any means to encourage or give a sanction to such acts as any of them count profane.

Many are of opinion that besides all this, the magistrate ought to make public provision for the worship of God in such manner as is agreeable to the great body of the society, though at the same time all who dissent from it are fully tolerated. And indeed there seems to be a good deal of reason for it, that so instruction may be provided for the bulk of common people, who would many of them neither support nor employ teachers unless they were obliged. The magistrate's right in this case seems to be something like that of a parent: they have a right to instruct, but not to constrain.

2. The second preliminary remark is that laws should be so framed

as to promote such principles in general as are favorable to good government, and particularly that principle, if there be one, that gave rise to the constitution and is congenial to it.

Such a principle as I have in view is generally the point of honor in a country, and this lawgivers and administrators of law should endeavor to preserve in its full vigor, for whenever it is undermined, the constitution goes to ruin.

Of these principles, sobriety, industry, and public spirit are the chief. Some states are formed to subsist by sobriety and parsimony, as the Lacedemonians.

Industry is the prevailing principle in others, as in Holland. Public spirit in others, as in Greece, ancient Rome, and Britain. Only public spirit may be diversified; sometimes it is a passion for acquiring glory and dominion, as in Rome, and sometimes for preserving liberty, as in Greece and Britain.

When I say that in the management of a state the utmost attention should be given to the principle of the constitution to preserve it in its vigor, I mean that though all other crimes are bad, and in part tend to the ruin of a state, yet this is much more the case with crimes against that principle than any other. Any act of immorality was bad at Sparta, but to make poverty and parsimony reproachful and to introduce fine houses and furniture and delicate entertainments would have been instant ruin.

Any act of immortality would be hurtful in Holland, but to make fraudulent bankruptcy less infamous than it is would immediately destroy them.

Sobriety, industry, and public spirit are nearly allied and have a reciprocal influence upon one another. Yet there may be a great degree of some of them in the absence of the others. In Sparta there was much sobriety and public spirit, but little industry. In Athens, industry and public spirit with very little parsimony.

In opposition to the whole of this, Mandeville wrote a book called *The Fable of the Bees,* which seems to be leveled against sobriety, industry, and public spirit all at once; his position is that *private vices are public benefits,* and that the waste and luxury of one man supplies the wants of another; but it is easy to overthrow his reasoning, for though sober and industrious persons spend each less than a profuse person, yet sobriety and industry tend much more to population, and by that means they are mutually serviceable to each other. Luxury and vice only waste and destroy, they add nothing to the common stock of property or of happiness. Experience fully justifies this, for though from the luxury of one man another may reap some gain, the luxury of a nation always tends to the ruin of that nation.

3. A third preliminary remark is that laws may be of two kinds, either written or in the breasts of magistrates. In every constitution of note, there is something of each of these kinds. It is uncertain whether it is better to have many or few special laws. On the one hand, it seems to be the very spirit of a free constitution to have everything as strictly defined as possible and to leave little in the power of the judge. But on the other hand, a multiplicity of laws is so apt to lead to litigation and to end in ambiguity that perhaps judges of equity, chosen by the district in which they live and are to act, and chosen but for a time, would be a more just and equitable method of ending differences. But the difficulty of settling a constitution so as always to secure the election of impartial judges has made modern states where there is liberty prefer a multiplicity of written laws.

4. The last preliminary remark is that no human constitution can be so formed, but that there must be exceptions to every law. So that there may be in every nation oppression under form of law, according to the old maxim, *summum jus summa injuria.* This further shows the necessity of forming the manners of a people.

After having laid down these preliminaries, we may observe that the object of civil laws may be divided into the three following particulars.

1. To ratify the moral laws by the sanction of the society. The transgression of such laws are called *crimes,* as profanity, adultery, murder, calumny, etc. And they are prosecuted and punished by order of the public according to the spirit of every constitution.

2. To lay down a plan for all contracts in the commerce or intercourse between man and man. To show when a contract is valid, and how to be proved. The transgressions of such laws are called *frauds.* They chiefly regard the acquisition, transmission, or alienation of property.

3. To limit and direct persons in the exercise of their own rights, and oblige them to show respect to the interfering rights of others. This contains the whole of what is called the police of a country, and the transgression of such laws are called *trespasses.* A number of things in this view may become illegal which before were not immoral.

Of the Sanction of the Moral Laws

In all polished nations there are punishments annexed to the transgression of the moral laws, whether against God, our neighbor, or ourselves; in the doing of which, the three following things are chiefly necessary.

1. To determine what crimes and what degree of the same crime are to be inquired into by the civil magistrate. It is of necessity that in a free state crimes should be precisely defined that men may not be ignorantly

or rashly drawn into them. There are degrees of every crime—profanity, impurity, violence, slander that are blameable in point of morals, nay, even such as may fall under the discipline of a religious society—that if they were made cognizable by the civil magistrate would multiply laws and trials beyond measure.

2. To appoint the methods of ascertaining the commission of crimes. This is usually by testimony in which we are to consider the number and character of the witnesses. Generally through Christendom, and indeed most other parts of the world, two witnesses have been esteemed necessary to fix crimes upon an accused person, not but that the positive evidence of one person of judgment and untainted character is in many cases sufficient to gain belief and often stronger than two of unknown or doubtful credit, but it was necessary to lay down some rule, and two are required to guard against the danger of hired evidence and to give an opportunity of trying how they agree together. To have required more would have made a proof difficult or impossible in many cases.

It seems to be a maxim in law, and founded on reason, that in the case of what are called occult crimes, such as murder, adultery, forgery, and some others, where the nature of the thing shows that there must be a penury of evidence, they sometimes content themselves with fewer witnesses if there are corroborating circumstances to strengthen their testimony.

It seems to be a matter not easily decided whether it be agreeable to reason and justice in the case of very atrocious crimes that on account of the atrocity less evidence should be sufficient for conviction, or that more should be required. On the one hand, the more atrocious the crime, the greater the hurt to society, and the more need of public vengeance. On the other hand, the more atrocious the crime and the heavier the punishment, it seems agreeable to justice that the conviction should be upon the more unquestioned evidence. Lawyers are seen to take their common places, sometimes the one way, sometimes the other. It is often thought that in practice, less evidence is suffient to convict a man of murder, forgery, rape, and other crimes of a deep dye. But I am persuaded that the appearance is owing to the greater and more general eagerness to discover the perpetrators of such crimes. Others are suffered to escape more easily, not that more evidence is necessary, but that it is more difficult to get at the evidence.

Evidence may be distinguished into two kinds, *direct* and *circumstantial*. Direct evidence is when the witnesses swear to their sight or knowledge of the accused committing the crime. Circumstantial, when they only swear to certain facts which cannot be supposed to have existed unless the crime had been committed, as a man found dead, another found near the place with a weapon bloody or clothes bloody, etc. Some have affirmed that circumstantial evidence is stronger than direct, but it must be taken with very great caution and judgment.

3. The law is to proportion and appoint the punishment due to every crime when proven.

Punishment in all regular states is taken wholly out of the hands of the injured persons and committed to the magistrate, though in many or most cases the injured party is suffered to join the magistrate in the prosecution and to have a certain claim, by way of reparation, as far as that is practicable.

Therefore the punishment in general must consist of two parts, (1) reparation to the sufferer, (2) the *vindicta publica,* which has sometimes two ends in view: to be an example to others and to reclaim and reform the offender, as in corporal punishment less than death; sometimes but one, the good of others in the example, as in capital punishments and banishment.

The kind of punishment and the degree is left wholly to different lawgivers and the spirit of different constitutions. Public utility is the rule. Punishment is not always proportioned to the atrociousness of the crime in point of morals, but to the frequency of it and the danger of its prevailing.

Some nations require and some will bear greater severity in punishments than others.

The same or similar conduct often produces opposite effects. Severe laws and severe punishments sometimes banish crimes, but very often the contrary. When laws are very sanguinary, it often makes the subjects hate the law more than they fear it, and the transition is very easy from hating the laws to hating those who are entrusted with the execution of it. Such a state of things threatens insurrections and convulsions, if not the dissolution of a government.

Another usual effect of excessive severity in laws is that they are not put in execution. The public is not willing to lend its aid to the discovery and conviction of offenders, so that in time the law itself becomes a mere *brutum sulmen* and loses its authority.

I may make one particular remark, that though many things are copied from the law of Moses into the laws of the modern nations, yet so far as I know none of them have introduced the *lex talionis* in the case of injuries, an eye for an eye and a tooth for a tooth, etc; and yet perhaps there are many instances in which it would be very proper. The equity of the punishment would be quite manifest, and probably it would be as effectual a restraint from the commission of injury as any that could be chosen.

The concluding remark shall be that it is but seldom that very severe and sanguinary laws are of service to the good order of a state, but after laws have been fixed with as much equity and moderation as possible, the execution of them should be strict and rigorous. Let the laws be *just* and the magistrate *inflexible*.

Lecture XV

THE second object of civil laws being to regulate the making of contracts and the whole intercourse between man and man relating to the acquisition, possession and alienation of property, we must consider carefully the nature of

Contracts

A contract is a stipulation between two parties, before at liberty, to make some alteration of property or to bind one or both parties to the performance of some service.

Contracts are absolutely necessary in social life. Every transaction almost may be considered as a contract, either more or less explicit.

The principle thing which constitutes a contract is consent. But in some kinds of contracts, viz. the gratuitous, the consent of the receiver is presumed. In the transmission of estates by donation or testament this is presumed, and those who are incapable of giving their consent through infancy may notwithstanding acquire property and rights. When a man comes into a settled country and purchases property, he is supposed, besides every other part of the bargain, to purchase it under such conditions and subject himself to such laws as are in force in that country.

Contracts are said to be of three degrees in point of fullness and precision: (1) A simple affirmation of a design as to futurity, as when I say to anyone that I shall go to such a place tomorrow; this is not properly binding, and it is supposed that many things may occur to make me alter my resolution, yet a frequent alteration of professed purposes gives the character of levity; therefore a prudent man will be cautious of declaring his purposes till he is well determined. (2) A gratuitous promise of doing some favor to me. This is not made binding in law, nor does it usually convey a perfect right, because it supposes that the person who was the object of goodwill may by altering his behaviour forfeit his title to it, or that the person promising may find it much more inconvenient, costly, or hurtful to himself than he supposed; or, lastly, that what was intended as a service if performed appears plainly to be an injury. In the last case everyone must see that it cannot be binding, but in the two former, I apprehend that in all ordinary cases a distant promise is binding in conscience, though it may not be necessary to make it binding in law. I say all ordinary cases because it is easy to figure a case in which I may make a promise to another, and such circumstances may afterwards occur as I am quite confident, if the person knew, he would not hold me to my promise. (3) The third degree is a complete contract, with consent on both sides and obligation upon one or both.

The essentials of a contract which render it valid, and any of which being wanting it is void, are as follow: That it be (1) free, (2) mutual, (3) possible, (4) careful, (5) with a capable person, (6) formal.

(1) It must be free. Contracts made by unjust force are void always in law, and sometimes in conscience. It must however be unjust force because in treaties of peace between nations, as we have seen before, force does not void the contract; and even in private life sometimes men are forced to enter into contracts by the order of a magistrate, sometimes by the threatening of legal prosecution, which does not make them void.

(2) They must be mutual; that is, the consent of the one as well as that of the other must be had. Contracts in this view become void either by fraud on one side or by essential error. If any man contrives a contract so as to bind the other party and keep himself free, this fraud certainly nullifies the agreement—or if there is an essential error in the person or the thing, as if a person should oblige himself to one man supposing him to be another.

(3) Contracts should be of things evidently possible, and probably in our power. Contracts by which men oblige themselves to do things impossible are no doubt void from the beginning, but if the impossibility was known to the contracting party, it must have been either absurd or fraudulent. When things engaged for become impossible by the operation of Providence without a man's own fault, the contract is void, and he is guiltless—as if a man should covenant to deliver at a certain place and time a number of cattle, and when he is almost at the place of destination they should be killed by thunder or any other accident out of his power.

(4) Contracts must be of things lawful. All engagements to do things unlawful are from the beginning void, but by unlawful must be understood the violation of perfect rights. If a man oblige himself for a reward to commit murder, or any kind of fraud, the engagement is void; but it was criminal in the transacting, and the reward ought to be returned or given to public uses. There are many contracts, however, which are very blameable in making that must, notwithstanding, be kept, and must not be made void in law—as rash and foolish bargains, where

there was no fraud on the other side. If such were to be voided, great confusion would be introduced. The cases of this kind are numerous and may be greatly diversified.

(5) Contracts must be made with a capable person, that is to say of age, understanding, at liberty, etc. It is part of the civil law, or rather municipal law, of every country to fix the time of life when persons are supposed capable of transacting their own affairs. Some time must be fixed, otherwise it would occasion numberless disputes difficult to be decided. A man at the age of fourteen and a woman at twelve may choose guardians, who can alienate their property, and at the age of twenty-one they have their estates wholly in their own hand.

(6) Contracts must be formal.

The laws of every country limit a great many circumstances of the nature, obligation, extent, and duration of contracts.

Having pointed out something of the essential characters of all lawful contracts, I observe they may be divided two different ways. First, contracts are either absolute or conditional. The absolute are such as are suspended upon no condition, but such as are essential to every contract, which have been mentioned above. Such as when a person makes a settlement upon another without reserve, then whether he behave well or ill, whether it be convenient or inconvenient, it must be fulfilled. Conditional contracts are those that are suspended on any uncertain future contingency, or some performance by the opposite party. Of this last sort are almost all transactions in the way of commerce—which leads to the second way of dividing contracts, into beneficent and onerous. The first is when one freely brings himself under an obligation to bestow any favor or do any service, as donations or legacies and undertaking the office of guardian of another person's estate.

The onerous contract is when an equal value is supposed to be given on both sides, as is the case for the most part in the alienation of property, and the transactions between man and man and between society and society.

To this place belongs the question about the lawfulness of lending money upon interest. If we consider money as an instrument of commerce and giving an opportunity of making profit, there seems plainly to be nothing unjust that the lender should share in the advantage arising from his own property.

The chief thing necessary is that the state or governing part of the society should settle the rate of interest, and not suffer it to depend upon the necessity of the poor or the covetousness of the rich. If it is not settled by law, usury will be the certain consequence.

The law of Moses does not seem to have admitted the taking of interest at all from an Israelite. It is thought however that the main reason of this must have been drawn from something in their constitution as a state that rendered it improper, for if it had been in itself immoral, they would not have been permitted to take it of strangers.

Of the Marks or Signs of Contracts

All known and intelligent marks of consent are the signs and means of completing contracts. The chief of these however are words and writing, as being found the most easy and useful. Words are of all others the most natural and proper for giving immediate consent, and writing to perpetuate the memory of the transaction. There are however many other signs that may be made use of, and wherever there is a real purpose of signifying our intention by which others are brought to depend upon it, the engagement is real, and we are bound in conscience, though the law in every country must of necessity be more limited. The whole rests ultimately on the obligation to sincerity in the social life.

This obligation arises from the testimony of conscience, and from the manifest utility and even necessity of sincerity to social intercourse.

Signs are divided into *natural, instituted,* and *customary.* Natural signs are those which have either a real likeness to the thing signified, or such a known and universal relation to it that all men must naturally be led from the one to the other—as a picture is a natural sign because a representation of the thing painted. An inflamed sullen countenance and fiery eyes are natural signs of anger because they are the universal effects of that passion.

Instituted signs are those that have no other connection with the thing signified than what has been made by agreement, as if two persons shall agree between themselves that if the one wants to signify to the other at a distance that he wishes him to come to his assistance, he will kindle a fire upon a certain hill or hang out a flag upon a certain pinnacle of his house or some part of his ship. Words and writing are properly instituted signs, for they have no relation to the thing signified but what original agreement and long custom has given them.

Customary signs are no other than instituted signs which have long prevailed, and whose institution has either been accidental or has been forgotten. It is also usual to apply the word customary to such signs as depend upon the mode and fashion of particular countries. There are some signs and postures which, though they may seem perfectly arbitrary, have obtained very generally, perhaps universally, as bending down the body or prostration as a sign of respect and reverence, kneeling and lifting up the hands as a sign of submission and supplication. Perhaps both these are natural, as they put the person into the situation least capable of resistance.

Sometimes there is a mixture of natural and instituted signs, as if a man sends a pair of wings or the figure of them to a friend to intimate his danger and the necessity of flying.

In the use of signs, the great rule of sincerity is that wherever we are bound, and wherever we profess to communicate our intention, we ought to use the signs in the least ambiguous manner possible. When we have no intention and are under no obligation to communicate anything to others, it is of small moment what appearances are; it is their business not to make any unnecessary or uncertain inferences. A light in a house in the middle of the night will perhaps suggest most probably to a traveler accidently passing that there is somebody sick in that house, yet perhaps it is extraordinary study or business that keeps some person awake.

Nay when there is no obligation to give, nor any reason for the party to expect true information, it is held generally no crime at all to use such signs as we have reason to suppose will be mistaken, as when one who does not desire to be disturbed keeps his chamber close shut that people may conclude he is not there, or when a general of an army puts a fire in the camp to conceal his march or retreat. And probably none would think it faulty when there was an apprehension of thieves to keep a light burning in a chamber to lead them to suppose the whole family is not at rest.

There are some who place in the same rank evasive phrases when there is an apparent intention to speak our mind but no right in the other to obtain it. Such expressions may be strictly true, and yet there is all probability that the hearer will misunderstand them. As if one should ask if a person was in any house and should receive for answer, he went away yesterday morning, when perhaps he returned the same evening. I look upon these evasions, however, as very doubtful, and indeed, rather not to be chosen because they seem to contain a profession of telling our real mind.

Some mention ironical speech as an exception to the obligation to sincerity. But it is properly no objection at all because there is no deception. Truth lies not in the words themselves, but in the use of them as signs. Therefore if a man speak his words in such a tone and manner as the hearer immediately conceives they are to be taken in an opposite sense, and does really take them in the sense the speaker means them, there is no falsehood at all.

Mr. Hutchinson and some others allow a voluntary intended departure from truth on occasion of some great necessity for a good end. This I apprehend is wrong, for we cannot but consider deception as in itself base and unworthy, and therefore a good end cannot justify it.

Besides, to suppose it were in men's power on a sufficient occasion to violate truth would greatly destroy its force in general, and its use in the social life.

There are two sorts of falsehood which, because no doubt they are less aggravated than malicious interested lies, many admit of, but I think without sufficient reason.

1. Jocular lies, when there is a real deception intended, but not in anything material, nor intended to continue long. However harmless these may seem, I reckon they are to be blamed because it is using too much freedom with so sacred a thing as truth. And very often such persons, as a righteous punishment in Providence, are left to proceed further, and either to carry their folly to such excess as to become contemptible, or to go beyond folly into malice.

2. Officious lies, telling falsehoods to children or sick persons for their good. These very seldom answer the end that is proposed. They lessen the reverence for truth and particularly with regard to children are exceedingly pernicious, for as they must soon be discovered, they lose their force and teach them to deceive. Truth and authority are methods infinitely preferable in dealing with children, as well as with persons of riper years.

Lecture XVI
Of Oaths and Vows

AMONG the signs and appendages of contracts are oaths and vows.

An oath is an appeal to God, the searcher of hearts, for the truth of what we say and always expresses or supposes an imprecation of his judgment upon us if we prevaricate.

An oath therefore implies a belief in God and his Providence, and indeed is an act of worship, and so accounted in Scripture, as in that expression, "Thou shalt fear the Lord thy God, and shalt swear by his name." Its use in human affairs is very great when managed with judgment. It may be applied, and indeed has been commonly used, first, in the contracts of independent states who have no common earthly superior. In ancient times it was usual always to close national treaties by mutual oaths. This form is not so common in modern times, yet the substance remains; for an appeal is always supposed to be made to God against the breach of public faith.

Second, it has been adopted by all nations in their administration of justice in order to discover truth. The most common and universal application of it has been to add greater solemnity to the testimony of witnesses. It is also sometimes made use of with the parties themselves for conviction or purgation. The laws of every country point out the cases in which oaths are required or admitted in public judgment. It is, however, lawful and in common practice for private persons voluntarily on solemn occasions to confirm what they say by oath. Persons entering on public offices are also often obliged to make oath, that they will faithfully execute their trust.

Oaths are commonly divided into two kinds, *assertory* and *promissory,* those called *purgatory* fall under the first of these divisions. There is perhaps little necessity for a division of oaths, for they do not properly stand by themselves; they are confirmations and appendages of contracts and intended as an additional security for sincerity in the commerce between man and man.

Therefore oaths are subject to all the same regulations as contracts, or rather oaths are only lawful when they are in aid or confirmation of a lawful contract. What therefore voids the one will void the other and nothing else. A contract otherwise unlawful cannot be made binding by an oath, but there must be a very great caution used not to make any unlawful contract, much less to confirm it by an oath.

It is easy to see the extreme absurdity of our being obliged to fulfill a criminal engagement by oath, for it would imply that out of reverence to God we ought to break his commands; but nothing can be more abominable than the principle of those who think they may safely take an unlawful oath because it is not binding: this is aggravating gross injustice by deliberate profanity.

I have said that oaths are appendages to all lawful contracts, but in assertory oaths which are only confirmations of our general obligation to sincerity, it is necessary not only that what we say be true, but that the occasion be of sufficient moment to require or justify a solemn appeal to God. Swearing on common occasions is unnecessary, rash, profane, and destructive of the solemnity of an oath and its real use.

From the general rule laid down, that oaths are lawful when applied to lawful contracts, it will follow that they become unlawful only when the fulfilling of them would be violating a perfect right; but perhaps an additional observation is necessary here. Contracts must be fulfilled when they violate an imperfect right, whereas some oaths may be found criminal and void, though they are only contrary to imperfect rights, as for example some persons bind themselves rashly by oath that they will never speak to or forgive their children who have offended them. This is so evidently criminal that nobody will plead for its being obligatory, and yet it is but the violation of an imperfect right. The same persons however might in many ways alienate their property to the prejudice of their children by contracts which the law would oblige them to fulfill.

In vows there is no party but God and the person himself who makes the vow; for this reason, Mr. Hutchinson relaxes their obligation very much: supposing any person had solemnly vowed to give a certain part of his substance to public or pious uses, he says if he finds it a great inconvenience to himself or family, he is not bound; this I apprehend is too lax. Men ought to be cautious in making such engagements, but I apprehend that when made, if not directly criminal, they ought to be kept.

Of the Use of Symbols in Contracts

Besides promises and oaths, there is sometimes in contracts a use of other visible signs called symbols, the most common among us are signing and sealing a written deed. There is also in some places the delivery of earth and stone in making over land—and sundry others. In ancient times it was usual to have solemn symbols in all treaties— mutual gifts, sacrifices, feasts, setting up pillars. The intention of all such things, whenever and wherever they have been practiced, is the same. It is to ascertain and keep up the memory of the transaction. They were more frequent and solemn in ancient times than now because before the invention of writing they were more necessary.

Of the Value of Property

Before we finish the subject of contracts, it may be proper to say a little of the nature and value of property, which is the subject of them. Nothing has any real value unless it be of some use in human life, or perhaps we may say, unless it is supposed to be of use, and so becomes the object of human desire—because at particular times and in particular places, things of very little real importance acquire a value, which is commonly temporary and changeable. Shells and baubles are of great value in some places; perhaps there are some more baubles highly valued in every place.

But though it is their use in life that gives things their value in general, it does not follow that those things that are of most use and necessity are therefore of greatest value as property or in commerce. Air and water, perhaps we may add fire, are of the greatest use and necessity; but they are also in greatest plenty, and therefore are of little value as a possession or property. Value is in proportion to the plenty of any commodity and the demand for it. The one taken in the inverse, and the other in the direct proportion.

Hence it follows that money is of no real value. It is not wealth properly but the sign of it, and in a fixed state of society the certain means of procuring it. In early times, traffic was carried on by exchange of goods; but being large, not easily divided or transported, they became very troublesome. Therefore it soon became necessary to fix upon some sign of wealth to be a standard by which to rate different commodities.

Anything that is fit to answer the purpose of a common sign of wealth must have the following properties. It must be (1) valuable, that is have an intrinsic commercial value, and rare, otherwise it could have no comparative value at all; (2) durable, otherwise it could not pass from hand to hand; (3) divisible, so that it might be in larger or smaller quantities as are required; (4) portable, it must not be of great size, otherwise it would be extremely inconvenient.

Gold and silver were soon found to have all these properties, and therefore are fixed upon as the sign of wealth. But besides being the sign of the value of other commodities, they themselves are also matters of commerce, and therefore increase or decrease in their value by their plenty or scarceness.

It may seem to belong to the ruling part of any society to fix the value of gold and silver as signs of the value of commodities, and no doubt they do fix it nominally in their dominions. But in this they are obliged to be strictly attentive to the value of these metals as a commodity from their plenty or scarceness; otherwise their regulations will be of little force: other nations will pay no regard to the nominal value of any particular country, and even in internal commerce, the subject would fix a value upon the signs according to their plenty.

It is as prejudicial to commerce to make the nominal value of the coin of any country too small as too great.

We shall close this part of the subject by speaking a little of the

Rights of Necessity, and Common Rights

These are certain powers assumed both by private persons and communities which are supposed to be authorized by the necessity of the case and supported by the great law of reason.

There will remain a great number of cases in which those rights of necessity are to be used, even in the best regulated civil society, and after the most mature deliberation and foresight of probable events, and provision for them by specific laws.

Were a man perishing with hunger and denied food by a person who could easily afford it him, here the rights of necessity would justify him in taking it by violence. Were a city on fire and the blowing up of a house would save the far greater part, though the owner was unwilling, men would think themselves justified in doing it whether he would or not. Much more would men in cases of urgent necessity make free with the property of others without asking their consent, but presuming upon it.

In our own government, where, by the love of liberty general among the people and the nature of the consitutions, as many particulars have been determined by special laws as in any government in the world; yet instances of the rights of necessity occur every day. If I see one man rob another upon the highway or am informed of it, if I have courage and ability, I pursue the robber and apprehend him without any warrant and carry him before a magistrate to get a warrant for what I have already done. Nothing is more common in Britain than to force people to sell their inheritance or a part of it to make a road or street straight or commodious. In this instance it is not so much necessity as great utility.

The question of the greatest moment here is whether the establishing these rights of necessity does not derogate from the perfection and immutability of the moral laws. If it be true that we may break in upon the laws of justice for the sake of utility, is not this admitting the exploded maxim that we may do evil that good may come? I answer that these rights of necessity have in general property as their object, or at most the life of particular persons, and it seems to be inseparable from the establishment of property in the social state that our property is to be held only in such manner, and to such a degree, as to be both consistent with and subservient to the good of others. And therefore these extraordinary cases are agreeable to the tacit or implied conditions of the social contract.

In rights of necessity we are to consider not only the present good or evil but for all time to come, and particularly the safety or danger of the example. Where the repetition of the thing in similar circumstances would have a fatal effect, it ought not to be done. If a city were under all the miseries of famine and a ship or two should arrive with grain, the owner of which would not sell it but at a most exhorbitant price, perhaps equity might admit that they should be compelled; but if any such thing were done, it would prevent others from going near that place again.

It would be of no consequence to determine these rights of necessity by law. If the law described circumstantially what might be done, it would be no longer a right of necessity but a legal right. To forbid them by law would be either ineffectual, or it would abolish them altogether and deprive the society of the benefit of them when the cases should occur. Things done by the rights of necessity are by supposition illegal, and if the necessity does not excuse, the person who pretends them may be punished. If I am aiding in pulling down a man's house on pretence of stopping a fire, if he afterwards makes it appear that there was not the least occasion for it, or that I, being his enemy, took the opportunity of this pretence to injure him, he will obtain reparation.

As property, or at most life, is concerned in the rights of necessity, still the moral laws continue in force. Whatever expresses an evil disposition of mind does not fall under the rule because it can never be necessary to the doing of any good. The pretense of its being necessary in some cases is generally chimerical, and even were it real, the necessity could not justify the crime—as suppose a robber very profane should threaten a man with death unless he would blaspheme God or curse his parents, etc.

There are certain things called common rights which the public is supposed to have over every member: the chief of them are (1) diligence. As a man must eat, the community have a right to compel him to be useful—and have a right to make laws against suicide. (2) They have a right to the discovery of useful inventions, provided an adequate price be paid to the discoverer. (3) They have a right to insist upon such things as belong to the dignity of human nature. Thus all nations pay respect to dead bodies, though there is no other reason for it but that we cannot help associating with the body, even dead, the ideas which arise from it and belonged to the whole person when alive.

The third and last object of civil laws is limiting citizens in the exercise of their rights, so that they may not be injurious to one another, but that the public good may be promoted.

This includes giving directions in what way arts and commerce may be carried on, and in some states extends as far as the possessions of private persons.

It includes the whole of what is called the police of a community— the manner of traveling, building, marketing, time and manner of holding all sorts of assemblies. In arts and commerce, particularly, the police shows its power.

It will only be necessary here to make a few remarks on the nature and spirit of those laws.

1. Those things in themselves are arbitrary and mutable, for there is no morality in them but what arises from common utility. We may sometimes do things in a way better than that appointed by law, and yet it is not allowed.

2. Men in general have but a very light sense of the malignity of transgressing these laws, such as running of goods, breaking over a fence, etc.

3. In the best constitutions some sanctions are appointed for the breach of these laws. Wherever a state is founded upon the principles of liberty, such laws are made with severity and executed with strictness.

Finally, a man of real probity and virtue adopts these laws as a part of his duty to God and the society, and is subject not only for wrath, but also for conscience sake.

Recapitulation

HAVING gone through the three general divisions of this subject, ethics, politics, and jurisprudence, I shall conclude with a few remarks upon the whole and mention to you the chief writers who have distinguished themselves in the branch of science.

1. You may plainly perceive both how extensive and how important moral philosophy is. As to extent, each of the divisions we have gone through might have been treated at far greater length. Nor would it be unprofitable to enter into a fuller disquisition of many points, but this must be left to every scholar's inclination and opportunities in future life. Its importance is manifest from this circumstance, that it not only points out personal duty, but is related to the whole business of active life. The languages, and even mathematical and natural knowledge, are but handmaids to this superior science.

2. The evidence which attends moral disquisitions is of a different kind from that which attends mathematics and natural philosophy, but it remains as a point to be discussed whether it is more uncertain or not. At first sight it appears that authors differ much more, and more essentially, on the principles of moral than natural philosophy. Yet perhaps a time may come when men, treating moral philosophy as Newton and his successors have done natural, may arrive at greater precision. It is always safer in our reasonings to trace facts upwards than to reason downwards upon metaphysical principles. An attempt has been lately made by Beatty, in his *Essay on Truth,* to establish certain impressions of common sense, as axioms and first principles of all our reasonings on moral subjects.

3. The differences about the nature of virtue are not in fact so great as they appear: they amount to nearly the same thing in the issue when the particulars of a virtuous life come to be enumerated.

4. The different foundations of virtue are many of them not opposite or repugnant to each other, but parts of one great plan—as benevolence and self-love, etc. They all conspire to found real virtue: the authority of God, the dictates of conscience, public happiness, and private interest all coincide.

5. There is nothing certain or valuable in moral philosophy but what is perfectly coincident with the scripture, where the glory of God is the first principle of action, arising from the subjection of the creature—

where the good of others is the great object of duty, and our own interest the necessary consequence.

In the first dawn of philosophy, men began to write and dispute about virtue. The great inquiry among the ancients was, what was the *summum bonum*? By which it seems they took it for granted that virtue and happiness were the same thing. The chief combatants here were the Stoics and Epicureans. The first insisted that virtue was the *summum bonum,* that pleasure was no good and pain no evil; the other said that the *summum bonum* consisted in pleasure, or rather that pleasure was virtue; the Academics and Platonists went a middle way between these.

I am not sensible that there is anything among the ancients that wholly corresponds with the modern dispute upon the foundation of virtue.

Since the disputes arose in the sixteenth and seventeenth centuries, some of the most considerable authors, chiefly British, are Leibnitz, his *Theodicee* and his letters; Clark's *Demonstration* and his letters; Hutchinson's *Inquiries into the Ideas of Beauty and Virtue,* and his *System;* Woolaston's *Religion of Nature Delineated;* Collins *On Human Liberty;* Nettleton *On Virtue and Happiness;* David Hume's *Essays;* Lord Kaims's *Essays;* Smith's *Theory of Moral Sentiments;* Reid's *Inquiry;* Balfour's *Delineation of Morality;* Butler's *Analogy* and sermons; Balguy's tracts; Theory of agreeable sensations from the French; Beattie *On Truth, Essay on Virtue and Harmony.*

To these may be added the whole deistical writers and the answers written to each of them in particular, a brief account of which may be seen in Leland's *View of the Deistical Writers.*

Some of the chief writers upon government and politics are Grotius, Puffendorf, Barberac, Cumberland, Selden, Burlamaqui, Hobbes, Machiavelli, Harrington, Locke, Sydney, and some late books, Montesquieu's *Spirit of Laws,* Ferguson's *History of Civil Society,* Lord Kaims's political essays, grandeur and decay of the Roman empire, Montague's rise and fall of ancient republics, Goguet's rise and progress of laws, arts, and sciences.

LECTURES ON
ELOQUENCE

Lecture 1

Gentlemen,

WE are now to enter on the study of eloquence, or as perhaps it ought to be called from the manner in which you will find it treated, composition, taste, and criticism.

Eloquence is undoubtedly a very noble art, and when possessed in a high degree has been, I think, in all ages one of the most admired and envied talents. It has not only been admired in all ages, but if I am not mistaken among all ranks. Its power is universally felt, and therefore probably the talent more universally esteemed than either genius or improvement in several other kinds of human excellence. Military skill and political wisdom have their admirers, but far inferior in number to those who admire, envy, or would wish to imitate him that has the power of persuasion.

Plato in his *Republic,* or idea of a well regulated state, has banished orators under pretense that their power over the minds of men is dangerous and liable to abuse. Some moderns have adopted the same sentiments.

Sir Thomas More in his *Utopia,* I believe (though I am not certain), has embraced it. But this is a manner of thinking and reasoning altogether superficial. It would militate equally against all cultivation of the mind, and indeed against every human excellence, natural and acquired. They are, and have been, and may be abused by men of vicious dispositions. But how shall this be prevented? It is impossible. How shall it be counteracted? Only by assisting the good in the cultivation of their powers, and then the same weapons will be used in defense of truth and virtue with much greater advantage than they can be in support of falsehood and vice. Learning in general possessed by a bad man is unspeakably pernicious, and that very thing has sometimes made weak people speak against learning; but it is just as absurd as if in the confines of a country exposed to hostile inroads, the inhabitants should say we will build no forts for protection because if the enemy get into possession of them they will become the means of annoyance; we will use no arms for defense, for if the enemy take them from us, they will be turned against us.

Perhaps it may be proper to take notice of what the apostle Paul says in his first epistle to the Corinthians in several places, particularly from the beginning of the second chapter, "and I brethren," etc. and in the fourth chapter, verse 11, "And my speech, and my preaching was not," etc. I have mentioned this to prevent any of you mistaking or being prejudiced against the subject and shall observe upon it that the meaning of the apostle in this and other similar passages is fully comprehended in one or more of the following particulars: (1) that he came not to the Corinthians with an artful delusive eloquence, such as the sophists of these days made use of to varnish over their foolish sentiments; (2) that he came not to show his skill in speaking for and against anything, as many of them did not to discover or communicate truth but to display their own talents; (3) that the truths he had to communicate needed no ornaments to set them off and were not by any means adapted to the proud spirit of the world; and (4) that he would use the greatest self-denial, and not by any means attempt to recommend himself as a man of ability and learning, but content himself with the humble and simple doctrine of the cross. And the truth is after the highest improvement in the art of speaking, there must be the greatest reserve and self-denial in the use of it, otherwise it will defeat its own purpose. Rhetoricians do usually give it among the very precepts of the art to appear to be in earnest, and to have the subject or the interest of the audience at heart and not their own fame; and this can never be attained to so great perfection as when there is the humility of a true disciple and the disinterested zeal of a faithful minister of Christ. That this is not contrary to the most diligent application for the improvement of our powers is manifest in itself and appears from the many exhortations of the same apostle to his young disciples, Timothy and Titus: 1 Tim. 4:13, "Till I come, give attendance," etc., and 5:15, "meditate," etc.

I know not whether any apology is necessary for my undertaking to speak on this subject or the manner of treating it. Some may expect that discourses on eloquence should be distinguished examples of the art of which they treat. Such may just be pleased to observe that a cool, plain, and simple manner of speaking is necessary in teaching this, as well as every other art. No doubt a justness and precision of expression will be of great benefit in these discourses, but there will be no need of that high and complete polish that might be expected in what is prepared for publication. Nor would the same brevity and conciseness be any advantage to discourse once delivered that would be reckoned a beauty in what is in everybody's hands and therefore may be often read.

Before entering on the strict and methodical discussion of the subject, I have commonly begun the course by two or three preliminary discourses, containing such general observations as may be most intelligible and may serve to prepare the way for what shall be afterwards introduced.

The subject of the first preliminary discourse shall be the following question: whether does art or nature contribute most to the production of a complete orator?

This is a question often asked, and many things have been said upon it; yet to discuss it as a matter of controversy and adduce the arguments on each side in order to a decision in favor of the one and prejudice of the other, I take to be of very little consequence, or rather improper and absurd. It seems to be just as if one should propose an inquiry whether the soil, the climate, or the culture contributes most to the production of the crop? Therefore, instead of treating the question as if one side of it were true and the other false, I shall make a few observations on the mutual influence of nature and art in order to your forming just apprehensions of the subject and to direct you in your future conduct and studies.

1. Some degree of natural capacity is evidently necessary to the instruction or study of this art in order to produce any effect. A skillful laborer may subdue a very stubborn or meliorate a very poor soil; but when there is no soil at all, as on a bare and solid rock, his labor would be impossible or fruitless. There must therefore doubtless be some capacity in general and even some turn for this very branch of knowledge. In this sense it is true of every other art, as well as oratory, a man must be born to it.

There are some so destitute of oratorical powers that nothing can possibly be made of them. It will be strange however if this is not easily discovered by themselves and if it does not make the study as unpleasant as it is difficult, so that they will speedily give it over. I have known some examples, but very few, of ministers whose principal defect was mere barrenness of invention. This is exceedingly rare because the far greatest number of bad speakers have enough to say, such as it is, and generally the more absurd and incoherent, the greater the abundance.

When speaking on this observation, I must make one remark, that a total want of capacity for one branch of science is not inconsistent even with a great capacity for another. We sometimes see great mathematicians who make miserable orators. Nay it is reckoned by some of the best judges that this study is unfriendly to oratory. The definite precision of mathematical ideas, which may all be ultimately referred to mensuration, seems to be contrary to the freedom and boldness of imagination in which the strength of oratory lies. There are, however, exceptions to this in fact. Dr. Clark and Dr. Barrow, two of the most eminent mathematicians of the last age, were also eminent orators; that is to say, the first was a very accurate writer, the other a very fervent preacher.

I have only further to observe that many have thought academical teaching not to be favorable to oratory; that is to say, those who are accustomed to the cool dispassionate manner of speaking usual and necessary in the instruction of youth frequently lose a good deal of that fire and impetuosity which they might naturally possess, and which is of so much importance in speaking to a large and promiscuous assembly.

2. To make what is called a complete orator, very great natural powers are necessary, and great cultivation too. The truth is, when we speak of a complete orator, we generally form an idea of perfection superior to anything that ever existed by assembling together all the excellencies of every kind that have been seen in different persons, or that we are able from what we have seen to form an imagination of. We can easily enumerate many of these; for example, great penetration of mind, great literature and extensive knowledge, a strong and lively imagination reined in by a correctness of judgment, a rich invention and retentive memory, tenderness and sensibility of affection, an acquaintance with the world, and a thorough knowledge of the human heart. To these we must add all external perfections, an open countenance, a graceful carriage, a clear articulate strong melodious voice. There is not one of these but is capable of great improvement by application and study, as well as by much practice. In all the great orators of whom we read, there appears to have been a union of natural talents and acquired skill, Pericles, Demosthenes, Cicero, Hortentius. To these you may add all the speakers mentioned by Cicero and Quintilian, taking their talents and performances to have been as related by these authors.

3. Perhaps the most extraordinary appearances in this as well as in other branches have been from nature wholly, or but with little study. These spontaneous productions are as so many prodigies. It is commonly believed that the orators and sages at the first formation of society were more powerful in their elocution than in more polished times. This, however, I am apt to think is in some degree founded on a mistake. There might be more extraordinary effects of eloquence because the ignorant or superstitious herd were then more easily moved, but this was as much owing to the state of the audience as the power of the

speakers. The same fire that would burn a heap of dry brush would not make any impression upon a heap of green logs. It might also be owing to another circumstance, which I shall have occasion afterwards to explain more fully, the narrowness of language and the use of figures, which have so great an effect upon the imagination.

But allowing very great force to uncultivated prodigies of genius in every kind, I am apt to think it is less powerful, comparatively speaking, in oratory than in poetry. It has been an old saying, "Poeta nascitur et non fit." There are two reasons why the poetry of nature without art seems to be so much admired. (1) That in such a poet a strong unbounded fancy must be the prevailing character, and this is what chiefly captivates the mind. It must be a very strong inward impulse that induces a man to become a poet without example and without instruction. (2) It is found in fact that the knowledge of the rules of art somehow cramps and deters the mind and restrains that boldness or happy extravagance that gives such general delight. It is an observation of an ingenious author that in no polished nation after the rules of criticism were fully settled and generally understood was there ever any great work of genius produced. This, however, must be understood chiefly of what are called the higher species of poetry, epic poetry and tragedy, and for the reasons just now given, it must be so in them. Homer is the great poet of nature, and it is generally thought that there is greater fire in him than in Virgil, just because he lived at a time when the rules of writing were unknown. The same thing is said of Shakespeare of our own country, and perhaps the late discovered poems of Ossian may be considered as another example. After all, perhaps the comparison made between the effects of nature and art is at bottom wrong, and that they produce beauties of different kinds: a wild uncultivated forest, a vast precipice, or steep cataract or waterfall is supposed to be an object more august and striking than any ornaments produced by human skill. The order and symmetry however of architecture and gardening are highly pleasing and ought not properly to be compared with the other, as pleasing the imagination in a different degree, so much as in a different kind.

The effects of the poetry of nature therefore in one view are very great and continue to be so in all ages because they touch the soul in one way which continues to be universally felt, but I doubt much whether eloquence ever arrived at much excellence without considerable study, or at least previous patterns, on which to form. The first great poets were before all criticism, and before even the polishing of human manners; but the first great orators appeared in improved, civilized states and were the consequence of the knowledge of mankind and the study of the human heart.

4. When persons are meanly qualified in point of natural capacity for any art, it is not very proper to attempt to instruct them in it. It is not only difficult to instruct those who have a radical incapacity for any study, but sometimes they are much the worse for application, just as fine clothes and a courtly dress upon a clown render him unspeakably ridiculous. Some who are utterly void of taste for speaking after long study, and sometimes even by great literature, become more obscure, more tedious, and more given to swelling and bombast than the most uncultivated person in the world. The want of a fund of good sense and genuine taste makes ignorant persons fools, and scholars pedants. A plain man will tell you of taking a purge or a dose of physic, and you neither mistake him nor laugh at him. A quack of a physician will tell you of a mucilaginous decoction to smooth the acid particles and carry off the acrimonious matter that corrodes and irritates the internal coats of the stomach.

5. In the middle regions of genius there are often to be found those who reap the greatest benefit from education and study. They improve their powers by exercise, and it is surprising to think what advances are to be made by the force of resolution and application. I might give you many examples of this in the annals of literature, but the one most suited to our purpose is that Demosthenes himself is said at first to have labored under almost insuperable difficulties. It is said he could not even pronounce at first all the letters of the Greek alphabet, particularly the letter R, the first letter of his art as the critics have called it.

Persons of the middle degrees of capacity do also, perhaps generally, fill the most useful and important stations in human life. A very great genius is often like a very fine flower, to be wondered at, but of little service either for food or medicine. A very great genius is also often accompanied with certain irregularities, so that we only consider with regret what he might have been if the lively sallies of his imagination had been reined in a little and kept under the direction of sober judgment.

On the whole, you may plainly perceive what great encouragement there is for diligence in your studies, and be persuaded to attend to the instructions to be given you on this subject in particular with assiduity and care.

Lecture II

IN this, which as the former I consider as a preliminary discourse, I will endeavor to give you some general rules, which as they belong equally to all sorts of writing would not come in so properly under the divisions of the subject.

1. Study and imitate the greatest examples. Get the most approved authors for composition, read them often and with care. Imitation is what commonly gives us our first ideas upon any subject. It is by example that ambition is kindled, and youth prompted to excel. It is by remarks upon actual productions that criticism itself is formed. Men were not first taught by masters to speak, either in oratory or poesy; but they first felt the impulse and did as they could, and their reflection and observation by making the comparison found out what was best. And after the existence of precepts, it is by examples that precepts are made plain and intelligible. An acquaintance with authors will also be the best mean of determining what is your own turn and capacity, for you will probably most relish those writers and that manner that you are best able to imitate.

For this purpose, let the best authors be chosen, ancient and modern. A controversy has often risen among critics and men of letters upon the preference being due to ancient or modern writers. This question was debated *ex professo* in the last age, and some very great men engaged in it. The famous M. Fenelon, archbishop of Cambray, has written a treatise upon it called the *Wars of the Poets,* and Dean Swift wrote his account of the *Battle of the Books in St. James's Library* on the same subject. I reckon it is wrong to be opinionative in such a controversy, and very easy to push it to excess on both sides. No doubt the few remains of remote antiquity have survived the wrecks of time in a great measure by their excellence itself, and therefore will always be considered as standards. And as they are chiefly works of imagination that have been so preserved, and true taste is the same in all ages, they must deserve real esteem, and this will be somewhat augmented by the veneration felt for their antiquity itself. Homer is the first and great pattern of writing, to whom the highest commendations have been given in every age. Horace says, "Vos exemplaria Graeca (meaning chiefly Homer) nocturna versate manu, versate diurna"; and Mr. Pope says:

> Be Homer's works your study and delight,
> Read him by day, and meditate by night.

Now the beauties of Homer we are easily capable of perceiving, though perhaps not his faults. The beauty of a description, the force of a similitude, we can plainly see, but whether he always adhered to truth and nature we cannot tell because we have no other way of knowing the manners and customs of his times but from what he has written.

The powers of mankind, however, are certainly the same in all ages, but change of circumstances may create diversity in the appearance and productions of genius. These circumstances tend to produce excellence of different kinds. The boldness and almost excessive flights of imagination in uncultivated times give way to beauties of a different nature, to order, judgment, and precision. A masterly judgment will endeavor to understand the reasons on both sides. It is certain, however, that there are great and excellent patterns to form upon both ancient and modern. And it is very proper for young persons to read authors after they have heard criticisms and remarks made upon them. These criticisms you may take at first either from books or conversation. Try if you can to observe the genius, or peculiar and characteristic turn of an author, not only his excellencies but wherein they are peculiar to him and different from those of others. Cicero is flowing, fervent, ornate—somewhat vain and ostentatious, but masterly in his way. Demosthenes is simple, close, nervous, rapid, and irresistible. Livy has a bewitching knack of telling a story; he is so expressive and descriptive that one cannot help being pleased with it, even after several times reading.

Sallust excels in giving characters, which he strikes off in single epithets or very concise remarks. Tacitus is chiefly remarkable for judicious and sagacious observations on human life, and Xenophon is superior to almost every author in dignity, elegance, and sweetness in the narration.

Of modern authors in our own language, Mr. Addison is a noble pattern of elegance, dignity, and simplicity. Swift in his political pieces writes with great strength and force and is perhaps a pattern of style which has scarcely been exceeded since his time. Hervey in his meditations has a great deal of very lively and animated description, but it is so highly ornamented that it is somewhat dangerous in the imitation. Dr. Robertson in his history has as just a mixture of strength and elegance as any other author I know in the English language. I cannot help here cautioning you against one modern author of some eminence, Johnson, the author of the *Rambler*. He is so stiff and abstracted in his manner and such a lover of hard words that he is the worst pattern for young persons that can be named.

It has been given sometimes as a rule to form one's self upon a particular author, who may be most agreeable to a student's taste, and perhaps congenial (if I may speak so) to his capacity. It is pretty common to fall into this without design by a natural propensity. It is said that Demosthenes wrote over the history of Thucydides eight times that he might the more effectually form himself to his style and manner. I cannot say I would recommend this; it seems to be too much honor to give to any one person. I would not be guilty of idolatry of any kind. A comprehensive knowledge of many authors, or at least a considerable number of the best, is certainly far preferable. If there be any advantage in particular imitation, it is that it is the easiest way of coming to a fixed

or formed style. One will soon run into an imitation of an author with
whom he is much conversant and of whom he is a great admirer, and
in this view, to some persons of moderate capacity it may not be an
improper method. But persons of real and original genius should be
rather above such a practice, as it will certainly make them fall short of
what they would otherwise attain.

To this we may add that particular imitation is liable to several very
great dangers. (1) It leads to servility of imitation. Such person often
may be said to borrow the piece instead of imitating the pattern. When
a servile imitation is perceived, which it always will be, it is certain to be
despised. Even a manner ever so excellent, if merely a copy, brings no
credit to a speaker. And if a writer retail the very sentiments and
language of another, it is considered as an absurdity. (2) Servile imitation
leads to copying defects. There neither is nor ever was any speaker or
writer free from defects or blemishes of some kind. Yet servile imitators
never fail to copy the defects as well as beauties. I should suppose that
anyone who made Cicero his particular model would very probably
transfuse a proportion of his vanity and ostentation, and probably more
of that than of his fire.

But of all sorts of imitation the most dangerous is the imitation of
living speakers, and yet to this young scholars are most prone, sometimes by design and sometimes quite insensibly. It is attended in the
highest degree with the disadvantage of copying defects. In living speakers, there are not only peculiarities of style and blemishes in composition
to copy, but in looks, tone, and gesture. It is a matter of constant
experience that imitators catch the blemishes easiest and retain them
longest. And it is to be observed that defects, when they are natural and
undesigned, appear very inconsiderable; but when they are copied and
adopted voluntarily, we cannot help despising the folly and absurdity
of one that judges so ill. Further, when defects are occasional and
undesigned, they are generally inconsiderable; but when they are copied, they are commonly aggravated and overcharged, and so appear
quite monstrous. This must be so; for even the very best manner looks
silly in the imitator, although just and graceful in the original.

2. An excellent general rule is to accustom yourselves early and much
to composition and exercise in pronunciation. Practice is necessary in
order to learn anything to perfection. There is something to be learned
from practice which no instruction can impart. It is so in every other
art as well as this—mathematics, geometry, and in navigation; after you
have learned the theory in the most perfect manner, there is still a
nameless something which nothing but experience can bestow. You
must not wait till you are masters of the rules of art before you begin
to put them in practice. Exercise must go hand in hand with instruction,

that the one may give meaning, force and direction to the other. I do not mean that you should be fond of entering very soon upon real life, but that you should be assiduous in preparatory exercises. This is a rule given by Cicero in his book *De Oratore*, which he reckons of great importance—"Scribendum quam plurimum," and he declares it to have been his own practice.

Since we are upon private exercises of composition, it may perhaps give you a clearer view of the matter to mention some of the various ways in which it may be separately tried. It may be tried in translation, perhaps it may be best to try it first here. Translation will accustom you to attend to the various idioms of language and to understand the genius of your own language; for when translating you will speedily find that to render out of any one language into another, *ad verbum*, would be very sorry composition. It may be tried also in narration. This I think should be the next step to translation to learn to give a naked account of facts with simplicity and precision. This also, though certainly in itself more obvious and easier than some other kinds, yet it is by no means so easy as some imagine. Imitation of a particular passage or composition of some author by writing upon something quite similar may perhaps be the next in order. To understand what this is, you need only look into an admirable example of it in poetry, Mr. Pope's imitation of a satire in Horace beginning "Quae virtus et quanta," etc. After this comes description, painting scenes, or drawing characters. Then argumentation; and lastly persuasion. I believe it would be a great improvement of the laudable practice in this college of daily orations if they were chosen with more judgment and better suited to the performers. Almost all the pieces we have delivered to us are of the last or highest kind, warm passionate declamations. It is no wonder that some should perform these ill who have never tried the plainer manner of simple narration. Supposing a student to have tried all these ways of composition for his own improvement, would he not be by that means sensible in what way he is most able to excel? As also having made trial of them separately, he is more able to vary his diction and give compass to his discourse upon a general subject. These are like an analysis or simple division of composition; and as persons read best who have first taught to resolve words into syllables and syllables into letters, so the easiest and completest way of any to composition is to begin it in this order.

In such exercises let me by all means recommend to you early to acquire and always to preserve a certain patience and resolution of mind, which will enable you to apply with vigor not only for a time, but to review and correct your pieces and bring them to some degree of perfection, and your taste to some degree of accuracy. To explain this a little, there are three things equally contrary to it, and perhaps equally prejudicial. (1) Mere weakness and want of courage, which finding one attempt unsuccessful will hardly be brought to make another. When a young person first goes to exercise himself in composition, he finds the thing so uncouth and difficult that he is apt to consider it as altogether impossible. (2) There is a fault contrary to this, a vanity of mind which is so pleased with anything it does, as neither to see its own faults nor be willing to hear them. There are some who from the beginning of life think it a great pity that any of their productions should be blotted or erased. It is not to be supposed that they will make great progress in knowledge or taste. (3) There is another sort perhaps distinct from both who are of a loose, desultory disposition, so unstaid that they cannot spend long enough time upon anything to do it well, or sometimes even to bring it to a conclusion. They will begin an essay upon a subject but are presently out of conceit with it, and therefore will do it very carelessly, or before it is finished must away to another which struck their fancy more lately.

That steady application which I have recommended some of the ancients were very remarkable for. Some of them indeed seemed to carry it to an excess. They would sometimes spend as much time in polishing an epigram, or little trifling panegyric, as might have been sufficient for the production of a work of extensive utility. However, this is not the most common error; running over a great deal in a superficial way is the bane of composition. Horace with his usual elegance ridicules this disposition when he says, "Detur nobis locus," etc.; and somewhere else he brings in a vainglorious poet boasting how many verses he had made, or could make, while standing upon one foot.

Lecture III

IN this discourse I intend to finish what I began in the last, viz. laying down some general rules to form the taste and direct the conduct of a student.

3. Be careful to acquaint yourselves well, and to be as perfect as possible in the branches that are subordinate to the study of eloquence. These, because they ought to be learned in the earliest stages, if they are then neglected, some are unwilling or ashamed to go back to them. What I have here in view chiefly are the grammar, orthography, and punctuation of the English language. It is not uncommon to find orators of considerable name, both in the pulpit and at the bar, far from being accurate in point of grammar. This is evidently a very great blemish. Perhaps it may be occasioned in some measure by the English seldom

or never being taught grammatically to children. But those who have learned the principles of grammar in the Greek and Latin languages should be more ready to attend to it. I am sensible that the grammar of every language is ultimately fixed by custom, with regard to which, Horace says, "Quem penes arbitrium est," etc. But even here we must attend to the meaning of the sentiment. It is not the custom of the vulgar that establishes either the grammar or pronunciation of any language, but that which is received and established by the best writers. You will say, how do these writers determine themselves? Are not they also guided by practice? They are in a great measure, and it is generally said that the practice of the capital of a nation or of the court in that capital settles the grammar. This must in substance be agreed to, yet judgment and analogy will frequently suggest improvements, and introduce a good or abolish an ill custom. You must not suppose that all the phrases of the vulgar in London are therefore agreeable to the grammar of the English, or even that at court all the nobility male and female speak with perfect propriety. It is in the last resort the men of literature, particularly the authors, who taking custom as a general rule, give it all the direction they can by their reasoning and example.

To make you understand this by some instances, you see Mr. Addison, Dean Swift, and Mr. Pope have endeavored to attend to the genius of the English language to show where it was harsh and unpolished and where improprieties might be corrected, and they have succeeded in a great measure. It was observed by all those great men that the English and all the northern languages are harsh by the numbers of consonants meeting without intervening vowels; therefore, that it is a great barbarism to strike out the vowels that we have, as in these words, *don't, can't, didn't, wouldn't, shouldn't, rebuk'd, drudg'd, fledg'd.* Several of these words may yet be heard in some places, and I have even seen them in print in America; but no good speaker or tolerable writer would use them in Great Britain. I give another example when the sense and analogy of the word suggests the improvement. *Averse* and *aversion* were often formerly used with *to* or *at:* he is very averse to it; he has a great aversion at it. But as averse properly signifies turned away, it seems an evident improvement to say averse from. What I mean by this observation is to turn your attention to such remarks when you meet with them in reading or conversation.

I will make an observation or two more. It is of some importance to attend to the use of words, nearly related or in some degree synonymous. It is not uncommon to hear people say a man is incident to such or such a thing; the evil is incident to the person—the person liable to the evil, or subject to it; this may be seen by the original meaning of the word of Latin derivation and signifies to fall upon. The word *notify* is often used wrong, particularly in America: they speak of notifying the public, that is to say making known the public. Instead of this, we should say notify anything, or make it known to the public. You advertise a person, or inform him of a thing—acquaint him with it. The verb *consist*, in English, has two distinct meanings and two constructions: when it signifies to agree or correspond, it is joined to *with*. It consists with my knowledge. When it signifies to compose or make up a total, it is constructed either with *in* or *of:* as his estate consists of, or in houses, lands, etc. *This* and *that* and *these* and *those* when together in a sentence are used with distinction: *this* and *these* for the nearest, and *that* and *those* for the most remote antecedent; but otherwise, *these* and *those* are used indiscriminately, but *those* more frequently—as those authors who are of different opinions.

In all matters doubtful, you ought to observe how the current of good authors go. So far as I have been able to observe, collective words in English are indifferently constructed either with a verb singular or plural, as number, multitude, part—a great number were present, or was present, though I should prefer the last.

As to orthography, it is of the utmost moment, not but that a man may be supposed to speak though he cannot spell, but because a public speaker must be always in some degree conversant in public life, and then bad spelling is exceedingly reproachful. It is not only necessary to understand in all ordinary cases the orthography of our own language, but a scholar and critic, I think, should be able to observe the variations that have been made in spelling from time to time. Between thirty and forty years ago, an attempt was made to alter the spelling of the English language very considerably by bringing it nearer to the way of pronouncing, but it did not succeed, being opposed by some of the greatest eminence as likely to destroy or hide the etymology of words. There have some small alterations obtained a good deal in my remembrance, such as taking away the final *k* in public, eccelesiastic, etc. There is also just now an attempt making to change the spelling of several words; I have seen an example of it in a very late edition if Middleton's life of Cicero: such as *revele, repete, explane; honor, favor, candor,* etc. This seems upon the principle of bringing words nearer to their Latin derivation.

Punctuation is a thing that a scholar should strive to understand a little, though there are few gentlemen or scholars who use it much, either in letters or in their composition. The reason of this is that it is looked upon as too formal, and unnecessary to use it in writing letters, except a full stop. It is always the best language that has least need of points to be understood. Points are, I believe, a modern invention subsequent to the invention of printing, very useful however in teaching young persons to read with proper pauses. Another reason why points are little used in private writing is that such papers as are sent to the press (in Britain) do not need them, the printers themselves understanding that matter at least as well if not better than any writer.

4. It is a good rule to observe early and study to guard against some of the most remarkable blemishes in writing and speaking, which are fallen into by design or accident and continued by habit. It is not difficult for any person as soon as he begins to observe and reflect to discover these in others, and as he will perceive the absurdity clearly in them, let him be very careful to find out whether there is not something of the same kind in himself. That you may understand what I mean, I will mention some particulars.

(1) Peculiar phrases—such as have nothing in them but what is just and decent and proper when used once, or now and then; but when a speaker falls so into any of them that the practice is known for his own, and he is known by it, they become unspeakably ridiculous. It is very difficult to avoid something of this kind; there are few, if any, but in common discourse use some phrases more than others. A cautious person, as soon as he perceives a habit of using any one coming upon him, will endeavor to alter or avoid it. Even the greatest men are not wholly free from this defect. It is observed of Cicero that *esse videatur* occurs in almost every three or four sentences, be the subject what it will. I knew a preacher that used the word *sedate* so very frequently that he was called generally where he was known by the name of the sedate preacher. I say the same thing of particular motions and gestures, which if they be in any degree out of the way are a great blemish in a speaker: both the one and the other of these are commonly at first taken up as graces and retained so long in that view that they acquire an irresisitible power from habit.

(2) Another blemish of this kind is using improper epithets. This is very common; some, especially young persons, are apt to think a discourse lean and poor unless there be a great number of epithets; and as they will let no substantive go without an adjective, it is a great chance that some of them are improper: they cannot say the sky, without the azure sky, or the lofty sky, or the wide expanded sky; and though all these epithets may belong to the sky, they may not be equally proper in the place where they are introduced. A certain gentleman of not mean rank in Great Britain in drawing an address from a borough to his majesty on the peace told him that the terror of his arms had spread to the most distant parts of the *terraqueous* globe; now, though it be certainly true that the globe is terraqueous, it was exceedingly ridiculous to tell the king so; it looked as if his majesty were a boy, and the borough magistrates were teaching him; or they themselves were boys who had

just learned the first lesson in geography, that the globe consists of land and water, and therefore were desirous of letting it be known that they were so far advanced.

(3) Another visible blemish is a multitude of unnecessary words of any kind, particularly the vain repetition of synonymous phrases. Some do not think their sentences full and round enough without a number of these phrases. But though it be true that there is a fullness of a sentence and the clauses of a sentence which is necessary to please the ear, yet it is but an ill way to make up the shape with what is without sense or force. The most common of this kind are the double epithets, which men are led into by the introduction of words derived from the Latin or Greek into the English language. These words, differing in sound, are often coupled together, as if different in meaning also: as *happiness* and *felicity, fruition* and *enjoyment, greatness* and *magnificence, ease* and *facility, way* and *manner, end* and *conclusion, small* and *minute, bountiful* and *liberal,* etc. Sometimes from your lofty speakers, we hear a whole string of words of so little difference in meaning that it is almost impossible to perceive it. Thus I have lately heard, "This grand, capital, important, and fundamental truth"—all proper epithets, and though any one of them would have made the discourse nervous as well as just, by the addition of them all, it becomes swelled and silly.[1]

1. *List of synonymous terms frequently to be met with*

Speakers and writers	Worth and value
Motives and arguments	Lasting and abiding
Benefit and advantage	Command and order
Small and minute	Order and appoint
Bountiful and liberal	Sin and guilt
Right and title	Cheerfulness and alacrity
Order and method	Greatness and magnificence
Sharp and acute	Joy and delight
Pain and anguish	Fruition and enjoyment
Moment and importance	Just and righteous
Delight and satisfaction	End and design
Joy and pleasure	Open and explain
Profit and advantage	Lasting and durable
Resolution and purpose	Clear and manifest
Justice and equity	Marks and signs
Truth and sincerity	Plain and perspicuous
Wealth and riches	Ease and facility
Penury and want	End and conclusion
Odious and hateful	A final issue
Poor and indigent	Motives and reasons
Order and regularity	Diminished and lessened
Rules and regulations	Excellence and perfection
Causes and reasons	Benevolence and goodwill

(4) Vulgarisms. I have been surprised to see some persons of education and character introduce the mere vulgarisms of discourse in the
pulpit, or at the bar, such as "I an't," "I can't," "I shan't." An author
who entitles his book *Lexiphanes* and has very successfully exposed Johnson's long and hard words let slip a vulgarism into his own discourse,
for which he was severely handled by the reviewers: "*between you and I.*"
I there is a governed case, and if it were to be used, it should be "between
you and me." But the truth is the phrase is altogether a vulgarism, and
therefore not to be used except in particular circumstances describing
familiar chat. There are also certain cant phrases which come into
repute or use in the course and the changes of fashion.

These have been sufficiently exposed by Swift and Addison, and
therefore I shall say nothing at all further on them at present as an
opportunity will afterwards occur of mentioning them to advantage.

5. The fifth and last general rule I shall just mention is to follow
nature. This is a rule often given and greatly insisted on by the ancients.
Everybody has heard of it; nay sometimes those who have not heard of
it will speak as if they had, and say, "This was quite natural. This
was altogether unnatural." But it is somewhat difficult to understand.
Nature seems in this rule to be opposed to art. Is following nature then
to do as untaught person generally do? Will the most ignorant persons
make the most plain and the best connected discourse? Will they tell
a story with the most genuine simplicity, and at the same time with
perspicuity? We find it is quite otherwise. Perhaps it would be best to
say it is following truth, or following that which is easiest and plainest,
and probably would be followed by all, but for affectation.

On this subject I can think of nothing so good as to say, realize and
suppose you saw the thing you would describe, and put yourself in the
very state of him whose sentiments you would speak. Clear conceptions
make distinct expressions, and reality is a great assistant to invention.
If you were bid to study a subject abstractly, it would be with great
difficulty that things proper and suitable to it would come into your
mind. But if you yourself were in the situation that is to be supposed,

---

Useful and profitable	Demonstrate and prove
Amiable and lovely	Cover and conceal
Wise and prudent	Foolish and unwise

Terms and phrases to be noted for remarks

Happifying—susceptive,—fellow-countryman—selicitos—to be found in the Monitor.
"Unsexed thy mind" in a poem, "Sensibilities," Aikin's Magazine, Oct. vol. I. 468–69.
"These commendations will not I am persuaded make you vain and coxcomical. Knick-
knackically, simplify, domesticate, pultpitically."

the sentiments pertinent to it would crowd upon you immediately. Let me try to make this familiar by an example: suppose I were to ask any of you just now what are the circumstances that aggravate sin, or make it more heinous and deserving of severe punishment; it is highly probable he would either be at a loss altogether, or at least would omit many of them. But if any of you had received an injury from another, in explaining of it, he would not fail to come over them every one. He would say it was unprovoked. If he had done him service, he would not fail to upbraid him with it, and nothing would be forgotten between the two that could aggravate the crime.

Supposing the reality of everything also serves particularly to deliver a speaker from affected ornaments and everything in language or carriage that is improper. If you were pleading the cause of one accused of a capital crime, it would be best to suppose that you yourself were the accused person and that you were speaking for your own life. This would give an earnestness of spirit and a justness and correctness to the manner infinitely distant from that threatrical pomp which is so properly said to be a departure from the simplicity of nature.

Lecture IV

HAVING given you some preliminary discourses on such points as I thought would serve to prepare you for what might be afterwards said, I proceed to treat the subject more methodically and more fully. There are various ways of dividing the subject, which yet may each of them be said to take in the whole in one way or other. Several of these must be combined together, as it is not sufficient to view a building only from one station. If you would understand it thoroughly, you must view it from different stations, and even take it in profile and learn not only its outward appearance, but its inward structure. The method I have resolved to follow, and which seems to me as complete as any I could fall upon, is this:

1. To treat of language in general—its qualities and powers, eloquent speech, and its history and practice as an art.

2. To consider oratory as divided into its three great kinds—the sublime, simple, and mixed; their characters, their distinctions, their beauties, and their uses.

3. To consider it as divided into its constituent parts—invention, disposition, style, pronunciation, and gesture.

4. To consider it as its object is different—information, demonstration, persuasion, entertainment.

5. As its subject is different—the pulpit, the bar, and the senate, or any deliberative assembly.

6. To consider the structure and parts of a particular discourse—their order, connection, proportion, and ends.

7. Recapitulation, and an inquiry into the principles of taste, or of beauty and gracefulness, as applicable not only to oratory, but to all the other (commonly called) the fine arts.

In the first place then, I am to treat of language in general—its qualities and powers, eloquent speech, and its history and practice as an art.

Language is what in a great measure distinguishes man from the inferior creatures. Not but that almost all animals have certain sounds by which they can communicate something to one another. But these sounds are evidently only simple, and sometimes single exertions, differing in one creature from another according to the different conformation of their organs. Articulate speech has a far greater compass and is able to express not only a vast multitude of complex, as well as simple ideas; perhaps we may even say that articulate speech is little less extensive than thought itself, there being hardly any idea that can be formed but it may be expressed, and by that means communicated. In this there is a wide and manifest distinction between the rational and irrational creatures.

Articulate language is intended to communicate our sentiments one to another. This may be considered as fully explained by saying it includes information and persuasion. A conception in my mind, when spoken, its excellence consists in making another perceive what I perceive, and feel towards it as I feel. They may be afterwards amplified and extended, but these two particulars show the true original purpose of speech. Eloquence is commonly called the art of persuasion, but the other must be taken in. We must inform before we can persuade, or if there be any such thing as persuasion without information, it is only a blind impulse.

Articulate speech is representing our ideas by arbitrary sounds. That is to say, there is no real or natural connection between the sound and signification, but what is the effect of compact and use. In this articulate speech is distinguished from signs or natural sounds, as alphabetical writing (of which more afterwards) is distinguished from hieroglyphical. Natural sounds may signify joy, fear, anger; but language in general has no such natural connection with its meaning. The words *sun* and *moon* might have had different meanings and served the same purpose. The word *bieth* in Hebrew, *oikos* in Greek, *domus* in Latin, *maison* in French, and *house* in English, though all of them different, are equally proper for signifying the same thing when once they are fixed by the custom of the several nations. Some have attempted to reduce the original words of a supposed original language and even the letters of the alphabet to a natural resemblance of the things to be signified, but their attempts have been fruitless and ridiculous. It was in ancient times a pretty general imagination that there was a certain language that was original and natural to man, that this was the first language in use, and that if men were not taught another language by example, they would all speak this language. But experience, after trial had been made by several curious persons, showed this imagination to be vain; for those who were brought up without any communication with men were always dumb and spoke none at all, except sometimes imitating the natural sounds of some beast or birds which they might occasionally hear. Herodotus's story is either a fable, or it proves nothing, of a king of Egypt having two children nourished by goats and pronouncing the word *Bec,* or *Beecos,* which they said signified bread in the Phrygian language. This was a thing merely accidental, if true; yet at any rate of very doubtful authority.

The words in articulate speech therefore are arbitrary, nor is there any possibility of their being otherwise; for words are only sounds, and though it is possible in some few particulars to fix upon words with a natural relation, as for example perhaps the names of animals might sometimes be given them with some resemblance of sound to the natural sounds which these animals utter, yet even this with disadvantages, as anybody may perceive, by trying to make a word that shall resemble the neighing of a horse, the lowing of a bull, etc. But as to all inanimate visible objects, it is impossible to represent them by sound, light and sound, the eye and the ear, being totally different in kind. I can recollect nothing that makes any difficulty in this matter, unless that some may say, how then do you find place for that particular beauty of poetry and other descriptions in making the sound an echo to the sense? But this is easily resolved. In some cases the passions give a modulation to sound, and in the quantity of the syllables and ease or difficulty of pronouncing them, there may be a resemblance to slowness and labor, or their opposites, or both. As in the famous passage of Homer, "Ton men Tissiphon"; or in Mr. Pope, who exemplifies the rule in giving it. "Tis not enough, no harshness gives offence, etc."

If words are arbitrary, it may be asked how language came first into use, in which the opinions are various, but the controversy is not of any great moment. Some think it was in the same way as other creatures exert their natural powers that man by practice gradually came to the use of speech, and settled the meaning of words by custom. Others think that this would either never have happened or have taken a very long time, and suppose that their Maker taught them at least some degree of practice, which should open the way to a more extensive use of the faculty. And the consideration that sounds in language are arbitrary in some degree favors this supposition because it may be observed that as mankind are capable by instruction of the greatest and most multifarious improvement, so without instruction they are capable of doing least. A human infant when first brought forth is more helpless and longer helpless than any other animal that we know. It does not seem to be of much importance to form a determinate opinion of this question. It occurs in the very same way again, and may be reasoned upon the same principles, whether alphabetical writing was an invention and discovery of man or revealed by God. Those who hold the last opinion observe that hieroglyphic writing, or writing by signs or pictures, was before alphabetical, and that the improvement of hieroglyphics does not lead to, but from alphabetical writing. That the one consists of natural emblems and visible signs of sentiments, and the other of arbitrary or artificial signs for simple sounds, so that the more complex you make the hieroglyphic, you differ the more from the alphabet. It seems probable that this, and indeed the radical principles of all great discoveries, were brought out by accident, that is to say by Providence; therefore, it is probable that God gave to our first parents who were found in a state of full growth all the instruction necessary for proceeding upon and exercising the faculty of speech, the length that was necessary for the purposes of human life. It is also probable from the analogy of Providence that he left as much to the exercise of the human powers as experience and application could conveniently supply.

I will not enter much into the formation and construction of language in general. It is formed by a certain number of simple sounds which when variously combined produce that variety of words which, though certainly not strictly infinite, yet have been hitherto inexhausted by all the languages in the world. The letters are divided into vowels and consonants, the first having a sound of themselves, and the other giving only a sort of modification to that sound. Some great philologists are of opinion that in the Hebrew and several other ancient languages, their whole letters are consonants, tending to mark the different configurations of the organs of sound at the beginning of pronunciation, and the vowels are the sounds themselves, which they say men were taught to adopt by habit, first in speaking, and then in writing, and afterwards were distinguished by marks of signs for the sake of readers. Hence the controversy about the Hebrew points, and indeed reading the dead languages in general, which is attended with great uncertainty, particularly from the following circumstances. Vowels have in general been but five or six in number, which should express all the simple sounds, and yet they do not, and perhaps there is not a language in which there is greater confusion in this matter, than our own, which makes the English so exceedingly difficult for a foreigner to attain. Several English vowels have three or four different sounds, and as Sheridan says, some of them the length of five: *I* has three in one word, viz. *infinite*. These things not being necessary to my main purpose, I only point at them without enlarging.

It is plain that in whatever manner languages were first formed, we can easily see that they came slowly and by degrees to perfection. An eminent French author, Father Lamy, says the Hebrew language was perfect in its original; but he advances no proof of this, but showing indeed by very just historical remarks and criticisms that the Hebrew was anterior in point of time to the Greek, and that in writing, the letters were taken from the Hebrew and employed in the Greek. History says that Cadmus was a Phoenician, and he has generally among the Greeks the honor of introducing letters. It is also observed that as the letters of the alphabet were used in expressing numbers, the Greeks after they had in process of time altered or left out the letter vau in Hebrew, which stands sixth in order, they put a new mark s for six that the rest might retain their powers, which plainly shows that the Hebrew alphabet was older than the Greek as it now stands.

But for my part, I do not understand the meaning of saying that the Hebrew language was perfect at first: it might be fitted for all the purposes of them that used it first, and is probably at this day as good as any other language so far as it goes, but it is plain that this and all the other languages of the first ages were narrow, short, and simple. They must have been so from the nature of the thing; most probably they consisted chiefly of monosyllables representing simple ideas. What occasion had they for complex or compound words when they had few if any complex or compounded ideas? This appears very plainly from the state of the Hebrew language, some of the other orientals, and the language of all uncultivated people. It holds likewise in the case of the Chinese language, which though the people are not uncultivated properly speaking, is yet in an unimproved state from their having had little intercourse with other nations. All such languages have few adjectives, and when they do use words as adjectives, they are commonly figurative. There is an ingenious and probable deduction how a scanty narrow language might be first used in Shuckford's connections. They might express qualities by the name of some animal remarkable for them—as a lion-man for a valiant or fierce man. This is wholly agreeable to the genius of the Hebrew language. The Hebrews describe everything that is very great by adding the name of God to it, as "the trees of God," "the river of God." It follows that in all uncultivated languages the figures are frequent and very strong. The Indians in America have a language full of metaphors. They "take up the hatchet," for going to war, and they "brighten the chain," when they confirm a peace.

Hence it appears that in the earliest times, if they used figures, it was the effect of necessity rather than choice. But what men did at first out of necessity, orators afterwards returned to from choice in order to increase the beauty or force of their diction or both. In fact figures do make the greatest impression on men's minds. They are sensible, and therefore level to every person's capacity; for the same reason they make a strong impression on the imagination. They likewise leave a great deal of room for the creative power of fancy to make additions. A sign or symbol seen by a multitude on a subject that is understood carries the contagion of enthusiasm or rage exceedingly far. In the nineteenth chapter of Judges you see the Levite took his concubine and cut her into twelve parts and sent them to all the tribes of Israel. The Roman also holding up the stump of his hand which he had lost in the service of the public pleaded for his brother with a power vastly superior to any language whatever.

Lecture V

HAVING given you a short view of language in general, if it were not too long, I would consider the structure of particular languages, instead of which take the few following short remarks.

1. The nature of things necessarily suggests many of the ways of speaking which constitute the grammar of a language, and in every language there is nearly the same number of parts of speech as they are enumerated in the Latin grammar: noun, pronoun, verb, participle, adverb, preposition, interjection, conjunction.

2. In the use of these, there is a very great variety. Nouns to be sure are declined nearly the same way in all by cases and numbers, though the Greeks in this differ a little, using three numbers instead of two, having a particular inflection of the word when there are but two persons meant, and another for the plural or more; but in the verbs, there is a very great diversity: in the active and passive signification they generally agree, but some express the persons by terminations, and some by pronouns and nominatives expressed. Some have moods which others have not. The Greeks have an optative mood; the Latins have gerunds; the Hebrews with fewer differences of moods have conjugations that carry some variety of signification to the same word. In one word *maser,* "he delivered," there is not only this and its passive, but another, "he delivered diligently," and the passive; another, "he made

to deliver;" another, "he delivered himself." The Greeks, besides the active and passive, have a *media vox,* of which perhaps the use is not now fully understood; since some of the best grammarians say it signifies doing a thing to one's self: *Tupsomai,* "I shall strike myself." Most of the modern languages decline their verbs, not by inflection of the termination, as the Greek and Latin, but by auxiliary verbs, as the English and French. The Chinese language is perhaps the least improved of any language that has subsisted for any time; this probably is owing to their want of alphabetical writing: every word among them had a character peculiar to it, so that letters and words were the same in number in their language. This rendered it of immense difficulty to understand their writing among themselves, and quite impossible to foreigners; but they were vastly surprised to find that the Jesuits from Europe that came among them could easily write their language by our alphabet; and as they use the same word in different tones for different meanings, these fathers also soon found a way of distinguishing these in writing by certain marks and accents placed over the word, differing as it was to be differently taken.

3. Some have amused themselves with inventing a language with such a regular grammar as might be easily understood and having this language brought into general use. We have a remark of this kind in Father Lamy's rhetoric in French, and he says the grammar of the Tartar language comes nearest to it. We have also had some schemes and propositions of this kind in English, but it seems wholly chimerical. I shall only observe further that some few have imagined that the Hebrew language itself was originally and when complete a perfect language, and that we now have it only maimed, and but a small part of it. These suppose the language to be generated thus, by taking the letters of the alphabet, and first going through them regularly by two, and then by three, ab, ag, ad, etc.; aba, abb, etc. All these schemes are idle because no person can possibly lay down rules beforehand for everything that may hereafter be thought and spoken, and therefore, when they are brought out, they will be expressed as those to whom they first occur shall incline, and custom will finally fix them and give them their authority.

Leaving these things therefore as matters of more curiosity than use, I proceed to speak of eloquent speech and its history as an art. It is plain that in the progress of society and the commerce of human life, it would soon appear that some spoke with more grace and beauty, and so as more to incline the hearers to their sentiments, than others. Neither is it hard to perceive that it would be early in repute. In the first associations of mankind, they must have been chiefly governed by those who had the power of persuasion. In uncultivated societies, it is so still:

in an Indian tribe, the *sachem* or wise man directs their councils. The progress of oratory towards perfection must have been evidently in fact like the progress of all other human arts, gradual, and in proportion to the encouragement given to its exercise. It prevailed where the state of things and constitution of government favored it, but not otherwise.

It is to be observed here that by the consent of all, and by the memorials of antiquity that are left, poetry was more ancient than oratory; or perhaps we may rather say that the first exertions of genius in eloquent expression were in poetry, not in prose. It has frequently been made matter of critical inquiry why poetry was prior to oratory, and why sooner brought to perfection. I do not perceive very clearly what great advantage there is in determining this question, supposing we should hit upon the true reasons. One reason I take to be that the circumstance in poetry that gives generally the highest pleasure, viz. a strong and vigorous fancy, is least indebted to application, instruction, or time for its perfection; therefore poetical productions in general, and that species of them in particular which have most of that quality, must be as easily produced in uncultivated times as any other; and for some reasons given in a former discourse must appear then with the greatest effect. Whereas, to success in oratory some knowledge of the human heart, and even some experience in the ways of men, is necessary. Another difference is plain: poetical productions, having generally pleasure or immediate entertainment as their design, may produce that effect in any age, whereas the circumstances that rendered the orator's discourse interesting are all gone.

Perhaps to this we may add that the incitements to poetry are more general. A poet pleases and obtains fame from every single person who reads or hears his productions, but an assembly, business, and an occasion are necessary to the orator. This last is likewise limited in point of place and situation. Oratory could not thrive in a state where arbitrary power prevails because then there is nothing left for large assemblies and a diffusive public to determine, whereas poetry is pleasing to persons under any form of government whatever.

Those who have given the history of oratory have rather given us the history of the teachers of that art than its progress and effects. It must be observed, however, that in this as well as in poetry, criticism is the child and not the father of genius. It is the fruit of experience and judgment by reflection upon the spontaneous productions of genius. Criticism inquires what was the cause of things being agreeable after the effect has been seen. Ward brings a citation from Cicero to show that the orator's art was older than the Trojan war. The purport of this is that Homer attributes force to Ulysses's speeches and sweetness to Nestor's; perhaps also he has characterized Menelaus's manner as simple, short, and unadorned. There is not, however, any certainty in this art being much studied or explained in these early times from this citation, for though Homer is an excellent poet, of inimitable fire and great strength of natural judgment, it is not certain that he kept so perfectly to propriety as to describe only the manner and style of things at the time of the Trojan war, which was 250 years before his own. I should be more apt to conclude that he had described manners, characters, and speakers as they were in his own time, with a little air of antiquity.

We are, however, told by Pausanias that the first school of oratory in Greece was opened in the school of Theseus, the age preceding that war. If there be any certainty in this, its being taught in Greece has been very ancient indeed; but these being fabulous times, it is scarcely to be depended upon. However, it is certain that oratory flourished early and was improved greatly in Greece. Many circumstances concurred to produce this effect: the spirit and capacity of the people, the early introduction of letters, but chiefly their political situation—the freedom of their states, the frequency of public enemies, and the importance of their decisions. There is much said of the spirit and capacity of the Greeks for all the arts, and to be sure their climate, so serene and temperate, might have all the effect that a climate can have; but I reckon the two other causes much more considerable. The introduction of letters is necessary to the improvement and perfection of a language, and as they were early blessed with that advantage, they had the best opportunity of improving. However, the last cause of all is much more powerful than both the former, though perhaps literature is necessary to be joined with it to produce any great effect. As to some of the other arts, particularly painting and statuary, an eminent modern critic says the Greeks could not but excel because they, of all others, had the best images from nature to copy. He says that the games in Greece, in which the best formed bodies for agility and strength in the whole country were seen naked and striving and exerting themselves to the very utmost, must have presented to persons of genius originals to draw from such as in most other nations never are to be seen. If this remark is just in the other arts, the influence of eloquence in the public assemblies of these free states must have had a similar effect in the art of speaking.

The art of speaking in Greece, however, does not seem to have risen high till the time of Pericles, and he is said to have been so powerful an orator that he kept up his influence in the city as much by his eloquence as tyrants did by their power. There is a passage of Cicero which seems to say that he was the first who prepared his discourses in writing, and some have been simple enough to believe that he read them; but nothing can be a more manifest mistake because action or pronunciation was by all the ancients considered as the great point in oratory. There were to be seen in Cicero and Quintilian's times orations said to be of Pericles, but both these great orators seem to be of opinion that they were not his because they did not at all seem to come up to the great fame of his eloquence. Mr. Bayle, a very eminent critic, says justly that these great men might be mistaken in that particular, for a very indifferent composition may be the work of a very great orator. The grace of elocution and the power of action might not only acquire a man fame in speaking, but keep up his influence in public assemblies. Of this we have two very great British examples, Mr. Whitefield in the pulpit, and Mr. Pitt in the senate.

After Pericles there were many great orators in Greece, and indeed all their statesmen were orators till the time of Demosthenes, when the Grecian eloquence seems to have attained its perfection. The praises of this great speaker are to be so generally met with that I shall not insist upon them at all further than reminding you that though no doubt eminently qualified by nature, he needed and received great improvement from art.

The Roman eloquence was of much shorter duration. It is true that the Roman state being free and the assemblies of the people having much in their power, it seems, according to the principles we have gone upon, that public speaking must have been in esteem; but there is something peculiar. The Romans were for many ages a plain, rough, unpolished people. Valor in war was their idol, and therefore though to be sure from the earliest times the assemblies must have been managed in their deliberations by their speakers, yet they were concise and unadorned, and probably consisted more of telling them their story and showing their wounds, which was of frequent practice among them, than any artful or passionate harangues. The first speakers of any eminence we read of in the Roman history were the Gracchi. Cicero I believe makes little mention even of them. Anthony and Crassus were the first celebrated orators among the Romans, and they were but in the age immediately before Cicero himself, and from his time it rather fell into decay.

I have said above that genius and excellence was before criticism. This is very plain, for though we read of schools and rhetoricians at different times and places, these are considered by the great masters as persons quite contemptible. Of this kind there is a remarkable passage in Cicero in his Brutus. "At hunc [speaking of Pericles] non declamator," etc. The first just and truly eminent critic in Greece was Aristotle, who flourished as late as the time of Demosthenes. And Cicero himself was the first eminent critic among the Romans. Aristotle has laid open the principles of eloquence and persuasion as a logician and philosopher, and Cicero has done it in a still more masterly manner as a philosopher, scholar, orator, and statesman; and I confess unless he has had many authors to consult that we know nothing of, his judgment and penetration are quite admirable, and his books *de Oratore,* etc. more finished in their kind than any of his orations themselves.

As to the effects of oratory, they have been and are surely very great but, as things seen through a mist or at a great distance, are apt to be mistaken in their size. I am apt to think many say things incredible, and make suppositions quite contrary to nature and reason, and therefore to probability. Some speak and write as if all the ancient orators had a genius more than human, and indeed by their whole strain seem rather to extinguish than excite an ardor to excel. Some also seem to me to go upon a supposition as if all the people in the ancient republics had been sages, as well as their statesmen orators. There is a remark to be found in many critics upon a story of Theophrastus the philosopher, from which they infer the delicacy of the Athenians. That philosopher it seems went to buy something of an herb-woman at a stall, and she in her answer to him it seems called him stranger. This they say shows that she knew him by his accent not to be a native of Athens, although he had lived there thirty years. But we are not even certain that her calling him stranger implied any more than that he was unknown to her. Besides, though it were true that she discovered him not to be an Athenian born, this is no more than what happens in every populous country that there is something in the accent which will determine a man to be of one country or province rather than another, and I am somewhat of the opinion that this would be more discernible in Greece than anywhere else. The different dialects of the Greek tongue were not reckoned reproachful, as many local differences are in Britain, which therefore people will endeavor to rid themselves of as well as they can. In short I take it for granted that an assembly of the vulgar in Athens was just like an assembly of common people among us, and a senate at Athens in understanding and taste was not superior to the senate of Great Britain, and that some of them were but mere mobs; and that they were very disorderly is plain from what we read of Plato being pulled down from the desk when he went up to defend Socrates.

The most remarkable story of the effect of oratory is that told of Cicero's power over Caesar in his oration for C. Ligarius. This is very pompously told by some critics that Caesar came to the judgment seat determined to condemn him, and even took the pen in his hand to sign his condemnation, but that he was interested by Cicero's eloquence and at last so moved that he dropped the pen and granted the orator's request. But supposing the facts to have happened, I am very doubtful of the justness of the remark. Caesar was a great politician, and as we know he did attempt to establish his authority by mercy, it is not unlikely both that he determined to pardon Ligarius and to flatter Cicero's vanity by giving him the honor of obtaining it. In short, oratory has its chief power in promiscuous assemblies, and there it reigned of old, and reigns still by its visible effect.

Lecture VI

WE now proceed to consider eloquence as divided into its three great kinds—the sublime, the simple, and the mixed. This is very unhappily expressed by Ward, who divides style into the low, the middle, and the sublime. Low is a word which, in its first and literal sense, signifies situation, and when applied metaphorically, never is in any instance used in a good sense, but always signifies what is either unhappy, or base and contemptible, as we say a man's or a state's finances are low. We say a man is in a low state of health. We say he is guilty of low, mean practices—has a low, mean, paltry style. It was therefore conveying a very wrong idea to make low one of the different kinds of style. You may observe that I have introduced this distinction in a manner somewhat different from him and some other authors. They consider it as a division of style. I choose rather to say there are three different great kinds into which eloquence and composition may be divided. The reason is I believe the word style, which was used both by the Greeks and Romans but especially the latter, has like many others gradually changed its meaning. At first it signified the manner of writing in general and is even sometimes used so still, but more commonly now in English it is confined to the diction. Nothing is more common than to say sublimity in sentiments and style, so as to distinguish the one from the other. I am sensible that even in this confined sense there is a sublimity, simplicity, and mediocrity in language itself, which will naturally enough fall to be explained, but it is better upon the whole to consider them as different kinds of eloquence for several reasons.

Sublimity in writing consists with all styles, and particularly many of the highest and most admired examples of sublimity are in the utmost simplicity of style. Sometimes they are so far from losing by it that they owe a great part of their beauty and their force to it. That remarkable example of sublimity in the Scripture is wholly in the simple style. "Let there be light, and there was light." There are also many others in Scripture: "The gods of the Gentiles are vanity and lies"; "I am that I am."

Some of the other kinds also, even the simplest, do sometimes admit great force of expression, though more rarely, and there is a great danger in the simple manner of writing by admitting lofty expressions to swell into bombast. The mixed kind frequently admits of sublimity of style, and indeed is called mixed as consisting, as it were, alternately of the one and the other, or being made up of a proportion of each.

The sublime kind of writing chiefly belongs to the following subjects: epic poetry, tragedy, orations on great subjects, and then particularly the peroration. Nothing can be too great for these subjects, and unless they are treated with sublimity, they are not treated suitably. The simple kind of writing belongs to scientific writing, epistolary writing, essay and dialogue, and to the whole inferior species of poetry, pastorals, epigrams, epitaphs, etc. The mixed kind belongs to history, system, and controversy. The first sort must be always sublime in sentiment or language, or both. The second may be often sublime in sentiment, sometimes, but very rarely, in language. The mixed admits of both sorts with full propriety, and may be often sublime both in sentiment and language.

Let us now consider these three great kinds of composition separately in the order in which I have named them.

Of the sublime manner of writing—this is very difficult to describe or treat of, in a critical manner. It is very remarkable that all writers on this subject, not excepting those of the greatest judgment, accuracy, and precision, when they come to explain it, have used nothing but metaphorical expressions. It is however certain in general that metaphor should be kept as much as possible out of definition or explication. These all agreeing therefore in this circumstance seems to show that sublimity is a single or simple idea that cannot be resolved, divided, or analyzed, and that a taste for it is in a good measure a feeling of nature. The critics tell us that sublimity is that which surprises, ravishes, transports. These are words frequently applied to its effects upon the hearers; and greatness, loftiness, majesty are ascribed to the sentiments, to the character, to the person. An oration or the sublime parts of a poem have been compared to the voice of thunder or penetration of lightning, to the impetuosity of a torrent. This last is one of the best metaphorical expressions for sublimity in eloquence because it carries in it not only the idea of great force, but of carrying away everything with it that opposes or lies in its way. That may be said to be sublime that has an irresistible influence on the hearers, and when examined, carries in it the idea of great power and abilities in the speaker; yet even this is not sufficient, it has the character of greatness, as distinct from that of beauty, sweetness or use. Burke on the sublime has endeavored to show that sublimity and beauty, though generally united in our apprehensions, are distinct qualities and to be traced to a different source. Of sublimity in particular, he says it is always allied to such things as raise the passion of terror; but of this I will speak more fully upon a head I have reserved for that purpose, in which I propose to inquire into the first principles of taste or approbation common to this and all other arts.

Longinus mentions no less than five different sources of the sublime: (1) greatness or elevation of mind, (2) pathos or passion, (3) figure, (4) nobleness of language, (5) composition or arrangement of words. But though the last two of these are of considerable moment and greatly contribute to augment the force as well as beauty of a discourse, I do not think they are of that nature as to be considered upon the same footing with the other three. Therefore leaving what is to be said upon them to the next head, when it will properly occur, I shall consider the others in their order.

Greatness or elevation of mind—this is the first and radical source of sublimity indeed. It is quite impossible for a man to attain to sublimity of composition unless his soul is great and his conceptions noble, and on the other hand, he that possesses these can hardly express himself meanly. Longinus gives it as an advice that a man should accustom his mind to great thought. But if you ask me what are great thoughts, I confess myself unable to explain it; and unless the feeling is natural, I am afraid it is impossible to impart it; yet is seems to be pretty generally understood. It is commmon to say such a man has a great soul, or such another has a mean or little soul. A great soul aspires in its hopes, is not easily terrified by enemies or discouraged by difficulties. It is worthwhile to consider a little the effect of a man's outward circumstances. The mind to be sure cannot be wholly made by any circumstances. Sentiments and state are different things. Many a great mind has been in narrow circumstances, and many a little rascal has been a king; yet education and manner have a sensible effect upon men in general. I imagine I have observed that when persons of great rank have been at the same time men of real genius, they have generally excelled in majesty and dignity of sentiments and language. This was an advantage generally enjoyed by the ancients whose writings remain to us; having but their own language to study and being early introduced into public life, and even into the conduct of the greatest affairs, they were led into nobleness of sentiment. Xenophon, Demosthenes, Cicero, Caesar were all of them great statesmen, and two of them great generals as well as writers. In modern times, there is a more complete partition of employments, so that the statesman, general, and scholar are seldom found united in the same person; yet I think it appears in fact that when statesmen are also scholars, they make upon the whole greater orators and nobler writers than those who are scholars merely, though of the greatest capacity. In every station, however, this remark has place, that it is of importance to sublimity in writing to endeavor to acquire a large and liberal manner of thinking. While I am making use of this language, I would caution you against thinking that pride and vanity of mind are at all allied to greatness in this respect. There is a set of men called free-thinkers who are pleased to arrogate to themselves a large and liberal manner of thinking, and the generality of them are as little creatures as any on the face of the earth. Mr. Addison compares them to a fly, which lighting upon a great building and perceiving the small interstices between the stones, cries out of vast chasms and irregularities, which is wholly owing to the extreme littleness of his sight that is not able to see the dignity and grandeur of the whole building.

When I am upon this subject of greatness and elevation of thought as one source of the sublime, you will naturally expect that I should give some examples to illustrate it. I shall begin with some out of the scriptures, where indeed there is the greatest number, and these the noblest that can well be conceived. "I am God alone, and besides me there is no saviour." "Who is this that darkeneth counsel by words without knowledge?" "Who will set the briars and thorns against me in battle?" etc. See also two passages inimitably grand—Isa. 40:12, and 5:21, and onwards.

To mention some of the sayings in heathen antiquity, Alexander's saying to Parmenio is certainly of the great kind, yet perhaps with a considerable mixture of pride as well as greatness. Parmenio told him if he were Alexander he would act in a certain manner. Answer, "So would I, if I were Parmenio." That of Porus, the Indian king, to Alexander however was much greater. When he was Alexander's prisoner and was asked by that prince how he expected to be treated, he answered, "like a king." Caesar's famous saying of "veni, vidi, vici" has often been quoted as a concise and noble description of the rapidity of his conquests; yet I confess I think it very dubious. It has not only an air of improper vanity but looks like an intended and silly play upon the words and what we call alliteration. They are three words of the same length, the same tense, and the same beginning and ending. Cicero, in one of his orations, I believe in that for Marcellus, has a very noble compliment to Caesar when he says the gods had given nothing to men so great as a disposition to show mercy. But of all great sayings on record, there is none that ever made such an impression upon me as that of Ayliffe to King James the III. He had been detected in some of the plots, etc. The king said to him, "Mr. Ayliffe, don't you know 'tis in my power to pardon you?" "Yes [says he], I know it is in your power, but it is not in your nature!"

It is necessary to put you in mind in reading books of criticism that when examples of greatness of sentiment are produced from Homer and the other ancient writers, that all circumstances must be taken in, in order to form a just opinion concerning them. We must remember his times and the general belief of his countrymen with regard to theology and many other subjects. There must be a probability to make a thing natural, otherwise it is not great or noble, but extravagant. Homer in describing the goddess Discord says her feet were upon the earth, and her head was covered with the clouds. He makes Pluto look up and affirm that Neptune would open hell itself, and make the light to shine into that dark abode. There are some of these that appear to me suspicious even in Homer himself, such as when he makes Jupiter brag that if all the other gods were to hang at the bottom of a chain, and earth and sea and all along with them, he would toss them all up as easily as a ball. However it was with regard to him, who was taught to believe in Jupiter sitting upon Mount Olympus or quaffing nectar in the council of the gods, modern and Christian writers and speakers should be careful to avoid anything that is extravagant and ridiculous, or even such allusions to the heathen theology as could only be proper to those who believed in it.

There is the more reason to insist upon this, that as grandeur and sublimity is commonly a great object of ambition, particularly with young persons, they are very ready to degenerate into bombast. You ought always to remember that the language ought to be no higher than the subject, or the part of the subject that is then immediately handled. See an example of the different ways of a simple and a turgid writer upon the very same sentiment: where the Roman empire was extended to the western coast of Spain, Sextus Rufus simply tells it thus—"Hispanias per Decimum Brutum obtinuimus et usque ad Gades et oceanum pervenimus." Florus taking a more lofty flight says, "Decimus Brutus aliquanto totius," etc.

I have only further to observe that in sublime descriptions great care should be taken that they be all of a piece, and nothing unsuitable brought into view. Longinus justly blamed the poet Hesiod that after he had said everything he could to render the goddess of darkness terrible, he adds that a stinking humor ran from her nose—a circumstance highly disgusting, but no way terrible.

Lecture VII

I COME now to the second source of the sublime, which is pathos, more commonly called in English the pathetic, that is the power of moving the passions. This is a very important part of the subject: a power over the passions is of the utmost consequence to a poet, and it is all to an orator. This everyone will perceive if he only recollects what influence passion or sentiment has upon reason, or in other words inclination upon the practical judgment. He who possesses this power in a high degree has the highest capacity of usefulness, and is likewise able to do the greatest mischief. Sublime sentiments and language may be formed upon any subject, and they touch the heart with a sense of sympathy or approbation; but to move the passions of others so as to incline their choice or to alter their purpose is particularly the design of eloquence.

The chief passions eloquence is intended to work upon are rage, terror, pity, and perhaps desire in general, though occasionally he may have occasion to introduce every affection. In a heroic poem every affection may be said to take its turn, but the different species of oratory, or the different object and subjects of it, may be said to divide the passions. A speaker in political or deliberative assemblies may be said to have it in view to excite the passion of rage: he may naturally desire to incense his hearers against their enemies, foreign and domestic, representing the first as terrible and dangerous to excite aversion and hatred, and the other as weak or worthless to excite contempt. An example of this you have in the great subject of Demosthenes's orations, Philip king of Macedon, another in Cicero's discourses against Cataline and Antony. Pity is the chief passion attempted to be raised at the bar, unless in criminal cases, where indignation against villainy of every kind is the part of the accuser. Terror and its attendants belong very much to a speaker in the pulpit; rage he has nothing to do with but in an improper sense, to raise a strong and steady but uniform indignation against evil. But even this a speaker from the pulpit should endeavor to convert into compassion for the folly and wretchedness of the guilty person. Pity seems to be the single object in tragedy.

One talent of great moment towards raising the passions is a strong and clear imagination and a descriptive manner of speaking to paint scenes and objects strongly and set them before the eyes of the hearers. To select such circumstances as will have the most powerful effect and to dwell only upon these, we have not anywhere in English a finer example of the pathetic, and the choice and use of circumstances, than the speech which Shakespeare has made for Anthony in the tragedy of Caesar. It appears from the history that Anthony did successfully raise the fury of the Romans against those who killed Caesar, and I think he could hardly select better images and language than those we have in the English poet. "But yesterday," etc.

1. To raising the passions with success, much penetration and knowledge of human nature is necessary. Without this every attempt must fail. In confirmation of this remark, though there are persons much better fitted for it by nature than others, the most powerful in raising

the passions have generally been those who have had much acquaintance with mankind and practice in life. Recluse students and professed scholars will be able to discover truth, and to defend it, or to write moral precepts with clearness and beauty; but they are seldom equal for the tender and pathetic to those who have been much in what is called the *world*—by a well known use of that word though almost peculiar to the English language. There is perhaps a double reason for persons well versed in the ways of men having the greatest power upon the passions. They not only know others better, and therefore how to touch them, but their own hearts it is likely have been agitated by more passions than those whose lives have been more calm and even.

2. To raising the passions of others, it is necessary the orator or writer should feel what he would communicate. This is so well-known a rule that I am almost ashamed to mention it, or the trite quotation commonly attending it: "Si vis me flere dolendum est primum ipsi tibi." You may as well kindle a fire with a piece of ice as raise the passions of others while your own are still. I suppose the reason of this, if we would critically examine it, is that we believe the thing to be a pretense or imposition altogether if we see that he who wishes us to be moved by what he says is notwithstanding himself unmoved. The offense is even something more than barely negative in some cases. If we hear a man speaking with coldness and indifference where we think he ought to be deeply interested, we feel a certain disappointment and are filled with displeasure; as if an advocate was pleading for a person accused of a capital crime, if he should appear with an air of indifference and unconcern, let his language and composition be what they will, it is always faulty or disgusting; or let a minister when speaking on the weighty subject of eternity show any levity in his carriage, it must weaken the force of the most moving truths; whereas, when we see the speaker wholly engaged and possessed by his subject, feeling every passion he wishes to communicate, we give ourselves up to him without reserve and are formed after his very temper by receiving his instructions.

3. It is a direction nearly allied to this that a man should never attempt to raise the passions of his hearers higher than the subject plainly merits it. There are some subjects that if we are able are of such moment as to deserve all the zeal and fire we can possibly bestow on them, of which we may say, as Dr. Young, "Passion is reason, transport, temper here." A lawyer for his client whom he believes to be innocent, a patriot for his country which he believes to be in danger, but above all, a minister for his people's everlasting welfare may speak with as much force and vehemence as his temper and frame are susceptible of; but in many other cases it is easy to transcend the bounds of reason and make the language more lofty than the theme. We meet often for example with

raised and labored encomiums in dedications, a species of writing the most difficult to succeed in of any almost that can be named. The person honored by this mark of the author's esteem is very seldom placed in the same rank by the public that he is by him. Besides, though he were really meritorious, it seldom comes fairly up to the representation: the truth is, to correspond to the picture he should be almost the only meritorious person of the age or place in which he lives. Now, considering how cold a compliment this is to all the rest, and particularly to those who read it, there is little wonder that such rhapsodies are treated with contempt. I have often thought the same thing of funeral panegyrics: when a man dies, whose name perhaps was hardly ever heard of before, we have a splendid character of him in the newspapers, where the prejudice of relations or the partiality of friendship do just what they please. I remember at the death of a person whom I shall not name, who was it must be confessed not inconsiderable for literature but otherwise had not much that was either great or amiable about him, an elegiac poem was published which began with this line, "Whence this astonishment in every face?" Had the thing been really true and the public had been deeply affected with the loss, the introduction had been not inelegant; but on such a pompous expression, when the reader recollected that he had seen no marks of public astonishment, it could not but tempt him to smile.

4. Another important remark to be made here is that a writer or speaker in attempting the pathetic should consider his own natural turn as well as the subject. Some are naturally of a less warm and glowing imagination, and in themselves susceptible of a less degree of passion than others. These should take care not to attempt a flight that they cannot finish, or enter upon such sentiments and language as they will probably sink as it were, and fall away from in a little time. Such should substitute gravity and solemnity, instead of fire, and only attempt to make their discourse clear to the understanding and convincing to the conscience. Perhaps this is in general the best way in serious discourses and moral writings because, though it may not produce so strong or ardent emotions, it often leaves a deeper and more lasting impression.

Of Figurative Speech

It is common to meet with this expression: "The tropes and figures of rhetoric." This expression is not just: the terms are neither synonymous, nor are they two distinct species of one genus. Figure is the general expression; a trope is one of the figures, but there are many more. Every trope is a figure, but every figure is not a trope. Perhaps we may say a trope is an expedient to render language more extensive and copious and may be used in tranquility, whereas a figure is the effect of passion. This distinction, however, cannot be universally maintained; for tropes are oftentimes the effect of passion as well as of the narrowness of language. Figures may be defined as any departure from the plain direct manner of expression, and particularly such as are suggested by the passions, and differ on that account from the way in which we would have spoken if in a state of perfect tranquility. Tropes are a species of figures in which a word or phrase is made use of in a sense different from its first and proper signification, as "The Lord is a sun and shield," where the words "sun and shield" are used tropically. There are several different tropes.

1. Metonymy—this is a very general kind of trope, comprehending under it several others. The meaning of it is a change of name, or one name for another; this may be done several ways. (1) The cause may be put for the effect, or the effect for the cause: as when we say, "cold death" because death makes cold; "old age kept him behind," that is made him weak, etc. (2) The author for his works. (3) The thing containing, for the thing contained: as "drink the cup," that is the liquor in the cup. (4) A part is taken for the whole, or the whole for a part: as "my roof" for my house—"my house is on fire," when only a small part of it burns. This is called synecdoche. (5) A general term for a particular: "a hundred reasons may be given," that is, many reasons may be given. (6) A proper name for a characteristic name: as he is a "Nero" for a cruel man, or a Sardanapalus for a voluptuous monarch. All these and many more are metonymies.

2. Metaphor—this might as well have been the general term as trope; for it also signifies change of expression. It is a species of trope by which any term is applied in a sense different from its natural import: as when we say "a tide of pleasure" to express the impetuosity of pleasure; when the heavens are said to be over our heads as brass, and the earth under our feet as iron.

3. Allegory—this is continuing the metaphor and extending it by a variety of expressions of the same kind: as "The Lord is my shepherd, he maketh me to lie down in green pastures, he maketh me to feed beside the still waters."

4. Irony—in using words directly contrary to their meaning: as, "No doubt you are the people and wisdom shall die with you."

5. Hyperbole—when things are carried beyond their truth to express our sentiments more strongly: as "Swifter than the wind, whiter than snow."

6. Catachresis—is the first trope of all, when words are used in an opposite, and sometimes in an impossible sense: as when chains and shackles are called "bracelets of iron."

Figures

Figures cannot be fully enumerated because they are without number, and each figure may be used several different ways. (1) Exclamation—this is nothing else than a way of expressing admiration or lamentation, as "Oh! Alas! Heavens!" etc. used by persons much moved. (2) Doubt—this is frequently the expression of a doubtful mind in suspense what to do. This is described by Virgil, in the distress of Dido when Aeneas left her: "Shall I go to the neighboring kings whom I have so often despised?" Sometimes it is a beautiful figure and obliges persons to take notice of it, and sometimes of what they would otherwise have omitted: "Who is this that cometh from Edom?" (3) Epanorthosis—this is a correction or improvement of what has been said: "You are not truly the son of a goddess, nay you must have sucked a tigress." (4) Pleonasm—this is a redundancy, as "I have heard it with my ears, he spake it with his mouth." (5) Similitude—this is comparing one thing with another, as "he shall be like a tree planted," etc. (6) Distribution—this consists of a particular enumeration of several correspondent images: "Their throat is an open sepulchre, their tongues have used deceit." (7) Prosopopeia—when persons dead or absent, or different from the speaker, are brought in speaking, as Cicero supposes his country, or Italy, and all the public saying to him, "Marcus Tullius what are you doing?" (8) Apostrophe—when persons dead or absent, or any inanimate things are spoken to, as Cicero says, "O vos!" or "Hear O Heavens, and give ear O earth!" (9) Communication—when a speaker calls upon his hearers to say what advice they would give or what they would have done different from what he or the person whom he defends has done: "What could you have done in this case?" "What should I do now?" (10) Interrogation—putting a thing home to the readers, as "What fruit had you then in those things of which you are now ashamed?"

Lecture VIII

I HAVE now gone through the account given in the systems of the tropes and figures of rhetoric, by which you will sufficiently understand the meaning of both. The proper applications however of them is a matter of much greater moment, and of much greater difficulty. I will make a few remarks before I close the subject, in addition to what has been already interspersed through the different parts of it.

1. Perhaps it will not be improper to consider what is the purpose intended by figures. I have introduced them here as a means of giving sublimity to a discourse, but may there not be some little analysis and

resolution of that purpose; may we not inquire what are the particular effects of figures? Are the effects of figures in general, and of all figures the same? It is certain that figurative speech is very powerful in raising the passions. And probably different figures are proper to express or excite different passions: admiration, desire, pity, hatred, rage, or disdain. This appears from the explication of figures formerly given. But besides this, we may observe that there are some effects of figures that seem to be wholly unconnected with passion, of these I shall mention three: ornament, explication, conviction. Sometimes figure is made use of merely for ornament. Of this Rollin gives us an example in which an author says, "The king, to give an eternal mark of the esteem and friendship with which he honored a great general, gave an illustrious place to his glorious ashes amidst those masters of the earth who preserve on the magnificence of their tombs an image of the lustre of their thrones." Under this head may be reckoned all the examples of the use of figures to raise things that are mean and low in themselves to some degree of dignity by the phraseology or to give a greater dignity to anything than the simple idea or the proper name would convey, as if one should say looking round the scene and observing the bounteous gifts of Providence for the support of innumerable creatures, instead of the grass and corn everywhere growing in abundance. Perhaps also under the same head may be reckoned the clothing in other terms anything that might be supposed disagreeable or disgusting: as when Cicero confesses that the servants of Milo killed Clodius, he does not say *intersecerunt* but he says, "They did that which every good man would wish his servants to do in like circumstances." I shall only observe that the greatest delicacy and judgment imaginable is necessary in the use of figures with this view because they are very apt to degenerate into bombast. Young persons in their first compositions, and especially when they have a good deal of ancient literature fresh in their heads, are very apt to be faulty in this particular. A common word or sentiment which anybody might use, and everybody would understand, they think mean and below them, and therefore they have recourse to unnecessary figures and hard or learned phrases. Instead of walking about the fields, they *perambulate* them; they do not discover a thing, but *recognize* it. Johnson, the author of the *Rambler*, is the most faulty this way of any writer of character. A little play of wit, or a few strokes or raillery, he calls a "reciprocation of smartness."

Another use of figures is for explication, to make a thing more clearly conceived. This in general may be said to be the use of the similitude; only I think when figures are used for illustration it is as much to assist the imagination as the judgment, and to make the impression which was before real and just very strong. For example when Solomon says,

"Let a bear robbed of her whelps meet a man, rather than a fool in his folly." "If you bray a fool in a mortar, he will return to his folly." "The foolish man walketh by the way, and he saith to everyone that he is a fool."

A third use of figures may be said, although improperly, to be for conviction, or to make us more readily or more fully yield to the truth: as when to support what we have said that persons of sound judgment are reserved in speech, we add "Deep waters move without noise," or that men in eminent stations are exposed to observation and censure, "A city that is set on a hill cannot be hid." In all such cases therefore it is certain that a similitude is not an argument, yet the analogy of nature seems to carry in it a good deal of evidence and adds to the impression made upon the mind.

2. A second remark is that figures of every kind should come naturally and never be sought for. The design of explaining the several kinds of figures is not to teach you to make them, but to correct them. Arguments and illustrations we must endeavor to invent, but figures never. If they do not flow spontaneously, they are always forced. If a man having proceeded too far in a subject bethinks himself that he will here introduce a similitude, or an allegory, or a prosopopeia, etc., he will either miss of it altogether, or he will produce something vastly more jejune and insipid than it is possible for any man to make without figures. It puts me in mind of the ridiculous chasms that some persons bring themselves to in conversation when they offer to bring a similitude which has not yet occurred to them. They will say, "He raged, and raved, and roared just like . . . I don't know what." Figures should be the native expression of passions or conceptions already felt, as they are the means of raising passions in those to whom you speak. They should therefore be posterior in point of time to the feelings of the speaker, although prior to those of the hearers. The great purpose therefore of criticism on this part of the subject is to prune the luxuriancies of nature and see that the figures be just and natural.

3. I have already in speaking upon the tropes had occasion to give some rules as to the use of them, particularly as to the propriety and consistency of them. But there are some things to be observed further for explaining them. There are two characters frequently given to tropes, especially to metaphors, which deserve to be considered. The one is strength, the other is boldness. These are by no means the same. That is a strong metaphor or image that gives us a very lively impression of the thing represented. As that of the wise man, "A stone is heavy, and the sand is weighty, but a fool's wrath is heavier than them both." A bold image or metaphor is that which upon the whole is just and strong, but is considerably removed from common observation and

would not easily or readily have occurred to another. It is also called a bold image when the resemblance is but in one single point. There is not anywhere to be seen a collection of bolder images than in the book of Job, particularly in the description of the war-horse, among which in particular the following seems to excel: "Hast thou clothed the neck with thunder." To liken the mane of a horse to thunder would not have occurred to every one; neither in idea does the resemblance hold but in one particular, that the flowing and waving of the mane is like the sheets and forked flakes of lightning.

Lecture IX

I NOW come to consider the simple manner of writing. If I could explain this fully so as to make everyone clearly to understand it and at the same time incline you to admire and study it, I should think a very difficult and important point was gained. It is exceedingly difficult to bring young persons especially to a taste for the simple way of writing. They are apt to think it of little moment, not so much the object of ambition as an exercise of self-denial, to say a thing plainly when they might have said it nobly. I would observe therefore in the very beginning that it is a mistake to consider simplicity and sublimity as universally opposite, for on the contrary there is not only a great excellence in some performances, which we may call wholly of the simple kind such as a story told or an epistle written with all the beauty of simplicity, but in the most sublime and animated compositions; some of the greatest sentiments derive their beauty from being clothed in simple language. Simplicity is even as necessary to some parts of an oration as it is to the whole of some kinds of composition. Let the subject be ever so great and interesting, it is prudent, decent, necessary, to begin the discouse in a cool and dispassionate manner. That man who should begin an oration with the same boldness of figure and the same high pitch of voice that would be proper towards the close of it would commit one of the greatest faults against propriety, and I think would wholly prevent its effect upon the hearers.

But how shall we explain the simple manner of writing? It is, say many authors, that which is likest to and least removed from the language of common life. It must be therefore easy and obvious—few or no figures in the expression, nothing obscure in the sentiments or involved in the method. Long sentences are contrary to it; words either difficult or uncommon are inconsistent with it. Cicero and Horace have both said, and all critics have said after them, it is that which when men hear, they think that they themselves could only have said the same, or that it is just a kind of expression of their own thoughts. They generally remark further that it is what seems to be easy, but yet is not: as Horace says, "ut sibi quivis speret idem," etc. We may further observe that what is truly simple always carries in it the idea of being easy in its production, as well as in imitation; and indeed the one of these seems necessarily to suppose the other. Whatever seems to be the effect of study and much invention cannot be simple. It is finely exemplified in the introduction of Anthony's speech in Shakespeare: "I am no orator as Brutus is," etc. Rollin has given us an admirable example of a story told with a beautiful simplicity from Cicero's Offices. There is an example also in Livy's account of the battle of the Horatii and Curiatii, only with a little more force of expression, as the importance and solemnity of the subject seemed to require it. But it requires a very masterly knowledge of the Latin language to perceive the beauties fully that are pointed at by Rollin in the the first instance, or might easily be mentioned in the last. There is no author in our language who excels more in simplicity than Addison. The *Spectator* in general indeed, but especially the papers written by him, excel in this quality. Ease and elegance are happily joined in them, and nature itself, as it were, seems to speak in them. If some of the later periodical writers have equaled, or even excelled them in force or elegance, not one has ever come up to them in simplicity.

The subjects or the species of writing in which simplicity chiefly shines are narration, dialogue, epistolary writing, essay writing, and all the lighter species of poetry, as odes, songs, epigrams, elegies, and such like. The ancients were remarkable for a love and admiration of simplicity, and some of them remain to us as eminent examples of its excellence. Xenophon in his institution of Cyrus is particularly remarkable for a sweet and dignified simplicity. He uses neither language nor ideas that are difficult and farfetched. In the smaller compositions of the ancients, as odes, epigrams, etc. they were at prodigious pains to polish them and make them quite easy and natural. They placed their great glory in bestowing much art, and at the same time making it to appear quite easy and artless, according to the saying now grown into a proverb, "artis est celare artem." The beauty of simplicity may not appear at first sight, or be at all perceived by persons of a vitiated taste, but all persons of good judgment immediately, and the bulk of mankind in time, are charmed with what is quite easy, and yet truly accurate and elegant.

It ought to be carefully observed that simplicity is quite a different thing from lowness and meanness, and the great art of a writer is to preserve the one without degenerating into the other. It is the easiest thing in the world to speak or write vulgarisms, but a person of true taste will carefully avoid everything of that kind. For example, one who would write simply, and as near the language of plain people in ordinary discourse as possible, would yet avoid every absurdity or barbarism that obtains a place in common conversation, as to say, "This here table, and that there candle." It is also quite contrary to simplicity to adopt the quaint expressions or cant phrases that are the children of fashion, and obtain for a little, or in some particular places, and not in others. The *Spectator* attacked with great spirit and propriety several of those that were introduced into conversation and writing in his time, such as *mob, rep, pos, bite, bamboosle,* and several others. Most of them he fairly defeated, but one or two of them got the better of him and are now freely introduced into the language, such as *mob.* Johnson also has put *bamboosle* in his dictionary, which he calls indeed a low word. Arbuthnot is his authority, but it was plainly used by him in the way of ridicule, and therefore it should either not have been in the dictionary at all, or such an authority should not have been given for it.

It is exceedingly difficult and requires an excellent judgment to be able to descend to great simplicity, and yet to keep out every low expression or idea. I do not think it is easy to be a thorough judge of pure diction in any language but our own, and not even in that without a good deal of the knowledge of human life and a thorough acquaintance with the best authors. Writers and speakers of little judgment are apt at times to go into extremes, to swell too much on the one hand, and to fall into what is vulgar and offensive on the other.

When speaking on simplicity, I observe that there is a simplicity in the taste and composition of a whole discourse different from simplicity of sentiment and language in the particular parts. This will incline a man to avoid all unnecessary ornament, particularly the ornaments of fashion and the peculiar dress or mode of the times. We say in architecture that a building is in a simple style when it has not a great multiplicity of ornaments, or is not loaded with beauties, so to speak. It is very remarkable that books written in the same age will differ very much one from another in this respect, and those which have least of the ornaments then in vogue continue in reputation when the others are grown ridiculous. I will give you an instance of this. A small religious treatise, Scougal's *Life of God in the Soul of Man,* which is written with great simplicity and yet dignity, and may now be read with pleasure and approbation by persons of the best taste, while most of the other writers of his age and country are ridiculous or hardly intelligible.

Perhaps it may help us to form right notions of simplicity to consider what are the opposites or the greatest enemies to it.

1. One is abstraction of sentiment, or too great refinement of any kind: of this the greatest example in an author of merit is the writer of the *Rambler*; almost every page of his writings furnishes us with in-

stances of departure from simplicity, partly in the sentiment and partly in the diction.

2. Another is allegory, and especially farfetched allusions, as in the example which the *Spectator* gives of a poet who speaks of "Bacchus's cast coat": this is little better than a riddle, and even those who discern it will take a little time to reflect that according to the heathen mythology Bacchus was the God of wine; wine is kept in casks, and therefore an empty cask, or at least a useless one, may be called Bacchus's cast coat.

3. A third enemy to simplicity is an affectation of learning. This spoils simplicity many ways; it introduces terms of art, which cannot be understood but by those who are adepts in a particular branch. Such persons have been long exposed to ridicule under the name of pedants. Sometimes indeed the word pedantry has been in a manner confined to those addicted to classic literature, and who intermix everything they say with scraps taken from the learned languages; but this is quite improper, for lawyers, physicians, dunces, or schoolmasters are equally ridiculous when they fill their discourse with words drawn from their particular art.

4. The only other enemy to simplicity I shall mention is an ambition to excel. This perhaps should not have been so much divided from the rest as made the great principle from which the rest proceed. Nothing more certainly renders a man ridiculous than an over forwardness to display his excellence; he is not content with plain things, and particularly with such things as everybody might say, because these would not distinguish him.

On the whole, as I observed on sublimity that one of the best and surest ways to attain it was to think nobly, so the best way to write simply is to think simply, to avoid all affectation, to attempt to form your manner of thinking to a noble self-denial. A man little solicitous about what people think of him, or rather having his attention fixed upon quite another purpose, viz. giving information or producing conviction, will only attain to a simple manner of writing, and indeed he will write best in all respects.

As to the mixed style or manner of writing, as it consists of the mixture of the other two, I shall not need to say anything by way of explaining it, but only make a remark or two of the use and application of it. The mixed kind of writing chiefly consists of history and controversy. The great quality necessary to execute it properly is soundness of judgment to determine on what subjects, and on what parts of subjects, it is proper to write with simplicity, and on what with force. One would wish not to go beyond, but just to gratify a reader's inclination in this respect.

There are many cases in history where the greatest sublimity both of sentiments and language is both admitted and required; particularly all the beauty and all the force that can be admitted into description is of importance in history. Those who will read in Robertson's history of Scotland the account he gives of the astonishment, terror, and indignation that appeared in the English court when news was brought of the massacre at Paris, or in the same author the account of the execution of Mary Queen of Scots, will see the force and sublimity of description. The difference between sublimity of sentiment and language in a historian and in a poet or orator seems to me to resemble the difference between the fire of a managed horse when reined in by the rider and marching with a firm and stately pace, and the same when straining every nerve in the eager contention in a race. We shall enter a little into this matter if we consider the different images that are made use of in the different arts. In poetry we say a beautiful, striking, shining metaphor or fervent, glowing imagery. In oratory we say warm, animated, irresistible. In history we use the words force, nobleness, dignity, and majesty, particularly those last attributes of dignity and majesty. Herodotus has been often called the father of history, though I confess I apprehend he has obtained this title chiefly because of his antiquity, and his being the first that ever gave anything of a regular history; but though he has some things august enough, yet he has admitted so many incredible stories and even peculiarities into his work as very much detracts from its dignity. We must indeed impute a good deal of this to the age in which he lived, and the impossibility of their distinguishing truth from falsehood so well as those of later ages, who have had the advantage of all past experience.

History indeed is not only of the mixed kind of writing, so as to admit sometimes sublimity and sometimes simplicity, but those styles should be really blended together in every part of it. The most noble and animated sentiments, characters, or descriptions in history should yet be clothed with such a gravity and decency of garb, so to speak, as to give an air of simplicity to the whole. It is an advantage to a poem that the author says but little in his own person, but makes the characters speak and say all; and in an orator it is an advantage when he can carry the hearers off from himself to his subject; but above all, a historian should not so much as wish to shine, but with the coolness of a philosopher and the impartiality of a judge should set the actors and transactions before the reader.

Controversy is another subject of the mixed kind, which ought to be in general written with simplicty, yet will sometimes admit of the ornaments of eloquence—of this I shall speak a little more afterwards, and therefore shall now only add that controversy differs from history in that it sometimes admits of passion and warmth when there seems to be a sufficient foundation laid for it. A controversial writer will endeavor to interest his reader and excite either contempt or indignation against his adversary.

After having given you this view of the three great kinds of writing, or as they are sometimes called different styles, it may not be amiss to observe that there are distinctions of style which it is proper that an able writer should observe that do not range themselves, at least not fully and properly, under these three heads but may be said to run through all the kinds of eloquence.

Many eminent authors have said that the climates have some effect upon the style, that in the warmest countries the style is more animated, and the figures more bold and glowing; and nothing is more common than to ascribe a peculiarity of style, and that particularly elevated and full of metaphor, to the orientals, as if it belonged to that part of the globe; but if I am not mistaken, both this and other things, such as courage, that have been attributed to the climate belong either not to the climate at all, or in a small measure, and are rather owing to the state of society and manners of men. We have before had occasion to see that all narrow languages are figured. In a state where there are few or no abstract ideas, how should there be abstract terms? If anybody will read the poem of Fingal, which appears to have been composed on the bleak hills of the north of Scotland, he will find as many figures and as bold as in anything composed in Arabia or Persia. The state of society then is what gives a particular color to the style, and by this the styles of different ages and countries are distinguished. That the climate does but little may be seen just by comparing ancient and modern Italy: what difference between the strength and force of the ancient Latin tongue and the present Italian language in the expression of sentiments? It must therefore vary with sentiments and manners, and what difference between the stern and inflexible bravery of a free ancient Roman and the effeminate softness of a modern Italian? Yet they breathed the same air, and were nursed by the same soil. I will just go a little off from the subject to say that a very late author (Lord Kaimes) seems to think that the courage of mankind is governed by the climates. He says that the northern climates produce hardened constitutions and bold and firm minds, that invasions have been made from north to south; but I apprehend he may be mistaken here both in his facts and the reasons of them. Invasions have not always been made from north to south, for the Roman armies penetrated very far to the north of their territory. The first great conquerors of the east in Egypt and Babylon carried their arms to the north, and where the conquest ran the other way, it was owing to other circumstances; Dean Swift says much nearer the truth, it was from poverty to plenty.

The design of this digression is to show that not only the circumstances that appear in a language, but several others that have also been attributed to climate, owe very little to it, but to the state of mankind and the progress of society. The maxim of that great modern writer, Montesquieu, which he applies to population is also true of language: that natural causes are not by far so powerful as moral causes. Allowing, therefore, as some have affirmed that the northern climates may give a roughness and harshness to the accent and pronunciation, I believe it is all that we can expect from climate; the distinction of styles and composition must come from another original.

Lecture X

HAVING in a great measure rejected the supposition of the style in writing being affected by the climate, and shown that it rather takes its color from the state of society and the sentiments and manners of men, it follows that all the great distinctions that take place in manners will have a correspondent effect upon language spoken or written. When the manners of a people are little polished, there is a plainness or a roughness in the style. Absolute monarchies and the obsequious subjection introduced at the courts of princes occasion a pompous swelling and compliment to be in request different from the boldness and sometimes ferocity of republican states.

Seneca in remarking upon the Roman language says, "Genus dicendi mutatur per publicos mores," etc. This he exemplifies in the Roman language, which was short and dry in the earliest ages, afterwards become elegant and ornate, and at last loose and diffuse.

The style of an age also is sometimes formed by some one or more eminent persons, who, having obtained reputation, everything peculiar to them is admired and copied and carried much into excess. Seneca has remarked this also that commonly one author obtains the palm, and becomes the model and all copy him: "Haec vitia unus aliquis inducit." And he gives a very good example of it, of which we may now judge in Sallust. He also very properly observes that all the faults that arise from imitation become worse in the imitator than in the example, thus reproving the fault just now mentioned in our ancestors.

It is remarkable that Seneca himself was another example of the same thing. His manner of writing, which is peculiar, came to be the standard of the age. His manner has been called by critics point and antithesis. A short sentence containing a strong sentiment, or a beautiful one, as it were like a maxim by itself. For an example or two of this, to express the destruction of Lyons he says, "Lugdunum quod ostendebatur," etc. That "Lyons, which was formerly shown, is now sought." And on the same subject—"Una nox," etc. "There was but one night between a great city and none." "Quid est eques Romanus," etc. "What is a Roman knight, a freed man or slave, names generated by ambition or oppression."

The fault of this sententious manner of writing does not lie in the particulars being blamable, but in the repetition and uniformity becoming tedious: when every paragraph is stuffed with sentences and bright sayings generally having the same tune, it wearies the ear. The most remarkable book in the English language for putting continual smartness, sentence and antithesis for elegance is the *Gentleman Instructed*. I shall read you one paragraph: "the misfortune of one breathes vigor into the others: they carry on manfully the attack—their heads run round with the glasses. Their tongues ride post. Their wits are jaded. Their reason is distanced. Brutes could not talk better, nor men worse. Like skippers in a storm, they rather hallowed than spoke. Scarce one heard his neighbor, and not one understood him; so that noise stood for sense, and everyone passed for a virtuoso because all played the fool to extravagance."

I shall not enlarge much farther upon the difference of style arising from the character of an age: as in the ages before the reformation called the times of chivalry, when military prowess was the great thing in request, their gallantry and heroism were to be seen in every writer. At the time of the reformation and the revival of learning, their citations of the ancient writers and allusions to the classic phrases distinguished every author. In the age of the civil wars in England, of which religion was so much the cause, allusions to singular expressions and theological opinions are everywhere to be met with, of which the great Milton is an example.

But there is another distinction of styles which is chiefly personal and will distinguish one author from another in the same age, and perhaps of the same or nearly the same abilities. There are several different epithets given to style in our language which I shall mention in a certain order, which I suppose will contribute something to explain the meaning of them. We call a style simple or plain, smooth, sweet, concise, elegant, ornate, just, nervous, chaste, severe. These are all different epithets which will each of them convey to a nice critical ear something different, though I confess it is not easy to define them clearly or explain them fully. (1) Plainess and simplicity is when the author does not seem to have had anything in view but to be understood, and that by persons of the weakest understanding. That ought to be in view in many writings, and indeed perspicuity will be found to be a character of many styles when there are other great qualities; but we call that plain and simple when there is no discovery of literature, and no attempt at the pathetic. Scougal's *Life of God in the Soul of Man* and Dr. Evans's *Sermons* are admirable patterns of this manner. (2) I would call that a smooth style when the utmost care had been taken to measure the periods and to consult the ear on the structure of the sentence, for this I know no author more remarkable than Hervey in his *Meditations*. (3) Sweetness seems to me to differ from the former only in that the subjects and the images are generally of a pleasing or soothing nature, such as may particularly be seen in Mrs. Rowe's *Letters*, perhaps also in a more modern composition by a lady, Lady Mary W. Montague's *Letters*. And indeed when female authors have excelled, they generally do excel in sweetness. (4) The next is conciseness. This is easily understood; it is just as much brevity as is consistent with perspicuity. It is a beauty in every writing when other qualities are not hurt by it. But it is peculiarly proper for critical or scientific writing because there we do not so much expect or want to know the author's sentiments, but as soon as possible to learn the facts, to understand them fully, and range them methodically. There are many more authors who excel in this respect in the French than in the English language. Not only the scientific writings, but even political and moral writings are drawn up by them with great conciseness. There cannot be greater conciseness than in Montesquieu's *Spirit of Laws*. Brown's *Estimate of the Manners and Principles of the Times* seems to be an imitation of that author in his manner. In essay writing, David Hume seems to have as happily joined conciseness and perspicuity as most of our English writers. Some pious writers have been as successful this way as most of our nation, such as Mason's *Sayings* and Mason *On Self-knowledge*. (5) A style is called elegant when it is formed by the principles of true taste, and much pain is taken to use the best and purest expressions that the language will afford. It is very common to join together ease and elegance. The great patterns we have of these are Addison and Tillotson. Seed's *Sermons* too may be mentioned here as very much excelling in both these qualities, so also does David Hume. The other Hume, author of the *Elements of Criticism,* though a very good judge of writing, seems in point of style to be very defective himself. If he has any talent, it is conciseness and plainess; but he is at the same time often abrupt and harsh. (6) An ornate style may be said to be something more than elegant, introducing into a composition all the beauties of language where they can find a place with propriety. I mentioned before that Hervey's style in his *Meditations* was exceedingly smooth and flowing. I may add it has also the qualities of elegant and ornate. That style is elegant which is correct and free from faults; that is ornate which abounds with beauties. (7) The next character of style is that it is just. By this I understand a particular attention to the truth and meaning of every expression. Justness is frequently joined with or otherwise expressed by precision, so that (if I may speak so) together with a taste which will relish and produce an elegance of language, there is a judgment and accuracy which will abide the scrutiny of philosophy and criticism. Many well-turned periods and showy expressions will be found defective here. This justness of style is scarcely ever found without clearness of understanding, so that it appears in accuracy of method in the whole discourse, as well as in the style of particular parts. Dr. Samuel Clark was a great example of this. He was one of those few mathematicians who were good writers and, while he did not lose the life and fervor of the orator, preserved the precision of the natural philosopher. (8) Nervous or strong is the next character of style, and this implies that in which the author does not wholly neglect elegance and precision. But he is much more attentive to dignity and force. A style that is very strong and nervous might often receive a little additional polish by a few more epithets or copulatives, but cannot descend to such minuteness. It is a fine expression of Richard Baxter upon style, "May I speak plainly and pertinently, and somewhat nervously, I have my purpose." Baxter was a great example of a nervous style with great neglect of elegance, and Dean Swift is an illustrious example of the same sort of diction with a very considerable attention to elegance. Both the one and the other seem to write in the fullness of their hearts, and to me without scruple those terms are commonly best that first present themselves to a fertile invention and warm imagination without waiting to choose in their room those that might be more smooth or sonorous, but less emphatic. (9) Chastity of style I think stands particularly opposed to any embellishments that are not natural and necessary. Nay, we generally mean by a very chaste writer, one who does not admit even all the ornaments that he might, and what ornaments he does admit are always of the most decent kind, and the most properly executed. (10) Severity of style has this title only by way of comparison. That is a severe style which has propriety, elegance, and force, but seems rather to be above and to disdain the ornaments which everybody else would approve and the greatest part of readers would desire.

Lecture XI

WE come now to the third general head, which was to speak of oratory as it is divided into the several parts which constitute the art. These have been generally the following: invention, disposition, style or composition, pronunciation, including gesture.

1. Invention. This is nothing else but finding out the sentiments by

which a speaker or writer would explain what he has to propose, and the arguments by which he would enforce it. This subject is treated of very largely in most of the books of oratory, in which I think they judge very wrong. In by far the greatest number of cases, there is no necessity of teaching it, and where it is necessary, I believe it exceeds the power of man to teach it with effect. The very first time indeed that a young person begins to compose, the thing is so new to him that it is apt to appear dark and difficult, and in a manner impossible. But as soon as he becomes a little accustomed to it, he finds much more difficulty in selecting what is proper than in inventing something that seems to be tolerable. There are some persons I confess whom their own stupidity, or that of their relations, forces to attempt public speaking who are entirely barren and not able to bring out anything either good or bad; but this is exceedingly rare, and when it does happen, it will be so burdensome to the man himself that he must speedily give over the attempt. There are infinitely more who have plenty of matter, such as it is, but neither very valuable in itself nor clothed in proper language. I think it happens very generally that those who are least concise and accurate are most lengthy and voluminous.

I will therefore not spend much time upon invention, leaving it to the spontaneous production of capacity and experience; only observe that it is called a commonplace from whence you draw your argument. That principle of law, nature, taste, experience from which you fetch your topic and apply it to your particular case is a commonplace; as for example, if I want to prove that a strict discipline in a society is best, I say that discipline which will in the most effectual manner restrain offenses is certainly the best; this is the topic or commonplace.

It would be needless to point out the sources of invention or show from whence arguments may be drawn, for they may be drawn from all the characters and qualities of an action or person, and from all the circumstances that accompany it. If I mean to aggravate a crime or injury, I say it was done deliberately, obstinately, repeatedly, without temptation, against many warnings, and much kindness; that its effects are very bad to a man's self, to others, to the character, the person, the estate, etc. If I want to speak in praise of a free government, I mention its happy effects in giving security and happiness, promoting industry, encouraging genius, producing value; and then I apply to experience and show the happiness of free states, and the misery of those that have been kept in slavery; but I repeat the remark that invention need not be taught, unless it be to one that never yet composed a sentence. There have been books of commonplaces published containing arguments and topics for illustration and even similitudes—sayings of the ancients, etc.; but they are of very little use, unless to a person that has no fund of his own, and then one that makes the use of them is like a man walking on stilts: they make him look very big, but he walks very feebly.

2. The next division of the oratorial art is disposition or distribution. This is a matter of the utmost moment, and upon which instruction is both necessary and useful. By disposition as a part of the oratorial art I mean order in general, in the whole of a discourse or any kind of composition, be it what it will. As to the parts of which a single speech or oration consists, they will be afterwards considered. Before I proceed to explain or point out the way to attain good order, I would just mention a few of its excellencies.

(1) Good order in a discourse gives light and makes it easily understood. If things are thrown together without method, each of them will be less understood, and their joint influence in leading to a conclusion will not be perceived. It is a noble expression of Horace, who calls it "lucidus ordo," clear order. It is common to say when we hear a confused discourse, "It had neither head nor tail; I could not understand what he would be at." (2) Order is necessary to force, as well as light. This indeed is a necessary consequence of the other, for we shall never be persuaded by what we do not understand. Very often the force of reasoning depends upon the united influence of several distinct propositions. If they are ranged in a just order, they will all have their effect and support one another. If otherwise, it will be like a number of men attempting to raise a weight, and one pulling at one time and another at another, which will do just nothing, but if all exert their power at once, it will be easily overcome.

(3) Order is also useful for assisting memory. Order is necessary even in a discourse that is to have a transient effect, but if anything is intended to produce a lasting conviction, and to have a daily influence, it is still more neccessary. When things are disposed in a proper order, the same concatenation that is in the discourse takes place in the memory, so that when one thing is remembered, it immediately brings to remembrance what has an easy and obvious connection with it. The association of ideas linked together by any tie is very remarkable in our constitutuion, and is supposed to take place from some impression made upon the brain. If we have seen two persons but once, and seen them both at the same time only, or at the same place only, the remembrance of the one can hardly be separated from the other. I may also illustrate the subject by another plain instance. Suppose I desire a person going to a city to do three or four things for me that are wholly unconnected, as to deliver a letter to one person, to visit a friend of mine and to bring me notice how he is, to buy a certain book for me if he can find it, and to see whether any ship be to sail for Britain soon. It is very possible he may remember some of them and forget the others, but if I desire him to

buy me a dozen of silver spoons, to carry them to an engraver to put my name upon them, and get a case to put them in, if he remembers one article, it is likely he will remember all of them. It is one of the best evidences that a discourse has been composed with distinctness and accuracy if after you go away you can remember a good deal of it; but there are sometimes discourses which are pompous and declamatory, and which you hear with pleasure and some sort of approbation, but if you attempt to recollect the truths advanced or the arguments in support of them, there is not a trace of them to be found.

(4) Order conduces also very much to beauty. Order is never omitted when men give the principles of beauty, and confusion is disgustful just on its own account, whatever the nature of the confused things may be. If you were to see a vast heap of fine furniture of different kinds lying in confusion, you could neither perceive half so distinctly what was there, nor could it at all have such an effect as if everything was disposed in just order and placed where it ought to stand; nay, a much smaller quantity elegantly disposed would exceed in grandeur of appearance a heap of the most costly things in nature.

(5) Order is also necessary to brevity. A confused discourse is almost never short and is always filled with repetitions. It is with thought in this respect as with things visible, for to return to the former similitude, a confused heap of goods or furniture fills much more room than when it is ranged and classed in its proper order, and everything carried to its proper place.

Having shown the excellence of precision and method, let us next try to explain what it is, and that I may have some regard to method while I am speaking of the very subject, I shall take it in three lights. (1) There must be an attention to order in the disposition of the whole piece. Whatever the parts be in themselves, they have also a relation to one another and to the whole body (if I may speak so) that they are to compose. Every work, be it what it will, history, epic poem, dramatic poem, oration, epistle, or essay, is to be considered as a whole, and a clearness of judgment in point of method will decide the place and proportion of the several parts of which they are composed. The loosest essay, or where form is least professed or studied, ought yet to have some shape as a whole, and we may say of it that it begins abruptly or ends abruptly, or some of the parts are misplaced. There are often to be seen pieces in which good things are said, and well said, and have only this fault that they are unseasonable and out of place. Horace says in his art of poetry what is equally applicable to every sort of composition, "Denique fit quod vis simplex duntaxat et unum," and shortly after "In felix operis summa, quia ponere totum nesciet."

This judgment in planning the whole will particularly enable a person to determine both as to the place and proportion of the particular parts, whether they be not only good in themselves but fit to be introduced in such a work, and it will also (if I may speak so) give a color to the whole composition. The necessity of order in the whole structure of a piece shows that the rule is good which is given by some that an orator before he begin his discourse should concentrate the subject as it were, and reduce it to one single proposition, either expressed or at least conceived in his mind. Everything should grow out of this as its root, if it be in another principle to be explained, or refer to this as its end, if it be a point to be gained by persuasion. Having thus stated the point clearly to be handled, it will afford a sort of criterion whether anything adduced is proper or improper. It will suggest the topics that are just and suitable, as well as enable us to reject whatever is in substance improper or in size disproportionate to the design. Agreeably to this principle, I think that not only the subject of a single discourse should be reducible to one proposition, but the general divisions or principal heads should not be many in number. A great number of general heads both burdens the memory and breaks the unity of the subject, and carries the idea of several little discourses joined together, or to follow after one another.

(2) Order is necessary in the subdivisions of a subject, or the way of stating and marshalling of the several portions of any general head. This is applicable to all kinds of composition, and all kinds of oratory— sermons, law pleadings, speeches. There is always a division of the parts, as well as of the whole, either expressed formally and numerically, or supposed though suppressed. And it is as much here as anywhere that the confusion of inaccurate writers and speakers appears. It is always necessary to have some notion of the whole of a piece, and the larger divisions being more bulky, so to speak, disposition in them is more easily perceived, but in the smaller, both their order and size is in danger of being less attended to. Observe, therefore, that to be accurate and just, the subdivisions of any composition—such I mean as are (for example) introduced in a numerical series, 1, 2, 3, etc.—should have the following properties: (1.) They should be clear and plain. Everything indeed should be clear as far as he can make it, but precision and distinctness should especially appear in the subdivisions, just as the boundary lines of countries in a map. For this reason the first part of a subdivision should be like a short definition, and when it can be done, it is best expressed in a single term; for example, in giving the character of a man of learning, I may propose to speak of his genius, his erudition, his industry or application.

(2.) They should be truly distinct, that is everybody should perceive that they are really different from one another, not in phrase or word only, but in sentiment. If you praise a man first for his judgment and then for his understanding, they are either altogether or so nearly the same, or so nearly allied, as not to require distinction. I have heard a minister on John 17:2. ("Holy Father," etc.) in showing how God keeps his people say, "(1) He keeps their feet. He shall keep thy feet from falling. (2) He keeps their way. Thou shalt keep him in all his ways." Now it is plain that these are not two different things, but two metaphors for the same thing. This indeed was faulty also in another respect, for a metaphor ought not to make a subdivision at all.

(3.) Subdivisions should be necessary, that is to say taking the word in the loose and popular sense, the subject should seem to demand them. To multiply divisions, even where they may be made really distinct, is tedious and disgustful, unless where they are of use and importance to our clearly comprehending the meaning or feeling the force of what is said. If a person in the map of a country should give a different color to every three miles, though the equality of the proportion would make the division clear enough, yet it would appear disgustingly superfluous. In writing the history of an eminent person's life, to divide it into spaces of ten years perhaps would make the view of the whole more exact; but to divide it into single years or months would be finical and disagreeable. The increase of divisions leads almost unavoidably into tediousness.

(4.) Subdivisions should be coordinate, that is to say those that go on in a series—1, 2, 3, etc.—should be as near as possible similar, or of the same kind. This rule is transgressed when either the things mentioned are wholly different in kind, or when they include one another. This will be well perceived if we consider how a man would describe a sensible subject, a country for example: New Jersey contains (1) Middlesex, (2) Somerset County, (3) the townships of Princeton (4) Morris County. So, if one in describing the character of a real Christian should say faith, holiness, charity, justice, temperance, patience, this would not do because holiness includes justice, etc. When, therefore, it seems necessary to mention different particulars that cannot be made coordinate, they should be made subordinate.

(5.) Subdivisions should be complete and exhaust the subject. This indeed is common to all divisions, but is of most importance here where it is most neglected. It may be said, perhaps, how can we propose to exhaust any subject? By making the divisions suitable, particularly in point of comprehension, to the nature of the subject. As an example, and to make use of the image before introduced of giving an account of a country, I may say the province of New Jersey consists of two parts, East and West Jersey. If I say it consists of the counties of Somerset, etc., I must continue till I have enumerated all the counties, otherwise the division is not complete. In the same manner in public speaking, or any other composition, whatever division is made, it is not legitimate if it does not include or exhaust the whole subject, which may be done let it be ever so great. For example, true religion may be divided various ways so as to include the whole: I may say that it consists of our duty to God, our neighbor and ourselves; or I may make but two, our duty to God and man, and divide the last into two subordinate heads, our neighbor and ourselves; or I may say it consists of faith and practice; or that it consists of two parts, a right frame and temper of mind, and a good life and conversation.

(6.) Lastly, the subdivisions of any subject should be connected, or should be taken in a series or order if they will possibly admit of it. In some moral and intellectual subjects it may not be easy to find any series or natural order, as in an enumeration of virtues, justice, temperance, and fortitude. Patience perhaps might as well be enumerated in any other order, yet there is often an order that will appear natural, and the inversion of it unnatural: as we may say, injuries are done many ways to a man's person, character, and possessions. Love to others includes the relation of family, kindred, citizens, countrymen, fellow creatures.

(3) In the last place there is also an order to be observed in the sentiments, which makes the illustration or amplification of the divisions of a discourse. This order is never expressed by numerical divisions, yet it is of great importance, and its beauty and force will be particularly felt. It is, if I may speak so, of a finer and more delicate nature than any of the others, more various, and harder to explain. I once have said that all reasoning is of the nature of a syllogism, which lays down principles, makes comparisons, and draws the conclusions. But we must particularly guard against letting the uniformity and formality of a syllogism appear. In general, whatever establishes any connection so that it makes the sentiments give rise to one another is the occasion of order; sometimes necessity and utility point out the order as a good measure: as in telling a story, grave or humorous, you must begin by describing the persons concerned, mentioning just as many circumstances of their character and situation as are necessary to make us understand the facts to be afterwards related. Sometimes the sensible ideas of time and place suggest an order, not only in historical narrations and in law pleadings, which relate to facts, but in drawing of characters, describing the progress and effects of virtue and vice, and even in other subjects where the connection between those ideas and the thing spoken of is not very strong. Sometimes, and indeed generally, there is an order which proceeds from things plain to things obscure. The beginning of a paragraph should be like the sharp point of a wedge which gains admittance to the bulky part behind. It first affirms what every body feels or must confess and proceeds to what follows as a necessary conse-

quence. In fine, there is an order in persuasion to a particular choice, which may be taken two ways with equal advantage: proceeding from the weaker to the stronger or from the stronger to the weaker. As in recommending a pious and virtuous life, we may first say it is amiable, honorable, pleasant, profitable even in the present life, and, to crown all, makes death itself a friend, and leads to a glorious immortality; or, we may begin the other way and say it is the one thing needful, that eternity is the great and decisive argument that should determine our choice, though everything else were in favor of vice, and then add that even in the present life it is a great mistake to think that bad men are gainers, etc. This is called sometimes the ascending and descending climax. Each of them has its beauty and use. It must be left to the orator's judgment to determine which of the two is either fittest for the present purpose, or which he finds himself at that time able to execute to the greatest advantage.

Lecture XII

THE next branch of this division is style or composition. This, which is so great a part of the subject, has already been considered in one view under the three great kinds of writing and will again be mentioned under the two following heads, as well as the remarks at the close; yet I will drop a few things upon it in this place.

1. It is necessary that a writer or speaker should be well acquainted with the language in which he speaks, its characters, properties and defect, its idioms or peculiar terms and phrases, and likewise with as many other languages as possible, particularly such as are called the learned languages—the Latin and Greek. Our own language is the English. A thorough acquaintance with it must be acquired by extensive reading in the best authors, giving great attention to the remarks made by critics of judgment and erudition, and trying it ourselves in practice. Our language, like most of the northern languages, is rough with a frequent meeting of consonants difficult of pronunciation; it abounds in monosyllables. You may write a whole page and scarce use one word that has more than one syllable; this is a defect and to be avoided when it can be done consistently with other properties, particularly simplicity and perspicuity. Our language is said to have an over proportion of the letter *S*, and therefore called a hissing language. This a writer of judgment will endeavor to avoid, wherever he can do it with propriety and elegance. A thorough acquaintance with the genius and idioms of our own language can scarcely be attained without some acquaintance with others because it is comparison of one with another which illustrates

all. There are not only smaller difference between one language and another, but there are some general differences in the arrangement of words in the ancient and modern languages: in the Greek and Latin, the governed words are pretty generally before the verb. It is a mistake for us to say that the English order is the natural order, as some have done. It is certain that they are either both alike natural and equally obvious when once custom has fixed them, or that the ancient order is the more natural of the two. There are two things, the action and the object, to be conjoined, and it is fully as proper to turn your attention first to the object, before you tell what you are to say of it or what you would have done with it, as after. "Istud scalpellum quod in manu habes, commoda mihi paulisper, si placet"; and in longer and more involved sentences, the suspending the sentiment for some time till it be completed is both more pleasing and more forcible. Our own language admits of a little transposition and becomes grander and more sonorous by it, both in poetry and prose.

2. We may attend to the arrangement of the clauses of a sentence and their proportion and sound. Every sentence may be considered as having so many clauses or members, which have each of them some meaning, but which is not complete till it is closed. Every sentence is capable of receiving some degree of harmony by a proper structure; this it receives when the most important ideas and the most sonorous expressions occupy the chief places; but what, you will say, are the chief places? We naturally, says an eminent French author on this subject, love to present our most interesting ideas first; but this order, which is dictated by self-love, is contrary to what we are directed to by the art of pleasing: the capital law of this art is to prefer others to ourselves, and therefore the most striking and interesting ideas come with the greatest beauty as well as force in the close. Where the difference does not lie in the ideas, the words or phrases that are most long and sonorous ought to be so distinguished. This rule however will admit some exception when we are to persuade or instruct, for we must never seem to have sweetness and cadence chiefly in view.

The rule of placing in a sentence the most important ideas and expressions last was taken notice of by ancient writers. "In verbis observandum est," says one of them, "ut a majoribus ad minus descendat oratio, melius enim dicetur, vir est optimus, quam vir optimus est." Sometimes several monosyllables terminate a sentence well enough because in pronunciation they run into one and seem to the hearers little different from a single word. It is an observation that the ear itself often directs to the rule upon this subject. Some French critics observe that some syllables in their language which are usually short are produced in the end of a sentence, for instance, "Je suis votre serviteur monsieur,

je suis le votre," where votre is short in the first sentence and long in
the second; and I believe the same thing would happen in translating
that sentence literally into English.

The harmony of sentences is preserved either by a measured proportion or regular gradation of the clauses: Cicero says upon this subject,
"Si membra," etc. In every sentence consisting of two members only,
everybody's ear will make them sensible that the last clause after the
pause of the voice ought to be longest, as in Shakespeare, "but yesterday," etc. In longer sentences there must be a greater variety, and
several causes must contribute to determine the length of the clauses;
but it is plain the last must be longer than the preceding; and sometimes
a regular gradation of more than two clauses has a very happy effect
such as these of Cicero, "Quorum quaestor fueram," etc. Again he says
in the same oration, "Habet honorem," etc. There is another order in
which there are two equal and one unequal member, and in that case
when the unequal member is shortest, it ought to be placed first. When
it is longest, it ought to be placed last, as in the two following examples:
"Testis est Africa," etc. and "Eripite nos ex miseris," etc. There is another structure of the members of a sentence in which this rule is
departed from and yet it pleases because of a certain exact proportion,
as that of Monsieur Fenelon, "Dans sa douleur," etc. The first and last
members are equal, and that which is in the middle is just double to
each of them.

Perhaps it will be asked, must an author then give attention to this
precise measure? Must he take a pair of scales or compasses to measure
every period he composes? By no means. Nothing would be more frigid
and unsuccessful, but it was proper thus to analyse the subject and show
in what manner the ear is pleased; at the same time there is so great a
variety and compass in the measures of prose, that it is easy to vary the
structure and cadence, and make everything appear quite simple and
natural. This leads me to the third remark upon style.

3. That variety is to be particularly studied. If a writer thinks any
particular structure necessary and forces everything he has to say just
into that form, it will be highly disagreeable, or if he is much enamored
with one particular kind of ornament and brings it in too frequently, it
will immediately disgust. There is a mixture in the principles of taste,
a desire of uniformity and variety, simplicity and intricacy; and it is by
the happy union of all these that delight is most effectually produced.
What else is necessary upon style will fall very properly under some of
the following heads.

The last part of the oratorial art is pronunciation, including gesture.
This is of the utmost, and indeed of universally confessed importance.

The effects of the different manner of delivering the same thing are very great. It is a famous subject, largely treated of by all critical writers. It seems to have been nicely studied by the ancients, and if we may judge from some circumstances, their action has been often very violent. We are told of Cicero that when he first went to the bar, the violence of his action, and what is called "contentio laterum," was such as endangered his consitution so that he took a journey for his health, and on his return took to a more cool and managed way of speaking. There is also somewhere in his writings an expression to this purpose, "nec fuit etiam, quod minimum est, supplosio pedis," as if stamping with the foot had been one of the least violent motions then in use. We cannot judge of this matter very well at such a distance. There is a difference in the turn of different nations upon this subject. The French and Italians have much more warmth and fire in their manner than the British. I remember once to have been told that no man could perceive the beauty of Raphael's picture of Paul preaching at Athens unless he had seen a Frenchman or Italian in the pulpit. Leaving you to read and digest all the criticisms and remarks upon this subject to be met with in different authors, I shall only give a few directions that I esteem most useful for avoiding improprieties and attaining some degree of excellence in this respect.

1. Study great sincerity; try to forget every purpose but the very end of speaking, information and persuasion. Labor after that sort of presence of mind which arises from self-denial, rather than from courage. Nothing produces more awkwardness than confusion and embarrassment. Bring a clown into a magnificent palace and let him have to appear in the presence of person of high rank, and the fear and solicitude he has about his own carriage and discourse make both the one and the other much more absurd and awkward than it would have otherwise been.

2. Learn distinct articulation, and attend to all the common rules or reading which are taught in the English grammars. Articulation is giving their full force and powers to the consonants as well as the vowels. The difference between a well-articulated discourse and one defective in this respect is that the first you will hear distinctly as far as you can hear the voice; the other you will hear sound enough, yet not understand almost anything that is said. Practice in company is a good way to learn this and several other excellencies in discourse.

3. Another rule is to keep to the tone and key of dialogue, or common conversation, as much as possible. In common discourse where there is no affectation, men speak properly. At least, though even here there are differences from nature—some speaking with more sweetness and

grace than others, yet there is none that falls into any of those unnatural rants or ridiculous gestures that are sometimes to be seen in public speakers.

4. It is of considerable consequence to be accustomed to decency of manners in the best company. This gives an ease of carriage and a sense of delicacy, which is of great use in forming the deportment of an orator.

5. In the last place, everyone should consider not only what is the manner, best in itself or even best suited to the subject, but what is also best suited to his own capacity. One of a quick animated spirit by nature may allow himself a much greater violence of action, than one of a colder disposition. If this last works himself up to violence or studies to express much passion, he will not probably be able to carry it through, but will relapse into his own natural manner, and by the sensible difference between one part of his discourse and another render himself ridiculous. Solemnity of manner should be substituted by all such persons in the room of fire.

Lecture XIII

WE come now to the fourth general division of this subject, which is that its object or end is different. The ends a writer or speaker may be said to aim at are information, demonstration, persuasion and entertainment. I need scarce tell you that these are not so wholly distinct, but that they are frequently intermixed, and that more than one of them may be in view at the same time. Persuasion is also used in a sense that includes them all. The intention of all speech or writing, which is but recorded speech, is to persuade, taking the word with latitude. Yet I think you will easily perceive that there are very different sorts of composition, in some of which one of the above mentioned purposes, and in others a different one, takes the lead and gives the color to the whole performance. Great benefit will arise from keeping a clear view of what is the end proposed. It will preserve the writer from a vicious and mistaken taste. The same thoughts, the same phraseology, the same spirit in general running through a writing is highly proper in one case, and absurd in another. There is beauty in every kind of writing when it is well done, and impropriety or bad taste will sometimes show themselves in pieces very inconsiderable. If it were but inditing a message card, penning an article in a newspaper, or drawing up an advertisement, persons accustomed to each of these will be able to keep to the common form or beaten track; but if anything different is to be said, good sense and propriety or their contraries will soon show themselves.

The writings which have information as their chief purpose are history, fable, epistolary writing, the common intercourse of business or friendship, and all the lower kinds. The properties which should reign in them are the following: (1) plainness, (2) fullness, (3) precision, and (4) order. (1) Plainness it is evident they ought to have, and indeed not barely perspicuity, so as to be intelligible, but an unaffected simplicity, so as not to seem to have anything higher in view than to be understood. (2) When we say that fullness is a property of writings which have information as their purpose, it is not meant to recommend a long or diffuse narration, but to intimate that nothing should be omitted in giving an account of anything which is of importance to its being truly and completely understood. Let a writer be as large as he pleases in what he says; if he omits circumstances as essential as those he mentions, and which the reader would naturally desire to know, he is not full. Many are very tedious, and yet not full. The excellence of a narrative is to contain as many ideas as possible, provided they are interesting, and to convey them in as few words as possible, consistently with perspicuity. (3) Precision as a quality of narration belongs chiefly to language. Words should be chosen that are truly expressive of the thing in view, and all ambiguous as well as superfluous phrases carefully avoided. The reader is impatient to get to the end of a story, and therefore he must not be stopped by anything but what you are sure he would be glad to know before he proceeds further. (4) The last particular is order, which is necessary in all writings, but especially in narration. There it lies chiefly in time and place, and a breach of order in these respects is more easily discerned and more universally offensive than in any other. Common hearers do not always know when you violate order in ranging the arguments on a moral subject, but if you bring in a story abruptly, or tell it confusedly, either in a letter or a discourse it will be instantly perceived, and those will laugh at you who could not tell it a whit better themselves.

Imagination is not to be much used in writings of the narrative kind. Its chief use in such writings is in description. A man of a warm fancy will paint strongly, and a man of a sentimental turn will interest the affections even by a mere recital of facts. But both the one and the other should be kept in great moderation, for a warm fancy is often joined to credulity, and the sentimental person is given to invention, so that he will turn a real history into half a romance. In history a certain cool and dispassionate dignity is the leading beauty. The writer should appear to have no interest in characters or events, but deliver them as he finds them. The character which an illustrious historian acquires from this self-denial and being, as it were, superior to all the personages how great soever of whom he treats has something awful and venerable in it. It is distinguished by this circumstance from the applause given to the poet or orator.

Demonstration is the end in view in all scientific writings, whether essays, systems, or controversy. The excellencies of this kind of writing may be reduced to the three following: perspicuity, order, and strength. The two first are necessary here as everywhere else, and the composition should be strong and nervous to produce a lasting conviction. More force of language is to be admitted, at least more generally in this kind than in the former; but a great deal less of imagination and fancy than even there. Whenever a scientific writer begins to paint and adorn, he is forgetting himself and disgusting his reader. This will be sensibly felt if you apply it to the mathematics. The mathematician is conversant only with sensible ideas, and therefore the more naked and unadorned everything that he says is, so much the better. How would it look if a mathematician should say, do you see this beautiful, small, taper, acute angle? It always approaches to this absurdity when in searching after abstract truth, writers introduce imagination and fancy. I am sensible that, having mentioned controversy as belonging to this class, many may be surprised that I have excluded imagination altogether, since commonly all controversial writers do to the utmost of their ability enlist imagination in the service of reason. There is nothing they are so fond of as exposing the weakness of their adversaries by strokes of raillery and humor. This I did on purpose that I may state this matter to you clearly. Controversy should mean, and very generally such writers pretend to mean, weighing the arguments on each side of a contested question in order to discover the truth. What strong professions of impartiality have we sometimes from the very champions of a party quarrel, while yet it is plain that searching after truth is what they never think of, but maintaining by every art the cause which they have already espoused.

I do not deny that there are sometimes good reasons for making use of satire and ridicule in controversies of the political kind, and sometimes it is necessary in self-defense. If any writer in behalf of a party attempts to expose his adversaries to public scorn, he ought not to be surprised if the measure he metes to others is measured out to him again. What is unlawful in the aggressor becomes justifiable, if not laudable, in the defender. Sometimes it is necessary to expose tyrants or persons in power, who do not reason but punish, and sometimes it is necessary to bring down self-sufficient persons, with whom there is no dealing till their pride is leveled a little with this dismaying weapon. Dr. Brown has set this matter in a very clear light in his *Essays on the Characteristics*, where he says that ridicule is not the test of truth, but it may be very useful to expose and disgrace known falsehood.

But when controversy is really an impartial search after truth, it is the farthest distant imaginable, either from passionate declamation on the one hand or sallies of wit and humor on the other. There is one instance of a controversy carried on between Dr. Butler and Dr. Clark upon the subject of space and personal identity in which there did not seem to be any design upon either side but to discover the truth. It ended in the entire conviction and satisfaction of one of them, which he readily and openly acknowledged; and I think in such an instance there is much greater glory to be had in yielding than in conquering. There is great honor in candidly acknowledging a mistake, but not much in obtaining a victory in support of truth. It is worthwhile just to mention that this was far from being the case in another controversy before two who were also very great men, Mr. Locke and Dr. Stilling-fleet, upon innate ideas. They not only supported each his sentiments with warmth and keenness, but descended to all the malice of personal reproach, and all the littleness of verbal criticism.

The next great end that may be in view is persuasion. This, being the great and general subject of oratory, has had most said upon it in every age. That you may understand what I mean by distinguishing it from information, demonstration, and entertainment, observe that persuasion is when we would bring the reader or hearer to a determinate choice, either immediately upon the spot for a particular decision, as in an assembly or court of justice, or in a more slow and lasting way, as in religious and moral writings. But particularly persuasion is understood to be in view as the effect of a single discourse. When this is the purpose, there are opportunities for all the ways of speaking within the compass of the oratorial art. There are times when an orator must narrate simply; there are times when he must reason strongly; and there are times when he may wound satirically. It must be remembered, however, that too great an infusion of wit takes away both from the dignity and force of an oration. We shall see under the next head that it cannot be admitted in religious instruction, but when you are speaking against an adversary that is proud and conceited, or when you want to make your hearers despise any person or thing as well as hate them, wit and satire may be of use. A minister of state is very often attacked in this way with propriety and success. It is sometimes allowed to relieve the spirits of the audience when they begin to flag. In this view Cicero recommends the *urbanitas,* and practices it himself; but at the same time he intimates that it should be done sparingly, and with caution: "Quo tamquam sale conspergatur oratio." Wit, therefore, is to be absolutely excluded from scientific writings and very rarely to be used in serious persuasion.

The last end of speaking and writing I shall mention is entertainment. This includes all such writings as have the amusement or entertainment of the hearers or readers as the only, the chief, or at least one great end of the composition. This is the case with all poetical compositions. They may pretend to write for the instruction of others, but to please them and obtain their favor is probably more their purpose. At any rate they must content themselves with taking in both, and say with Horace, "Et prodesse volunt et delectare poetae." Sweetness, tenderness, and elegance of style ought to characterize these sorts of composition. Here is the greatest room for imagination and fancy. Here is the dominion of wit and humor. It is an observation of some that the word *humor* is peculiar to the English language; that the *eutrapelia* in Greek, *sales* and *urbanitas* in Latin have all the same meaning with our general term *wit,* but that *humor* denotes a particular kind of wit consisting chiefly of irony. But if the word is peculiar to the English language, it is certain that the thing itself is far from being peculiar to the English nation. Perhaps Homer's Batrychomachia may be said to be the most ancient example of it upon record. Lucian's *Dialogues* have it in high perfection, though it must be owned that it seems particularly to have flourished in modern times. Fontenelle's *Dialogues of the Dead,* and Boileau's *Satires* are famous examples of it, but none ever exceeded Cervantes, the celebrated author of *Don Quixote.* That piece is highly entertaining to an English reader under two great disadvantages. One is its being translated into another language. Now, wit is more difficult to translate than any other subject of composition. It is easier to translate undiminished the force of eloquence, than the poignancy of wit. The other disadvantage is its being written in ridicule of a character that now no more exists, so that we have not the opportunity of comparing the copy with the original.

We must also observe that wit in general, and this species of it in particular, has often appeared in the highest perfection in Britain, both in prose and poetry; Shakespeare's dramatic pieces abound with it, and Dr. Donnes's *Satires.* It is in high perfection in Marvel's *Rehearsal Transprosed,* Alsop's *Melius Inquirendum,* but above all in Swift's writings, prose and verse.

It is observed sometimes that the talent of humor is often possessed in a very high degree by persons of the meanest rank, who are themselves ignorant of it; in them it appears chiefly in conversation, and in a manner that cannot be easily put upon paper. But as to those who think fit to try this manner from the press, they should be well assured before hand that they really possess the talent. In many other particulars, a real taste for it, and a high admiration of anything, is a considerable sign of some degree of the talent itself; but it is far from being so in wit and humour. Mr. Pope tells us that "Gentle dullness ever loves a joke," and we see every day people aiming at wit who produce the most miserable and shocking performances. Sometimes they do not excite laughter, but loathing or indignation; sometimes they do excite laughter, but it is that of contempt. There is a distinction which everyone should endeavour to understand and remember between a wit and a droll: the first makes you laugh at what he says, and the object of his satire, and the second makes you laugh at his own expense, from his absurdity and meanness.

Lecture XIV

WE come now to the fifth general division of eloquence, as its subject is different, under which we may consider the three great divisions of the pulpit, the bar, and promiscuous assemblies. All the general principles of composition are common to these three kinds, nor can any man make a truly distinguished figure in any one of them without being well acquainted with literature and taste. Some pecularities in different ways of writing have been already touched at, all which I suppose you gave attention to; but there are still some differences, as the scene in which a man is to move in life is different, which are highly worthy of observation. I will therefore consider each of these separately, and try to point out the qualities for which it ought to be distinguished or delineate the character of an accomplished minister, lawyer, and senator.

I begin with the pulpit. Preaching the gospel of Christ is a truly noble employment, and the care of souls a very important trust. The qualities of most importance I think are as follow.

1. Piety—to have a firm belief of that gospel he is called to preach, and a lively sense of religion upon his own heart. Duty, interest and utility all conspire in requiring this qualification; it is of the utmost moment in itself and what men will the least dispense with in one of that profession. All men good and bad agree in despising a loose or profane minister. It discovers a terrible degree of depravity of heart, and those that begin so seldom alter for the better. The very familiar acquaintance which they acquire with serious thoughts and spiritual subjects serves to harden them against the arrows of conviction, and it is little wonder that for such daring wickedness, God should leave them to themselves, or sentence them to perpetual barrenness; but while I think it my duty thus to warn you, I must beg leave to guard it against abuse, lest while we are aggravating the sin of profane ministers, others should think themselves at liberty who have no view to that sacred office. We have even seen persons decline the sacred office because they did not think they had true religion, and then with seeming ease and quiet-

ness set themselves to some other business as if in that there was no
need of religion at all. Alas! After all that can be said of the guilt and
danger of an irreligious minister, there is an infinite danger to everyone
who shall go out of this life an irreligious man. Will it not be poor
consolation think you in the hour of sickness or death, that though you
must perish everlastingly, you go to hell not as a minister but a lawyer
or a physician. I do truly think this has been a pillow of security to many
poor thoughtless souls, and that they have actually rid themselves of
conviction by this mistaken comfort, as if there was much merit in it,
that they would not be ministers because they wanted religion. Remember this then, in a single word, that there is neither profession nor
station, from the king on the throne to the beggar on the dunghill, to
whom a concern for eternity is not the *one thing needful*.

But let me just take notice of the great advantage of true religion to
one destined for the work of the ministry. (1) It gives a man the knowledge that is of most service to a minister. Experimental knowledge is
superior to all other, and necessary to the perfection of every other
kind. It is indeed the very possession or daily exercise of that which it
is the business of his life, and the duty of this office, to explain and
recommend. Experimental knowledge is the best sort in every branch,
but it is necessary in divinity because religion is what cannot be truly
understood unless it is felt.

(2) True piety will direct a man in the choice of his studies. The object
of human knowledge is so extensive that nobody can go through the
whole, but religion will direct the student to what may be most profitable
to him, and will also serve to turn into its proper channel all the knowledge he may otherwise acquire.

(3) It will be a powerful motive to diligence in his studies. Nothing
so forcible as that in which eternity has a part. The duty to a good man
is so pressing, and the object so important, that he will spare no pains
to obtain success.

(4) True religion will give unspeakable force to what a minister says.
There is a piercing and a penetrating heat in that which flows from the
heart, which distinguishes it both from the coldness of indifference and
the false fire of enthusiasm and vainglory. We see that a man truly pious
has often esteem, influence, and success, though his parts may be much
inferior to others who are more capable, but less conscientious. If then
piety makes even the weakest venerable, what must it do when added
to the finest natural talents and the best acquired endowments?

(5) It adds to a minister's instruction the weight of his example. It is
a trite remark that example teaches better than precept. It is often a
more effectual reprimand to vice, and a more inciting argument to the
practice of virtue, than the best of reasoning. Example is more intelligi-

ble than precept: precepts are often involved in obscurity, or warped by controversy; but a holy life immediately reaches and takes possession of the heart.

If I have lengthened out this particular beyond the proportion of the rest, I hope you will forgive it for its importance, and observe as the conclusion of the whole that one devoted to the service of the gospel should be *really, visibly,* and *eminently* holy.

2. Another character which should distinguish pulpit eloquence is simplicity. Simplicity is beautiful everywhere. It is of importance that young persons should be formed to a taste for it and more disposed to exceed here than in the opposite extreme, but if I am not mistaken, it is more beautiful, and the transgressions of it more offensive, in the pulpit than anywhere else. If I heard a lawyer pleading in such a style and manner as was more adapted to display his own talents than to carry his client's cause, it would considerably lessen him in my esteem, but if I heard a minister acting the same part, I should not be satisfied with contempt, but hold him in detestation.

There are several obvious reasons why simplicity is more especially necessary to a minister than any other. (1) Many of his audience are poor ignorant creatures. If he means to do them any service, he must keep to what they understand, and that requires more simplicity than persons without experience can easily imagine. It is remarkable that at the first publication it was a character of the gospel that it was preached to the poor. In this our blessed master was distinguished both from the heathen philosophers and Jewish teachers, who confined their instructions in a great manner to their schools, and imparted what they esteemed their most important discourses to only a few chosen disciples. (2) Simplicity is necessary to preserve the speaker's character for sincerity. You heard before how necessary piety is, which is the proper parent of sincerity in the pulpit. Now it is not easy to preserve the opinion of piety and sincerity in the pulpit when there is much ornament. Besides the danger of much affected pomp or foppery of style, a discourse very highly polished, even in the truest taste, is apt to suggest to the audience that a man is preaching himself and not the cross of Christ. So nice a matter is this in all public speaking that some critics say that Demosthenes put on purpose some errors in grammar in his discourses, that the hearers might be induced to take them for the immediate effusions of the heart, without art and with little premeditation. I doubt much the solidity of this remark, or the certainty of the fact, but however it be, there is no occasion for it in the case of a minister because preparation and premeditation are expected from him, and in that case he may make his discourses abundantly plain and simple without any affected blunders. (3) Simplicity is also necessary, as suited to the gospel itself, the subject of a minister's discourses. Nothing more humbling to the pride of man than the doctrine of the cross; nothing more unbecoming that doctrine than too much finery of language. The apostle Paul chose to preach "not with the words which man's wisdom teacheth" and again "not with excellency of speech or wisdom," which though I admit that it does not condemn study and sound knowledge, yet it certainly shows that the style of the pulpit should be the most simple and self-denied of any other.

3. Another qualification for a minister is accuracy, from the utmost diligence in his important work. I place this immediately after the other to guard it against abuse by excess. To avoid vain affected ornaments is a very different thing from negligence in preparation. The very same apostle who speaks with so much contempt of human wisdom yet greatly insists in writing to Timothy and Titus on their giving themselves to study, to exhortation, to doctrine: "Meditate upon those things," says he, etc.

Study and accuracy indeed is necessary that a minister may procure and keep up the attention of his hearers, that he may inform the judgment as well as convince the conscience. The ancient fathers have generally insisted upon this as of much moment. And in our own times I observe that it is necessary to avoid offending persons of finer taste, who are too much attached to the outside of things and are immediately disgusted with every error against propriety, and are apt to reproach religion itself for the weakness or absurdity of those who speak in its behalf. Let no man seek to avoid that reproach which may be his lot for preaching the truths of the everlasting gospel, but let him always avoid the just reproach of handling them in a mean, slovenly, and indecent manner.

4. Another quality of a minister's eloquence should be force and vehemence. I have in some former parts of the general subject shown you how and when this is to be most exerted. The design of the present remark is to let you know that there is no speaker who has a greater right to exert himself to the utmost, or who may properly interest his hearers more, than a minister of the gospel. No speaker has subjects or arguments more proper for producing this effect. To consider the subjects which a speaker from the pulpit has to handle, one would think that it must be the easiest thing imaginable to speak from them in a powerful and interesting manner. The eternal God, the greatness of his works, the universality of his Providence, his awful justice, his irresistible power, his infinite mercy and the wisdom of God in the mystery of redeeming grace, the condition of saints and sinners while on earth, and the final decision of their eternal state in the day of judgment. The truth is the subjects are so very great in themselves that it is not possible

to equal them by the manner of handling them. Probably for this very reason many fall short. Discouraged by the immensity of the theme, they fall below what they might have done on subjects less awful. This however shows with what a holy ambition those who are employed in the service of Christ in the gospel should endeavor to exert themselves in the glorious cause. Provided they are themselves in earnest, and take truth and nature as their guide, they can scarcely exceed in zeal and ardor for the glory of God and the good of precious souls.

5. Another excellent quality of pulpit eloquence is to be under the restraint of judgment and propriety. I place this after the former, as its counterpart and necessary to give it proper effect. And it may be observed that as religious and moral subjects give the surest and the fullest scope to zeal and fervor, so they need as much as any the strict government of prudence and experience. I do not mean only by this to guard ministers from the irregular fervors of enthusiasm, but to give if possible a degree of solidity and real truth to their instructions. They ought to avoid all turgid declamation, to keep to experience, and take things as they really are. Let some people, for example, speak of riches, and what shall you hear from them? Gold and silver, what are they but shining dross, sparkling metals, a thing of no real value? That in the eye of reason and philosophy they are of no extensive use and altogether contemptible. And indeed to take things in a certain philosophical abstraction, they are good for nothing. Mere gold or silver you can neither eat nor wear: their value, you will say, depends all upon opinion, the changeable fancy of men; but this manner of speaking, and all that is related to it, seeming to be philosophy and reason, is really absurdity and nonsense. For though it be true that gold, abstracted from the opinion of mankind, is not a whit more valuable than stones, and that if I was in the midst of a forest surrounded with wild beasts, a whole bag full of gold would do me no service; yet it is as certain that in our present situation it is of that real value as to procure all the conveniences of life. The way then to treat such subjects is not to use these rhetorical phrases in contempt of riches, but to show from experience that they are good or evil according to the temper of him that uses them, and that we see discontent and ungoverned passion find as easy access to the antechamber of the prince as the cottage of the poor. The same thing I would say of fame, that it is easy to say fame is no more but idle breath, etc., but the great matter is to view those things in a sober and rational light, to give to every outward mercy its proper value, and only show how much they are counterbalanced by things of infinitely greater moment.

But what I have often observed with most regret upon this subject is young persons carrying the things that are really true and excellent to a certain excess or high pitch that is beyond nature and does not tend in the least to promote conviction, but rather hinders it. When men speak of virtue or true goodness, they are apt to raise the description beyond the life in any real instance, and when they speak of vice and its consequences, they are apt to draw the character so as it will apply only to a few of the most desperate profligates and the miserable state to which they reduce themselves. This rather seems to fortify the generality of persons, to whom these descriptions do not apply, in their careless and secure state.

Once more I have often observed young persons frequently choose as their subject afflictions of which probably they have had very little experience, and speak in such a high style as if every good man were, as the heroes of old, above the reach of every accident. And it is true that an eminent saint is sometimes made superior to all his sufferings, but generally speaking, we ought to be very tender of sufferers, till we ourselves have been in the furnace of affliction; and after that we shall not need be told so. On the whole, a strict adherence to truth and nature, and taking the world just as it is, will be an excellent mean to direct us in every part of our public service.

6. Lastly, a minister ought to have extensive knowledge. Everything whatever that is the object of human knowledge may be made subservient to theology. And considering that a minister is in public life and has to do with friends and enemies of all ranks, he ought to be well furnished with literature of every kind. At the same time I would have this well understood, it is not necessary, and I think it is not desirable, that a minister should be quite an adept in particular branches of knowledge, except those that are closely related to his proper work. The reason of this is it takes more time to be a perfect master of some of the particular sciences than he has to spare from his duty, and therefore with a taste of the several sciences, general knowledge is most suited to his circumstances, and most necessary to his usefulness.

Lecture XV

I PROCEED now to the eloquence of the bar. The profession of the law is of great importance in the British dominions. There is, therefore, great room for this sort of eloquence. This, indeed, may be said to be the country of law, not only on account of its being a free state, the character of which is that not man but the laws have dominion, which is our glory, but because by the great multiplicity of our statutes it becomes an important and difficult science. For both these reasons there are great hopes proposed to persons of ability in this department.

They have not only the reasonable prospect, if of tolerable abilities with diligence, to provide an honorable subsistence to themselves, but it is the direct road to promotion and the way of obtaining the highest offices in the state.

Here as in the former particular, we much consider everything as already said that belongs to the subject in general; and indeed by far the greatest number of valuable books on the subject of eloquence having been drawn up by pleaders at the bar, they must be at least as much or perhaps more directly applicable to this species as any other. I cannot help, however, taking notice of a preposterous practice in this country of some who take their children from literature before they have finished their course because they intend to put them to the law. This must be voluntarily confining them to the very lowest sort of practice in that profession, for if any whatever stand in need of literature, it must be the lawyers. Supposing therefore all that has been said of composition and speaking in general, there are a few particular characters of most importance in men of that class.

1. Probity or real untainted integrity. There can be no doubt that integrity is the first and most important character of a man, be his profession what it will; but I have mentioned it here because there are many not so sensible of the importance of it in the profession of the law, and think it is necessary to make a good man, but not a good lawyer. On the contrary, I am persuaded not only that a man loses nothing in any capacity by his intregity, but that a lawyer should in general study by probity and real worth to obtain respect from the public, and to give weight to everything he says. This integrity should show itself in undertaking causes. There are many who think there is no ground of scruple in this respect, and sometimes they are found to boast with what address they conducted, and with what success they carried through a very weak cause. I apprehend this is truly dishonorable, and as there are plenty of causes in which the equity is doubtful, everyone should make it a point of honor not to undertake a cause which they knew not to be just. It would give unspeakable influence to his management and pleadings. The same probity should appear in the manner of conducting causes. No sinister arts, no equivocation or concealment of the truth. Perhaps some may think that those who should be conscience bound in this manner would give roguish persons an evident advantage over them, but it is a great mistake. Let them use but prudence and firmness joined with integrity, and they are an over match for all the villains upon earth. The common proverb is certainly just, "Honesty is the best policy." The arts of chicanery can only succeed once or twice. As soon as a man gets the reputation of cunning, its effect is over, for nobody will trust him, and everybody counter-works him.

2. Another excellent quality for a lawyer is assiduity and method in business. This is of great advantage to the very best genius. I the rather insist upon it that there prevails often a supposition that it is not the quality of a great man. Because there are some persons of very middling abilities who give great application and are lovers of order, therefore some are pleased to call those dull plodding fellows, and think it is a mark of fire and vivacity to be irregular both in their business and in their lives. There are also some few men of real and great capacity who are negligent and even loose in their practice, who rise by the mere force of singular parts. These are an unhappy example to those superficial creatures who think by imitating them in their folly that they will become as great geniuses as they. But suffer me to observe to you that the greatest geniuses here have been remarkable for the most vigorous application, and the greatest men have been and are remarkable for order and method in everything they do. There is a certain dignity which arises from a man's word being sacred, even in keeping an appointment, or the most trifling circumstance; and for people of business, order and punctuality give so much ease to themselves, and pleasure to all who have to do with them, that it is a wonder there should be anybody that does not study it. Is there any genius, think you, in throwing down a thing so unthinkingly that you do not know how to take it up again? The great archbishop of Cambray looks upon it as one of the most important things to teach young persons to put everything in its proper place. As everything that belongs to furniture, dress, books, and implements must be in some place, they are always best disposed when each is in its own place. They will give least disturbance there when they are not used, and they will be most readily found when they ought to be used.

But when we come to loose and vicious practices, it is truly entertaining to meet with riotous disorderly fellows, who are pleased to speak with contempt of those who love form and good order, as if they themselves were men of great acuteness. Now I almost never knew an example of your mischief-workers, but they were thick skulls. I have known some who could neither write a jest nor speak a jest in all their life, but had tricks enough they could play to disturb a sober neighborhood. I have thus been led back to the irregularities of youth from speaking of method in business as of importance to lawyers. I shall conclude the observation with saying that there is no great prospect of a man's ever being lord chancellor who spends his time in scouring the streets and beating the watch when he is at the inns of court.

3. Another quality useful to a lawyer is address, and delicacy in his manners and deportment in general and the conduct of his business in particular, and above all in pleading and public speaking. The address

and delicacy I mean are such as are acquired by the knowledge of human nature and some acquaintance with human life. They are useful I admit for every public speaker, but if I am not mistaken, much more needful to the lawyer than the clergyman. The clergyman proceeds upon things of acknowledged moment, a certain dignity of character is allowed him and expected from him. A pretended delicacy is sometimes offensive in him. A certain firmness, not to call it boldness, and impartiality in administering instruction and reproof are ornaments in him. But a lawyer must always consider the propriety of time and place—what belongs to him who speaks, or to him or them who are spoken to, or who are spoken of. There are some fine examples of address and delicacy in Cicero, particularly in his orations *pro Roscio, pro Milone, et de lege agraria.*

4. A fourth quality necessary for a lawyer is extensive knowledge in the arts and sciences, in history and in the laws. A person who means to rise, or attain to some of the highest degrees of this profession, must strive to accomplish himself by knowledge in the arts and sciences. His business is of a public kind; the causes he may have occasion to treat are exceedingly various. What adversaries he may meet with he is altogether uncertain. I do not mean that a lawyer need to be an adept in particular branches of science, but the principles of knowledge in general are very necessary, otherwise he will frequently expose himself. Gross ignorance in the sciences will lay him open to blunders in language, which he could not otherwise avoid. History also is a branch of literature that a lawyer should make his favorite study; as his business lies in canvasing the various relations of men in social life, he will be best able to reason on the meaning and propriety of laws and their application if he be well acquainted with history, which points out the state of society and human affairs in every age. As to knowledge of the laws, this is what lawyers cannot do without, and what therefore they do necessarily study, but it would be much to their advantage if they would add to the knowledge of the municipal laws of their own country, a knowledge of the great principles of equity and of natural and political law as applied in general.

5. The last quality I shall mention as of use to a lawyer is quickness and vivacity. It is of use to him to have an acuteness and penetration to observe the turns of a cause. To detect the plots and fallacy of adversaries, as well as to answer upon the spot whatever may be thrown up. I am sensible that this quickness is entirely a natural quality and cannot be learned, but I thought it best to observe it because it is of more use to a lawyer than to most other men. A minister is only called to speak what he has deliberately prepared and fully digested, but a lawyer quite incapable of extemporary productions would not do so well. It is also certain that wit, which is intolerable in the pulpit, is often not barely

pardonable in a lawyer, but very useful. There is however such a difference in the capacity of men that one may be eminent in one branch and defective in another. A man of coolness, penetration, and application is often eminent in chamber councils; and one of vivacity, passion and elocution eminent in pleading causes, especially in criminal courts.

The third and last division of this class is the eloquence of promiscuous deliberative assemblies. I shall not be very long upon this subject, but as it is far from being improbable that some here present may in future life have occasion to act in that sphere and to be members of the provincial assemblies, I shall make a few remarks upon it to that purpose. In large deliberative assemblies of the political kind, there is nearly as much opportunity for fervor and passion as there is to the divine, and more scope for wit and humor than to the lawyer. For though no matters of a merely temporal kind are of equal moment in themselves with the things a minister has to treat of, yet men's passions are almost as much, and in many cases more excited and interested by them. The fate of nations, the welfare of our country, liberty, or servitude may often seem to want as violent an exertion of the passionate kind of eloquence as any subject whatever.

It is worthwhile to observe that several writers in speaking of the ancient and modern eloquence have taken it for granted that the circumstances of things are changed, that the violent passionate eloquence that prevailed in Greece and Rome would not do in modern times. They will tell you that in a modern senate or other deliberative assembly people come all prepared by private interest, and will vote just as they are engaged without regard to either eloquence or truth; but some very able writers have delivered a contrary opinion, particularly David Hume, who though an infidel in opinion, is of great reach and accuracy of judgment in matters of criticism. He has said that human nature is always the same and that the eloquence which kindles and governs the passions will always have great influence in large assemblies, let them be of what station or rank so ever. I apprehend that experience, since his writing the above, has fully justified it by two signal examples: one in the state, and the other in the church. Mr. Pitt, now Earl of Chatham, from being a colonel of dragoons rose to the highest station in the British Empire merely by the power of a warm and passionate eloquence. There was never anything in his discourses that is remarkable either for strength of reasoning or purity and elegance of style, but a very great impetuosity and fire that carried his point in the British House of Commons. The other instance is the late Mr. Whitefield, who acquired and preserved a degree of popularity to which the present age never saw anything that could be compared. The happy ends that were promoted by this in providence I omit as a subject of a different nature, but the immediate and second causes that produced it were a power of elocution and natural talents for public speaking superior by far to any that ever I saw possessed by any man on earth.

To succeed in speaking in public deliberative assemblies, the following are the most important qualities: (1) Dignity of character and disinterestedness. In public deliberations, it is not easy to procure attention unless there is some degree of character preserved; and indeed, wherever there is a high opinion of the candor and sincerity of the speaker, it will give an inconceivable weight to his sentiments in debate.

(2) There is a necessity of knowledge of the most liberal kind, that is the knowledge of men and manners, of history, and of human nature. The most successful speakers in senates are generally those who know mankind best, and if a man would uniformly preserve his character and influence in this light, he must addict himself to the study of history and the exercise of reflection.

(3) To this sort of eloquence is particularly necessary a power over the passions. This is one of the most important characters of eloquence in general; yet it is more peculiarly necessary, and more eminently powerful, in promiscuous deliberative assemblies than in any other. In religious discourses, the effect is expected to be cool, deep and permanent. Even preachers in single discourses rather choose to speak as writers than as pleaders, and lawyers, except in some few instances, may expect to have their assertions taken to pieces, canvased and tried one after another; but in meetings of the political kind, the decision is to be by a vote before the dissolution of the assembly and cannot be altered afterwards though the majority should change their sentiments. In these assemblies therefore, to be sure, a power over the passions must be of the utmost moment.

I shall conclude this particular by two subordinate remarks on the same subject. (1) That to succeed in speaking in senates or large assemblies, there is much need of great discernment, both to proportionate men's attempts to their capacity, and to choose the proper time for exerting it. When information is demanded, any person who can give it will be heard with patience upon it; but on subjects of high political importance, where there are many eminent champions on each side, even persons of moderate abilities would run a risk of being affronted. (2) The other direction is that all who intend to be speakers in political assemblies must begin early; if they delay beginning till years shall add maturity to their judgment and weight to their authority, the consequence will be that years will add so much to their caution and dissidence that they wil never begin at all.

We come now to consider the structure of a particular discourse— the order, proportion, and mutual relation of the several parts. Orators, or critics on oratory, very early learned to analyze a discourse and to enumerate the parts of which it is composed. They are a little differently stated by different authors: some reckon four, introduction, proposition, confirmation and conclusion; others, five adding narration; others, six, adding refutation; and there are some discourse in which you may easily have each of these different things; but considering that we must take this matter so generally as to include all kinds of composition, it would be I think as well to adopt the division in poetical criticism and say that every regular discourse or composition of every kind must have a beginning, a middle, and an end. Every performance, however short, must be capable of some such division, otherwise it is called abrupt and irregular. The reason why I would make the division in this manner is that the beginning is properly the introduction; the middle includes everything however various that is taken into the body of a discourse. Now these may be very many—proposition, narration, explication, confirmation, illustration, and refutation; but these are not all requisite in every discourse and are to be introduced in propositions variable and accidental according to the nature of every particular subject.

Let us speak first of the introduction. This is the more necessary that it is of very considerable importance, especially to an orator; it is also difficult, at least speakers have generally said so. We find it said in some of the books of oratory that the introduction, though first pronounced ought to be last composed, that it comes to be considered after the discourse is finished; but this does not appear to me to be either natural or necessary, except in a qualified sense. The introduction is commonly settled after the subject is pitched upon, the distribution planned and digested, and such reflection upon the whole as precedes writing.

The ends in an introduction are said by Cicero to be these, "Reddere auditorem attentum, benevolum et docilem:" to make the reader attentive to the discourse, favorable to the speaker, and willing to receive instruction upon the subject. These different views may not only be altered in their order at the judgment of the orator, but any of them may be left out when it is unnecessary. If, for example, I have no reason to suspect disaffection in any of my hearers, long apologies, especially if any way personal, are rather disgusting.

The ways of procuring either attention, a favor, or making the hearers teachable are so various that they can neither be enumerated nor classed. In this, the orator must exercise his invention, judgment, and good taste. The most usual manner of introduction is a commonplace upon the importance of the subject; the introduction drawn from the circumstances of time, place and person are generally the most striking. Sometimes an unusual stroke is happy in an introduction, as also a weighty reflection or bold sentiment on the subject itself. A funeral sermon was happily begun by Mr. Baxter in this manner: "Death is the occasion of our present meeting, and death shall be the subject of the following discourse; I am to speak of that which shall shortly silence me, and you are to hear of that which shall speedily stop your ears." Dr. Evans begins a sermon on Eccles. 12:10, "Rejoice O young man," etc., by telling a story of a soldier whose life was saved by a Bible in his pocket, and his conversion produced by the accident. The Bible saved him from being shot through with a bullet, and when he examined, it had just pierced the leaves through till it stopped at that passage, which no doubt he read with particular emotions. A discourse of a lawyer in a lawsuit is generally best begun by a narrative of the occasion of the quarrel, and the introducing of any commonplace topics would be reckoned affectation. A clergyman may often have an introduction to his subject with advantage and may also begin by a concise view of the context, or the occasion of the words he has chosen to discourse upon.

Perhaps what will be of most use here will be to point out several ways by which an introduction may be faulty; of these I shall mention the following.

1. An introduction may be faulty by being too pompous and extravagant. This is one of the most common faults in the prefaces or introductions to books. When an author is to write upon any subject, he thinks it necessary to show not only that his subject is worth the handling but that it is better than all other subjects. Weak and pedantic writers are often guilty of this to a degree that is ridiculous. A treatise on arithmetic sometimes is introduced by a pompous proof that the knowledge of numbers is either superior to, or the basis of all other knowledge; the same thing is done with grammar; and there is often a general truth or plausibilty from which the ridicule to which they expose themselves takes its rise; for to be sure, number is everywhere; everything that ever was or can be must be either one or more. As to grammar, all good sense must certainly be grammar; yet there are sometimes persons who would be thought to understand both these subjects very well who could not speak five sentences, or write a letter without being deservedly laughed at.

2. An introduction may be faulty by being general. We see often reflections in the introduction to a discourse that would be just as proper for one subject as for another. Such sentiments may be said to go before, but they cannot be said to introduce their subject. Sometimes you will hear the introduction almost out before you can conjecture what is to be the subject, and some are so unhappy in the choice of introductory sentiments that you would think they intend something that is very different from what really appears in the piece itself.

3. It is a fault in an introduction to be filled with remarks quite beaten

and hackneyed, if I may speak so. These may have been very good remarks or sentiments when first conceived and uttered, but by perpetual repetition have lost their force, and from the very commonness appear mean and despicable. They are many of them founded upon sayings in the classic authors, and in the past age were commonly produced as quotations with their paraphrase, such as "omne tulit punctum qui miscuit utile dulci." "Ingratum si dixeris, omnia dixeris."

4. An introduction may be forced and unnatural; that is to say, such remarks may be made as it requires a great deal of pains to show any relation between them and the subject to be treated.

5. It may be fanciful or whimsical. There was an age when these sort of introductions were to the taste of the public. This fancy or whim, or as I may call it a finical way of entering upon a subject publicly, may be best illustrated by an example. An author of the last age begins a discourse upon chapter 8 of the Epistle to the Romans, verse 28, to this purpose: The Scriptures may be considered as a large and rich garden. The New Testament is the most valuable division of that garden. The Epistle to the Romans is the richest compartment of that division. The eighth chapter is the most delightful border of the compartment, and the twenty-eighth verse the finest flower of that border.

6. An introduction may be faulty by being tedious. An introduction is designed to whet the attention and excite impatience for what is to follow. But when it is very long, it not only disgusts by the disappointment but wastes that attention which should be preserved in full vigor, or raises a high expectation, which is probably for that reason disappointed.

As to the middle or body of a discourse, the chief thing to be attended to in this place is to make you sensible of what it consists. The former discourses have all been intended to teach you the way of composition, both as to materials and structure; yet as to the method of conducting a particular discourse, I would make the three following remarks: (1) Be careful of the order of the several particulars mentioned. You may not see it proper to introduce all in the compass of a single discourse, but so far as they are introduced, they should be in the following order: proposition, narration, illustration, confirmation, refutation. You will speedily perceive this to be the order of nature, to lay down the method, narrate the facts, illustrate them by whatever may have that effect, adduce the proofs, resolve objections. A person of a clear head will range his sentiments in this order, yet there are some exceptions to be admitted. Sometimes it is useful in a cause to reserve a part of the story itself to apply or illustrate an argument, and in some few instances it is best to answer objections, or remove prejudices, before you adduce your proofs.

(2) It is a most useful direction to the greatest part of writers and speakers to guard against introducing everything that they might say, or being so formal that they will say something in the way of form in every one of their divisions. This analysis of a discourse is good for making the judgment clear; but if it be applied merely to make the invention copious, it will probably produce an unnecessary load. Some people will need answer objections on any subject, and frequently teach their hearers to make objections which they never would have thought of.

(3) Learn to keep close to a subject, and bring in nothing but what is truly of force to the point to be proved. I rather mention this as a rule for the middle or body of a discourse because the most are there apt to transgress it. In the introduction and the conclusion, everyone but those who are perfectly stupid keep their subject directly in their eye; whereas in the body, when they are entered upon argument and amplification, they are apt to be led astray, and either to fall into what may be called absolute digressions, or at least to lengthen some parts more than true proportion requires.

As to the conclusion or peroration, to this may be applied particularly all that was said upon pathos, or raising the passions, to which I add the following short observations.

(1) The conclusion should be by far the warmest and most animated part of the discourse. It is not, I think, desirable to attempt to raise the passions of an audience high till towards the close of a discourse because, if it be begun sooner, there is evident hazard of not being able to preserve them in the same pitch till the end.

(2) The conclusion should collect into one point of view, by some well-chosen expressions, the force of what has gone before, and the greatest skill in the speaker is shown by concentrating the whole in this manner. Before the illustration it could not be said so briefly; but by the help of what went before, it may be recalled to memory in less room.

(3) Towards the conclusion the sentences should be studied, the tone of voice higher, and the pronunciation more rapid than towards the beginning.

(4) Lastly, great care should be taken in moral discourses to have no farfetched inferences.

Lecture XVI

I AM now to conclude the discourses upon this subject by an inquiry into the general principles of taste and criticism. In the former discourses we have kept close to the arts of writing and speaking and have attempted to describe the various kinds of composition, their characters, distinctions, beauties, blemishes, the means of attaining skill in them, and the uses to which they should be applied. But is it not proper to consider the alliance, if there be any such, between this and other arts? This will serve greatly to improve and perfect our judgment and taste. It was very early observed that there was a relation between the different arts, and some common principles that determine their excellence. Cicero mentions this in the introduction of his oration for Archias the poet. "Etenim omnes artes quae ad humanitatem pertinent, habent quoddam commune vinculum, et quasi cognatione quadam inter se continentur."

These arts, which Cicero says, "Ad huminitatem pertinent," are called by the moderns the fine arts. This is to distinguish them from those commonly called the mechanic arts, making the utensils and conveniences of common life. And yet even these may be included, as taste and elegance or the want of it may plainly be discerned in every production of human skill. However, those called the fine arts are the following: poetry, oratory, music, painting, sculpture, architecture. It must be allowed that, though these arts have some common principles of excellence, there are some persons who have a strong inclination after, and even a capacity of performing in some of them, and not in others. There are good orators who are not musicians, or perhaps who have very little taste for the beauties of architecture. Yet commonly complete critics, and those who have a well-formed taste, are able to perceive the beauty of the whole and the relation of one to another. It is remarkable that the expressions in composition are frequently borrowed from one art and applied to another. We say a smooth, polished style, as well as a polished surface; and we say a building is sweet or elegant, as well as an oration. We say the notes in music are bold and swelling, or warm and animated.

One of our modern authors on eloquence has thought fit to take exception at the use of the word *taste,* as being of late invention, and as implying nothing but what is carried in judgment and genius. But I apprehend that the application of it, though it should be admitted to be modern, is perfectly just. It came to us from the French. The *bon gout* among them was applied first to classic elegance, and from thence to all the other arts. And as a sense of the beauty of the arts is certainly a thing often distinct from judgment, as well as from erudition, the term seems not only to be allowable, but well chosen. We find persons who can reason very strongly upon many subjects who yet are incapable of elegance in composition, and indeed of receiving much delight from the other fine arts. Nay, we find persons of uncommon acuteness in mathematics and natural philosophy who yet are incapable of attaining to a fine taste.

It has been sometimes said that taste is arbitrary. Some will have it that there is no such thing as a standard of taste, or any method of improving it. It is a kind of common proverb with many that there is no disputing about taste. That it is of this intellectual as of natural taste, according as the palate or organs are differently formed, what gives an agreeable relish to one, gives a disagreeable one to another. They say that the modes of taste are temporary and variable; that different nations, climates, governments, and ages have different ways of speaking and writing, and a different turn in all the arts; that chance or particular persons will be able to give a turn to the mode in all these. Even so great a man as Dr. Warburton has embraced this sentiment, and to those who attack the Scriptures as not being a complete model of eloquence, he answers there is no fixed standard of eloquence. That eloquence is one thing in Arabia, another in Greece, and another in England, for this reason he condemns those who, after the example of Mr. Blackwall in his sacred classics, vindicate the Scriptures from objections of this kind, or produce instances of their sublimity and beauty. But though I have shown you in some of the former discourses that the style and manner in vogue will receive some tincture, and be liable to some variation, from all the particulars mentioned, yet there is certainly a real beauty or deformity in nature independent of these partial changes, which, when properly explained and examples of it exhibited, will obtain more universal approbation and retain it longer than the others. The poetry and oratory of the ancients and their paintings and statuary are instances and proofs of this. It may also appear from what I mentioned to you formerly that those compositions which have most simplicity and such excellencies as are most solid, with fewest of the casual ornaments of fashion and the peculiarities of their own age, will please when their contemporaries are lost in oblivion. The same thing holds with pieces of furniture that are elegant but plain. Such have the beauties of nature, which belong to every age. But to show this more fully, even the remarks upon natural taste are not true in such a sense as to weaken what has been said. For though it is certain that persons used to the coarsest kind of food, which they have often eaten with relish, may show at first an aversion to the delicacies of cookery; yet after a person has been a little accustomed to that kind of preparation of victuals in which regard is had to the mixtures that are most proper to gratify the palate, he will not easily return to his slovenly provision. But though there were less in this remark, it seems plain that there is a taste in the fine arts, and a real foundation for it in nature.

But supposing that there is a foundation in nature for taste and criticism, there is another question that arises, viz. can we tell what it is? Can we reach the original principles which govern this matter? Can we say not only that such and such things please us, but why they do so? Can we go any further than we have already done as to composition? Some have refused that we can with certainty reach the source of the subject. When the cause is asked why one person, one thing, or one composition is more excellent than another, they say it is an immediate and simple perception, a *je ne sais quoi,* as the French say, which phrase seems to have taken its rise from the circumstance which often occurs that in a house, a garden, a statue or painting, or even in a person's countenance and carriage, you perceive something agreeable upon the whole, and yet cannot suddenly tell wherein it lies. The parts are not better proportioned perhaps, nor the features better formed than in another, and yet there is something in the composition of the whole that gives the most exquisite delight.

Others however, and the far greatest number, have thought it proper to go a great deal further and to inquire into human nature, its perceptions and powers, and endeavor to trace out the principles of taste, which apply in general to all the fine arts, or in greater or less proportion to each of them, for some apply more to one than to others. As for example, if the sense of harmony is an original perception, it applies chiefly to music, and remotely to the pronunciation of an orator, and still more remotely to the composition of an orator. These powers or perceptions in human nature have been generally called the powers of imagination. Mr. Hutchinson calls them reflex senses, finer internal sensations; and upon examination we shall find that besides the internal senses, there are certain finer perceptions which we are capable of which may be said to take their rise from outward objects and to suppose the external sensation, but yet to be additions to, and truly distinct from it. As for example, I see a beautiful person. My eye immediately perceives color and shape variously disposed, but I have further a sense of beauty in the whole. I hear the sound of musical instruments; my ear receives the noise; everybody's ear who is not deaf does the same. If I have a sense of harmony, I take a pleasure in the composition of the sounds. The way to examine the principles of taste is to consider which of these perceptions are simple, immediate, and original; which of them are dependent upon others; and how they may be combined and compounded and afford delight by such composition.

This is an extensive subject, and it is difficult to treat it concisely and yet plainly; and indeed after all the pains I can take, there will be reason to apprehend some obscurity will remain to persons not used to such kind of disquisitions. The way I shall take is to state to you critically or historically the way in which this matter has been treated by some of the most celebrated writers. The *Spectator,* written by Mr. Addison, on the pleasures of the imagination reduces the sources of delight or approbation to three great classes: novelty, greatness, and beauty. He says that such is our desire after novelty that all things that were before unknown are from this circumstance recommended to us, and that we receive a delight in the discovery and contemplation of what we never saw before, except such objects as are painful to the organs of sight. That children run from one plaything to another, not because it is better, but new; that it is the same case with men; and that authors in particular are at great pains to have something new and striking in their manner, which is the more difficult to be attained that they must make use of known words, and that their ideas too must be such as are easily intelligible. There is something here that would require a good deal of explication. I do not think that any object is, properly speaking, painful to the organs of sight except too much light; but we do not consider this as a fault in the object, but feel it as a weakness in ourselves. And further, if there be such a thing as beauty, one would think that if beauty be agreeable it must have a contrary, which is ugliness, and that must be disagreeable. As to greatness, this has been always considered as a source of admiration. The most ancient critics observe that we do not admire a small rivulet, but the Danube, the Nile, the ocean. This I will afterwards consider. As to beauty, it has been considered as of all other things most inconceivable, and therefore made a first and immediate perception.

Others have taken beauty and grace as the general terms, including everything that pleases us. Thus we say a beautiful poem, statue, landscape. Thus also we say a sublime and beautiful sentiment. Thus they have taken in under it novelty and greatness, and every other agreeable quality. Many eminent critics have acted in this manner, particularly the ancients. Longinus, *On the Sublime,* introduces several things which do not belong to it, as distinguised from beauty. Taking beauty as the general object of approbation or source of delight, and as applicable to all the fine arts, it has been variously analyzed.

A French writer, Crousaz, *Traite du Beau,* analyzes beauty under the following principles: variety, unity, regularity, order, proportion. Variety is the first. This seems to be related to, or perhaps in some respects the same with, novelty, which was formerly mentioned. It is certain that a dead uniformity cannot produce beauty in any sort of performance—poem, oration, statue, picture, building. Unity is, as it were, the bound and restraint of variety. Things must be connected as well as various, and if they are not connected, the variety is nothing but confusion. Regularity is the similarity of the correspondent parts; order is the easy gradation from one to another; and proportion is the suitableness of each part to the whole, and to every other part. I think it cannot be denied that all these have their influence in producing beauty.

One of the most celebrated pieces upon this subject is the famous painter Hogarth's *Analysis of Beauty*. He first produced his system in a sort of enigma, drawing one curved line with the title of the line of beauty, and another with a double wave, which he called the line of grace. He afterwards published his *Analysis of Beauty,* which he resolves into the following principles: fitness, variety, uniformity, simplicity, intricacy and quantity. The first principle is fitness, under which he shows that we always conceive of a thing as intended for some use; and therefore there must be a correspondence or suitableness to the use, otherwise whatever be its appearance, we reject it as not beautiful. He instances in sailors, who whenever there is a ship that sails well, they call her a beauty. The same thing will apply perfectly to all kinds of writing; for whatever fine sentiments and noble expression be in any composition, if they are not suited to the season and subject, we say with Horace, "Sed nunc non erat his locus." Variety and uniformity must be compounded together, and as he has made no mention of order and proportion, it is to be supposed that by variety he meant that which changes in a gradual and insensible manner; for variety without order is undistinguishable, and a heap of confusion. Simplicity means that which is easy, and which the eye travels over and examines without difficulty; and intricacy is that which requires some exercise and attention to follow it; these two must limit one another. In representing beauty as a visible figure, he observes that a straight line has the least beauty; that which has a wave or easy declination one way begins to be beautiful; that which has a double wave has still greater grace. The truth is, if these two things do not destroy the one the other, simplicity and intricacy improve and beautify one another. Mr. Hogarth observes that ringlets of hair waving in the wind have been an expression of grace and elegance in every age, nation, and language, which is just a contrasted wave, first that of the curls, and this again rendered a little more intricate by the motion of the breeze. If one would have a view of this principle as exhibited in a single kind, let him look at the flourishes with which the masters of the pen adorn their pieces, and he will see that if they are easy and gradual in their flections, and just as intricate as the eye can follow without confusion, anything less than that is less beautiful, and anything more destroys the beauty by disorder. I might show you how this principle applies to all the arts but shall only mention composition, where the simplicity must be combined with refinement, and when the combination is just, there results the most perfect elegance. Mr. Hogarth adds quantity; that a thing having the other qualities pleases in proportion as it is great, as we say a magnificent building where the proportions are truly observed, but every part is large.

I have only to observe that Mr. Hogarth has very well illustrated the principles of beauty, but at the same time he seems to have introduced two which belong to other sources of delight, viz. fitness and quantity, as will be shown afterwards.

It is to be observed that in the enumeration of the principles of beauty, there are to be found in some authors things not only different but opposite. A French author, not many years ago, to the principles mentioned by others adds strength, which he illustrates in this manner. He considers it as a principle of grace and beauty in motion, and says that everything that we do with great difficulty, and that seems to require our utmost effort, is seen with uneasiness, and not with pleasure. For this reason he says the motions of young people in general are more graceful than those of old, and agreeably to this we join the word *ease* to gracefulness as explicatory—a graceful, easy carriage. With this explication it seems abundantly proper to admit the remark. On the other hand, there are some who have made comparative weakness a principle of beauty, and say that the more light and slender anything is, unless it be remarkably weak, it is the more beautiful, and that things remarkably strong rather belong to another class. Thus we say a fine, tender, delicate shape; and on the contrary we say a strong, coarse, robust make—a strong, coarse, masculine woman. Perhaps we may reconcile these two, and say they are both principles because there should be just as much of each as is suitable to the thing in question, that a person may have either too strong or too weak a frame for being esteemed beautiful, that a pillar or dome may be too delicate to be durable, or too strong and bulky to be elegant.

Again, many writers as you have seen make greatness a principle of beauty; yet there are others who make littleness one of the constituents of beauty. Those who do so tell us that *little* is a term of endearment in every nation and language yet known, that it is the language of the vulgar, and therefore the undesigned expression of nature. They instance the diminutive appellations which are always used in fondling—*filiolus, filiola*—have more affection than *filius* and *filia*—my dear little creature, it is a pretty little thing. To enumerate these different appearances some, particularly Burke *On the Sublime*, affirm that the ideas of sublimity and beauty are ideas of a class radically different, that the first, sublimity, ultimately arises from the passion of terror, and the other from that of love and delight. He with a good deal of ingenuity resolves all the sources of the sublime into what is either terrible or allied to this passion, exciting it either immediately in some degree or by association. It is however uncertain whether we should reduce what we receive so much delight from to a passion, which in itself, or in its purity so to speak, is painful. This objection he endeavors to remove by showing that the exercise of all our passions in a moderate degree is a source of pleasure, but perhaps we may distinguish the ideas of sublime and beautiful without having recourse to the passion of terror at all by saying that there is an affection suited to the greatness of objects without considering them as terrible, and that is veneration. Nay, perhaps we may go a little further and say that veneration is the affection truly correspondent to greatness in innocent creatures, which becomes terror in the guilty. I cannot go through the particulars of Burke's theory. He seems rightly to divide the ideas of sublime and beautiful, by the union of which some have made one thing, others directly its contrary, to belong to beauty. One thing remarkable in Burke's *Essay* is that he denies proportion to be any of the cause of beauty, which yet almost every other writer has enumerated among them; and what he says of the infinitely various proportion in plants and animals seems to be much in support of his opinion; yet in works of art proportion seems of much moment, and it is difficult to say to what source to refer it. I view a building, and if the parts are not in a regular proportion, it offends my eye, even though I could suppose that the disproportion was voluntary in order to obtain some great convenience.

I should be inclined to think that there are a considerable number of simple principles or internal sensations that contribute each its part in forming our taste, and are capable of being variously combined, and by this combination are apt to be confounded one with another. One of the most distinct and complete enumerations we have in Gerard's *Essay on Taste,* and is as follows: a sense of novelty, sublimity, beauty, imitation, harmony, ridicule, and virtue. I cannot go through all these in order, but shall make a few remarks and show where the division is just or defective. His distinguishing all these from one another is certainly just, but there are some things that he introduces under wrong heads: fitness, for example, he introduces under the head of beauty; and this seems rather a source of approbation distinct in itself, as also proportion, if that is not included in fitness. Perhaps a more complete enumeration than any of them may be given thus: novelty, sublimity, beauty, proportion, imitation, harmony, ridicule, utility, and virtue.

We shall now proceed to those we have not spoken of before: imitation certainly gives great pleasure to the mind, and that of itself even independent of the object imitated. An exceedingly well-imitated resemblance of any object, of that which is indifferent or even disagreeable in itself, gives the highest pleasure, either from the act of comparison as some say, or from it suggesting the idea of skill and ingenuity in the imitator. The arts of painting and statuary derive their excellence from the perfection of imitation, and it is even thought that poetry and oratory may be considered in the same light, only that the first imitates form and passions by the means of form, and the other imitates actions and affections by language as the instrument.

Harmony is the most distinct and separate of all the internal senses that have been mentioned; it is concerned only in sound, and therefore must be but remotely applicable to the writer and speaker. What is remarkable that although harmony may be said to be of much importance in speaking, there are many examples of the most excellent speakers that yet have no musical ear at all, and I think the instances of those who have a remarkably delicate musical ear, and at the same time are agreeable speakers, are not many.

The sense of ridicule is not very easily explained, but it is easily understood when spoken of because it is universally felt. It differs in this from most other of our constitutional powers, that there is scarcely any man who is not sensible of the ridiculous or may be made easily sensible of it, and yet the number of good performers in the art of ridiculing others, or in wit and humor, is but very small. The multitude who cannot follow speculative reasoning, and are hard to be moved by eloquence, are all struck with works of humor. Most people are apt to think they can do something in the way of humor, and yet we have many who render themselves ridiculous by the attempt.

As to a sense of virtue, by mentioning it is by no means from my joining with those who would place moral approbation entirely on the same footing with the internal senses that are the foundation of taste. Hutchinson and Shaftesbury incline very much this way; on the contrary, I think we are evidently sensible that the morality of actions is a thing of a different species and arises from the sense of a law and obligation of a superior nature; yet I have mentioned it here because there is certainly a relation or connecting tie between the sentiments of the one kind and of the other. The beauties of nature, we are sensible, are greatly heightened by adding to their delightful appearance a reflection on their utility, and the benevolent intention of their author. In persons capable of morality, as in human nature, we consider fine features and an elegant carriage as indications of the moral disposition or the mental powers; and as the whole of the sources of delight mentioned above may be combined in a greater or lesser degree, as novelty, sublimity, beauty, etc., so the governing principle which ought to direct the application of the whole is what gives them their highest excellence, and indeed only is their true perfection. The gratification even of our internal senses is highly improved when united with taste and elegance. As the most delicious food when served up with neatness and order, accompanied with politeness of manners, and seasoned with sprightly conversation, in the same manner the fine arts themselves acquire a double beauty and higher relish when they are inseparably connected with, and made subservient to purity of manners. An admirable poem, or an eloquent discourse, or a fine picture would be still more excellent if the subject of them were interesting and valuable, and when any of them are perverted to impious or wicked purposes, they are just objects of detestation.

After having thus attempted the analysis of the principles of taste and elegance, I would observe that as nature seems to delight in producing many great and different effects from simple causes, perhaps we may find an ultimate principle that governs all these. A French author has written a treatise called the *Theory of Agreeable Sensations,* in which he says that the great principle is whatever exercises our faculties without fatiguing them gives pleasure, and that this principle may be applied to our bodily form, and to the constitution of our mind, to objects of external sensation, to objects of taste, and even to our moral conduct. It may no doubt be carried through the whole of criticism, and we may say this states the bounds between variety and uniformity, simplicity and intricacy, order, proportion, and harmony.

Neither would it be difficult to show that this principle may be applied to morality, and that an infinitely wise and gracious God had so ordered matters that the moderate exercise of all our powers should produce at once virtue and happiness, and that the least transgression of the one must prove of necessity an injury to the other.

You may see from the preceding remarks that the foundation is laid for taste in our natures; yet is there great room for improvement and cultivation. By investigating the grounds of approbation, by comparing one thing with another, by studying the best examples, and by reflection and judgment, men may correct and refine their taste upon the whole, or upon particular confined subjects.

Carrying taste to a finical nicety in any one branch is a thing not only undesirable but contemptible, the reason of which may be easily seen: when a person applies his attention so much to a matter of no great moment, it occasions a necessary neglect of other things of much greater value. After you pass a certain point, attachment to a particular pursuit is useless, and then it proceeds to be hurtful, and at last contemptible.

Landmarks in Rhetoric and Public Address

Also in this series